Female Philanthropy in the Interwar World

Female Philanthropy in the Interwar World

Between Self and Other

Eve Colpus

Bloomsbury Academic
An imprint of Bloomsbury Publishing Plc

B L O O M S B U R Y
LONDON · OXFORD · NEW YORK · NEW DELHI · SYDNEY

Bloomsbury Academic

An imprint of Bloomsbury Publishing Plc

50 Bedford Square	1385 Broadway
London	New York
WC1B 3DP	NY 10018
UK	USA

www.bloomsbury.com

BLOOMSBURY and the Diana logo are trademarks of Bloomsbury Publishing Plc

First published 2018

© Eve Colpus, 2018

Eve Colpus has asserted her right under the Copyright, Designs and Patents Act, 1988, to be identified as Author of this work.

British Library Cataloguing-in-Publication Data

A catalogue record for this book is available from the British Library.

ISBN: HB: 978-1-4742-5968-2
ePDF: 978-1-4742-5970-5
eBook: 978-1-4742-5969-9

Library of Congress Cataloging-in-Publication Data

A catalog record for this book is available from the Library of Congress.

Cover image: YWCA helpers during the General Strike in London, 1926 © Mary Evans / Sueddeutsche Zeitung Photo

Typeset by RefineCatch Limited, Bungay, Suffolk
Printed and bound in Great Britain

To find out more about our authors and books visit www.bloomsbury.com. Here you will find extracts, author interviews, details of forthcoming events and the option to sign up for our newsletters.

In memory of Jonathan Francis Colpus (1950–2008)

Contents

List of Illustrations viii

Acknowledgements ix

List of Abbreviations xii

Introduction 1

1 Relationships 31

2 Knowledge 65

3 Identity 97

4 Culture 129

5 Communication 163

Conclusion 193

Notes 201

Bibliography 251

Index 275

List of Illustrations

1. Illustration in UK Young Women's Christian Association Pamphlet, 1923   18
2. Photograph of Evangeline Booth in Scotland on a UK motorcade tour, 1936   21
3. Photograph of Emily Kinnaird, c. 1913   22
4. Photograph of Lettice Fisher by Bassano Ltd., 1919   24
5. Lantern slide (photograph) of Muriel Paget   26
6. Photograph of the Feeding Centre, Riga, opened by Muriel Paget's Mission to Eastern Europe   42
7. Map, 'Europe's Need: Save the Children Fund, October 1920', *The Record of the Save the Children Fund* 1, no. 3 (Dec. 1920): 41   43
8. Dinner party seating plan drawn up by Lettice Fisher   84
9. 'The X-ray apparatus' at the Anglo-Russian Hospital, Petrograd, photograph taken by Lyndall Pocock, 1916   87
10. The Young Women's Christian Association's eightieth anniversary image   98
11. 1937 UK Salvation Army international appeal, *This Brotherhood of Nations*   122
12. Watercolour painting of the *dacha* in Sosnovka, painted by Muriel Paget, 1936   140
13. Poster produced for the UK Young Women's Christian Association's World Fellowship Week, 1935   150
14. Photograph of Evangeline Booth and Frank O. Salisbury with Booth's portrait by Salisbury, November 1939   164
15. Still from *Unmarried* (1920), featuring members of the executive committee of the National Council for the Unmarried Mother and her Child, reproduced in *The Sketch*, 11 Feb. 1920, 227   174

Acknowledgements

Many people have extended hands of friendship, generosity and support over the long course of writing this book. I would like to thank first, and most, my former supervisor and now mentor and friend, Jane Garnett. Jane's intellectual generosity, kindness and wisdom has supported this project in its earlier iteration as an Oxford doctoral thesis to its end product. For all of this, and for much more, I pass on the warmest, affectionate thanks.

Financial and institutional support from an AHRC Doctoral Award (2008/140729) and a Bryce Research Studentship (Faculty of History, University of Oxford) sustained my research on the project in its early stages. The funding allowed me to pursue archival research in the United States, as well as Britain, and I remain in debt for the hospitality and kindness of Kerry and Tom Carter during my research trip to The Salvation Army National Archives and Research Center, Alexandria, VA, and to Mark Adomanis for arranging that. In later phases of the work, I have been very grateful for the support of the Faculty of Humanities at the University of Southampton in giving me the time on research leave to move forward the book, and an early career small award to purchase a number of the images used.

For their expertise, knowledge and unfailing help, I would like to thank Colin Harris in the Special Collections, and librarians especially in the Upper Reading Room at the Bodleian Library; Anna Towlson at the London School of Economics (LSE) Library: archivists at the Modern Records Centre, University of Warwick, the Cadbury Library: Special Collections, University of Birmingham, Somerville College, Oxford, and the Heinz Archive, National Portrait Gallery; Katie Ankers at the BBC Written Archives Centre; Rhianydd Davies at the National Library of Wales; Leslie Pitman at the UCL School of Slavonic and East European Studies and Grant Mitchell at the International Federation of Red Cross and Red Crescent Societies. Special thanks go to Richard Davies and Helen Price at Special Collections, Leeds University Library; Susan Mitchem, the Director at The Salvation Army National Archives and Research Center: and Steven Spencer, the Acting Director at the Salvation Army International Heritage Centre, London; Steven kindly traced and provided some of the images used in the book, for which I am so grateful.

I pass on formal thanks for permissions to use materials from the Salvation Army International Heritage Centre, London (photographs); The Salvation

Army National Archives and Research Center, Alexandria, VA (Evangeline Booth Papers); the Young Women's Trust, formerly the Young Women's Christian Association and Modern Records Centre, University of Warwick (Young Women's Christian Association Records); Gingerbread and the LSE Library, The Women's Library Collection (Papers of the National Council for the Unmarried Mother and her Child); Special Collections, Leeds University Library (Lady Muriel Paget Papers); Bodleian Libraries, University of Oxford (Papers of H. A. L. Fisher and Fisher family); the Imperial War Museum (Papers of G. M. and L. C. Pocock); Save the Children Fund and the Cadbury Research Library: Special Collections, University of Birmingham (Papers of Eglantyne Jebb and map from *The Record of the Save the Children Fund*); BBC Written Archives Centre (Papers relating to the *Week's Good Cause*); and the National Library of Wales (Letter from Lettice Fisher to Frances Stevenson).

Appreciative thanks to those who have given permissions as copyright holders to reproduce text and images are due to the following: Sir Richard Paget (Lady Muriel Paget Papers); Sophie Ilbert Decaudaveine (Papers of H. A. L. Fisher and Ilbert Family Papers); Susan Pares (Letter from Bernard Pares to Muriel Paget); Pete Blindell (photograph, 'The X-ray apparatus', taken by L. C. Pocock); Getty images (photograph of Evangeline Booth with Frank O. Salisbury); the National Portrait Gallery (photograph of Lettice Fisher by Bassano Ltd., 1919). Every effort has been made to trace copyright holders and to obtain their permission for the use of copyright material regarding the photograph of Evangeline Booth in Scotland on the 1936 motorcade tour. Moreover, while I have endeavoured to trace the owners of material used in preparing this book I apologize for any inadvertent infringement of copyright and trust that, in the event of such an oversight, a general acknowledgement of the value of being able to consult the papers I have used for this book will be accepted in lieu of more precise thanks.

It has been all to my benefit to work with inspiring and supportive colleagues. Thank you especially to those with whom I worked on the Religious Faith, Space and Diasporic Communities in East London, 1880 – the present project and on the Barnett House Centenary History project, both at the University of Oxford. At the University of Southampton, I have been supported enormously (formally) by mentors including Neil Gregor, Joan Tumblety, and David Brown and other colleagues and friends whose advice I have sought so frequently.

Conversations with many over the years have helped me to think in new ways about what I was researching and writing about: Aurelia Annat, Scott Anthony, Belinda Beaton, Gemma Clark, Niamh Cullen, Frances Flanagan, Charlotte Greenhalgh, Stuart Halifax, Alana Harris, Matt Houlbrook, Matt Kelly, Jane

McDermid, Eloise Moss, Stella Moss and Stephen Robinson. I was fortunate enough to meet the late Robin Ilbert, who shared his memories of one of the women in this book; I remain so grateful for his and Pat's kindness. I owe particularly large debts of gratitude to those who have generously read and commented on draft chapters: Liz Peretz, Kathryn Eccles, Joan Tumblety, Mike Hammond, George Gilbert, Priti Mishra, Helen Spurling and Jenny Crane. David Brown and Rachel Herrmann read the whole manuscript; thank you both for offering constructive criticisms with such good humour.

This book could not have been written without the close friendships that have sustained me in writing, and much beyond. Thank you especially to Sam Evans, Elin Leyshon, Stella Moss and Rachel Herrmann, who in addition to reading a draft of the book, has continually spurred on the long process of writing it; and to Kate Hallett, who has not only offered a London-base for work over now many years, but has been the most continually encouraging and loyal of friends.

Finally, I am only too aware of the support I have sought from my family 'at home'. Thanks to Rose, Adam and Poppy for your love and kindness and for allowing me the time to spend on this book; and above all, to Mum for whom there are not words enough to express my gratitude for everything. I have written this book in the memory of Jonathan Francis Colpus: a wonderful friend, a truly generous man and teacher and the most loving and supportive Dad.

List of Abbreviations

BBC	British Broadcasting Corporation
BL	Bodleian Libraries
BSRRA	British Subjects in Russia Relief Association
CBE	Commander of the Order of the British Empire
CMS	Church Missionary Society
COPEC	Conference on Christian Politics, Economics and Citizenship
COS	Charity Organization Society
DNB	*Dictionary of National Biography*
GPO	General Post Office
ICRC	International Committee of the Red Cross
IDC	Imperial Defence College
IKL	Invalid Kitchens of London
IMC	International Missionary Council
IWM	Imperial War Museum
JUC	Joint University Council for Social Studies
LCC	London County Council
LORCS	League of Red Cross Societies
LRA	Leeds Russian Archive, Special Collections, Leeds University Library
LSE	London School of Economics
MP	Member of Parliament
MR	Medical Research Council
MRC	Modern Records Centre, University of Warwick
MU	Mothers' Union
NCSS	National Council of Social Service
NCUMC	National Council for the Unmarried Mother and her Child
NCW	National Council of Women
NFWI	National Federation of Women's Institutes
NUSEC	National Union of Societies for Equal Citizenship
NUWSS	National Union of Women's Suffrage Societies
OBE	Officer of the Order of the British Empire
ODNB	*Oxford Dictionary of National Biography*

SAA	The Salvation Army National Archives and Research Center, Alexandria, VA
SCF	Save the Children Fund
TWL	London School of Economics Library, The Women's Library Collection
VOKS	All-Union Society for Cultural Relations with Foreign Cultures
WAAC	Women's Army Auxiliary Corps
WAC	BBC Written Archives Centre
WEA	Workers' Educational Association
YMCA	Young Men's Christian Association
YWCA	Young Women's Christian Association

Introduction

Female Philanthropy in the Interwar World: Between Self and Other explores the ideas, work practices and connections of four British-born women who were celebrated philanthropists in their lifetimes. Evangeline Booth, Lettice Fisher, Emily Kinnaird and Muriel Paget were each born in London in the middle decades of the nineteenth century and went on to occupy a global stage through networks of action that stretched across Central, Eastern and Southern Europe, North America and South and South East Asia. Each remarkable in their fields of operation and influence, there were distinct intellectual, ethical and social drivers to these women's work: Evangeline Booth and Emily Kinnaird contributed to international Christian missions that envisaged, respectively, a universal brotherhood of mankind and the progress of society through the mutuality of women's service; Muriel Paget's interventions in the Baltic States, Czechoslovakia and Russia were rooted in a developing humanitarian model of international friendship; and Lettice Fisher worked to reinvigorate principles of citizenship and civic action in Britain's new interwar mass democracy. Although the contribution of women's philanthropy to historical civic development is now understood well, the meanings and influences of women's philanthropy into the twentieth century (and beyond) remain under-appreciated. Focusing on the interwar years as a moment of transformative change, my approach in this book is to foreground how female philanthropists inhabited and represented society and culture to various audiences and publics; how they evaluated and interpreted the forces of contemporary society. In doing so, I show that female philanthropy – as a practice, a commitment, an ethics and a way of understanding social obligation and opportunity – tested and shaped the practical and imaginative extent of women's social action in these years as a vehicle for social development and for interpreting the cultural and political transformations of the era. I argue that female philanthropy was both more engaged with, and critical of, the project of early-twentieth-century modernity than has been acknowledged.

Between them, Evangeline Booth, Lettice Fisher, Emily Kinnaird and Muriel Paget had a great deal to say about what it meant to be a philanthropist and to do philanthropy. Their collective practice illuminates variation: while Evangeline Booth lead the Salvation Army and worked primarily with the poor and homeless, Fisher established and participated in charities and voluntary organizations that supported mothers and housewives, Kinnaird worked with the YWCA (Young Women's Christian Association) in its domestic and international outreach programmes and Paget provided food aid, medical and welfare support to the sick, refugees and children at home and abroad. The women have left behind them evidence of their thought, work and networks of action that spans personal and professional correspondence, memoirs, books, articles, speeches, newspaper and magazine stories, films, and radio broadcasts, as well as the reports and documents they produced in association with their organizations. In putting Booth's, Fisher's, Kinnaird's and Paget's stories centre stage, this book looks through the narratives that female philanthropists told to what has been to date the overlooked range of public discussions to which philanthropy was connected in the interwar years. Looking outwards from the choices and obligations Booth, Fisher, Kinnaird and Paget articulated, the relationships they forged and the explanatory logics they shaped for their commitments, I explore the contributions that philanthropy made in this period to a series of affective, cultural and intellectual engagements with modernity: of knowing populations (in Britain and the wider world); the construction of identities; and practices of public communication. My purpose in closely analysing the evidence of these four women's ideas and work, therefore, is not an act of retrieval that seeks to restore women's stories to the historical record; this book does not argue that these women were exceptionally significant, nor that we should now see them as four representative pillars of interwar female philanthropy. Rather, it is an attempt to explore the breadth of female philanthropists' contributions to contemporary understandings of human experience and the role the individual was to play in interwar society. More than a women's history or a study of women's philanthropy per se, the book aims to reveal philanthropy as part of the reflexive and communicative practices individuals used in the interwar years to make sense of the social, political and cultural changes in the world around them.

The image on the front cover of the book begins to open up some of the complexities of these themes. The photograph captures two young women moving furniture across Hyde Park in London on the eve of the first full day of the General Strike in May 1926.[1] The women, whose dress in the tailored fashions of the day connotes their relative privilege, were members of the YWCA, an evangelical organization founded over seventy years earlier by Emily Kinnaird's mother, Mary Jane Kinnaird, to provide social amenities and spiritual support to young women living and working away from home. The women's activity depicted in the image – the setting up of temporary administrative huts – was part of an immediate response during the strikes to the national communications emergency that stretched from the interventions of voluntary organizations (both old and new) to the young BBC (British Broadcasting Corporation).[2] This civic action, consciously aiming to galvanize a spirit of national purpose, illuminated a particular political and moral ambition to bolster the essential interdependency of social relationships. It was a distinctive response to contemporary social and economic pressures, as the strike itself was. As recent commentators have argued, the General Strike was a symbol of the conflicts of interwar modernity, in which the political force of the striking workers tested on the one hand the strength of modern projects of social engagement and on the other hand the emphases upon the aesthetic autonomy of self that were gaining hegemony through self-consciously Modernist movements.[3] The affirmation in the theatre of industrial politics of a vision of collective participation that attacked both corporatist and individualist approaches validated a distinctive understanding of the constitutive nature of social life.

In depicting the two women as cheerful in their purpose, the photograph also engaged with a specifically gendered conceit of the interwar period that positioned women's social contributions as facilitating the positive expression of selfhood. The 'active cheery worker' was a recurring idealized portrait of women's work – paid and unpaid – that exposed the ideological role of gender in the formulation of both individual agency and the development of the common good.[4] Invoking Christian conceptualizations of a purposeful life, the YWCA shaped a model of women's action around the teaching that working with others was the root to personal satisfaction and common benefit: as the Ministry of Labour employee, M. E. Marshall wrote in an article for the UK YWCA members' magazine published in May 1926, young women should seek opportunities for service that 'would exercise and *stretch* all the faculties of her nature'.[5] The organizational principle of the mutuality of service, formalized in 1914 by the international body of the YWCA, the World's YWCA, further expanded the idea of women's self-development as a *relational* process, one that women explored in conversation with each other. The photograph's representation of female companionship and solidarity speaks to this ideal: although the image eludes any understanding of documentary accuracy – were the baskets and chairs 'props' to be staged for the camera? – it intentionally portrays a sense of the collaborative principles driving the two women. Any one of the four women whose stories are centred in this book might just have easily appeared as the subjects of this photograph. In each case, the idiom of female solidarity and collaboration would differ from the image here – not least because the four women were in middle and older age in the 1920s – but nonetheless be palpable: Muriel Paget might have been photographed with the aid worker, Alice Masaryk, the daughter of the first President of Czechoslovakia, to whose pleas for aid for her country she responded in 1919 by setting up hospitals and welfare clinics; Evangeline Booth might have been shown (as she was in institutional publicity) holding a portrait of her late mother, Catherine Booth; Emily Kinnaird might have appeared with her sister, Gertrude or her friend Edith Picton-Turbervill, both of whom were companions in her social work in India; and Lettice Fisher with the working women in the Women's Institutes with whom she claimed identification. Still, and notwithstanding the broader patterns of female solidarity that can be discerned in these examples, the image of the YWCA helpers hints at the exclusions within female philanthropists' projects of social connection in the interwar period. In contrast to the proximity of the two young women, the depiction of their physical and emotional distance from the working-class men shown, inactive, in the background of the photograph, is striking. In multiple contexts, the personally- and socially-enabling principle of working *with* each other was still complicated during the interwar years by the material, moral and psychological practices of working *for* others.

***

The central focus of this book is upon the *ideas* of the women who carried out philanthropy, the identities they invoked and how their work and thinking was communicated and connected up to multiple cultural fields in the interwar period. It needs to be emphasized at the outset that this book is not about the experiences of those individuals or groups who were in receipt of philanthropists' attention. Although some very fine scholarship has shown how we might listen to the voices of those men, women and children who were reached by the work of philanthropy,[6] it remains the case that we still need to more audibly *hear* the philanthropist, herself, in the historical record. In making the choice to listen more closely, this book addresses the central roles played by language and presentational form in the history of philanthropy, and how the expressive domains of philanthropy were forged in relation to the sites of modern experience in the interwar years.[7] Examining the language through which women's philanthropy was accredited public meaning in the interwar period illuminates the comparative intellectual framework of the era, in which philanthropy was defined in relation to alternative modes of charitable and political engagement. The civic landscape was shifting in the interwar period, but philanthropy remained a critical and often testing feature.

The concentration upon language is also designed to illuminate the intellectual and cultural realms to which philanthropy was connected in this period, and how philanthropic practice was itself a vehicle for reflection upon the varied personal and social transformations that men and women experienced in the interwar world. Exploring the explanatory and representational devices that Evangeline Booth, Lettice Fisher, Emily Kinnaird, Muriel Paget and their publicists used, the book traces how language framed the shifting idea and practice of philanthropy; how that language was engaged with by philanthropists themselves, their supporters and critics; and how it connected to what these women were actually doing and where they were doing it. I am specifically interested in charting the interpretative registers and presentational strategies through which women's philanthropic practice was conceptualized as part of interconnected strands of social, political, economic, psychological, cultural and religious thought. In this respect, one of the main aims of the book is to trace the construction of the meanings of philanthropy within and beyond the philanthropic realm. The language Booth, Fisher, Kinnaird and Paget used was both in dialogue and confrontation with perceived standards of cultural modernity in the interwar years and enduring traditions of personal and social commitment, and shows how philanthropists sought to shift the significance of philanthropy between the work of documenting charitable need and provision (to institutional audiences and in the search for wider public support) and wider cultural, political, social and ethical impact. In exploring this presentational and interpretative work, the book treats metaphor and imagery as of central historical significance in revealing the meanings of philanthropy, and what it meant to be a philanthropist. Allusions were typically composite and used as commentaries both upon the self and the social work that philanthropy performed. For example, when Emily Kinnaird reflected in her autobiographical memoir in 1925 that she hoped she would remain a 'beggar all my life', she played not only with the terms of her reputation as financial secretary of the UK YWCA but also with the public knowledge of her long life of evangelical commitment, in which she felt humbled before God.[8] Metaphor and imagery spoke to both the projects of selfhood and social engagement that inhered in women's philanthropic practice.

The twin concepts of 'self' and 'other' in the book's title signal my particular attention to the conceptualization of women's philanthropic projects in the interwar years in terms of the contemporary search for social connectedness. The philanthropic sensibility of mediating between the 'giver' and 'receiver' is in one respect timeless, but the expressions and explanations of this ambition are always historically specific and could be redrawn across an individual's lifetime as part of a process of a philanthropist's own development in her thinking. I am interested in how, in the interwar years, philanthropic practice constructed particular models of socially-constructed selfhood. Such thinking was shaped fundamentally by the specific spaces and sites of a philanthropist's engagements. Booth's, Fisher's, Kinnaird's and Paget's philanthropic initiatives were transnational in scope; geographically the women ranged widely, and their ideas and work practices, in crossing territorial and imagined borders, involved both the re-articulation of national difference and the valuation of interracial reciprocity.[9] Growing out of their individual material and conceptual experiences, perceptions of social and cultural difference – as well as connection – modelled philanthropists' reflexive practice in looking between self and other. The four women whose stories are central to this book did not imagine or fantasize a classless society, or a society that did away with markers of difference. Indeed, their work was shored up by unequal gradations of cultural, ethnic, national and social difference: it should not be forgotten that these women, in most cases, were able to pursue their public commitments because of the domestic labour performed by other, less privileged women who worked as family servants for them, nor that their cultural authority was in part derived from the ideas of scientific, technological and anthropological superiority that pervaded late-nineteenth- and early-twentieth-century imperialist notions of thought.[10] Yet the women's acceptance of structural inequalities such as these went alongside their commitments to the idea and practice of inter-class subjectivity and cross-cultural friendship as much as the goals of social and political reform. Exploring the four women's searches for models of social connection the book argues that women's philanthropic practice actively shaped cultural imaginations of the relationships between peoples and societies in the interwar world. Female philanthropy was not only, or even always primarily, a response to remedial social need but was a decidedly creative force that opened up reflection upon the social, psychological, political and religious preoccupations of the age.

Centring on the stories of a small group of women gives a richness and texture to the broader argument about philanthropy. Although this book does not claim that Evangeline Booth, Lettice Fisher, Emily Kinnaird and Muriel Paget were representative of similar or related work in Britain or abroad, the public and intellectual networks of these four women encompassed many women and men.

The voices of a number of these figures will be important at various moments of the analysis. My interest is in what the study of a group of individuals' work and writings, contextualized in relation to these other voices, reveals about the developing historical force of women's social activism in the interwar period. The focus on the four women's varied contributions means that the book's examination of the influence of female philanthropy ranges both with greater breadth and depth than has been attempted to date across the social, cultural and intellectual history of the interwar period, and looks across analytical layers of historical meaning. One of the explicit aims of the book is to dislodge interpretations of women's philanthropy that take at face value historical constructions that placed women as concerned typically with the concrete rather than the abstract, and which have by extension construed women's philanthropic projects as driven by an 'anti-intellectual ethos'.[11] It was *because* women's philanthropic projects were embedded in practices of cultural storytelling, I argue, that female philanthropy was a mechanism for the conceptualization of social action as an intellectual project as much as practical intervention. A central goal of this book is to make this conceptual expansiveness and cultural incursion of female philanthropy apparent, and it accounts for the design and thematic focus.

***

I have stated above that this book seeks to read female philanthropy for its critical engagement with early-twentieth-century cultures of modernity. My interest is in tracing how Evangeline Booth's, Lettice Fisher's, Emily Kinnaird's and Muriel Paget's everyday commitments to philanthropy formed part of their wider operations in, and critiques of, the cultural politics of the interwar world. The women's responses to the manifold physical, political and social changes of early-twentieth-century modernity could be celebratory.[12] Muriel Paget, for example, embraced energetically new technologies of modernization both pragmatically, to further her own access to the spheres of international action (she travelled to the humanitarian field on chartered flights as well as by boat and train), and intellectually, notably in her interest in the development of the medical practices of modern health care systems. Other women who explored in the interwar years reformist modes of social and political engagement became targets of criticism of those Modernist thinkers who were reaching deliberately towards dissent from historical modernity. Writing in her diary in 1934, Virginia Woolf depicted her first cousin, H. A. L. Fisher and his wife, Lettice '[r]epresent[ing] culture, politics [and] world wisdom gilt with letters'; ultimately the embodiment of the urbane elites who 'spin along the grooves' and do their duty.[13] Framed by the formalist aesthetic of Bloomsbury Modernism, Woolf's portrait was also a critique of the 'functualist' ethic of academics and public intellectuals like the Fishers, and especially Lettice, who worked for the direct social, economic and political ends of intellectual projects as much as the projects themselves. Woolf had underscored this theme more pointedly in a diary entry two months previously when she decried the epistemological legacy that Lettice Fisher had passed on to her daughter Mary: a 'mean look, a sharp practical look'.[14] Female philanthropists' confrontations with the identities and experiences of modernity, as this book explores, were both more fluid and complex than the portraits of consciously independent-minded women of the interwar period allowed.

Where Evangeline Booth, Lettice Fisher, Emily Kinnaird and Muriel Paget sat in relationship to Modernism is an easier question to address, however, than *where exactly* they sat in relationship to modernity. Modernism's hostility to mass culture, its radical separation from the culture of everyday life and its distance from political, economic and social concerns, made it an unlikely partner of the socially-embedded and constitutive practice of female philanthropy. As we have seen, Lettice Fisher was critiqued 'from without' Bloomsbury Modernism. Muriel Paget, by contrast, was an active proponent of aesthetic modernity as a patron of early-twentieth-century avant-garde artists. Avant-gardism, as Andreas Huyssen has argued, represented a new stage of the culture of modernity. In artistic terms, it aimed at developing a new and alternative relationship between high art and mass culture, a stark contrast between the exclusive preoccupations of Modernism, and one which could harness explicitly political messages. Although there was common ground – both Modernism and the avant-garde were defined in relation to traditional bourgeois high culture and vernacular and popular culture – the results sought out differed markedly.[15] Similarly, as T. J. Jackson Lears has argued, both Modernist and *anti*-Modernist concerns shared common roots in the late-nineteenth-century yearning for the authenticity of experience but drew very different lessons from such heritage. The difference explains why, for example, the aggressively anti-Modernist critique of an organization such as the Salvation Army – that institutionalized a romantic and martial spirit of Christian activism in an attempt to move beyond the 'pleasure principles' of bourgeois, industrial society – could be blended with sleeker versions of modern culture, and connected by the end of the interwar period to emerging therapeutic cultures.[16] This book follows this process of cultural dialogue in relation to

Evangeline Booth's leadership roles in the Salvation Army, which modelled a hard-line evangelistic faith in combination with the interwar psychological discourse of self-realization. In this work, as in the YWCA's and Emily Kinnaird's extended concern with the conditions and challenges of contemporary life for young women, what emerged was philanthropists' programmatic *closeness* to material political, economic and social concerns in stark contradistinction to the way in which Modernist projects sought a programmatic *distance*.[17]

So what can be said about female philanthropists' relationship to modernity? Booth's, Fisher's, Kinnaird's and Paget's work to ascribe public meaning to social, economic, political and psychological change positions them as active proponents but also critics of the culture of modernity. This book traces the women as influential players in the interwar information age.[18] Their readiness to take up technological innovations and communication models shows their recognition of the scope for new sorts of social connections that could be drawn around philanthropic projects, and could be mediated by them. Moreover, the women's active concern to *shape* regimes of public communication in this era marks out their contributions within new and developing fields – in academic, public and media discussion – that registered increasing demand for expert knowledge. My interest is in how, in addressing these political, social and personal transformations of the age, female philanthropists' commitments focused afresh the enduring vitality of older traditions and mechanisms of social life in conformity with the new vehicles for social connectivity. Blending the old and the new – seeing not only ways to facilitate, but a requirement to bolster the enduring and constitutive bases of social relationships and the experiences of everyday life – was pivotal to these women's projects as philanthropists and thinkers, and to the meanings of modernity to which their practice subscribed.

***

The First World War had diverted what many commentators recognized to be a dormant spirit of social service into the causes of patriotism and peace, expanding in the process newly bureaucratized and professionalized approaches to social work. The Ministry of Munitions, set up under H. H. Asquith's UK government in 1915, and bringing under direct and indirect state control an unprecedented number of factories and factory workers employed in the manufacture of armaments, was a training ground for many social work practitioners and theorists, both men and women.[19] The voices of some of these individuals have surfaced frequently in historians' accounts of interwar social policy and social theory. Women like Elizabeth Macadam, who was asked by the wartime Ministry of Munitions to help devise training courses for welfare workers, had been debating and practicing training in social work for a number of decades. Macadam began her social work career in the 1890s when she lived and worked in women's settlements in London and later Liverpool, where she also played a central role in the establishment of early university level training in social work at the University of Liverpool. In 1911 she was appointed as the first salaried lecturer in Social Work at the University and in 1919 as the secretary of the recently formed JUC (Joint University Council for Social Studies).[20] Elizabeth Macadam's voice was certainly an important one in early-twentieth-century social work circles, and her contribution to interwar debates about both the enduring and the shifting bases of women's philanthropy and social work offers one insightful contemporary commentary against which the individual contributions of Booth, Fisher, Kinnaird and Paget will be read. This generation of women, who had begun their public careers in the last decades of the nineteenth century or the turn of the twentieth century, had developed by the interwar years individual reflexive repertoires on the meanings of philanthropic practice, which they sought to pass on in the interwar world. Elizabeth Macadam assessed the opportunities and tensions experienced by a new generation of middle-class women who, from the first years of the twentieth century, had been formally trained for the profession of social work in certificate and diploma courses in the social studies and training departments that were newly established in (or on the edges of) a number of British universities.[21] The varied practical methods of social work were addressed on these courses through observational visits and placements for students at statutory and voluntary welfare organizations. There were also vital conceptual and political dimensions to the work: programme curriculums were structured precisely so as to involve the unpicking of the relationship between the role of the state and the voluntary and industrial sectors.[22]

State-sponsored social service, which scholars now understand made up a large part of the total British welfare provision before the First World War, was not the only model of voluntary action that was harnessed by the demands of wartime. Peter Grant has shown the scale of the wartime renewal and extension of civilian models of voluntary and philanthropic effort beyond the boundaries of the state, from the knitting and stitching drives across the country to the establishment of around 18,000 new charities, half as many as had existed in total in Britain before the war.[23] Grant's argument that this massive wartime stimulus reinforced the 'integrative elements' of voluntary action, breaking down in some cases class barriers for the cause of a 'people's war',[24] is suggestive for a history that seeks to chart the significance of philanthropy in the two decades that followed the war. As this book explores, the centrality of an ethics of social integration to the shaping of the history of twentieth-century participatory citizenship developed pivotally in the interwar years. Wartime participation focused a new scale and urgency for the contribution of charitable activity to the project of social connectedness, but it is precisely its building upon and extending traditions and mechanisms of pre-war commitments for this new context that is key. As Grant inferred, women's membership in late-Victorian and Edwardian social service and political organizations was particularly important in laying vital groundwork for this intervention.[25] I argue that interwar ambitions for the integrative purpose of voluntary action were fundamentally shaped by traditions of female philanthropy that were both more socially-embedded and more malleable even than this context allows for. The dynamic *conceptual* influence of women's voluntary work, as well as its organizational practice, I argue, reveals the richness of this inheritance for the interwar spirit of social connection.

The developing taxonomies of philanthropy in the interwar period were one manifestation of these shifts. In the interwar years, definitions of philanthropy were formulated in dialogue with the meanings attached to the evolving categories of voluntary work, public service and social and economic practices. In *The New Philanthropy: A Study of the Relations Between the Statutory and Voluntary Social Services* (1934), Elizabeth Macadam defined 'Charitable or philanthropic organisations' in relation to 'Voluntary work in the public services'; 'Institutions and self-help bodies'; 'Research and experiment' initiatives; and 'Propaganda.'[26] In *The Voluntary Citizen: An Enquiry into the Place of Philanthropy in the Community* (1938), the Social Studies scholar, Constance Braithwaite argued that philanthropy held together a range of social practices, and comprised 'all that is included in both the terms "charity" and "voluntary social service"', where 'charity include[d] all voluntary gifts of money (or its equivalent in goods) for purposes which are of no direct economic benefit to the donor or his immediate family dependents.'[27] Braithwaite's interest in the relationship between the role of voluntary and statutory welfare work and industrial practice codified expansive definitions of philanthropic practice as 'supplementary', 'experimental', 'controversial' and 'international'.[28] However, like Macadam, Braithwaite worried about the dislocation of revisionist contemporary thought in relation to earlier re-conceptualizations of philanthropic commitment, notably by key thinkers of the nineteenth century, Charles Loch, Octavia Hill, Bernard and Helen Bosanquet.[29] Other commentators critiqued what was assumed to be the failures of older notions of benevolence to address the social and political relationships that denoted the new post-war mass democracy. In the wake of the national sacrifices of the First World War, the future Labour Prime Minister, Clement Attlee discussed the need for social work to replace an outdated practice of benevolence with the modern principle of social justice.[30] Addressing an audience of young women in 1927, the Conservative Prime Minister, Stanley Baldwin spoke of how 'the old fields covered by benevolence ... or philanthropy' had been narrowed by statutory activities and urged that older forms of 'emotional benevolence' be replaced by the work of 'both heart and brain.'[31]

Although women who undertook voluntary work themselves were centrally concerned with the development of models of modern citizenship, their consciousness of the shifting political landscape and the evolving scope for cultural transmission in the interwar years signalled an often personal and collective rawness in their responses to social change. In 1928 Lettice Fisher described herself rhetorically for a Liberal newspaper readership as 'belong[ing] to the pre-war period, and find[ing] it amazingly hard to think in terms of this puzzling new world.'[32] Having stood in 1919 as a candidate for the leadership of the NUWSS (National Union of Women's Suffrage Societies), Lettice Fisher moved with other suffragists in the post-war years to explore women's awkward and halting assimilation within Britain's mass democracy, and continued to critique the incompleteness of the parliamentary record on women's social and political rights. For suffragists and feminists crucial questions remained after the 1918 and 1928 Representation of the People Acts and the Sex Discrimination Removal Act (1919) about the scope for women's and men's self-development within any evolution of social structures that continued to be framed intellectually by the principles of 'sex differentiation.'[33] Lettice Fisher directed her energies after 1918 towards challenging the inequalities of economics, industrial practice and social welfare in her work to support voluntary and statutory provision for unmarried mothers and through her connection with the Women's Institutes. Fisher's comment in the late 1920s about the 'puzzling new world' registered, additionally, a wider interwar debate about how the passage of citizenship illuminated the concept of futurity.[34] In her popular writings she rehearsed the point repeatedly, in conversation with the interwar interest in what would be theorized later in the twentieth century as time-space compression, that collective national psychology and individual sensibilities were tested as the world grew smaller through the innovations of mass transport and communications.[35] Both the awareness and confrontation of such changes, as we will see, were to have profound effects upon the cultural and historical narratives female philanthropists produced between the wars, and upon the stories and contexts to which their philanthropy was connected. Like each of the women studied in this book, Lettice Fisher's appropriation of this thinking influenced the reach of her public discussion in the interwar years within and beyond the philanthropic realm.

***

The subject of female philanthropy has been fertile ground for historians. A vast amount of historical scholarship has been published exploring philanthropic practice as a conduit for the expansion of middle- and upper-class women's social and political freedoms, increasing visibility in public life and contributions to the development of the professionalization of social work.[36] It is now both very well understood that philanthropy was a critical site for the development of women's agency within the historical public sphere,[37] and that these efforts had influential legacies in the twentieth-century policy developments of welfare states.[38] Beneath both of these arguments – the former framed by the historiographical concern about cultures of domesticity and the latter by an interest from the 1990s onwards in 'maternalist' political cultures – lies the assumption that women's philanthropic commitment can be explained by female capacities for the provision of care. Interpreting the personal and social force of women's relationship to the economies of care-giving certainly remains a critical task for historians. However, the tendency to date has been to instrumentalize women's work of care as a concrete rather than a conceptual mode in ways that juxtapose the qualities of nature and reason (male) with matter and form (female), and therefore wholly downplay, if not ignore, the theoretical contributions of this practice.[39] A related problem to that of the juxtaposition of male and female 'natures' in the interpretation of women's philanthropic practice has been the over-readiness to accept historical rhetoric which, while treating men's philanthropic commitment in terms of the investment of economic capital (with respect to the sums of money an individual donated to a cause/s), measured women's philanthropy by an individual's dedication of emotional and moral energy (through time and commitment); an indication of the moral and cultural capital that middle-class and elite women ideally were expected to wield.[40] By the late-nineteenth and early-twentieth centuries, women's philanthropic emotion connoted satirical behaviour that could be related to critiques of 'unnatural femininity' that was more properly directed towards motherhood and other conventionally feminine work.[41] We need to look beyond these rhetorical representations, I argue, which themselves, were not static. In shifting attention from the assumed feminine, emotional qualities of women's philanthropy this book emphasizes how close attention to the depth of the convictions that drove women's philanthropic commitments illuminates philanthropists' endeavours as theoretical as well as practical projects. As the following chapters trace, female philanthropists not only engaged with contemporary debates and concerns, they posed vital intellectual questions about how knowledge, identity and relationships were to be constructed and understood.

The conceptual vitality of women's philanthropic engagement into the twentieth century has been especially overlooked. Although James Hinton's work on 1940s wartime Britain has shown the longevity of elite women's work of personal social service into the first half of the twentieth century, the assumption is still that such work was driven by the moral framework of a 'Victorian ethos of public service ... at odds' with the developing individualistic sensibilities seen to define modern culture.[42] The possibilities for a less rigid conception of female philanthropists' theory work for the interpretation of twentieth-century history have not yet been explored. The suggestive work of historians of the nineteenth century that considers how female philanthropy was embedded in wider cultural and intellectual discourses needs to be extended to address philanthropy as a tool for negotiating the social and cultural changes that accompanied early-twentieth-century modernity.[43] I have found scholarship on the role of religion in shaping nineteenth-century women's philanthropic cultures especially insightful in pointing to the need for more rigorous engagement with the conceptual histories of philanthropy. Susan Mumm has shown how by the end of the nineteenth century, women's religious observance refocused the female-dominated culture of philanthropy away from the direction of social control and religious conversion towards ideals of Christian mutuality in conformity with the aims of social uplift, and in ways that reveal how reformulated religious cultures in this period confronted the secular professions of education, medicine and social work.[44] The Christian theology animating nineteenth-century gendered theories of social service that Jane Garnett and Julie Melnyk independently have explored, additionally, needs consideration in the context of the twentieth century which, it has been argued, saw a 'reorientation of liturgy and theology based on women's experience'.[45] The wide resonance of Christian theology to the evolving social and psychological meanings of interwar philanthropy is explored especially in this book through the examples of Emily Kinnaird and Evangeline Booth's work and writings.

In all of this literature, historians have had to confront timeless stereotypes of the exercise of social and moral dominance of elite women over the working class and the poor in the form of the 'Lady Bountiful' or the 'Do-gooder'.[46] Despite Kathleen McCarthy's call over twenty-five years ago that the Lady Bountiful image 'often obscures more than it explains',[47] as Seth Koven has argued recently, the shadow of the Lady Bountiful, 'who talks sisterhood with the outcast poor in smug tones of condescending sympathy' still haunts scholarship and popular parlance about women's philanthropic practice.[48] Historical scholarship over the last two decades has done much to deepen understandings of the complexities of the personal, psychological and social dynamics underpinning the encounters of elite women's social work in the nineteenth and early twentieth centuries. Koven and Ellen Ross' studies of women slum visitors in this period, notably, have shown how women's social action shaped relationships between women and across boundaries of class, culture and sexuality.[49] While earlier work identified social conflict as defining these interactions, Koven and Ross maintain that the encounters could offer women – both the philanthropist and those in receipt of her charity – mutual support and routes to self-development. Mark Peel's work on the influential social work organization, the COS (Charity Organization Society) has underscored additionally how gender inflected the narratives of poverty and the poor constructed by female COS workers who were acutely perceptive of the appearance, demeanour and behaviour of their clients.[50] This scholarship reminds us that class identity, itself moulded around age, generational, regional, national and ethnic difference, was a central marker of women's philanthropic practice into the twentieth century in ways that informed the makings of modern socially-constructed selfhood. Indeed, in one respect the language of female philanthropy was always a language of class. The conceptual contributions made by the women examined in this book were the product of everyday experiences of the philanthropic relationship that were made sense of either through recourse to upper-middle-class access to higher education (Fisher); the social and cultural education of women of the aristocratic classes (Paget); or exposure from childhood to the political, social and religious elites (Booth; Kinnaird). Whether using vocabularies that could be understood and respected by members of the educated and politically-influential classes; consciously looking to speak across class divides; or to celebrate the authenticity of the labouring classes' everyday life, female philanthropists both marshalled the privileges of their class and sought out ways to be heard across class divides.

Notwithstanding these complicating insights about the social and psychological nature of the charitable encounter, the political commitments of women's philanthropy continue to present historians a problem. The political identities claimed by philanthropists have been interpreted either as cautious and moderate or chauvinistic. Writing about the nineteenth century, Susan Mumm has argued that, notwithstanding the examples of women who moved between charity work and political activism, including well-known figures such as the social reformer Beatrice Webb, '[r]adical political positions were rare among women philanthropists ... except for the far-from-universal support for suffragism'.[51] To delineate a 'radical' position risks, to my mind, obfuscating the transformative potential of philanthropy, however. Too often still in historical narratives, female philanthropy appears as 'an infliction on the poor', and a 'radical' practice only when it spoke a seemingly 'progressive' language that claimed social rights for the recipients of charity, or as declining and unable to face out the rising tide of secularization and specialization of social work practice.[52] Recent work has begun to explore philanthropy in relationship to alternative axes of progressive social and political activism. Here, it is notable that there has been a turn towards examining the legacies of dynamic religious and ethical traditions, in which the wider renewed interest in faith-based social policy, civic activism and social engagement amongst scholars of the sociology of religion and religious historians has suggested new fields for the exploration of political action. Seth Koven's recent account of cross-class female philanthropic relations as part of early-twentieth-century 'utopian Christianity' is one important model.[53] However, the post-secular turn in approaches both to the twentieth-century history of social engagement and in scholarship on women's agency has signalled the need for new interpretative lenses on the political drivers of women's social commitments, and not only of those women who inhabited self-consciously socially democratic worlds. The aims to extend social connectedness of those philanthropic women who chose to live by less outwardly progressive social and ethical principles, or who chose to speak sometimes though not always in these terms, also need to be readdressed to account for the ways in which enduring traditions of benevolence were reformulated in the early twentieth century in conversation with shifting political, religious and ethical cultures, and social changes. The category of 'radical', like 'conservative' – inflected with distinct meanings in historical, civic, cultural and political domains – now looks decidedly unstable as an explanatory model of women's philanthropy. In the interwar years, female philanthropy revealed the contested and much more complex search for meaningful affiliations, not only amongst citizens and between citizens and the state, but also between peoples and cultures.

***

I am unsure whether Evangeline Booth, Lettice Fisher, Emily Kinnaird and Muriel Paget knew each other personally. They have left no records or writings that indicate they did. It is possible that Fisher and Kinnaird met as part of their work for women's rights through their membership of the NCW (National Council of Women). Muriel Paget might have met Lettice Fisher at one of the international conferences on child welfare in the 1920s that they each attended; in 1903, Muriel Paget did attend a charity bazaar on behalf of the Zenana Bible and Medical Mission at which Emily Kinnaird's brother and sister, Arthur and Gertrude were present.[54] Although it would have been intriguing to find evidence of the women meeting or corresponding with each other, my interest here is in the value of tracing the individual and cumulative reflexivity in their stories (rather than necessarily the intersections), and the broader points of conceptual connection, comparisons and contrasts between their ideas and practice. The UK YWCA's 1923 publicity campaign literature, which featured an image of a young woman dressed in white holding the world in her arms, provides one indication of these encounters (see Fig. 1). The image, reminiscent of that used in the suffrage movement ten years previously in portraits of physically strong women, dressed in white to embody purity, was signed Paul Bissell and was reproduced as a poster and featured in a 1923 article in the YWCA's members' magazine.[55] Suffrage symbolism was extended here in a religious message of unity in difference; the inculcation of 'a living union with Christ' was illustrated by the transition between the faces of the globe and the variation in the skin tone of the young woman's arms. I first found this image amongst Muriel Paget's papers. There was no accompanying note, and whether Paget responded to the YWCA's campaign as a donor is unclear. The fact that she kept the pamphlet, however, points at least on one level to the constructive engagement between female philanthropists and their organizations; it indicates that virtual dialogue, if not direct conversations, did take place. It might also be suggestive of the wider processes of cross-cultural analysis that women's philanthropic practice encouraged: in parallel with the YWCA's work to extend the international understanding of young women, Muriel Paget's humanitarian engagements in war-torn and famine-stricken areas of Central and Eastern Europe post-1918 involved a series of cultural encounters in which English identity was explored in relation to the cultural and ethnic identities of European populations. In comparison with the YWCA's Christian message of universal experience, Paget's international projects reasserted cultural difference, notably as will be discussed, in the emphasis placed upon the passing on of expertise from English medical professionals to Eastern European nurses and doctors. The forms of identity and

Figure 1. Illustration in a UK YWCA Pamphlet, 1923. Image by P. Bissell. Reproduced with the permission of Special Collections, Leeds University Library, Box 38, LRA/MS 1405 (Lady Muriel Paget Papers).

exchange imagined in these two projects differed markedly but what these examples had in common was a concern to address the meanings of the cultural encounter that might be made possible in transnational social projects.

Female Philanthropy in the Interwar World places the women who undertook philanthropy in the interwar period centre stage in the historical analysis, but it differs from most previous work in one key respect. In tracing philanthropists' individual expressions of commitment and their lived experience, I foreground the conceptual scope and vitality of female philanthropy in this period, and female philanthropists' strategies for 'operating in the world'. Examining what philanthropists said, and the way they said it, is in one respect an attempt to respond to Natalie Zemon Davis' call for historians to address the '"look" of charity … The words, postures and gestures of giving and receiving', which harbour the meanings of social encounters.[56] In charting how philanthropy was constitutive of individuals' wider, varying personal and social expression, this book looks beyond the idea that there was a defining model of female philanthropy and explores how women's philanthropic practice reflected and refracted the culture and identities of contemporary society. In doing so, a central historical tension that this book addresses is the finding that female philanthropists' declared aspirations for social connectedness in the interwar period could leave social inequalities unchallenged. For some scholars, the evidence of Muriel Paget's commitment to projects of international relief work that were linked to imperial modes of operation would place her interventions beyond the scope of what can be understood as international 'friendship',[57] and yet Paget worked tirelessly and unswervingly for these causes as part of a commitment both to tackling severe disadvantage and to widening cross-cultural understanding. Acknowledging that the encounters Muriel Paget and other women explored in their projects were unequal should not be the end point of our enquiry. The finding asks us to address exactly what philanthropic relationships reveal about historical and social change and the bases for social and cultural understanding over time and place.

***

In centring the stories of four women, the book aims to open windows onto a series of contemporary transformations that defined interwar society. Studied as a group, Evangeline Booth, Lettice Fisher, Emily Kinnaird, and Muriel Paget merit attention because their trajectories and interests range so widely, both within and beyond philanthropy, and also because their reflections on the interwar world sit in such interesting dialogue and creative tension with each other; the differences, as well as the convergence in their approaches and interpretations, underscore the need to move beyond an analysis that classifies any one particular model of female philanthropy. Looked at as individuals, there are multiple ways that the lives and public contributions of these four women could be told; they told narratives about themselves and were the subject of public commentaries and memoirs. Evangeline Booth (1865–1950) is the best known of the four women in this book (see Fig. 2).[58] Born on Christmas Day, 1865, in Hackney, London, she was the seventh of eight children of William Booth and Catherine (née Mumford) who founded in 1865 a new evangelical drive amongst the poor and sinners in London, the Christian Mission, to be renamed the Salvation Army in 1878. Alongside her siblings, Booth formally entered the Salvation Army as a child; by the age of fifteen, she was a Salvation Army sergeant in London, where she worked amongst the poor in East London slums and preached as captain at the Salvation Army's Great Western Hall in Marylebone. Moving up the ranks in the 1880s and 1890s, Booth took charge of the Salvation Army in America temporarily in 1896, before being appointed national commander of the Salvation Army in Canada (1896–1904), and permanent commander of the Salvation Army in the United States (1904–34), where she settled in Hartsdale, New York. Evangeline Booth became a leading figure in the movement for constitutional reform of the leadership of the Salvation Army. She stood twice for World General, the key leadership role within the organization (the first time in 1929), and was elected in 1934, aged sixty-nine. She was the first woman in the organization to hold the position and it would be the 1980s before another woman did so again.[59]

In a newsreel broadcast in early September 1934, British audiences saw the new leader of the Salvation Army, who looked younger than her years, dressed in the organization's distinctive pencil skirt and long-lined jacket, and asserting that she would work 'in sacrificial service to the peoples of every land'.[60] Between 1934 and 1939 Booth campaigned across North America, in Australia, New Zealand, Norway, Sweden, Finland, Holland, France, Denmark, Switzerland, India, Ceylon, Singapore and Indonesia. Building on the platform she had carved out in North America, Evangeline Booth's international public recognition and celebrity was wide-ranging between the wars: she received many honours throughout her life for recognition of social work and services in wartime;[61] in 1919 she self-starred in a Lasky-Players produced feature film, *Fires of Faith*, exploiting a great upturn in public interest in the American Salvation Army's work during the First World War. Her celebrity expanded in the decades that followed and she became an international figure preaching a hard-line

Figure 2. Photograph of Evangeline Booth in Scotland on her 1936 UK motorcade tour. Photographer unknown. Reproduced with the permission of the Salvation Army International Heritage Centre, London, UK.

evangelistic faith of compassion and individual regeneration from sin through faith in the Holy Spirit. Evangeline Booth remained active in the Salvation Army until her death in New York on 17 July 1950. She never married, although the story of her 'many suitors' was reiterated throughout her life. In the late 1880s in London she adopted four children who moved with her to Canada.[62] Pearl Hamilton, the one unmarried child when Booth took over the Salvation Army in America, travelled with her to New York and in 1914 began her own career in the organization.[63]

Emily Kinnaird (1855–1947), like Evangeline Booth, never married and dedicated her life to pursuing the work of Christian social commitment with which she had been brought up in the Presbyterian Church (see Fig. 3). The evangelical fervour of the Kinnaird family was well known in the nineteenth century, both through the work of Kinnaird's father, the Gladstonian Liberal MP, Arthur Fitzgerald Kinnaird and her mother, Mary Jane Kinnaird, who pioneered a number of community provisions for women in London that preceded the founding of the YWCA, and medical and social support for Indian women. The family home at 2 Pall Mall Street East that Kinnaird remembered adjacent to London slums became a centre for evangelical campaigning.[64] The Kinnairds' lent their support to a series of missions including the 1871 campaign against

Figure 3. Portrait photograph of Emily Kinnaird, illustration in 'Girls of Yesterday and To-day. The Romance of the YWCA', by Lucy M. Moor c. 1913, 96. Reproduced with the permission of the Young Women's Trust (formerly the YWCA) and The Modern Records Centre, University of Warwick, MSS 243/15/2 (Young Women's Christian Association Records).

the slave trade on the east coast of Africa led by Lord Shaftesbury, the revival movements of 1859–60 and 1873–5, and the Mildmay Conferences. While her brother Arthur Kinnaird was educated at Eton College and the University of Cambridge, Emily Kinnaird and her four sisters were educated at home in what Kinnaird described as an expansive atmosphere.[65]

The evangelical culture underpinning the YWCA's work has attracted the interest of a number of scholars.[66] Growing from national beginnings, in the early 1890s the World's YWCA had 300 branches and nearly 100,000 members and associates in Europe; on its eightieth anniversary in 1935 it was established in fifty-six countries with a membership in excess of one million.[67] Emily Kinnaird began actively working for the UK YWCA in 1881, and was still doing so in the 1940s, by then known affectionately as 'Grandmother', and her close friends noted, still working a fourteen-hour day.[68] She was the first Honorary Secretary of the London YWCA and would go on to hold the offices of finance secretary of the UK YWCA, Vice-President of the World's YWCA, and Vice-President of the Executive Committee of the Scottish Zenana Bible and Medical Mission. Developing the work of her mother, Emily Kinnaird travelled with her sister, Gertrude on missions to India from the 1890s to the 1940s, and assisted in organizing the YWCA in India, Burma and Ceylon. She became a disciple of progressive nationalist thought in the tradition of the Indian poet and philosopher, Rabindranath Tagore and through her friendship with Mahatma Gandhi.[69] During the First World War Kinnaird worked to establish YWCA centres for the members of the WAAC (Women's Army Auxiliary Corps), munitions and other women war workers, and was awarded an OBE for the work in 1918 and a CBE in 1920.

On her death in 1956, the *Times'* obituary celebrated Lettice Fisher (1875–1956) as a 'great Oxford hostess' (see Fig. 4).[70] There was an irony in the epithet. Lettice Fisher was born into the elite political classes: the eldest daughter of the British lawyer, civil servant and clerk of the House of Commons, Courtenay Peregrine Ilbert, and his wife Jessie (née Bradley), whose commitment to upholding the family's reputation within the traditions of diplomatic hospitality was renowned.[71] In fact Lettice Fisher's own mode of hospitality was unconventional; guests and family members remembered her knitting through visits, how she took a rest after lunch (following her doctor's advice about her frequent 'heart attacks' as a young woman – probably what we would think of today as panic attacks) and had an uncompromisingly busy schedule of committee meetings, societies, and the writing for which she was publicly known. Although she spent much of her adolescence and adulthood in Oxford – as an undergraduate student in the 1890s; in North Oxford in the first years of married life, during which she worked as a tutor in economic history at the women's college, St Hugh's (1902–12); and from the mid-1920s to 1940 as wife of a College head – Oxford was not the defining environment of Lettice Fisher's life. She spent her childhood in London and North India and was energized both by the metropolitan and imperial circles of the political elites and the freedom that country-living provided, notably in the family home in Thursely, Surrey which was to be a haven from the 1920s onwards.

In the novel, *Lost Content* (1953), Lettice Fisher's younger sister Olive Heseltine looked back on elite women's position in the early-twentieth century

Figure 4. Portrait photograph of Lettice Fisher by Bassano Ltd., 1919. Copyright, National Portrait Gallery, London. Reproduced with the permission of the National Portrait Gallery.

and imagined Lettice Fisher's transformation from an intelligent child into 'the practical, progressive, democratic woman, careless in her dress, frugal in her habits, indifferent (except for music) to the fine arts'.[72] In 1899 Lettice married H. A. L. Fisher, one of her former History tutors at Oxford, and future member of Lloyd George's Coalition Government. The marriage sustained the couple's mutual intellectual interests; former students at Oxford remembered how in the early 1910s the Fishers shared their study with a basketful of kittens, while friends and associates recognized the couple's joint rewards in public life.[73] The constant stream of letters that H. A. L. Fisher wrote to his wife about life as a Lloyd George Liberal politician (1916–22) and public committee meetings, attest to a close political and professional partnership. They also shared a public commitment towards the cause for women's suffrage. Lettice Fisher was not an actively religious woman but was remembered within her family for her 'great vigour' and social conscience.[74] Her daughter, Mary, thought her mother's teetotalism was a personal response to the poverty she had seen when doing social work with poor families in East Oxford in the early 1900s.[75] From the relative modesty of the private comforts of North Oxford in the first years of her marriage, Lettice Fisher contributed to the establishment of a range of social work enterprises in Oxford for the poor. Having developed a particular concern with infant welfare that extended in the wake of the evidence of the rising wartime rate of illegitimate infant deaths, in February 1918 she became a founding member and the first chair of the NCUMC (National Council for the Unmarried Mother and her Child), and presided over the organization's combination of political lobbying initiatives and social work administration for single mothers and infants. In the interwar years Lettice Fisher was also well known for her work with the NFWI (National Federation of Women's Institutes) and in connection with the WEA (Workers' Educational Association).

Born in London, the eldest child and only daughter of Murray Edward Gordon Finch-Hatton, the twelfth earl of Winchilsea and his wife Edith, Muriel Paget (1876–1938) was brought up in an Anglican household and educated at home by governesses and later on a continental tour and social circuit befitting of a young aristocratic woman (see Fig. 5). In 1897 she married the barrister, diplomat and scientific engineer Sir Richard Arthur Surtees Paget, known to her as Artie. Early married life encompassed international travel, including to India and South Africa, as well as the establishment of a family: between 1898 and 1914, Paget gave birth to five children, four of whom lived.[76] Throughout her adulthood Muriel Paget, along with family members, featured in the pages of the international press, both for her fashionable connections and her philanthropic commitment.[77]

Figure 5. Lantern slide (photograph) of Muriel Paget. Photographer unknown. Copyright, Sir Richard Paget. Reproduced with the permission of Sir Richard Paget and Special Collections, Leeds University Library, Lantern slide box, LRA/MS 1405 (Lady Muriel Paget Papers).

Paget joined the British Red Cross Society in 1910. In 1915 she was appointed Honorary Organizing Secretary of the Anglo-Russian Hospital in Petrograd, which was officially opened on 1 February 1916, to attend to Russian soldiers fighting in the battles on the eastern front. Further projects in Russia, including the Women and Children of Russia Relief Fund (founded in December 1919) and the British Subjects in Russia Relief Association (BSRRA, for which she began fundraising in 1924), a charity that maintained British men and women who had lived and worked in Russia and were too old or infirm to leave the country, continued to absorb her attention. She was also celebrated for her relief work, developed in connection with the SCF (Save the Children Fund) in the years immediately following the end of the First World War, which established feeding centres and infant welfare clinics in war-torn areas of Central and Eastern Europe – in Czechoslovakia, Estonia, Latvia, Lithuania and Romania – to tackle the extreme poverty facing child populations. She was awarded an OBE in 1918 and CBE in 1938 as well as a range of international decorations.

In March 1938, a few months before her death, Muriel Paget was named in Russia and in Britain as associated with the British Intelligence Service. Although the assertion was denied in the highest of political circles, Muriel Paget's cultural politics were well known. She was a celebrated Russophile, a politico-cultural position that complemented her Conservative and imperialist heritage.[78] She was close to leading British Russianists and a member and supporter of a number of non-political societies fostering cross-cultural friendship and exchange in the early-twentieth century, including VOKS (All-Union Society for Cultural Relations with Foreign Cultures). She was also a close personal friend of the first Czechoslovakian President, Thomas Masaryk. Having fallen out of public discussion in the two decades following her death, Muriel Paget was reclaimed in the 1960s in a biography by Wilfrid Blunt which revealed her to have been an indefatigable philanthropist in Britain and internationally and in David Mitchell's treatment of Paget in his 1966 *Women on the Warpath*, which reaffirmed her reputation as a 'war heroine'.[79] Within the growing scholarship on post-First World War humanitarianism, and in the light of the centenaries of the Anglo-Russian Hospital and of the Russian Revolution, Muriel Paget has again been the focus of some attention.[80] Muriel Paget's cultural capital as part of an international aristocratic elite accorded her both very different personal opportunities and challenges to the other women in this book. Yet she emerges here sharing a common commitment with Evangeline Booth, Lettice Fisher and Emily Kinnaird to seeing the establishment of a 'better world', and dedicating a phenomenal energy and drive – as each woman did – to this endeavour.

***

Female Philanthropy in the Interwar World makes three key arguments. First, it argues that historians should move beyond interpretations that categorize women's philanthropy as a gendered practice and focus instead upon the outcomes – imagined and real – of the relationships that underpinned, and were stimulated by, women's philanthropic exchanges. Treating female philanthropy as a gendered category of analysis limits historical understandings of women's social activism and of philanthropy's influence. This book treats philanthropy, alternatively, as an expansive conceptual and practical enterprise – one which through the language and imagery upon which it drew, stretched between the fields of cultural, intellectual and political engagement, and personal and social experience. Female philanthropists did not simply proffer social or therapeutic tools, but also critiques of interwar society, culture and politics; ideas about how society should function; and models of personhood, that critically engaged with modern identities and social relationships in the search for social development. Second, this book charts how older assignations of middle- and upper-class women's cultural authority through philanthropy evolved in the interwar years in conversation with the history of women's professionalization, the reconfiguration of the state, and the intertwined politics of citizenship, communication and consumerism during the interwar years. Moving between the histories of social policy, religious faith, academic engagement, celebrity culture, media communications and the transnational sites of female philanthropists' commitments, I argue that women's philanthropic practices emerged as vital markers and interpretative models of the varied cultural and epistemological transformations that men and women lived through between 1918 and 1939 and illuminated philanthropy's wide significance as a marker of historical change. Third, in conceiving of philanthropic practice as a creative endeavour, I argue that philanthropy was a revelatory rather than a reactive practice. The search for deeper understandings of the self in relation to society was at the heart of female philanthropists' contributions between the wars, which I argue combined reflexive interest in imaginative, virtual and subjective encounters with concrete material, moral and social goals.

In tracing these interconnected themes, my analysis builds upon scholars' insights about the meanings of human exchange in social action. I have been influenced by the scholarship of Marcel Mauss on earlier historical periods,[81] and in a modern context, by the theories of contemporary economics advanced by Maurice Glasman. In the post-Keynesian and post-neo-Liberal world, Glasman maintains, we need an economic system that is both 'humane' and 'competitive', and which centres relationships over transactions. Glasman's contribution to this debate – voiced under the banner of 'Blue Labour' and reconfiguring older religious traditions of Catholic social thought, in conformity with recent perspectives on social entrepreneurship – is to state the need to look beyond either state (Keynesianism) or market (neo-liberalism) models of exchange to those present within 'intermediate institutions', including associational cultures, charities, vocational colleges and, for example, supporter-owned football clubs, in which an alternative logic of relationships is conceived.[82] Glasman sees these sorts of institutions as vehicles for furthering the texture of associational and durable relationships as a critical form of political and economic participation. For him, the recognition of these institutional energies, and the enduring, institutionally-embedded relationships which they foster, amount to democratic and vocational 'resistance' to modernity. My aim, instead, is to historicize the value that was accorded to the mechanisms of social engagement fostered by philanthropists' attention to human and social relationships that were developed in conversation with the shifting practices of the modern world. In the interwar world the results were wide-reaching, both within and beyond the philanthropic realm and in spheres that mediated the competitive and compassionate bases of philanthropic action. As I argue throughout this book, philanthropy was not only understood to work through modern relationships in the interwar years. Indeed, its modelling of the extensive reach of interpersonal encounter in this period actively shaped recognition of the potential for the much wider application of affective exchange in the modern world.

***

Evangeline Booth, Lettice Fisher, Emily Kinnaird and Muriel Paget come in and out of focus in the chapters that follow. They emerge at different moments engaging with the personal, intellectual and social significance of their work, and in ways that place their activities, beliefs and ideas in constructive conversation with each other. The value of an approach to writing the history of women's social action which relates personal stories to broader social and intellectual contexts has been shown by engaging critical work,[83] and this book seeks to build on the approach through its focus on multiple stories. The five chapters in this book are structured to follow cumulatively the four women's intellectual, moral and physical journeys as they refined their arguments about the principles underpinning their work, and moved between various political and cultural mechanisms to explain and represent these goals. Beginning by discussing the women's stories in relation to new reflections upon personal service in the interwar years and psychological discourses of 'relationships' (Chapter 1), subsequent chapters trace the evolving epistemological bases of women's philanthropy and its contribution to understanding knowledge (Chapter 2); female philanthropy and interwar ideas of democratic agency (Chapter 3); the role of philanthropists in international exchange and their composition of narratives of history and culture (Chapter 4); and female philanthropists' expertise in public communication (Chapter 5). In placing Booth's, Fisher's,

Kinnaird's and Paget's stories in proximity with one another, the book seeks to tease out the complexities in the conceptual, material and subjective engagements underpinning a generation of women's understandings of modern philanthropy and the role of social action in the interwar world. The differences as well as the comparisons between their stories are thus vital. The tensions experienced by these four women in reformulating the work of care between the wars illustrate that recalibrations of notions of duty, obligation and responsibility in social action were absolutely central to the project of challenging and shaping a modern future.

1

Relationships

When, in 1923, Vera Brittain examined the question of women's duty in an article for the feminist publication, *Time and Tide*, she argued provocatively that little, if anything, had changed since the stiff mid-Victorian days. The generation of middle-class women to which her mother belonged, 'brought up to believe in this supreme duty of individual service', Brittain claimed, had 'bound the consciences of their daughters to the same iron tradition'. There was little escape from the perpetual and thankless round of domestic work, even for those young women who took up university places, who if they were lucky might work uninterrupted for 'two vacations out of eight'.[1] Vera Brittain's provocation raised the question of whether there was in fact any room at all in the post-war landscape of public expectations about educated and elite women's social duty for the satisfactory development of personal initiative.

My starting point in this chapter is a simple question: how did female philanthropists and their publicists position projects of personal service in the interwar years against shifting configurations of women's service, the professionalization of voluntary commitment and in debates about the shifting role of the individual in society? I focus on Evangeline Booth's, Emily Kinnaird's and Muriel Paget's stories. These three women were part of the same generation as Vera Brittain's mother. They had been brought up in mid-to-late-nineteenth-century social and Christian principles that configured voluntary work as essential personal and civic commitment. Unlike Brittain, Booth, Kinnaird and Paget did not understand service ethics to be repressive, and their writings show how each of them in distinct ways conceptualized the work of service as contributing centrally to the development of selfhood within the evolving terms of women's professional practice and extra-professional activism. The women critically re-examined and reinforced nineteenth-century theories of gendered social service, grounded in many cases in Christian concepts of friendship and personal sympathy.[2] Equally, if not more fundamentally, their own performances of personal service became models for broader appropriation in the interwar years in the context of wide-ranging debates about the interdependencies of personal relationships for the effective functioning of society.

Others addressed the question of personal service differently to Vera Brittain. Winifred Holtby, a fellow member of the feminist organization, the Six Point Group and a close friend of Brittain, considered the ethics of women's obligation in another article for *Time and Tide* in 1926. She saw social commitment as vital both for the development of personality and for the contribution women and men were to make to the common good, and she recognized an alternative ethical motor for the work. Holtby, who regarded service as 'privilege', as much as obligation, looked forward to a time when feminist activism was no longer needed but for now, when it still was, she understood personal service as a vehicle for women to address inequalities and continue the search for a better society, one in which 'men and women work together for the good of all mankind [and for] a supreme regard for the importance of the human being'.[3]

The renewed reflection upon women's individual service, articulated with differing emphases by feminists and friends Vera Brittain and Winifred Holtby, was part of a wider debate in the 1920s and 1930s about the scope of women's service that addressed both shifting models of social service and women's particular contributions to this work in relation to the goals of individual and community development. The expansion of professional social work was one important context underpinning these debates. An article in the NUSEC's (National Union of Societies for Equal Citizenship) magazine the *Woman's Leader* in 1924 reported the JUC's identification of a swing amongst young people away from 'organized personal philanthropy' of the sort undertaken by the COS, in girls' and boys' clubs and university settlements towards the more obviously political or educational work undertaken through Labour Party membership, the trades union movement, the WEA, government departments and local administration.[4] A decade later, in 1934, Elizabeth Macadam, herself a leading member of the NUSEC, distinguished between personal service and charity, writing that 'social service means personal service, whether the personal service is supplemented by material gifts, or not', which she contrasted to charity, 'in the sense of almsgiving', the gifting of money that she believed comprised no personal sacrifice of time or thought.[5] Other female commentators sought to interpret the expansive political traditions of individual service and social work consciously for modern forms of social relationships. The Fabian Beatrice Webb, who began social work as a friendly visitor in London in the 1880s for Charles Booth's extensive social survey, looked back in *My Apprenticeship* (1926) to the example set in the late-nineteenth century by Samuel and Henrietta Barnett who founded the university settlement, Toynbee Hall in 1884 in London's

East End. She argued that the Barnetts 'had come to realize that the principles of personal service and personal responsibility for ulterior consequences, together with the application of scientific method' should be 'extended from the comparatively trivial activity of almsgiving to the behaviour of the employer, the landlord and the consumer of wealth without work'.[6] Writing in 1938 in *The Voluntary Citizen*, the socialist Constance Braithwaite maintained that the 'personal attitude towards clients' was vital in both the public and voluntary social services, and argued that charities and voluntary organizations historically had been more adept at such interpersonal work than public authorities.[7]

A central focus here is on the attention paid in the interwar period to the affective and social exchanges sustained by women's philanthropic practice as mechanisms for marshalling psychological insights upon interpersonal relationships. Particularly striking was the interest a diverse range of social commentators showed in examining female philanthropy as a model both for understanding the inequalities underpinning everyday social relationships and for harbouring ambitions for the achievement of social levelling. The growing importance attached to psychological thought in this period, framed partly in the terms of individual 'conscience' that Vera Brittain invoked, asked new and challenging questions about the contemporary relevance of personal service. Mathew Thomson has shown that, as well as a new vogue for self-management and 'brain training' in the interwar years, popular psychology was concerned precisely with an understanding of the functioning of individuality as part of the common good.[8] Building on this finding, I read Booth's, Kinnaird's and Paget's discussions about traditions of women's service, not as indicative of the unbending nor necessarily detrimental impact of duty upon women's subjective development (as in Brittain's critique), but for what they reveal about female philanthropists' contributions to shifting ideas about the constitution of the social self in the interwar years. Relational understandings of individual behaviour functioned as a broad psychological church attracting philanthropists from distinct intellectual and social traditions, and forming a shared common vocabulary for public explanations of their work. The emphasis upon philanthropy as a model for interpersonal encounters was not intended to confer a cozily conservative model of women in the role of care-giver, however, as will become clear. Evangeline Booth, Emily Kinnaird and Muriel Paget explored philanthropic selfhoods through their work with the poor and deprived, children and young women variously to address the institutional, political and psychological implications of their practice. The public significance attached to the modelling of their work around the theme of interpersonal encounter was contested but also had a coherence that can be illustrated in this chapter through the evidence of organizational literature, press and broader discussions which show contemporaries teasing out the contemporary registers of the 'philanthropic relationship' in dialogue with the professionalization of society; behavioural psychology; democratic subjectivity and mass politics. Women's philanthropic projects provided examples in the interwar years of the differential of emotional power, as well as the ambition for the interdependency, between the 'giver' and 'receiver' in the philanthropic relationship.

The organization of personal service

The family story had it that it was a gesture by her aunt, Lady Templetown that initiated Muriel Paget's philanthropic career in the first decade of the twentieth century. After her Society marriage to the polymath, Sir (Richard) Artie Paget in 1897, Muriel Paget suffered periods of illness (as she would throughout her life) and family tragedy on the death of her first child in 1898. Retreating from fashionable circles, the story goes, she re-emerged in 1905 as the Honorary Secretary of a charity to provide subsidized meals for convalescent men and women in Southwark, London, which had been established by Paget's great-aunt, Camilla Rice and which Lady Templetown chaired. Paget was to hold this position uninterrupted until her death in 1938.[9] At first glance, this was a typical entrée into the world of charitable work that Society women, with the domestic organizing skills appropriate for executive positions, were expected to inhabit: as an article in the 1901 New Year issue of the Society magazine, *The Queen, the Lady's Newspaper and Court Chronicle* stated, '[m]ost women have wonderful powers of organization', which could be transplanted from the conditions of managing a home and family to running a philanthropic enterprise.[10] Within five years, the charity established by Paget's relatives had expanded onto a larger scale, with kitchens operating in a number of boroughs in South and East London, including Bermondsey, Stepney and Hoxton under the auspices of the organization, the IKL (Invalid Kitchens of London). Newspaper reports specified the IKL was providing by 1911 around 11,000 1d. ready-cooked dinners a year to between 500 and 600 convalescents recovering from illness in their own homes.[11]

A modernizing practice

In its early years the IKL proceeded, as many philanthropic organizations established by women in the nineteenth century had done, through the institutionalization of personal methods of engagement and the local management of social work projects.[12] These practices facilitated an integrated approach to community action. IKL personnel liaised with London borough hospitals, church workers, health and aid societies about applications for support as part of an inter-agency approach towards poverty that systematized the cumulative establishment of local knowledge. In the process, the IKL emerged, independently, as an important source of data about the London infirm. There was some anxiety amongst the cultural and political elites about how the charity's data on the individuals whom it supported would be used. Press reports in the 1910s stressed the IKL's work of personal investigation by district visitors who concentrated on supporting men and women who were not in receipt of local parish provision. A report in the *Times* in February 1911 calibrated the charity's work in a notice that stressed the combination of personal investigation by district visitors 'with a proper organization under a central authority', thereby reassuring readers that provision was confined to those ineligible for Poor Law and other municipal sources of relief and was overseen by professionals.[13] In this respect, investigative casework, itself a mechanism of the professionalization of the social work sector in the early-twentieth century,[14] was both a way of reinforcing the terms of charities' specialist practice and a vehicle for voluntary bodies to claim legitimacy in gatekeeping definitions of poverty by means of the direct access to local community knowledge.[15]

Discussion in the Edwardian national and local press about specific *forms* of philanthropic practice was significant not only for tracing the developing organizational logic of philanthropic enterprises, but also in indicating how that logic was a response to perceptions of the shifting social affiliations and relationships of contemporary life. For a Society couple such as the Pagets, this discussion was closely bound up with their developing public reputation as part of the fashionable set. In 1911, the Pagets addressed a meeting of the Guild of Help branch in Dudley, Wolverhampton. By then widely recognized in the locality, having opened a garden suburb scheme on the outskirts of Wolverhampton in 1908, the Pagets attended the meeting as high-profile patrons of the 'modern' methods of social action embodied by the Guild of Help. In his 'Vote of Thanks', Sir (Richard) Artie Paget stated a concern not only for the means by which a charitable institution operated but also for the implications of the great problem of urban poverty for the preservation of the nation and the vigour of the race.[16] Addressing the mainly middle-class audience in the 'Capital of the Black Country', such rhetoric spoke to the Edwardian vogue of the educated classes for hereditary science and the broad political language of 'national efficiency'.[17] Muriel Paget spent more time in her talk than her husband did focusing upon the sorts of practical social work the Dudley branch had undertaken on the ground since its establishment in 1908, notably with families in local slums, but once again she was primarily interested in how the form and nature of institutional charitable practice built upon and reflected models of social relationships. She discussed the possibility for a distinctively modern practice that reformulated older methods of philanthropy to confront pressing social problems, in which 'personal instruction' was as vital as legislation in the wars against the social 'evils' of 'drink, wilful idleness, and the spread of infectious diseases', and against ignorance: '[i]t was only by personal service on an organised basis', she argued, that such problems could be overcome.[18] The Guild of Help offered a resonant image for repurposing the work of personal service around this model; the organization's motto, 'Not alms but a friend', at once part of a wide late-nineteenth- and early-twentieth-century critique of charity as almsgiving, also called upon memories of historical guild membership that advanced Christian ideas of community action.[19] In developing models of associational life that redirected indiscriminate charitable giving towards active participation, guilds modelled a creative and dynamic form of fraternity in which the relationships connecting individuals and society in civic life were to be fostered.[20]

IKL publicity in the years during and following the First World War shows how evolving models of social work were mapped onto imaginations of the philanthropic relationship in ways which further complicated the reprisal of nineteenth-century traditions of women's personal service for the development of both professional and extra-professional practice. Although outwardly, alleviation of distress remained the charity's priority throughout this period, the IKL also registered a concern with the psychological development of those whom the charity supported as a broader project requiring the managed intervention of social work. When, during wartime, the IKL extended its provision amongst soldiers' and sailors' families and in seventeen kitchens across London, publicity described the organization operating through a committee comprising a 'large proportion of practical social workers'.[21] By the late 1920s, fundraising literature stressed the role of the secretary of each branch, 'a trained welfare worker', who assessed individual applications, and then passed them on to a local committee of representatives of district health and welfare organizations who reviewed the claims on a case-by-case basis.[22] In her short piece on 'Welfare work' for the NUSEC's *Woman's Year Book 1923–1924*, Eleanor T. Kelly, the Vice-President of the Welfare Workers Institute, defined the aim of the welfare worker not '"to do things for" the workers but to make it possible for them to do the things themselves'. The IKL's statement about the employment of a trained welfare worker can be read as a device to combat the sort of critique of unregulated welfare work that Kelly observed as 'tend[ing] to patronage and so render[ing] the workers less independent than before'.[23] Certainly, IKL organizational literature in the 1920s stressed the end results of the charity's work in effecting personal transformations over and above the fulfilment of basic social need. The charity's balance sheet for 1926, for example, specified that all applications for support were reviewed via interviews and correspondence with medical and social agencies, precisely 'so that the benefit derived from them does not begin and end with the actual dinners given'.[24] The language spoke to the aims of welfare work to support industrial efficiency that required an understanding of the individual worker 'as a human being rather than as a unit of power or a cog in the industrial machine'.[25]

The emphasis upon the IKL's attention to individual behaviour was of critical importance in the developing public rhetoric about the charity from the war years onwards which signalled the complexities of the modelling of professionalization within the organization beyond the principles of bureaucratic systematization. The reinvigoration of the psychological metres of the *extra*-professional engagement of voluntary practice also vitalized the work around evolving conceptions of personal service. For example, in an article for the religious magazine, *The Quiver* in 1916, the popular writer Amy Barnard imagined the secretary of an IKL branch working through compassion, purchasing and paying for the food and giving freely of her sympathy to the 'pale-faced queue at the opening before her. "I might spend hours listening to the people", said one helper … Evidently she knew all about them, and accosted them by name, inquiring after this sick child or that invalided husband'.[26] The significance of Barnard's use of the term 'helper' – interesting itself in the wider context of charities' contribution to the political culture of wartime integration – was not that it defined the work as unpaid or amateur, and indeed leading figures in interwar social work training insisted that there was 'no essential difference between salaried and voluntary social work'.[27] Rather, the practice was shaped as pivotal to understanding the application of a model of the philanthropic relationship in which sympathy helped to construct a bond of trust between the secretary and the men, women and children using the service. The service encounter was to be born of individual feeling and commitment, not the outcome of a contract between the professional worker and her client.

Reclaiming self-help

In the late 1920s the interpersonal aspects of the philanthropic relationship emerged as a central framing device of the IKL's publicity in ways that register an important development in the configuration of women's service as the basis for personal psychological transformation, as well as the relief of distress. In October 1929, Muriel Paget broadcast a wireless radio fundraising appeal on behalf of the IKL to London listeners of the BBC's *Week's Good Cause* feature that articulated the charity's central ambitions to extend both men's and women's self-development. The IKL was in financial deficit in this period, having already closed a number of the kitchens that were opened during the war years,[28] yet Paget informed listeners that during the last twenty-one months 114,938 dinners had been served to nearly 4,000 infirm and convalescent men and women in London.[29] On the cusp of the Great Slump, it is possible that the London donating public was most focused upon the increasingly urgent plight of the British unemployed that was portrayed in so much journalism, fiction and documentary coverage of the period;[30] by 1930 it is notable that IKL publicity framed the charity's work explicitly within a language of class, oriented around the principle of the privileged classes assisting working men and women back into paid employment (as well as good health).[31] The *Radio Times*' advertisement for Muriel Paget's 1929 wireless radio appeal was illustrated by a sketch of the archetypal respectable working boy, wearing a flat, cloth cap, and reading a poster about the IKL, an affirmation of an idealized heroic, masculine working-class culture. Projecting a complementary ideal of personal improvement to that registered broadly by the work of the 'cultivated elites' (including at the early BBC),[32] the illustration supplemented the emphasis placed in Muriel Paget's script upon the IKL's policy of requiring men and women to contribute to the cost of the dinners according to their ability to pay: 'the system is based on self-respect and self-help'.[33] The message invoked for those who supported the charity an understanding of the relationship between the 'giver' and 'receiver' in the philanthropic relationship as a form of assisted self-help. While reinforcing established class distinctions, the broadcast stated the charity's ambition specifically to foster individual independence and self-development.

This reclaiming and reanimating of an ethic of self-help as relevant to the interwar philanthropic exchange reframed, in a new idiom, the emphases of late-nineteenth- and early-twentieth-century inter-class projects of mutuality and reciprocity. The broad currency of these ideas ranged from the sorts of organicist thinking about society advanced by social reformers such as Helen Bosanquet to the civic model of the Guild of Help.[34] Muriel Paget grew up with first-hand knowledge of another example. In 1893, following the great family tragedy of the death of their ten-year-old child, George Edward Henry Finch-Hatton, Viscount Maidstone, Muriel Paget's parents Lord and Lady Winchelsea had established The Children's Order of Chivalry to encourage aristocratic children to befriend the children of poor families in the East End of London. The ambition was to build personal connections between privileged and poor children – the former sending the London child clothes, boots and some of their pocket money and issuing invitations to holiday in the family home outside of London – while stimulating a broader sense of social and moral responsibility amongst the children of the wealthy classes. This enterprise, although limited in its engagement with the causes of urban and child poverty, had a distinct ambition, as sympathetic commentators acknowledged: 'in no way a charity', The Children's Order of Chivalry encouraged cross-class relations ('as one child should help another') and emphasized the responsibility of the elite classes to address the terms of their own behaviour as the basis for civic action.[35] These principles signalled the need for an ethical understanding on the part of children in privileged families, who, growing up in comfort, needed to be trained to social conscience. In the 1890s Muriel Paget's father wrote a pamphlet advertising The Children's Order of Chivalry that expressed the desire for 'a new era of personal love and sympathy between the children of the rich and the children of the poor' as a vision of spiritual connection as well as social cohesion. The ideal was for a social, economic and moral good framed around sympathy and large-heartedness. Christian allusions of personal relationships were central to this project: while gifts of alms that merely do 'good by proxy' were to be condemned, Lord Winchelsea envisaged instead the 'bind[ing] together with the threefold cord of Gentleness, Honour and Love' of young people growing up with very different life chances.[36]

In Britain in the early 1930s the discourse of social connection through mutuality was to be remoulded around an emphasis upon personal dignity in sympathetic commentaries about unemployment that called for active collective response to the human costs of the Slump. For example, in an article about unemployment in Northern England for the BBC's weekly commentary magazine, the *Listener* in January 1933, the writer and broadcaster Stuart Petre Mais claimed that '[i]t is not charity that the unemployed want, but a practical expression of understanding friendliness – and that at once. Charity does not begin to touch the problem; friendliness may indeed in the end solve it'.[37] 'Friendliness', for Mais, was a social process that would rebuild the confidence of those who were out of work, who should be seen as 'first-rate workmen' not 'unemployables', and whose needs were to be viewed beyond the essentializing and 'Victorian' categories of the 'deserving' or 'undeserving'.[38] Although the homogenizing rhetoric of such commentaries sought to stress the distance between Victorian and consciously modern modes of socio-political engagement (those that were derived from the evidence of the personal psychology of the unemployed), in fact there were vital ethical connections between older philanthropic practices of interpersonal encounter and the interwar idiom of community work as friendship that centred personal dignity and development. The goals of The Children's Order of Chivalry and the Edwardian Guild of Help both focused, specifically, upon the development of personal and civic relationships over the giving of alms and worked by encouraging an ethical understanding across classes. What was apparent in the late-Victorian and Edwardian contexts as well as in the 1930s was the attention paid to fostering the individual development of the 'giver' and 'receiver' in the philanthropic relationship. Self-consciously progressive calls in the interwar years for a new social model of friendliness to address contemporary social disadvantage in this respect came very close to the reprisal of older notions of the work of service in philanthropic projects of the era: both were concerned precisely for the extension of mechanisms to support the assumed psychological benefits of self-help. Both were fundamentally concerned with how the self was connected to others.

The humanitarian field

Warfare in Europe in 1914–18 and the continuance of the Allies' naval blockade of the Central Powers brought famine, disease and homelessness across much of Central and Eastern Europe in the years immediately after 1918. The unprecedented social crises unleashed across Europe by the Great War, as Bruno Cabanes has argued, triggered a profound transformation in the practice and discourse of humanitarianism: the establishment of an astonishing range of international agencies to aid the victims of war and to enshrine the idea of humanitarian rights.[39] Starving and displaced populations, alongside disabled soldiers and veterans, became the target of many European and American relief agencies' energies, now faced not only with an unprecedented scale of need but with the new challenge of working through distinctively transnational networks of practice in the transition from war to peace.[40] Between 1919 and 1923 Muriel Paget worked in Czechoslovakia and Romania with the LORCS (League of Red Cross Societies), and in collaboration with the SCF (established in January 1919 as the Fight the Famine

Council) to support the mainly Russian children who had been displaced in the conflict into the new republics of Estonia, Latvia and Lithuania; she became a member of the SCF's General Council and Executive Committee, holding the position of Vice-President. In the period up to 1922 the SCF allocated grants totalling £56,645 to advance a range of initiatives launched by Paget to provide food, clothing and medical supplies to populations distressed by war and its aftermath.[41] Initially, in February 1919 Muriel Paget responded to the pleas of her friend, the daughter of the first President of Czechoslovakia, Alice Masaryk for assistance in the provision of clothing and other necessities to populations in Slovakia. She went on over the next two years to set up hospitals (first in Turzovka and then Bytča), and infant welfare centres in Western Slovakia in the towns of Žilina, Caca and Mariková.[42] In May 1920 Paget's Mission to Eastern Europe was established with headquarters based in Dvinsk, Latvia and inaugurated a scheme of medical assistance to child populations in the new Baltic States. Paget had personal experience by this period of organizing emergency feeding centres to meet critical basic need: in February 1918 she had established a temporary kitchen in Kiev, Russia feeding 6,000 Russians who had been displaced during the revolution of 1917 – an example of her relief and medical work in Russia that spanned over two decades, against the background of shifting national political culture, that will be discussed in more detail in the following chapters.[43] Muriel Paget's clinics in Latvia (Dvinsk and Riga), Estonia (Reval and Petseri) and Lithuania (Kovno) in 1921–2 worked under the auspices of the New Zealand government, a key sponsor of the SCF's early schemes (see Fig. 6).

It has become commonplace amongst historians to describe international aid work as extending elite women's established authority in the philanthropic projects of district and parish visiting from a local, domestic context to a global one.[44] One commentator has described the welfare clinics Muriel Paget established in devastated areas of Eastern Europe, 'issu[ing] sulphur soap for the verminous', as directly applying to the humanitarian project the methods of the philanthropic work carried out by her organization, the IKL, in its work with the London poor and infirm.[45] Obvious parallels can be discerned. In January 1922 Muriel Paget met with the London committee of her Mission to Eastern Europe and reported that, in a similar method to that used by the IKL, at the child welfare centres open in Latvia and Estonia where sewing classes for mothers were run, 'an organized system was in operation whereby those attending clinics paid according to their needs'.[46]

There were evident connections between the methods female philanthropists used to assist populations in the international humanitarian field and those at

Figure 6. Photograph of the Feeding Centre in Riga, opened by Lady Muriel Paget's Mission to Eastern Europe. Copyright, Sir Richard Paget. Reproduced with the permission of Sir Richard Paget and Special Collections, Leeds University Library, Box 9, LRA/MS 1405 (Lady Muriel Paget Papers).

home, but the direction of influence upon the evolving practice was not one way. Beginning in the work in Czechoslovakia in 1919, Muriel Paget's relief work schemes used the vocabulary of self-help to express an ambition to support men's, women's and children's individual development that would only be foregrounded in the IKL's publicity in the later 1920s.[47] The first issue of the SCF's magazine, the *Record*, in October 1920, reported on Paget and the SCF representative, Mr Cournos' investigations of 'war-stricken lands' in Slovakia, Ruthenia and Carpathian Russia, where famine was worsened by poor and overcrowded living conditions and 'families are herded together in one-roomed shanties, in the utmost promiscuity, with pigs, rabbits and fowls.'[48] The visceral depiction of deprivation and squalour was characteristic of the emerging visual and moral language of twentieth-century humanitarian publicity.[49] It was used here to marshal a specific argument about humanitarian relief as a driver for the development of individual independence within the collective unit of society: the fear was that the poverty of living conditions stifled personal initiative, and the 'mere gifts of food and clothing' set up a vicious circle. Even the most emergency famine relief, from this perspective, needed to be given 'so as to stimulate at the same time the initiative and the power of self-help of those who receive it.'[50]

In the first instance, there was little time in the relief work projects that Muriel Paget established in Central and Eastern Europe for the sorts of personal encounters that writers such as Amy Barnard had romanticized in the wartime work of the IKL, though in fact interpersonal methods came to shape the developing practice of humanitarian politics in critical ways. At Paget's humanitarian relief centres, emergency provision – including curative medical care – was to be the first goal, but preventive medical attention to children and mothers was established as early as possible (see Fig. 7). The flexibility to develop constructive relief work was built in to the founding rationale of the SCF which, Dorothy Buxton and Edward Fuller reported, under the leadership of Eglantyne Jebb established its first relief programmes for children pragmatically with an ambition to 'creat[e] … as little new machinery as possible.'[51] Muriel Paget used the political space this opportunity opened up, comparatively to that of the sponsorship of other bodies, as a way to distinguish her work from the sorts of interventions made in

Figure 7. 'Europe's Need: Save the Children Fund, October 1920', map printed in *The Record of the Save the Children Fund* 1, no. 3 (Dec. 1920): 41. Reproduced with permission of The Save the Children Fund and the Cadbury Research Library: Special Collections, University of Birmingham.

the new European states by other international organizations, in particular American relief agencies. For example, in planning for the Mission's work in Estonia in early 1920, Paget's advisors observed that existing American agencies paid little attention to the population's needs for preventive medical care, which Paget's programmes would seek to do.[52] In 1920 the *Red Cross World* reported favourably that the clinics already established under the auspices of Muriel Paget's Mission to Eastern Europe were undertaking more developed application of the principles of child welfare work than either 'ordinary English' or American centres by providing pre-natal clinics, infant consultations, children's clinics and schools for mothers.[53] The emphasis here was placed upon the integrated methods. Reflecting primarily about the work in Czechoslovakia for the SCF journal, the *Record*, in 1922 Muriel Paget herself displayed growing confidence in defining child welfare as a 'comprehensive' practice, to be applied in the 'broadest' and most 'progressive' ways possible, and consistent with the national policy of the country in which the relief project was established.[54]

Muriel Paget's relief schemes were established in the new post-1918 states of Eastern Europe with the support of those governments who issued agreements that the clinics and hospitals would be transferred to state management relatively quickly. This was achieved in all cases in 1922, when the centres established in Latvia, Lithuania and Estonia were handed over and Paget's Eastern European Mission was disbanded. Within this context, the presentational strategy of claiming the goals of 'permanent' relief, in comparison with the 'temporary' measures provided by American relief agencies' schemes, became a way for Muriel Paget's international initiatives to shape the politics of personal service within the developing 'mixed economy' of humanitarianism.[55] In doing so, the model of the interpersonal encounter between the 'giver' and 'receiver' in the philanthropic relationship was transplanted to the fields of international interventionism underpinning humanitarian action and the 'internationalization of famine expertise'.[56] Imperial anxieties surfaced visibly in the transnational humanitarian field as European and American agencies sought to establish such expertise in dialogue with the policies of international governments. Notably, the SCF's sponsorship of clinics established under Muriel Paget's Mission was secured on the condition they should be supervised by the SCF Commissioner, and on the insistence of the governments of the new states that local medical practitioners should be trained by English doctors and nurses to carry on the work at the end of the grant.[57] Notwithstanding the political and institutional restrictions of this policy, actors such as Muriel Paget carved out the space to underscore the pivotal motor of personal service within the developing framework of transnational humanitarian governance. In a talk in 1921 to her English supporting committee, Paget found a way to visualize the ongoing centrality of personal service models to the success of humanitarian schemes in this regard. Now imagined on a more extensive scale, Paget advised how the interpersonal work of service ethics would be reprised by the English medical workers, who would pass on professional skills 'in sequence' to the local health workers who were to run the clinics once they had been taken over by national authorities.[58] The model was to be both a vehicle for celebrating the promotion of self- and collective development of the new European states and a route for the conscious politicization of models of personal service. International relief work of this sort provided an expansive opportunity to extend the philanthropic ethic of service and interpersonal encounter whilst negotiating the nexus of national, ethnic, political and social relations in transnational projects of exchange.

Saving souls and the emotional proximity of service

In October 1904, shortly before Evangeline Booth took over the leadership of the Salvation Army in the United States, her father, the Salvation Army's World General, William Booth, wrote to her expressing concern about the need to foreground the religious dimensions of all aspects of the organization's work and notably its expanding social service provision. Evangeline Booth's new appointment represented a great responsibility, as well as an opportunity, to establish the organization across America, and its reputation for a particular praxis of Christian social engagement. William Booth understood that the scope for extending social work in the United States was almost 'illimitable', including in the social policy areas of smoking, alcohol and white slavery in which Evangeline Booth would go on to launch organizational campaigns.[59] He wrote with reservations, however, about the prioritization of this work over the concern for saving souls and cautioned against too much publicity of social work – cinematography, lectures and public demonstrations he felt, hindered, rather than advanced the Salvation Army's cause – and he saw the additional risk that, as a new religious organization, the Salvation Army would get caught up promoting the churches and other Christian organizations. The letter moved on to urge Evangeline Booth to centre the organization's work upon the active process of religious conversion: 'Officers', the World General explained, 'must be taught to go after their own converts and people until they can pay their own way instead of living by selling *The War Cry* [the organization's newspaper] and making collections to which people contribute on the supposition that they are giving to Social Work'; social work, he maintained, 'which is not merely to help the people in their poverty or to do a large business in housing and the homeless', was 'to get at the peoples' souls and change their natures'.[60] This was a distinctive institutional configuration of the philanthropic relationship. The combative language invoking the encounter between Salvation Army members and the 'souls' and 'natures' of the public invoked the metaphor of militarism at the heart of the organization's founding rationale. William Booth was convinced his daughter had implemented the creed successfully to date, and he praised her efforts as Commander in Canada and elsewhere 'to make a real Blood-and-Fire Salvation Army to my very heart's highest satisfaction and content'.[61] However, the methods required constant reiteration to embed the forcefully transformative outcomes of spiritual work. William Booth had written in a letter to Evangeline Booth in 1897 that leaders needed to educate Salvation Army members into 'connecting their labour' with the right public; those who were capable, and most in need of, salvation.[62]

The Salvation Army's social service work had begun in London in 1884, led by women, in projects mainly with poor unmarried women and women working in the city's prostitution economy.[63] Forming part of the broader moral campaigns of late-nineteenth-century 'rescue work',[64] the schemes were high-profile from the beginning, and publicity was heightened by the organization's connection with notorious cases, notably the London journalist, W. T. Stead's 1885 newspaper exposé of child prostitution, the 'Maiden Tribute of Modern Babylon'.[65] However, anxieties surfaced quickly amongst Salvation Army personnel about the feasibility for social work projects adequately to address the work of evangelical conversion.[66] Pamela Walker has noted that already in the first decade of the twentieth century, Richard Haggard in his book *Regeneration* (1910) discussed the Salvation Army's social service provision without considering the theological impetus.[67] This was a fundamental misreading in the eyes of leading figures in the organization. In America in the first decade of the twentieth century, Evangeline Booth denounced any separation of the social and the spiritual in the Salvation Army's work and called for the two bases to be intertwined, precisely as an illustration of the workings of Christian love. As she implored an audience at the Woman's Club in Jersey City, New Jersey in 1912, those who 'speak of the Social being separated from the Evangelistic' were wholly misguided: '[h]ow can the Social be separated? Is not true Charity love – and is not Love God?'[68]

Evangeline Booth's examination in the early-twentieth century of the interdependencies between the social and the spiritual dimensions of the Salvation Army's work also reflected her conscious recognition of the organization's need to confront the materialism of the market economy. Booth's leadership of the American Salvation Army (1904–34) was formative in this context and forged a new model that connected the practical theology of personal evangelical work with modern commercial practices. The First World War provided an early opportunity to establish this process: during wartime Booth greatly expanded the American Salvation Army's financial base for welfare work through her cultivation of wide public support in an organizational appeal to raise a million dollars. The methods of large-scale advertisement and publicity used in this campaign, whilst hugely effective, were not accepted universally, however. In March 1918, William Bramwell Booth, who had succeeded his father as the World General, wrote to Evangeline expressing gratitude that the appeal for the American War Service League and War Fund had been so successful but echoed earlier fears that the religious work of individual regeneration was not being conveyed explicitly. It was a mistake, Bramwell Booth noted, only to advertise the Army and seek to 'please' the public (he was alluding to the celebratory response of many recruits to the American Expeditionary Forces); he thought that this had framed the 'spiritual' failure of the work of other Christian social organizations in America in wartime, notably the YMCA (Young Men's Christian Association). Rather, he underscored that '[s]alvation is the only thing that is worthy of a moment's consideration of the spending of a single dollar'.[69] William Bramwell Booth feared that in the mediation by popular devices of the goals of spiritual development, the organization's concentration upon personal salvation would be undermined.

Evangeline Booth, however, was becoming increasingly convinced of the value of bureaucratic methods and publicity, not only for the purposes of the organization's administrative development, but because they facilitated direct, interpersonal encounters between Salvation Army members and the wider public that were necessary for the work of salvation. In 1919 she launched in America the new Home Service Fund and the even more ambitious Thirteen Million Dollar campaign, in large part to free up the scope for the personal service of Salvation Army members (largely women) in the practical projects of social work schemes, rather than in fundraising drives.[70] In 1925 she wrote to another brother, Herbert Booth, then retired from formal action in the Salvation Army, that the conformity of personal work and administration had always been possible in the Salvation Army's enterprises, that the practice of soliciting funds was an 'institution as old as the Army itself', and that she had collected money at Canadian theatres, and had desired to do so in London, had civic practice not forbidden it. Her point was that the modern administration of fundraising required the forging of interpersonal encounters and spiritual emphases just as much as the work of regeneration and social work; there was little, if no, difference. She stressed that Salvation Army members could not be brought into the presence of people, even while they were collecting, without doing good.[71]

Emergency relief and moral rescue work

The personal methods of the Salvation Army's social work were refocused in the years immediately following 1918 in the context of the American Salvation Army's successful war. Not only had the organization's financial bases been extended significantly, Salvation Army members had also undertaken significant and well-received social work with American soldiers. In 1919, Evangeline Booth co-authored with the novelist Grace Livingstone Hill *The War Romance of the Salvation Army* in celebration of the wartime record. Booth began her section of the book by discussing the organization's relief work in North America during the earthquake and fire in San Francisco in 1906, 'the wild rush to the Klondike', and during the flood in Jamestown, Virginia (1889), storm in Galveston, Texas (1900) and the Great Dayton Flood, Ohio (1913).[72] Natural disaster became the setting for a narrative of personal service as exemplifying a quotidian, religious faith: Booth quoted the Salvation Army member and writer Arthur E. Copping's description of the 'simple, thorough-going, uncompromising, seven-days-a-week character of Christianity'.[73] It was the 'sweet, pure' Salvation Army women who attended the Klondike disaster, Booth wrote, who demonstrated, primordially, this model of personal service, and whose domestic model of action was to be extended during the floods in Ohio, Texas and Virginia by the example of the male Salvation Army officer, who, 'with his boat laden with sandwiches and warm wraps', was the first on the scene.[74] As in Muriel Paget's work with the IKL and in her Mission to Eastern Europe, the praxis of personal intervention that Booth portrayed in this example was by no means incompatible with the organizational logic of the Salvation Army's social service work. Indeed, in a number of cases first-support emergency care was extended in the establishment of permanent initiatives, for example the American Emergency Relief Unit was set up in the wake of the 1906 earthquake in San Francisco. Here, emergency relief work was configured as a compassionate response to human need that worked outwards from the inspiration of God's love towards an 'almost instantaneous service' of personal work that would be systemized in institutional schemes of social service.[75]

The setting of the war front in France, in which Salvation Army women undertook welfare work with allied troops, emerged in *The War Romance* as a central conceit in the early-twentieth-century configuration of personal service.

The war trenches provided an exciting new context for the organization's narrative about Christian empathy as a vehicle for the development of personal spiritual identification through welfare work: as Evangeline Booth wrote, in the brutal conditions of war, '[w]e look through the exterior, look through the shell, look through the coat, and find the man'.[76] It was in this ethical context that the methods of Christian encounter logically could be stretched, notwithstanding the horrors of warfare, where as Grace Livingston Hill declared, Salvation Army members won the confidence of American soldiers by showing themselves willing to share the hardships and dangers of the war by venturing themselves into the huts and trenches on the battlefields in France.[77] Grace Livingston Hill's description mirrored the narratives of emotional dependency soldiers articulated towards their immediate commanders that were popularized in accounts of life on the front line during the First World War.[78] But it threw into sharp relief the models of subjectivity constructed through homosocial and class-based hierarchies in such wartime writings. Her narrative developed instead an emphasis upon the emotional and spiritual strength provided specifically by the American Salvation Army women ('Sallies') who 'mothered' the American troops and other young men in France, who appeared subsequently 'more contented and more easily handled'.[79] Reviewers of *The War Romance* picked up on this emphasis as indicative of the book's primary concern with the homely character of the 'lassies' who, for the benefit of the men, 'fried so many doughnuts and baked so many pies under fire'.[80] The language also spoke to the wider popularizing discourse of child psychology, and specifically of the movement of child guidance coming out of America: the concern was to support the emotional and psychological health of children – or in this case the American troops that needed mothering – to prevent and attend to the sorts of 'maladjustments' that would otherwise threaten familial and social instability.[81]

Although *The War Romance* exploited a popular interest in the possibility on the one hand, of the domestic romantic encounter between Salvation Army women and American men and on the other, the emerging authority of child psychiatry, in its emphasis upon women's spiritual strength the book shaped the rescue work of the 'Sallies' around a specific model of female identification. In this context, it was the relationships of emulation and admiration between women that were most highly prized. Grace Livingstone Hill captured a key expression of these relationships following the announcement of the armistice, when many girls between the ages of fourteen and sixteen were being led into 'immoral[ity]' through contact with the troops at Des Moines, prompting Salvation Army women to open a home to offer shelter and companionship for the young women.

The portrait of a young, attractive woman of twenty-four, a former private secretary of a Salvation Army Brigadier in Chicago, who was placed in charge of the home for girls, personified the moral and psychological encounters perceived to be at the heart of this personal work. Grace Livingstone Hill wrote that:

> if you could look into her beautiful eyes you would have an understanding of the consecrations and strength of character that has made it possible for her to do this work with marvellous success . . . In her work she deals with the individual, always giving immediate relief for any need, always pointing the way straight and direct to a better life.[82]

This characterization played to the media and public interest in the Sallies' 'womanly appeal', and to the traditions of Salvation Army 'rescue work' that was dominated by middle-class women, in order to present the qualities of physical attractiveness as a message about women's moral fortitude.[83] But it also went further. Personal service, in this model, worked through the expression of psychological intimacies between women. Each young woman's needs were to be considered on an individual basis, according to her temperament. And wider social development was to be secured through the strength of the girls' personal relationships with the woman who ran the home, 'whom they easily love and trust'.[84]

Metaphors of touch

By the interwar period, metaphors of emotional proximity were well-established within the Salvation Army's international publicity as a symbol of the sorts of social levelling that was achieved through common spiritual purpose. In mid-to-late-nineteenth-century London, the imagery was located in the cultural symbolism attached to the sites of the Salvation Army's working-class neighbourhood activism. As Pamela Walker has argued, the physical proximity of human life in urban culture was a particular target for the organization's early evangelical work and, in competition with the Anglican churches' pastoral work, channelled the initiatives through the distinctive urban geographies of working-class neighbourhoods that cut across the established parish system.[85] Extending the metaphor of proximity in *The War Romance*, Evangeline Booth focused attention upon how emotional and spiritual contact preceded the sharing of individual burdens and broke down markers of social difference: she wrote that we 'never permit any superiority of position, or breeding, or even grace to make a gap between us and any who may be less fortunate'.[86] This emphasis spoke to the popular post-war discourse that used the example of the collaborative bases of the war effort and common losses to question the social force of class and social distinctions, while reinforcing Christian teachings of grace in which the principle of neighbourliness overcame self-righteousness. In the years before the outbreak of war, Evangeline Booth had drawn upon Biblical teachings specifically on neighbourliness to argue for the erosion of social distance in the everyday work of service to others. In January 1913 she rehearsed the parable of the Good Samaritan in an article published in the *Toronto Star* in which she was quoted as having said that 'the rapidity of the mark of the Salvation Army is down, almost in its entirety, to the close-touchness of its methods', and that '[y]ou can't bring great effectual help to bear upon anyone at a distance'.[87] In the foreword to *The War Romance*, she emphasized again that '[a]s a people we have felt that to be of true service to others we must be close enough to them to lift part of their load, this time to perform the "grand injunction of the Apostle Paul, 'Bear ye one another's burdens and so fulfil the law of Christ'"'.[88]

The narrative of the emotional proximity of the Salvation Army's encounter with the public was further extended in the interwar years through the popular representation of Evangeline Booth's embodiment of a distinctive style of leadership in relation to the urban crowd. In May 1924, the *New York Times* published a poem by Ella Fanning, entitled 'Evangeline Booth Goes on Tour'. The poem alluded to concerns about the autocratic style of Salvation Army leaders ('[n]ot as a queen she comes') that would reverberate loudly during the controversy of 1928–9 in which the Salvation Army's constitution was reformed and an electoral system for choosing successive World Generals was introduced.[89] But it was in her work for others in which Evangeline Booth, the 'Handmaiden of Service', was celebrated here, in her 'tender care'; 'zeal to cheer, uplift and share'; 'minister to scarred and wretched souls'. The gendered language in the poem worked in one respect to reaffirm Evangeline Booth's spiritual authority and it propelled the reader between acknowledgement of Booth's individual presence ('humble toiler'; 'self-forgetting'; and non-queenly) and the presence of the crowds ('surg[ing] and jostl[ing]'). As will be discussed at greater length elsewhere, publicity of Evangeline Booth often homed in on her bodily characteristics to justify her competence for leadership roles. It is significant that in the poem the only part of her body to be envisaged was her 'gentle hands'. It was the crowd that took centre stage, and the character of the crowd – its 'tense stillness' and hushed volume in relation to Booth's spiritual power – that was the poem's apparent subject.[90] What is interesting about this emphasis is that, while existing theories of the crowd emphasized the spirit of uniformity amongst crowd members, the limits to individuality and the animalistic instincts of the crowd,[91] the poem modelled Booth's haptic presence deliberately to cross-cut these perspectives. The interconnections between the affective and practical nature of the Salvation Army's work were inferred here as a project both of direct personal impact, and one working for wider social and spiritual ends. The audience was imagined waiting to 'see' and understand the work of the Salvation Army leader by *feeling* the power of her ministering hands.

Selling service

In conformity with such emphases upon her haptic presence, the significance of Evangeline Booth's psychological authority was one on which public commentators in America reflected frequently in the interwar years. Such interest demonstrates the further extension of the influence in twentieth-century society of the models of service she was made to embody. A notable context for the development of this thinking emerged in the 1930s and 1940s amongst American experts in the fields of behavioural and social psychology. They readdressed Evangeline Booth's work beyond the contexts of evangelical mission and spiritual ministry for the purposes of business management. The business psychologist Dale Carnegie, whose book *How to Win Friends and Influence People* was published in 1936, included Booth in his *Five Minute Biographies* (1937), noting her efficient working practices of keeping a pen and pad next to her bed at night and dictating correspondence for the duration of her one-hour car journey from home to office.[92] Carnegie rehearsed the well-known story of Evangeline Booth's meeting with the renowned gangster 'Soapy Smith', describing her visit to the Yukon River, Canada during the gold-rush of 1898 where she preached to 'twenty-five thousand lonely men' who sang songs with her until one o'clock in the morning. Soapy was in the crowd. Carnegie reported that, after speaking to Evangeline Booth about his grandmother joining the organization, 'Soapy Smith' prayed with her and another Salvation Army girl and, with tears rolling down his cheeks, promised that he would stop killing people and give himself up.[93] Narrating the story of personal conversion was central to the Salvation Army's praxis of sharing individual testimonies that recalled the experience of individual salvation as both psychological and physical change. The imagery mapped onto the organization's model of conversion that configured the permeability of human nature and the openness of all to redemption: as Pamela Walker has explained, this was a distinctive approach to conversion that combined an interpretation of bodily meaning with theological significance.[94]

The distinctiveness of Dale Carnegie's account was its emphasis upon Evangeline Booth's communication skills and emotional power in the relationship with the convert as a model for developing understandings of consumer behaviour. American advertising expert, Ewing T. Webb and Professor of Psychology, John B. Morgan interpreted her qualities in similar terms in 1930 in *Strategy in Handling People*. Published by the New York Garden City Publishing Company, the book was a study in applied psychology offering biographies of individuals who showed good business sense and strategy. The genre of business management writing was new in this period, and the novelty can be inferred from an advertisement of the book in the American daily press, describing it as '[e]xciting as detective fiction'.[95] Evangeline Booth was the only female subject to feature in the book, and one reviewer noted that in gendering the salesman male, Booth was made to occupy a lonely position amongst over a hundred 'characters'.[96] Evangeline Booth's inclusion in the book, although significant as part of this gendered debate about business success, was not framed in terms of her pioneering role as a woman, however, but rather in respect of the broader influence of her work methods upon developing understandings of the science of social interactions.[97] Appearing in the chapter, 'How to interest and convince people', Booth featured alongside the New York managing editor and philanthropist, John. D. Rockefeller and the sea captain, Charles W. Brown, amongst others. The chapter explored the talent 'to speak the other fellow's language', in which Booth exemplified an ability to appeal to other people's personal experience to engage trust and interest. Webb and Morgan concluded Evangeline Booth would 'send hardened convicts to their knees in tears after talking to them for only a few minutes':

> 'She would start with things the criminal did as a boy', says [advertising expert] Waldo Warren, 'by asking him questions about his mother, drawing him out about his own experiences. The convict could resist anything that came from outside, but against ideas that came from within himself he was powerless'.[98]

The perception of Booth's ability to read selfhood, and her own desire to project selfhood as constructed within family relationships, are consciously drawn in this excerpt. The encounter between self and other in this example was a direct and testing, as well as a dramatic, one. Furthermore, advertising experts' narration of Evangeline Booth's encounters specifically emphasized the control she exerted through personal intimacy with the public. In doing so, the principle of reaching the marginalized – long influencing the Salvation Army's religious and social work – was reformulated to consider the psychological effects of proximity in the context of everyday consumer culture. Celebrated stories of Evangeline Booth's meetings with renowned criminals had cultural capital precisely because they indicated Booth's own exceptional spiritual power and also how this power reflected upon and made malleable the construction of selfhood. For commentators such as Webb and Morgan, it was the emotional influence that Evangeline Booth was claimed to exert over former prisoners that illuminated the potential for the reconfiguration of models of women's social action by the developing advertising industry. The psychology of interpersonal relations was critical to the developing world of consumer advertising and Booth's mature practice of personal service offered one rich model for appropriation.

Personal religion: between the individual and the mass

In 1925 Emily Kinnaird celebrated her seventieth birthday and the UK YWCA, its seventy-year anniversary. The moment seemed auspicious to reflect upon the YWCA's history. In her autobiography, *Reminiscences*, Kinnaird charted the route the organization had taken, expanding her mother, Mary Jane Kinnaird's establishment in London in 1855 of the North London Home for young women, to the breadth of its current international projects supporting girls and young women through educational, workplace and social provision. *Reminiscences* was both an important piece of organizational storytelling and an account of the recent history of evangelicalism. Like many evangelical organizations in Britain and America, in the years immediately following 1918, the UK YWCA divided between 'conservative' and 'liberal' wings that clashed over the extent to which religious doctrine should be prioritized over the material demands of social life.[99] The period witnessed a number of inter-organizational splits, including the Irish Division (1917), the Scottish Division (1924) and the secession of a group in 1919 that went on to form the Christian Organization of Women and Girls.[100] Partly as a foil to the evidence of organizational fracture, alongside offering up examples of the YWCA 'pioneers', including her mother and Mary Robarts, who had formed a prayer union for women in mid-nineteenth-century London, in *Reminiscences* Emily Kinnaird framed her own commitment to the organization within a lineage of transatlantic evangelical fervour. The influence of mid-nineteenth-century American and British missionaries and scholars, Oswald Dykes, Dwight Moody, Ira D. Sankey and W. W. White and Christian evangelical social reformers, including Ellen Ranyard, George Holland, Annie Macpherson and Thomas Barnardo were all vitally meaningful to Kinnaird's thought and practice.[101] Perhaps to be expected, Emily Kinnaird expressly celebrated the broad evangelical consensus of the nineteenth century here, logically the more so in the wake of the post-war splits.

Within the wider context of post-war evangelical schisms, it is unsurprising that the principal conceit of *Reminiscences* was the dialogue between nineteenth-century principles of spiritual commitment and the methods animating lay Christian voluntary organizations in reaching out to new audiences. Susan Mumm has argued that in the organizational schisms of 1917–19, 'the question of philanthropy's core purpose – whether conversion or assistance – tore the YWCA apart', before the organization re-emerged in the post-war years espousing a doctrine of 'civil Christianity' that centred justice and compassion above the teachings of original sin.[102] The rethinking of original sin, stimulated in the nineteenth century by scientific thought on evolution, was a critical issue of interpretative debate within British and American Protestant traditions in the early-twentieth century. For proponents of the new view, theologies of action needed to assume forms of progressive social development rather than remain grounded in the understanding of social meaning as caused, in a determinant sense, by an individual's sinfulness.[103] It remained to be debated from 1919 onwards within the YWCA exactly what form and purpose personal religion would assume specifically in this new consensus upon sin.

More broadly, Emily Kinnaird consciously addressed the shifting contexts of theological perspectives in a chapter in *Reminiscences* entitled, 'Change', where she discussed the example of books owned by her late brother, including once inspirational texts by the Scottish Episcopal clergyman Donald McIntosh and F. R. Havergal, which were now outdated in their language – 'even the early Keswick books' – and useless for addressing a generation of young women accustomed to reading the publications of the Student Christian Movement or the New York Women's Press.[104] At the same time as embracing theological shifts, Emily Kinnaird lamented, additionally, the fear of the 'danger of emotion' within contemporary society that blighted the scope for the development of the sorts of religious selfhood that she had experienced as a young woman. Derived through spiritual revelation and the teachings of divine immanence, Kinnaird had witnessed God's Spirit working in camps for girls; in the Navvy and Moody Missions; and in the nineteenth-century evangelical revivals of William Hay Aitken, the Canon Body Missions and in the Welsh and Kassia (India) Hills.[105] Furthermore, she regretted the anxiety and reluctance of young women to forge personal attachment to female religious leaders in the ways that she and others of her generation had done with British evangelical women such as Catherine Marsh and Elizabeth Garnett, who established Christian welfare drives for manual labourers in Yorkshire in the mid-nineteenth century. Emily Kinnaird's remembered reverence for the 'quiet influence' of women like Catherine Marsh, Elizabeth Garnett, Mary, Countess of Harrowby, a governor of the Bible Society and the Countess of Aberdeen illuminated a conscious impetus to reprise the methods of personal and social transformation of mid-nineteenth-century evangelical missions for the reconfigured organization. In 1918, those leaders who had defended internal criticisms that there had been a 'worldly drift' in the organization since the wartime expansion of the work, emphasized the contemporary need for social work enterprises amongst working-class communities, not as separate or 'new' ends in themselves, but as part of a 'pioneer missionary effort' that sought to renew the groundwork for projects once again of a 'more definitely religious character'.[106] Reorganizing following the initial splits, the YWCA redrew the spiritual emphases of the work and launched a new Evangelistic campaign for the year 1919–20 through the Religious Work Committee.[107]

Christian friendship and the whole person

The YWCA's vision of service had always involved the search for a holistic approach to the developing challenges of young women's lives that attended equally to the provision of social amenities and support for spiritual development. Emily Kinnaird had addressed the implications of the YWCA's personal methods of service since the 1880s, when she took up her first leadership positions within the UK organization. In 1884, in the inaugural issue of the YWCA members' monthly magazine, *Our Own Gazette*, Kinnaird outlined the centrality of the principle of Christian friendship ('[w]hich of us does not know the pleasure of having a friend, and a good one too?') to the YWCA's configuration of a unifying model of associational work which, in crossing classes and churches, stood at a membership of over 40,000 comprising young British women 'of all ranks of society, and of every section of the Church of Christ', a figure which would grow by 1900 to 94,000 women.[108] Having established the Guild of Helpers scheme for young women of the leisured classes in 1902, in 1905, the year of the UK YWCA's fiftieth anniversary celebrations, in an article for the fashionable women's publication, *The Gentlewoman*, Kinnaird set out the YWCA's 'fourfold method' of the Christian project of social activism – 'physical' (food and lodgings), 'intellectual' (lectures, etc.), 'social' (in place of family), and 'spiritual' (the 'development of the spiritual as a protest against the materalis[m] of the time').[109]

In the first decades of the twentieth century, YWCA leaders' awareness of the need to map evangelical missionary ambitions onto a diversifying landscape of belief, nonetheless, focused an evolving set of questions about the work of personal religion in the construction of women's citizenship and active service. In the 1910s leading personnel recognized a new challenge to adapt the principles of the association to the concerns of a world characterized both by religious pluralism and growing secularization, in which individual Christian commitment could no longer be assumed. In the years immediately before the outbreak of the First World War, leaders identified the central task of understanding how young women's religious faith was to be developed within the context of the shifting material pressures of social and political life. The tension about whether to foreground religious doctrine or the methods of civil Christianity that would become entrenched over the course of the decade emerged as a key problem in this period. In the foreword to the YWCA publication, 'Girls of Yesterday and To-day. The Romance of the YWCA' (c.1913), the missionary, William Hay Aitken observed the risk of the subordination of spiritual ambitions to social work. Aitken was sanguine about the situation so far as the YWCA was concerned, believing that in all such organizations 'there must ever be an unspiritual, as well as a spiritual element', in as much that the work encouraged young women to the Christian faith as well as supporting those who were already committed: he maintained that the YWCA remained 'a centre of spiritual influences wherever its branches extend'.[110] Nevertheless, Aitken observed a new urgency for the spiritual work in respect of the widening civic opportunities that were opening up to young women: 'if they [women] are to come more and more to the front in the social, the commercial, the literary, and even in the political life of the country, how doubly important that they should themselves be won for Christ'.[111]

In 1910–13 an internal YWCA Commission met to develop a strategy to improve the organization's public image amongst British girls and young women as a means to further the association's contribution to the nation's civic life and extend the national purpose of the Christian church. A key finding of the Commission was the need to attend to the family and leisure time of young women working in the industrial sector and, in a phrase anticipating a wartime idiom, 'the future home-makers of the nation', whose health and outlook was suffering under the 'strain and stress of factory labour'.[112] This vision of civic life, whilst on the one hand bolstering cultural expectations of women's domestic experience, indicated firm commitment to a 'whole' understanding of the individual. Expanding earlier constructions of the YWCA's holistic method, the Commission recommended an organizational restructuring in eight new divisions with departments that attended to the overlapping individual and community needs of young working women. The ambition to extend the scope of the work of personal religion in individual and collective life was pivotal to this project, and three interlocking departments – the Religious Activities Department, the Social Service Department and the Education Department – were planned to coordinate the YWCA's overlapping religious and social work enterprises. Such ambition expressed a model of spirituality that had been advanced in organizations including the Student Volunteer Movement for Foreign Missions from the 1890s onwards, which combined individual and corporate prayer life, alongside the zeal for world missions.[113] The Religious Activities Department, which Emily Kinnaird was to lead, aimed, through this model, both to deepen members' 'prayer life' and establish bonds of fellowship through group activities and religious education classes. The goal, as Kinnaird refined it in 1913, was 'to incite to devotion and intercession those who feel the need for a corporate spiritual life'.[114]

Building personality

Although there were vital continuities from its earlier history in the focus of the YWCA's work, addressing young women's personal spiritual development within community engagement projects and through the principles of Christian friendship raised a new series of questions during wartime and in the years that followed. Above and beyond the splits within evangelical groups, the concern was focused upon the wider social debate about the development of individual personality. In the mid-to-late-nineteenth century, building on the earlier work at the North London Home and later the homes and institutes established under the United Association for the Christian and Domestic Improvement of Young Women, the organization's initiatives took shape around the proposed cultivation of girls' personal friendships at hostels, restaurants and clubs. In the nineteenth century the work reverberated clearly within the confident projections of Christian civility. The wartime fracturing of such assertions – when Christian civilizations were at war with each other – marked a new urgency for emphasizing the work of spiritual revelation and connection. At the Stockholm Conference of the World's YWCA in 1914 a new principle was added to the constitution 'to enlist the service of young women for young women in their spiritual, intellectual, social, and physical advancement, and to encourage their fellowship and activity in the Christian Church'.[115] In 1915 the executive sought clarity about the year's work ahead to call British girlhood 'to come into personal contact with Jesus

Christ and to know Him as a Saviour who not only pardons sin, but equips for life and service'.[116]

This newly accented language of self-development spoke to a maturing emphasis within women's groups upon the need for the conformity of community development and the effective and full expression of individual personality.[117] At a conference for UK YWCA Secretaries in Bangor, Wales in April 1916, discussions centred upon how Christian faith and practice could be built up through sustained attention to girls' personality and call to wider fellowship and faith in terms that addressed both individual and 'corporate' expressions.[118] Embodying liberal evangelicals' wider interest in the development of thought and doctrine, at the UK YWCA Conference in October 1922 delegates discussed 'education of Christian personality for service' through planned activities at clubs, including recreations, team games and study sessions, and the example of branch and club leaders' 'co-operative leadership'.[119] Encouraging the expression of personal freedoms directed by Christian faith was at the heart of a vision for the modern educational value of interpersonal work. Bible study and prayer circles remained central to the YWCA's programme for the 'freeing of personality', but now it was considered vital that self-expression was to be explored as part of personal, social and spiritual experience.[120] In this context, the emphasis upon the development of young women's personality was an integral part of the social campaigns undertaken by the YWCA in the 1920s – including around inadequate housing for single women, rates of pay, limited job opportunities, occupationally-compromised health, lack of education opportunities and industrial conditions – and an essential aspect that linked the aspiration for individual spiritual development to those of collective social progress. The goals positioned the YWCA within a developing stream of Christian thought in the interwar years that re-evaluated individual commitment for collective participation, seen for example in the discussions at COPEC (Conference on Christian Politics, Economics and Citizenship) that took place in Birmingham in 1924. The YWCA focused their discussions around a refinement of the organization's holistic method of personal religion that spoke to the concern for young women's material, psychological and spiritual health. As a pamphlet produced in 1935 for the organization's eightieth anniversary underlined, while a visitor returning from 1855 might think the YWCA was now chiefly concerned with 'material things ... he would quickly realise [sic] that the value set on the indivisible whole of human personality was implicit in the first seeking of salvation through faith in Christ'.[121]

Interpersonal relations in an inclusive church

The wide appropriation of the language of personality in the interwar period reflected a common challenge amongst Christian organizations and churches to address the work of spiritual commitment within the evolving conditions of modern life and mass citizenship. Lucy Delap has argued that such language, applied for example in interwar debates about female marital obedience (wives' capacity to 'obey' their husbands), posed a critical challenge to conservative gender discourse, both within and beyond the Anglican church, which continued to seek recourse in the criteria of biological difference as the explanation for social and subjective behaviour.[122] A broader concern, shared widely across Christian groups, was how to combine the expression of individuality and personality with the shifting political and spiritual vision of collective engagement. Within the YWCA, a key debate in the years before and immediately after the First World War focused on how to address the needs of corporate spiritual life (of the organization, women and internationally), whilst attending to the development of the personality of each individual member of the association. In 1919 Mina Gollock, a leading figure within the CMS (Church Missionary Society) and Emily Kinnaird's Private Secretary, addressed the interdependency of personal development and corporate spiritual life in a discussion paper on the future direction of the UK YWCA. Gollock observed the changing contexts of young women's economic, social and political experiences, whose selective pre-war calls for enfranchisement, she observed, had shifted towards universal expectations during wartime, and now needed to be guided in the post-war world in a contemporary image of a community of the faithful. Against this background, Gollock discussed how the work of the YWCA now had to address a combination of social and psychological priorities that might cut across the divisions of social class and project alternative affiliations and models of collective behaviour. She identified a new tension in the work to configure a community of believers around the principles of personal religion: she wrote that whereas in the past the organization's chief effort had been to 'reach individuals', with the hope of achieving such interpersonal connection in large numbers, now, 'when the value of the individual is in no degree lessened, the value of the mass is paramount'. While large numbers, and their 'corporate' action could be 'unreasoning', as Gollock discussed in the example of the impulses of the crowd, they nevertheless demanded the YWCA's close consideration. What was required, Gollock argued, was flexibility in the approach to individuals within a collective body: 'no wholesale treatment of the mass can ever suffice. Diversity exists and involves diversity of method.'[123] In exploring the effective expansion of the work of personal religion, there was to be a flexible accommodation of difference. There was to be a new interrogation of the work of Christian universalism. There was to be a critical distinction between the principles of 'unity' and 'uniformity', as Gollock explained: '[u]niformity can always be secured by the simple expedient of keeping very small … True unity loves to include all. Uniformity of method, on the other hand, is a matter of exclusion.'[124]

This emphasis upon the complementarity of individual and collective expression for the achievement of civic purpose reinforced the YWCA's commitment to understanding the work of personal religion as an expression of broad theological thinking. In *Reminiscences*, Emily Kinnaird described the YWCA's work as 'interdenominational … international and … inter-class'.[125] Kinnaird celebrated the heritage of these methods, writing that the organization was established with 'no ecclesiastical bias', a breadth of outlook she observed in her parents' broad commitment to an interdenominational enthusiasm of the style of nineteenth-century American revivalism and their open hospitality in the London family home.[126] Such broadness, resonating within the developing momentum attached to ecumenical thinking in the interwar years, was itself part of the wider interdenominational commitment that had characterized evangelical missionary work since the mid-1850s.[127] In *Reminiscences*, Emily Kinnaird would claim a widespread tolerance, if not accommodation, with the idea of an inclusive church if only for the fact that 'it would be difficult for this generation to conceive [as] possible' the great chasm between High, Low and Broad church, and between Churchmen and Dissenters out of which Wesleyan Methodism had emerged in the eighteenth century.[128] In 1927 she specifically encouraged flexibility of thinking amongst YWCA members both about Christian devotional practices and those of other faiths in a pair of articles in the organization's members' magazine that addressed Hindu teachings of karma, contemplation and mediation and a wide range of historical Christian devotional texts.[129] The focus of Kinnaird's writings at this moment stressed an interest in the shifting application of the work of personal religion; while there was still an educative basis to the work of personal service, the ambition encouraged greater independence amongst young women in approaching their own religious selfhood. It was this aim, once driven by direct emotional expression and now embodied in the language of personality and rooted in the particular conditions of contemporary life, that YWCA leaders invoked in the interwar years as the model of a broad Christian approach to immediate political concerns. As an article in the 1931 YWCA *Review* stated: only 'interdenominationalism' could enable religious social activism to face the complexities of 'modern life'.[130]

Conclusion

Historians have tended to assume that the public influence of British women's philanthropic projects was at its highpoint in the Victorian period, when local parish work and district visiting were widely energized by the personal service undertaken by middle- and upper-class women.[131] Linked rhetorically by nineteenth-century commentators to women's assumed expertise in domestic and caring roles, these methods of charitable work foregrounded women's capacities in forging social relationships that extended familial and friendship bonds within the wider community. It is unsurprising that individuals who were brought up in mid-to-late-nineteenth-century principles of personal work and ethics of service should have continued to reflect upon the value of such models into later life, but the cultural and political distances between the contexts of their practice in the late-nineteenth and early-twentieth centuries and the interwar period called for an engagement with explanatory models that reconciled old and new emphases. Delineating the shape of the 'philanthropic relationship' was at the heart of this tension. Constance Braithwaite discussed the multiple motives for social services in 1938 around four key principles – the 'emotion of pity and sympathy with distress'; 'the conviction that all members in a certain group are "members one of another"'; ideals of equality; and economic reasons – but stressed the central conviction of 'a realization of the facts of economic, social and cultural interdependence'.[132] The transformative encounter that had always been central both to the conceptualization and practice of female philanthropy was appropriated in the interwar years as a central aspect of the politics of citizenship and governance and of the role of religious expression in negotiating the integration of the self within society. Women's service was not an 'iron tradition', as Vera Brittain asserted, but was to have challenging legacies – personal, political and social – in the interwar years and beyond.

One of the central goals of this chapter has been to reveal how, in reprising the ethics of personal and individual service in the interwar period, female philanthropists contributed to the popularization of understandings of relational psychology as a vehicle for social development. Addressing the relational behaviour underpinning models of service was in one respect a counterpoint to Modernist perspectives of the period that advanced the interiority of the self.

Female philanthropists explored socially-embedded selfhood as a tool for achieving material, social and political change and personal satisfaction. Aged seventy in 1925, Emily Kinnaird wrote that it was 'personal work' that had always brought her the 'greatest of pleasure [and] when later the business side of the Association [YWCA] service occupied most of my attention, I clung to my first love, the "navvies".[133] As the anecdote underscored, female philanthropists evaluated individual service as moving far beyond repressively gendered models of female duty. The interpersonal influence women exerted through philanthropy was as keenly debated in the interwar period as it had been in the nineteenth-century expansion of middle-class and elite women's local charitable work, but here the emphasis was upon psychological development, both of the 'giver' and 'receiver' in the philanthropic relationship, as much as upon women's public influence. Neither cozy nor pious, women's philanthropic practice between the wars involved the confrontation of everyday emotional power relationships, as well as the search for selfhood and for the interconnectedness of society that a rigorous commitment to service compelled.

2

Knowledge

Elizabeth Macadam's *The New Philanthropy* begins in a revealing way. Even before reaching the short preface (in which Macadam stated that a successful book about the relationship between statutory and voluntary welfare provision 'would require a writer who is at once a historian, a philosopher, and an experienced administrator'[1]), the reader is alerted to the notion that the book connects to a broad intellectual landscape, in which a social scientific model intersects with the older disciplines of philosophy and the physical sciences. In the epigraph to the book, Macadam quoted the French chemist and microbiologist Louis Pasteur on the science of 'observation' and the poet laureate Robert Bridges' portrait of the 'alliance of living entities', in *The Testament of Beauty* (1929).[2] Historians have read Macadam's *The New Philanthropy* in the light of debates about the professionalization of social service,[3] and separately, of the interwar mixed economy of welfare provision.[4] What has not been observed about Macadam's work, and what I argue is revealed by the juxtaposition of the two quotations in her epigraph, is her contribution to interwar understandings of the epistemologies of philanthropy, especially those projects undertaken by women.[5] The two allusions point to the conceptual elasticity animating female philanthropy. The quotation from *The Testament of Beauty* presented a strikingly different conception of knowledge formation compared to Pasteurian scientific observation, because it gestured to the significance of organic and embedded forms of lived experience. What Macadam was exploring was the need for the *combination* of these different types of knowledge in women's modern philanthropic projects, and specifically the value of study in combination with practice. She had refined this argument over some years, first in her work in settlements in London and later Liverpool, and subsequently through her teaching on university social work and social administration courses. In 1914, she wrote an article for the Oxford-published *Hibbert Journal* arguing that the learning and knowledge derived from 'experiences of real life' was essential for students of social work who must go beyond 'learning in libraries'.[6] In *The*

Equipment of the Social Worker (1925), she advocated 'goodwill, kindly feeling and instinctive tact', to be applied in combination with the studied knowledge of social conditions.[7]

As well as documenting the shifting relationship between the statutory and voluntary social services, Elizabeth Macadam's *The New Philanthropy* contributed to a different debate in the interwar period, one that would be of equal if not more fundamental importance to understanding the future direction of social service, about the sorts of knowledge that preceded and were derived from philanthropic and voluntary work. The conceptualization of female philanthropy, specifically, as a mode for producing and interpreting knowledge in the interwar years in one respect reflected women's distinctive relationship to the specialist authority that had been attached to the social sciences in the nineteenth century.[8] Eileen Yeo found that in the nineteenth century, middle-class and elite women 'carved a pathway into public scientific work' by mobilizing the concepts of social motherhood and the 'sexual communion of labour' alongside men's activism in social policy formation, and saw this as pushing educated and academic women in the interwar years almost exclusively into social work.[9] A number of excellent contributions to the scholarship on nineteenth-century social science have reinforced how the debates were about more than simply the intellectual calibration of the field: that the questions that arose around the authority of the social sciences encompassed wide psychological, moral and religious concerns about the basis of modern society.[10] I argue that this reading, too, needs some qualification with reference to the interwar years as a period in which the authority of the social sciences was maturing alongside women's professional and social status that combined to provide new opportunities for philanthropists to debate the formulation of knowledge. Female philanthropists were well-versed by the interwar period in claiming the legitimacy of social (and other) scientific methods for their work. This chapter shows how they addressed the sciences in ways that both engaged with and contested the logic of academic methods. As Henrietta Barnett – well-known within the university settlement movement – put it first in 1903, the pursuit of knowledge and rejoicing in learning needed to be balanced by the education of care-giving that was spread through actions 'more effectively than books, classes or lectures'.[11]

The focus of this chapter, then, is on questions of epistemology and language. I argue that paying attention to the intersecting intellectual and ethical fields in which female philanthropists produced and evaluated social knowledge in relation to scientific disciplines in the interwar period opens up a more complex understanding of interwar epistemologies of philanthropy and social work. This chapter considers how Evangeline Booth, Lettice Fisher and Muriel Paget articulated three distinct sets of engagement with this debate. Lettice Fisher was one of a number of university-educated women whom, Eileen Yeo argues, in partnership with their academic husbands, personified a gendered model of social science.[12] Yeo's critique of the 'feminized margins of an academic map of learning' which educated women inhabited framed an interpretation of the separation in the early-twentieth century of husbands' and wives' work spheres: both were public spaces, but whereas men created new social knowledge, women supposedly kept busy with practical social work.[13] As we will see, this framing of the distinction between theory and practice downplays the extent to which Lettice Fisher herself actively shaped theoretical reflections on social and economic questions both in and beyond her direct philanthropic practice; regardless of the varying emphases upon the intellectual and the practical, at any one time Fisher combined the two motivations of public work. Furthermore, examining Lettice Fisher's writings alongside those of Evangeline Booth and Muriel Paget illustrates that there was more than one model being used in the interwar period to explore the intersections between the sciences, other philosophical engagements and the practical elements of women's public commitments. Evangeline Booth was more cautious than Lettice Fisher in emphasizing the theoretical credentials of the Salvation Army's social work, but she still drew upon variously scientific and theological perspectives to foreground visceral experience and the force of Christian conscience. Muriel Paget prioritized the vocabulary of medical science and scientific psychology in the projection of her philanthropic and relief work at home and internationally, both to assert the professionalizing bases of women's voluntary work, and as part of the developing discourse of humanitarian governance.

A critical debate that this chapter explores is the movement between the theoretical and the practical in constructions of women's social service in the interwar years. As will be explored through the examples of Fisher's, Booth's and Paget's writings, distinct traditions of women's philanthropy and social work focused this debate differently; however, there were overarching themes. Even in relation to individuals who operated within the world of academia, anxieties emerged with respect to women's claims to intellectual status. C. V. Butler, a former student of Lettice Fisher, and herself influential in interwar social work, would reflect in the 1920s upon the 'human' (rather than theoretical) aspects of Fisher's scholarship in part as a way of finessing Fisher's academic contributions in conformity with her social work practice.[14] Elizabeth Macadam had made a similar point in her article for the *Hibbert Journal* in 1914, arguing it was to be 'hands-on experience', rather than 'second hand' learning (including in libraries), that would define the future of women's social work.[15] As we have seen with respect to Evangeline Booth's publicity in the interwar years, the metaphor of women's hands signalled particular sorts of competencies that were assumed to be associated with women's philanthropic practice. 'Lending a hand' was an older and recurring motif of women's philanthropy and civic practice. The Society magazine *The Queen, the Lady's Newspaper and Court Chronicle* fashioned women's charitable activity in these terms in its regular column, 'Queen's Helping Hand', while a June 1932 article in the Anglican *Mothers' Union Journal* implored women 'to lend a hand' within the organization and join branch committees.[16] In earlier periods, the work of women 'lending a hand' voluntarily in the community was not devoid of intellectual reflexivity or application: in 1866 the social commentator Charlotte Ward wrote a book of that name that considered contemporary philanthropic practice and policy and evidenced her own expertise though the practical application of highly specialist knowledge.[17] The act of writing was also an act of knowledge creation.

It is, then, the interrelationship between claims to practical, intellectual and ethical knowledge in women's philanthropic projects that needs to be explored further.[18] It is my argument here that in drawing upon the conceptualization of 'experiential knowledge' female philanthropists in the interwar years found a flexible legitimating language for their public work.[19] Bridging professional and extra-professional concerns, female philanthropists claimed access to, and the production of, knowledge through expertise in embedded lived experience. Working often upon the edges of the professional fields of the social and medical sciences, female philanthropists were able to critique established, formal ideas about how knowledge should be understood. They appropriated variously the authenticating perspectives of reason, imagination and instinct in their claims to authentic understanding of human nature. Furthermore, they showed that there were distinctive facets of knowledge to be gleaned respectively through the pursuit of observation, understanding and, separately, though 'practice'.

The power of the heart and embedded experience

Evangeline Booth did not regard herself as academic. Schooled at home in a strict evangelical faith and the tenets of 'practical Christianity', she was brought up to enjoy music and sports (notably horse-riding and swimming) more than academic disciplines. The deliberate evoking of the practical, rather than the intellectual, in this tradition carried positive connotations, and indeed was to be publicly celebrated. Booth's non-academic background became a notable feature of her public reputation as Salvation Army leader: her biographer, P. W. Wilson wrote that 'Piccadilly Circus [London] was the campus of the only college that Booth ever attended.'[20] The rhetoric spoke to the populist ambitions of the Salvation Army and its historical targeting of groups that were marginalized from educational and other social opportunities. Evangeline Booth's early leadership roles training Salvation Army officers, dating to 1892 when she took up the office of managing the International Training Centre based in Clacton, Essex, provided a particular context for promoting the message of learning as a pragmatic tool.[21] An article in the spring 1906 issue of the journal for Salvation Army officers *The Field Officer* discussed how Booth prepared her speeches, and it was not through scholarship:

> [s]he has little taste for it [reading], even if she had time. She is inclined to the theory that after one has undergone the education that best fits him for the position in his life he is called to fill, he should then be free from the trammels and errors of book-reading.[22]

The depiction of Evangeline Booth's denunciation of extended 'book-reading' was not itself anti-intellectual – it is worth noting that Booth's approach was projected in the article as a 'theory' in its own right. Rather, it was part of a conscious institutional narrative that emphasized spiritual revelation as the principal form of Christian learning. Explored in everyday settings, this was a logic that moved beyond scholarship to experience. The challenge was to translate Christian teachings into a meaningful vocabulary: to interpret, as her biographer wrote, 'the Scriptures into the English of the English'.[23]

The limitations of Evangeline Booth's own literary interest is inferred from her speeches and writings. Booth relied on only a very small range of intellectual reference points drawn from Biblical texts, the writings of celebrated historical authors (William Shakespeare and Thomas Carlyle) and political statesmen (Abraham Lincoln), a fact that was perhaps reflected in the evidence of a public sale of her estate, held at O'Reilly's Plaza Art Galleries in New York, in April 1951, following her death, where of a total of twenty-seven lots, books numbered only thirteen.[24] (Then again it is worth noting that, on her death, books amounted to sixty per cent of Evangeline Booth's worldly possessions.) The authorities that Booth did choose to draw upon helped to focus a quotidian moral code. In her pamphlet on female enfranchisement, *Woman*, published in America in 1930 and in Britain in 1936, she quoted Thomas Carlyle (who defined 'human life as a supreme choice between the Everlasting Yea and the Everlasting Nay'), William Shakespeare ('[a] victory is twice itself when the achiever brings home full numbers') and Abraham Lincoln (addressing Harriet Beecher Stowe as having precipitated the modern fight for American women's equal rights).[25] The reference to Abraham Lincoln's speeches is particularly illuminating of the symbolism of Booth's literary repertoire: Martha Nussbaum has argued that allusions to Lincoln's work have been used historically by commentators seeking to inspire an emotional response amongst listeners and readers.[26] More broadly in her speeches and writings Evangeline Booth called upon a distinctively visceral vocabulary as a way of affecting the hoped for goal of individual spiritual revelation. In 1920 she wrote an article for the American *National Geographic Magazine* that discussed the principles of officer training in terms of the sought-after evidence of visceral transformation, a process 'which transfigures a sheet of cold, gray canvas into a throbbing vitality, and on its inanimate spread visualizes a living picture'.[27] She would use similar imagery in a sermon in the published collection, *Toward a Better World* (1929), in which she spoke of reaching a 'heavenly' world beyond a better country (Heb. xi. 16), and imagined herself standing at her office window, where 'I saw the sun, with fingers of flame, painting on the sky groups of white angels in robes of amber fastening with crimson ribbons the black mantle of the night'; she theorized: '[t]his is God's artists'.[28]

In the context of such emphatic appropriation of the revelatory aspects of religious faith, the authority of the social sciences was not absent from the Salvation Army's public vocabulary in the interwar years, but it was contested. Evangeline Booth appropriated the cultural and intellectual clout associated with the evidence of 'facts' in a number of talks and writings aimed at both Salvation Army members and the wider public.[29] In 1933 she was invited to receive an award from the American Institute of Social Sciences, where she talked about the Salvation Army 'penetrat[ing] appearances and produc[ing] facts'.[30] However, the *moral* authority that was attributed to social science methods was always contingent within the organization. In one respect, the shifts in emphasis from visceral to scientific creeds gestured towards the elasticity in the formal presentation of the Salvation Army's social service work, and showed how the organization, with Evangeline Booth at its head, strategically related its work to fluid public discourses about the structural and spiritual bases of social knowledge. There was an express tension between the argument for the scientific understanding of society and the projections of divine illumination used in internal communications, however. Indeed, finding ways to configure the movement between these positions was at the heart of the Salvation Army's public work in this period, and required sustained engagement with the critical terms used by contemporaries in the project of knowledge formation. Evangeline Booth exemplified the challenge in 1945 in a speech accepting the American Humanitarian Award. There she would claim the practical mediation of studied approaches in the Salvation Army's methodology, 'not so much of the ascetic or monastic type', but 'tak[ing] the form of a practical and instructed pity for every phase of human need ... We reduce theory to action, apply faith to deeds.'[31]

Motherhood, intuition and reciprocal understanding

In exploring the composite bases of action and theory, Evangeline Booth spent much time in her public work in the interwar years elaborating women's social expertise, specifically. Women's social work, she wanted to convey, combined qualities of understanding and compassion that broke down the binaries of everyday engagements and the higher principles of religious activism. In *Woman*, Evangeline Booth tapped into an established narrative in the social sciences that traced the movement of women's actions from the domestic sphere to the professional and the extra-professional spheres through the roles of motherhood, nursing and missionary work.[32] Booth framed the debate in terms of personal and social transformations working through the love of Christ to reconfigure gender normative models; she wrote of '[t]he mother bending over her babe, the Red Cross nurse binding up a wound, the Salvation Army lassie kneeling by a penitent' and the formulation of opportunities for women's influence to stretch from a 'homely' countenance to a 'chance and a career, eternal in never-ending satisfaction'.[33] The metaphor worked in part to position the Salvation Army's work outside of the potential narrowness of professional and specialist knowledge, and within the well-rehearsed evangelical language of social motherhood. The label, 'Mother of Israel' was used in the nineteenth century by Methodist groups and by the Salvation Army to affirm the influence of women's religiosity (which was elevated in specific contexts distinctively above that of men's), and was extended in the twentieth century into an argument within the women's movement about the bases for women's political emancipation.[34] Mothers were also the most significant family members in Salvation Army conversion stories from the beginning of the organization's work, and the role of motherhood in these narratives explicitly ascribed women spiritual and social, as well as domestic, authority.[35]

In addressing Salvation Army women, Evangeline Booth configured intuition and insight (rather than the knowledge derived from study) as key markers of women's engagement and central to the effective functioning of human fellowship. The representation of female understanding as derived from everyday experience was a recurring conceit in Booth's talks. In a number of presentations, the imagery marshalled a broader argument about women's distinctive capacities over men's. In September 1939, Booth prepared a talk to British Salvation Army women as part of her planned Farewell Ceremony in Earls Court, London, to celebrate her retirement as World General, in which she claimed women's essential capacities for reciprocal understanding.[36] Booth's notes for the event show that she planned to speak of how women's gifts of mutual empathy surpassed any devotion men might show women: 'there is a breadth of understanding, and a source of sustenance and comfort that can alone come from a woman to a woman'.[37] She had made a very similar point in a talk to an audience of women's clubs in Tokyo in 1929 that promoted the model of 'holy womanhood' and distinguished women's mutual 'service [as] the best interpreter [of] life'.[38] Historians of social work have observed the centrality of women listening to the poor as a critical vehicle for the developing practices of professional social work, in ways which show a depth of understanding amongst female practitioners of the questions of 'unfairness, injustice and unearned disadvantage' that their male colleagues typically did not reach.[39] Evangeline Booth used the metaphor of female-centred conversation to configure women's mutual service as both a levelling and strengthening practice. Holiness theology, which stressed the fulfilment of social relationships through divine inspiration, taught that true conversion enabled an individual to know and act upon God's will.[40] As a marker of holiness, women's expertise in the trials and celebrations of life not only levelled relations between women, they also challenged men's monopoly on spiritual authority.

Female iconographies

Evangeline Booth was often quoted in the popular interwar press describing herself as a 'chip off the old block' of her father, William Booth; however, it was the weight of her mother's example that needed to be addressed as Booth moved towards the highest rank within the organization. It was well-known during William and Catherine Booth's lifetimes that Catherine was better educated and theoretically capable than her husband and that she made central intellectual contributions both to the nineteenth-century development of the Salvation Army's radical Christian theology and to developing Christian feminist thought.[41] In her pamphlet, *Female Teaching* (1861) Catherine Booth had set out an argument that women were suited by nature to preaching and to the Christian ministry. In texts including *Popular Christianity* (1887), *Papers on Practical Religion* (1879), *Papers on Aggressive Christianity* (1880) and *The Salvation Army in Relation to Church and State, and Other Addresses* (1883), she addressed the theology of salvation and atonement as expressing the harmony between the justice and love of God. Catherine Booth's reputation as an educated woman known for theological seriousness continued long after her death in 1890, and was translated in the early-twentieth century into the popular, though rather reductive, portrait of her as a 'suburban blue-stocking' – a bookish, intellectual woman.[42] It was a reputation that Evangeline Booth sought to complicate in the interwar period. In a sermon 'The Gardener' (John 20.15), published in the collection, *Toward a Better World* (1929), Booth consciously portrayed her mother denouncing theoretical abstractions, arguing: "'[a]way with arguments of your theoretical religion which would drive from the world all practical Christianity!" And so I say here – Away with them! Away with cold, stiff forms … I must have more than theory and form.'[43] The anecdote played up to the Salvation Army's populist ambitions but only when Evangeline Booth's mother was portrayed eschewing theory for practical faith. The model of quotidian religion, celebrated in 'The Gardener' in the portrait of 'a working-day Christ, in working-day clothes, for working-day hardships', needed to be reaffirmed and reinforced for the appreciation of the organization as a religion of the labouring classes.[44]

Under Evangeline Booth's leadership, Catherine Booth's example was of central importance to the public debate of how the theoretical and practical could be combined in the contexts of women's social work. In *Woman*, Evangeline Booth appealed to the image of her 'sainted Mother', hoping her influence would be passed on to the next generation, as it had been to her through her wearing of her mother's ring, a 'talisman'.[45] This family memory formed part of a wider female iconography – extending internationally and historically – that Booth called upon in the pamphlet to celebrate pioneers of modern medical, scientific and philanthropic practices, including Josephine Butler, St Elizabeth of Hungary, Elizabeth Fry, Florence Nightingale, Edith Cavell and Marie Curie. I have written elsewhere about how in the interwar years women's organizations consciously reverenced past female luminaries. In groups ranging from Christian bodies (the YWCA and the MU (Mothers' Union)) to organizations of professional women, discussions illuminated not only the cultural authority that exemplary Victorian women continued to wield, but also how the cultures of interwar civic practice allowed for the possibility of ascribing multiple identities to these women.[46]

Evangeline Booth's celebration of her mother's memory reveals, additionally, the process through which women who were well-known for social service were ascribed a *composite* public identity as part of the formulation of philanthropic epistemologies. Although Evangeline Booth was keen to prioritize a mode of experiential authority embedded in the domestic, she nevertheless tied in the theoretical and the practical resonances of women's contributions within and outside of the home. In a talk at a meeting for American Salvation Army women in September 1935 Evangeline Booth celebrated Harriet Beecher Stowe, Josephine Butler and Frances Willard as 'heroines of emancipation', and 'the heroines of service', Elizabeth Fry and Florence Nightingale, and configured her mother's qualities as a writer and her talents as a speaker in conformity with 'her marvellous efficiency in the arts of the home'.[47] In the planned talk to British Home League women in 1939, Booth drew again upon the examples of Elizabeth Fry and Florence Nightingale to argue that theory and practice were not mutually exclusive but rather intertwined in the everyday and embedded work of women's social service: '[w]oman deals not with theories alone, not with science alone, not with art alone', she argued, 'but with the innermost secrets of life itself'.[48] The audience's possible reception of this imagery is not my focus here so much as Booth's self-presentation in the conscious construction of her argument. Booth chose the rhetoric precisely to instruct members of the Salvation Army's Home League – a group that trained women in child and home management – that good motherhood could be extended but never wholly enacted through the theoretical insights promoted in contemporary movements of domestic science.[49] The art of home life, she argued, was to be revealed through experience, at least as much as it was to be explained through theory.

Love triumphant

In 1935 P. W. Wilson wrote in his sympathetic biography of Evangeline Booth that public interest in the Salvation Army was neither simply the response of propaganda, publicity and learning, nor 'conspicuous ability and wisdom or knowledge by [Salvation Army] officers and soldiers'. Rather, it was indicative of the organization's methods of facilitating popular understanding through 'raising to people's conscience of human duty to mankind'.[50] The appeal to deriving conscience had assumed a pivotal significance in the nineteenth century in the evolving creed of salvation to which Catherine Booth had contributed centrally. In 1879 in *Papers on Practical Religion* she had defined the agency of Christian conscience, using the teachings of St Paul's letter to the Romans, as the 'faculty of the soul which pronounces on the character of our actions' (Rom. ii. 15).[51] In her address 'Aggressive Christianity', Catherine Booth wrote of the exemplification of consciousness, channelled vigorously though Paul's teachings, to 'open the eyes of the converted and turn them from darkness to light'.[52]

Evangeline Booth would draw upon Pauline teachings about spiritual revelation and conscience repeatedly in the interwar years to juxtapose theological emphases and the principles of new scientific thought in explaining the influence of Christian social action. She specifically explored the correlation between the power of knowledge and truth by calling for the reorientation of the new psychological authority attributed to the 'brain' and a renewed emphasis upon the workings of the soul. In her sermon, 'Charity', published in the 1935 collection *Love is All*, Evangeline Booth drew upon the teachings of Paul's first epistle to the Corinthians (13:1–3) to reassess the authority of scientific psychology:

> How could KNOWLEDGE make up for LOVE?
> How could KNOWING make up for BEING?
> How could THINKING make up for FEELING?
> How could the BRAIN – glorious as it is – take the place of the SOUL? ...
> Knowledge springing from, revolving around, and resolving itself into Charity, is one of Heaven's mightiest forces. Knowledge without Love dwarfs the soul, narrows sympathies and minimizes character.[53]

The assertion of the subordination of learning and knowledge to the greater purpose of love in this example presented a different set of emphases to those that in 1906 had been used to project Booth as denouncing book learning: here there was a vital recognition of the 'glori[es]' of the work of the brain. But Booth projected a wider critical discourse in her sermon which targeted the privileging of scientific knowledge over the authority that was to be derived from faith. Her prioritization of the soul as the organ through which knowledge could be derived from love voiced a direct challenge to contemporary scientific studies of the development of the brain.[54] She expressed a related point in her talk in September 1935 to American Salvation Army women that celebrated Florence Nightingale, Elizabeth Fry and Josephine Butler when she also spoke about an Irish-born domestic servant, Margaret Graffa, who had lived an extraordinary life of service with orphaned children in New Orleans. Graffa, an uneducated and illiterate woman, exemplified not 'the triumphs of intellect, or the attainment of learning, or even militant bravery', but rather the power of love and compassion, in which women's gifts surpassed masculine modes of education. This female iconography – perhaps most poignantly, because it celebrated the example of a woman of poor background – exemplified a model of knowledge for the practice of social work that, proceeding from lived experience, romanticized a lack of formal education, and indeed poverty. Evangeline Booth told her audience that Margaret Graffa 'could not so much as write her name – signing with a cross the will by which she made her last gift – all her possessions – to the little orphans'. The point Booth wanted to make to the female listeners was that this was a strength, not only of exceptional women, like Graffa, but of the whole of womanhood, itself exalted over the world of men: '[w]oman can always write on the heart, whereas man often has to be satisfied with writing on the brain. This is powerful', Booth conceded, 'but what is the power of the brain, in comparison with the power of the heart?'[55]

Economics for life: combining theory and practice

In 1898 Lettice Fisher took up a postgraduate scholarship at the LSE (London School of Economics) where she studied economic history. It was still unusual at this time for women to take up these posts and Lettice Fisher was supported by family example; her father, Courtenay Peregrine Ilbert was an early visiting lecturer at the LSE.[56] However, as Maxine Berg has argued, the new subject of economic history offered distinctive intellectual opportunities for women within social and political spheres, ranging from feminist politics, adult education, Fabian socialism, the peace movement, the League of Nations and, later, the 1930s anti-fascist movement.[57] Furthermore, studying a new discipline (and at the LSE, which opened in 1895, at a new university) afforded women students the chance to assess the practical application of theory in an academic programme. The first prospectus for the LSE declared how alongside economic and political theory, the curriculum incorporated 'study and investigation of the concrete facts of industrial life and the actual working of economic and political relations as they exist or have existed, in the United Kingdom and in foreign countries'.[58] This founding rationale goes some way to explaining why it would be 1912 before the LSE established a separate Social Study Department, following, like a number of other institutions, the lead of the University of Liverpool, which founded the first Department of Social Studies in Britain in 1904.[59]

Lettice Fisher's postgraduate work illuminates the composite methodology of economic history at the LSE that combined emphasis upon practical, moral and intellectual engagements with direct implications for the development of contemporary social policy.[60] Beginning in 1899, Fisher published a series of articles on her research on urban housing in *The Economic Journal*. The articles addressed the municipal policies of the housing of the urban labouring classes – a question that H. H. Asquith's Liberal government would pick up in town planning proposals – especially the problems of tenements in slum areas and the exploitative rents of 'house jobbers'; Fisher questioned the wisdom of building houses with 'large rooms, elaborate appliances [and] ornamental appearance' which commanded high rents and inevitably priced out the poor labourer.[61] The evidence of empirical data derived from personal observation was understood to be critical to the forging of this argument. Lettice Fisher's mother had passed on to her daughter the value of such engagement: Jessie Ilbert (née Bradley), who had worked in London as a rent collector for Octavia Hill and trained as a nurse at St Thomas' Hospital in London, before marrying in 1874, published in 1885 in India six lectures on 'Practical Nursing' as an appeal for the direct exposure to factual knowledge on 'the sick room'; dress and hygiene; feeding the patient and administering medication; medical applications and bathing; and diseases and infections.[62] In the early 1900s Lettice Fisher worked as a rent collector amongst poor families in East Oxford, and through personal exposure to working-class poverty in the city developed first-hand knowledge to critique, as well as to support, local government measures in public health.[63] Reviewing the LCC (London County Council) report, *The Housing Question in London* (1900), she argued that it was 'scarcely possible to over-emphasize the importance of the preventive side of a local authority's work' in public sanitation,[64] which needed to cooperate with the work of voluntary agencies. In her article on 'Local Authorities and the Housing Problem in 1901' (1902), Fisher praised the movement in Birmingham which had produced a voluntary Sanitary Aid Committee. She was herself to become a founding member of the Oxford Sanitary Aid Committee (1902), and in 1912 an executive member of the newly formed Oxford Health and Housing Association.[65]

Theories of education

Eileen Yeo has argued that the relationship between thought and action emerged in a distinctively gendered subset of debates amongst public-spirited academics in the early-twentieth century, in which the pursuit of academic learning was gendered male and the practice of social work was gendered female.[66] The Fishers offer an interesting commentary on this model. In his posthumously published autobiography, H. A. L. Fisher reconsidered the purpose of intellectual learning for its own sake and wrote that 'from my own experience there is always a haunting feeling that learning and scholarship and the lettered life can bring content only if combined with some more practical form of active service to the community'.[67] H. A. L. Fisher's reflections revealed a set of privileges that were available to the male don, who might be at risk of boredom with the intensity of the focus upon academic work. The context was different for women academics who, if they married and had children (a minority),[68] typically found it very difficult to combine university work with marriage and family life (when the Fishers' daughter, Mary, was born in 1913, Lettice Fisher gave up tutoring). Moreover, as Carol Dyhouse has shown, the obstacles placed in women academics' paths in the early-twentieth century, both in terms of the sorts of knowledge it was deemed respectable for them to possess and the inferiority of the working environments in which many found themselves, further undermined the feasibility of the distinction between scholarship and wider social engagement.[69] As such, these inequalities – whilst real and frustrating to women academics – also played a part in allowing for flexibility in epistemological engagement through which female scholars were able to communicate to a broad public.

Lettice Fisher translated the conviction in the public role of scholarship and learning into a more specific argument about the futility of casting economic knowledge as disembodied theoretical abstractions; for her there was only meaning in economic thought if it could be applied to projects with clear social implications. Her consideration of theories of education beyond university life complicated her husband's assessments and revealed her own more attuned sense of the work of the social application of ideas. In her projects from the late 1890s, in both academic and social work settings, she experienced from the beginning of her career the sorts of interconnection between the spheres of thought and action that H. A. L. Fisher claimed was yearned for amongst male academics who were well-established in their careers. In her textbook for economic students, *Getting and Spending* (1922), Lettice Fisher defined economics as 'worth studying' as a part of training for citizenship because it made 'the ordinary affairs of life . . . so infinitely more interesting if we know a little about the intricate and wonderful organization in which each small transaction is a part'; she believed that getting used to thinking in a scientific manner would 'help us to be good citizens, to be interested in the work of our daily lives, and to be sensible, reasonable human beings'.[70] Addressing the book to school pupils, students, study circles and citizens' associations, Lettice Fisher configured education as a holistic enterprise, 'very much more than just book-learning: it means the training of every part, of body, mind, and soul'.[71] There were connections here with the arguments that Elizabeth Macadam and Evangeline

Booth were making independently, from the early 1900s onwards, about the value of learning outside of the library, but also distinctions: in contrast to Booth's emphases, Fisher's comments stressed a greater parity of attention upon physical, mental and spiritual development.[72]

For Lettice Fisher, the rationalism of the social sciences was a route to social progress, yet this was not a reductive project: she argued that 'economic science will not tell us that certain things are right or wrong', but would help facilitate understanding of the construction of knowledge and 'courses of action'.[73] In this respect, her thinking demonstrated a distinctive attribute of those who had embraced the new discipline of economic history in consciously moving beyond the work of the 'great' economic thinkers. Some reviewers claimed this feature of the work funnelled Fisher's public contributions through personal, rather than theoretical, methods. C. V. Butler, who studied under Lettice Fisher in the 1910s and herself became a tutor in social science and social work in Oxford after the First World War and author of social surveys, saw Fisher's economics as rooted in a methodological interest 'in human things' as distinct from the broader practice of the 'researcher'.[74] In a review of *Getting and Spending* for *The Economic Journal* in 1922, Butler praised Fisher's line of argument as a stimulus to investigate the 'things not seen', the economic structures and systems of everyday life. Butler elaborated the book's method with reference to Lettice Fisher's portrait of a pet goat – illustrating the frustration of 'the machinations of a typical milk-ring' and 'the relationship of substitution to monopolistic gains' – which she claimed exemplified Fisher's interest in the practical application of economic theory and everyday economic activity.[75]

Other intellectuals read into Lettice Fisher's interwar writings the affirmation of models of classical economic theory. In a review for the *Times Literary Supplement*, the writer E. St John Brooks discussed the economic historian, Sir William Ashley's introduction to *Getting and Spending* as evidence of Fisher's discipleship to 'the great masters of English political economy', including Ricardo, whose theory of rent and other classical economic theories was to be found in the book 'simpl[y] and intelligibl[y]' expressed.[76] The political edges of Fisher's work were more strongly assumed in this review than in C. V. Butler's and, in this sense, St John Brooks showed a greater willingness to acknowledge the social application of the theories Fisher discussed. He identified Lettice Fisher's endorsement of free trade arguments for the education of 'working men', who would 'learn the force of the arguments against the socialistic theory of production'.[77] As was inferred in this review, Lettice Fisher's economic thought was not anti-theoretical, rather it demanded attention to the relationship between domestic and political economy in building effective social relationships. Like other early female economists, she was interested in labour as a tool in economic exchanges other than, and additional to, those of production, an issue signalled in the title *Getting and Spending* (changed in 1938 to *Earning and Spending*), and which other contemporary female economists explored through an interest in the consumption practices of different social classes and in the functioning of labour within a mixed economy.[78] In Fisher's case, this was partly a critique of (predominantly male) economists who paid too much attention to the market economy.[79] But there was a broader relevance to the terms of her emphasis that reinforced the work as embedded in the forces of social life. Fisher made the point clearly in *Earning and Spending* when considering the usefulness of the unpaid work within the community undertaken by mothers, magistrates, those on town councils and other local bodies, 'and by all sorts of people in all sorts of ways'.[80] Inferring her own experiences as a mother and in voluntary work, Fisher indicated here the perceived continuum between theory and lived experience that drove her own practice and thinking.

Infant welfare work

Lettice Fisher's route into public work involved a commitment to voluntary enterprises with poor and working-class families alongside scholarship in economics that combined an engagement with social theory, public policy and practical response to human need. In April 1918, she took up the chair of a new organization, the NCUMC, and headed a committee in which men outnumbered women. The NCUMC was an example of the sort of inter-agency and cross sector cooperation that the guild socialist, G. D. H. Cole argued characterized the new social services of the post-1918 period, perhaps most obviously embodied by the NCSS (National Council of Social Service),[81] that aimed to bring together representatives of locally- and centrally-administered public authorities, national organizations, local committees and councils and private individuals.[82] Founded in the same year as the Maternity and Child Welfare Act (1918), the NCUMC initially comprised fifty-three organizations,[83] and worked as both a supporting agency for unmarried women having babies and a platform for policy lobbying. It aimed to secure reform of the laws defining the status of illegitimate children (Bastardy Acts) and the system for financial support from fathers of illegitimate children (Affiliation Acts); to secure provision of accommodation to support keeping together mothers and babies; and act as an information bureau for unmarried mothers or those seeking to support them.[84] The organization's campaigning and lobbying work, as Pat Thane has recently shown, from its origins illuminated the dynamic interrelationship between voluntary action and state welfare provision, and the recognition of the need for the two mechanisms to be brought into constructive partnership in response to the scale of the problem of unmarried mothers and their children.[85] From the beginning, both the policy and educational work was grounded in quantitative research methods that spoke to the urgent interest from the late-nineteenth century in the high infant mortality rate.[86] A notice produced in 1920 to accompany the NCUMC's campaign in support of a new Bastardy Bill included statistics drawn from the Register-General of the illegitimate birth rate in England and Wales (1918: 41.153); the illegitimate death rate (1917: 201 per 1,000 infants under 1 year); the legitimate death rate (1917: 90 per 1,000 under 1 year); and the number of affiliation orders in 1913 (the 'last normal year' before the outbreak of war: 6,914 out of 37,909 births). The statistics were made to tell a woeful story: the notice reported that the majority of illegitimate children were not only left fatherless; 'nearly 8,000 every year find an early death'.[87]

Early debates within the NCUMC show the organization's appropriation of a public vocabulary that stressed the composite moral and social policy ends of the charity, but also indicated lack of consensus over whether to foreground the social scientific or the compassionate logic of the work. In 1917 representatives of the Child Welfare Council of the Social Welfare Association for London, out of which the NCUMC emerged, discussed the need for an organization that would campaign for legislative reform in regards to the problem of illegitimacy as not only a 'humane' issue but an 'economic' one, that tackled the prohibitive costs that mothers of illegitimate children currently faced in bringing affiliation cases against fathers.[88] In seeking to advance the charity's rootedness in social scientific methods, early notifications from the NCUMC inferred the recognition of the limitations of using quantitative analysis in publicity. The 1920 notice about the revised Bastardy Bill underscored that 'there is an amount of undeserved suffering which cannot be estimated in statistics'.[89] Such language expressed the anxiety of some leading NCUMC members that the dignity of the unmarried mother might be overlooked in the focus purely upon the social scientific determinants of the problem of illegitimacy. Developing the emphasis upon qualitative reasoning, one of the early tasks the executive committee discussed was the need to communicate to statutory and voluntary agencies just how critical it was to interpret the new Maternity and Child Welfare Act both *humanely*, in ways that did not undermine the woman's self-esteem, and to point out the danger to life of refusing to attend to unmarried mothers.[90]

The pursuit of scientifically rigorous social classification, long a central concern amongst bodies charting demographic trends and birth and mortality rates,[91] was addressed in the NCUMC's early work in ways which indicate the further complexity of the organization's engagement with social scientific frameworks. Although scholars have argued that voluntary organizations and state authorities took a bleak approach towards unmarried mothers, based upon a rigid classification of 'first offenders',[92] discussions within the NCUMC demonstrate a broader concern to examine critically the classificatory systems used in infant welfare work in the period. Here the debate moved between consideration of sociological models and those used in the developing schools of psychiatry. Between 1918 and 1920 organizational discussions appropriated social scientific vocabularies to explain the problem of illegitimacy through the language of social types, where illegitimate children were categorized as 'ill or well, normal or abnormal, good or naughty' and unmarried mothers were grouped by age and occupation.[93] A key issue arose over the social category of 'unmarried'. At a conference at Mansion House, London in February 1918 at which the NCUMC was formally established, a Special Committee agreed '[t]hat any scheme for the assistance of unmarried mothers should not exclude any mothers left with the responsibility of the care and maintenance of their children (i.e. widowed and deserted mothers in need)'.[94] At the second meeting of the NCUMC executive in July 1918, committee members discussed whether the word 'unmarried' might be deleted from the organization's name altogether, though no obvious alternatives were raised and the suggestion was defeated.[95] The NCUMC's policy that support was to be given to unmarried mothers with one illegitimate child (and not more) did not, therefore, signal an uncritical approach to the practice of social classification. Rather the policy needs to be understood as formed within an assessment of the differentiated categories of motherhood and women's varying relationships to marital status through widowhood, separation and other forms of desertion as well as non-marriage. Despite these early debates, nonetheless the term 'unmarried' was retained by the organization until 1970, when the charity was renamed the National Council for One Parent Families.

The College mother

'Democratic' in sensibility so far as her closest associates were concerned, Lettice Fisher's reformist ambitions were themselves a product of the social and political privilege that she enjoyed as an elite and educated woman, and her concomitant access to particular sites of debate and discussion. A new opportunity arose for such expression in the mid-1920s. In 1925, seven years into her work with the NCUMC, and between writing projects for the Home University Library, Lettice Fisher moved with her husband and daughter into 'the beautiful rooms' of the Warden's lodgings of New College, Oxford, that were to become the family's home during the working week until 1940.[96] The family's relocation in 1925, like the previous one from Oxford to Sheffield, was to further H. A. L. Fisher's career; he had been appointed the Warden of the College. For Lettice Fisher, creative engagement with the opportunities, as well as the restrictions, of elite women's scope for influential public conversation became of critical personal, social and political importance. The New College Wardenship combined an administrative and academic role with the commitments of professional entertaining. While Lettice Fisher appreciated the pleasure this public aspect of the role brought her husband, her daughter recalled she was only too glad to leave behind the 'unceasing' round of entertaining on weekends to go to the family home in Surrey.[97] The draft seating plans for the supper parties held in the Warden's lodgings, drawn up by Lettice Fisher, testify to the unrelenting schedule of entertaining, typically at least one supper party a week in term time, on top of student tea parties, alumni dinners and College receptions (see Fig. 8).[98]

Lettice Fisher was well-versed in the social and psychological expectations that accompanied the wifely role of a public figure. In December 1916, H. A. L. Fisher had been appointed President of the Board of Education in David Lloyd George's wartime coalition cabinet, a role that placed new demands upon the family within the circles of the British political classes. That month, Lettice Fisher's former Oxford tutor, the historian Edward Armstrong wrote with congratulations that she, herself, would become a Queenly figure in the Westminster 'Salon' culture.[99] The endorsement rooted Lettice Fisher's identity within the culture of elite political hospitality in which she had been brought up in Imperial India and London.[100] Although self-consciously independent-minded women in the early-twentieth century decried the salon as stifling the development of women's personhood,[101] it offered a site for the performance of formal hospitality that continued to be valued as a mechanism for elite women's influence and social activism.[102] In the interwar years, those who celebrated the salon as bridging the scientific and intuitive bases of women's personal interactions conceived the particular sorts of knowledge and understanding that women could display in this setting. In *Conversation* (1927), Lettice Fisher's sister, Olive Heseltine, would describe the necessity for such attributes for the 'modern hostess', who needed to be 'an acute psychologist [and] who knows by

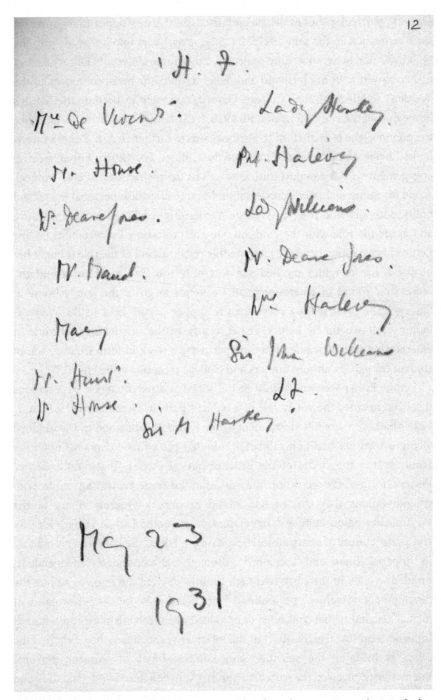

Figure 8. Seating plan drawn up by Lettice Fisher for a dinner party at the Warden's lodgings, New College, Oxford. Copyright, Sophie Ilbert Decaudeveine. Reproduced with the permission of Sophie Ilbert Decaudeveine and the Bodleian Libraries, University of Oxford, MS Eng.d.3780 (Additional Papers of H.A.L. Fisher).

instinct the kind of people who are likely to get on together and those who will unconsciously paralyse their neighbours'.[103] Lettice Fisher disclosed such a fine-tuned sense of her own subjectivity in relation to these various models: in a letter to her friend Frances Stevenson in the mid-1920s she confided apprehension about the prospect of a forthcoming supper party at the Warden's lodgings for the historians, Lawrence and Barbara Hammond, the philosopher and historian Élie Halévy and his wife Florence and the Bishop of Winchester: 'an odd mixture but I expect it will work'.[104] Yet Fisher remained in conversation, for intellectual and/or administrative ends, with all of these guests: she reviewed Halévy's *History of the English People in the Nineteenth Century* (1924–34); Lawrence Hammond reviewed her publications and Cyril Garbett, the Bishop of Winchester, went on to become a Vice-President of the NCUMC.[105] Instinct, intuition and personal knowledge were a critical part of the performance of academic, administrative and social work, as well as practical psychology, so far as Lettice Fisher was concerned.

The role of Warden's wife might have functioned as a set of 'incorporated' obligations,[106] but Lettice Fisher exploited it as an expansive opportunity and one which further illuminates the movement between the intellectual and practical bases of her social activism. The wifely duties of the hostess extended Fisher's personal networks through which she gathered and exchanged information for her own public causes and shaped her theory of social action. Throughout the 1920s and 1930s visitors at the Warden's lodgings included, amongst many others, fellow academics (Cyril Bailey, George Macaulay Trevelyan, Isaiah Berlin), politicians and economists (H. H. Asquith, William Beveridge) and advocates of women's causes (the writer Ray Strachey and the actress Lillian Baylis).[107] The exchanges on such occasions functioned within the shared rhythm of the social life of the educated and political classes. (Fisher often drew up the seating plans for dinner parties at the Warden's lodgings on the reverse of invitations to 'At Homes' and garden parties hosted by members of the Oxford and London elites.[108]) But more than this, the forms they took embodied particular opportunities for Fisher to combine thought and action. In addition to urging guests to engage with the social and political causes for which she and her husband worked, Lettice Fisher's personal correspondence reveals that formal entertaining was a site in which practical, political and intellectual engagement was mutually reinforcing. Isaiah Berlin, tutor at New College and a family friend, observed her publicizing forthcoming fundraising events for the NCUMC at supper parties at the Warden's lodgings, and New College alumni Michael Crum remembered Fisher encouraging undergraduates to attend

NCUMC sales in the College garden.[109] Lettice Fisher's everyday influence was thus a marker of the combined intellectual and practical goals of her public engagement. Appropriating what might have been limiting spheres of operation, she modelled a distinctly political and radicalizing social practice.

Philanthropy as scientific vocabulary

In 1915 the historian, Russian scholar and friend of Muriel Paget, Bernard Pares returned to England from Russia and Galicia, where he had been based since the outbreak of war in 1914 on the eastern front as an official observer of the Russian army. In Galicia, where Russian peasant soldiers of the White Russian Army were fighting against Austria-Hungarian forces, Pares found a terrible lack of medical supplies. In 1915 anaesthetics in military hospitals were wholly inadequate and Pares witnessed doctors undertaking surgical operations on patients who had not been sedated.[110] Bernard Pares found in Muriel Paget a pro-active sympathizer to this evidence: her response was the fundraising and organizing for the Anglo-Russian Hospital in Petrograd, that opened officially in February 1916, and three field hospitals on the eastern front.[111] My interest in the exchange between Bernard Pares and Muriel Paget is in what it reveals about Paget's developing commitment to the advancement and publicity of modern medical practice. British publicity for the Anglo-Russian Hospital shows how the vocabulary of clinical medicine was used immediately as a central legitimizing device for Paget's humanitarian practice. Reports in the medical press about the initial work of the hospital emphasized its contribution to contemporary medical research and surgical practice: in February 1916 the *British Medical Journal* ran a short report specifying the hospital's provision of 200 beds, an operating theatre, X-ray installation and a 'bacteriological outfit', and its staffing by radiographer, bacteriologists, anaesthetists and surgeons.[112] There were many limitations still to be overcome both with respect to medical practice and resources. Notes kept by medics at the hospital recorded the failures of early surgical apparatus; the British doctor, Lyndall Pocock, for example, noted in his diaries the flawed functioning of the X-ray equipment in 1916, though it was largely effective for work in the field hospitals by 1917–18 (see Fig. 9).[113] Yet the social aspirations for modern medical practice were widely emphasized in reports of the relief programmes Paget set up around this time. Articles in non-specialist publications also appropriated clinical vocabulary to discuss the work as a form of preventive medical care: in 1919 *The Christian World* reported on

Figure 9. 'The X-ray apparatus' at the Anglo-Russian Hospital, Petrograd. Photograph taken by Lyndall Pocock and included in his MS Diary (Nov. 1916). Reproduced with the permission of Pete Blindell and the Imperial War Museum, Documents.3648 (Papers of G. M. and L. C. Pocock).

the clinics set up in Czechoslovakia, established in connection with the Anglo-Czech Relief Fund, as launching a vaccination programme on top of the work of feeding kitchens and clothing centres.[114]

Women's medical professionalization

A striking element of Muriel Paget's relief work in the immediate post-war period, especially child welfare work, is the validation it attached to models of women's medical expertise. Paget's connection with the Red Cross (she joined the British Red Cross in 1910) was an important vehicle for her appreciation of this practice and had been extended by the evidence of the work women undertook in the Red Cross Voluntary Aid Detachments during the First World War. Paget's legitimization of the authority of women medical *professionals*, specifically, emerges clearly in respect of the women she appointed to oversee her own relief programmes. Dr Isabel Emslie, one of the leading figures, joined Muriel Paget's Mission for Children in the Crimea in the summer of 1920 where she managed a children's hospital in a converted school building in Sebastopol.[115]

The project was short-lived, and the hospital closed in November 1920 after only a few months of operation, following the defeat of Wrangel's White armies by the Bolsheviks. Isabel Emslie had trained in the women's medical school at the University of Edinburgh, graduating in 1910 in medicine, and had gained her doctorate in 1912, specializing in the treatment of nervous disorders. In 1915, she joined the Scottish Women's Hospitals organization, where she took up posts firstly in France and then Thessaloniki.[116] The appointments of doctors such as Emslie with the Scottish Women's Hospitals and later Muriel Paget's Mission in the Crimea exemplified the value placed by humanitarian organizations upon women's medical professionalization as a vehicle for experimental models of constructive and preventive relief work. Medical professionals' willingness to show initiative whilst applying their medical training was vital in this context. In her memoirs, published in 1960, Isabel Emslie would present the trajectory of her own professional career in the Mission hospitals in exactly these terms as expanding her early involvement in psychiatric medicine; initially satisfying her 'hankering after the practice of surgery', but also confirming her love of clinical research, to which she subsequently returned.[117] She acknowledged how the drivers of her work in the hospitals combined the search for self-growth and commitment to furthering specialist expertise. Looking back on her decision to join anti-malaria work in Albania in the mid-1920s following the disbandment of Muriel Paget's Mission, Emslie conceded: 'I realise that it was not only pity for a suffering people that had urged me to volunteer for Albania; it was a longing to go back to that wild countryside, to lead the primitive life and use to the full my initiative and experience.'[118]

Professionalization in the field of medicine, in common with the majority of spheres in which women's professional contributions expanded from the mid-nineteenth century onwards, was a 'gendered affair'.[119] In interwar Britain, the rhetorical emphasis placed upon women doctors' personal and moral characteristics, as well as specialist knowledge, was widely used to legitimate women's authority within the medical profession. The physiologist and feminist Winifred Clara Cullis would use such a model in her article on the medical surgeon, Dame Mary Scharlieb in the 1922–30 supplement of the *DNB*, which associated Scharlieb's professional competence with the 'thorough knowledge of human nature', acquired through her experience of motherhood.[120] The blurring of the professional, personal and moral bases of female doctors' experience can be seen too in a brief comment in a letter that Muriel Paget wrote to Eglantyne Jebb in August 1920 about the forthcoming inspection of conditions in Petrograd that was to be undertaken by Mr Webster and Isabel Emslie, in Paget's words: 'a good lady doctor'.[121] Correspondence between Paget and Isabel Emslie in 1920 shows more fully the central place Paget accorded clinical knowledge in the formalization of humanitarian practice.[122] However, the authority derived from personal insight still retained a central place in Muriel Paget's admiration for Emslie's expertise. Writing to the doctor soon after her appointment with the Mission, Paget asked explicitly for Emslie's 'personal views' of the conditions in which children lived in Serbia and the Crimea, over and above the work of the Mission, that could form the basis for a submission of comparative evidence of the relative needs of children in Ruthenia and Central Europe to be presented to the SCF.[123]

Interpreting the methods of personal observation as a bridge for professional and extra-professional bases of authority became an important part of Muriel Paget's wider argument for the necessity for female expertise in international child welfare projects. Although my focus here is upon epistemologies, rather than politics, political contexts were central to the developing formulation of these methods. In 1922, the year in which Paget's relief centres in Eastern Europe had been taken over by the new national governments, she returned her energies to working with child populations in Russia, and visited the Soviet Department of Education in Moscow. There she received sympathy amongst officials (that she would not in two years' time) for a programme of constructive national child welfare provision, but she felt that the administrative changes required to implement the policy were hampered 'by [a] total lack of executive female personnel'.[124] She reiterated the point in a report to her London committee about medical and social conditions in Russia at the time, writing that 'so long as we only send business men and amateur workers, however excellent they may be, to administer funds subscribed by the British public for the saving of child life in Russia, presumably in the most efficient and economic way, I consider that the organization of the work leaves great room for improvement'.[125] Effective humanitarian work was not to be restricted by narrow measures of efficiency and economy. It required the performance of both specialist skills and embedded forms of personal experience which, Paget projected, were combined uniquely amongst women in executive roles.

The logic of inspection

In recent decades historians have read narratives about the practices of inspection in the humanitarian project for what they reveal about the claims to public authority made by humanitarian actors. Showing both first-hand experience of the conditions and rhetoric of empathy for the suffering and wretchedness of war-torn and famine-stricken communities was a critical tension in the reporting of humanitarian news stories in the nineteenth and twentieth centuries, as James Vernon has found.[126] What interests me is the language through which, in Paget's case, visual authority was constructed in this context as a marker of modern healthcare practice. British news reports of Muriel Paget's relief work in the early 1920s signalled how her authority was formulated in the period partly as a function of social class, through which she gained direct access as an intrepid and committed aristocratic woman to the social and political spheres of humanitarian need. In 1922, the *Manchester Guardian* reported on Paget's witnessing of the local conditions of poverty and hunger in her recent visit to the Baltic States as a route to public education and collective compassion; she was claimed to have said it was 'impossible' for anyone who had not seen the conditions to realize the distress that existed: '[s]he could not have imagined the scenes, for example, at the welfare centres in Dvinsk, to which starving exhausted people come from great distances for supplies of milk and bread'.[127] The legitimating authority of visual inspection was constructed in these accounts as an ethnographic practice that was rooted in Paget's personal connections with international policymakers (in Czechoslovakia, through her friendship with the Masaryk family) in the work to advance modern healthcare systems. Muriel Paget's ideas about health policy, welfare policy, food aid policy and child welfare policy were interlinked, if distinct, initiatives in this context but the method of observational inspection was an important tool for their connection. Furthermore, the value placed upon the empirical evidence of visual access for the development of these policies was transmitted through various layers of organizational practice. In September 1920, Isabel Emslie wrote to Paget from the Crimea about the prospect of the harsh winter in Sebastopol and the implications for the child welfare work. She reported on the children's hospital that now looked smart, having been freshly painted, and she hoped to send photographs to give a fuller idea of it and the patients to Paget.[128] Muriel Paget herself passed on photographs and reports from the sisters and social workers at the children's clinics in the Baltic States to SCF authorities, who in turn presented them to international sponsors.[129]

The work of inspection carried out by women medical and social work professionals framed more extensively the daily operation of the child welfare centres run by Paget's Missions, which themselves became an important cog in the wheel of international humanitarian data collection systems on the health of local populations. The appropriation of social scientific methods for the practice of humanitarian governance was key.[130] Quantitative evidence was used to measure the 'need' to which any particular venture attended. In August 1920, the two medical sisters overseeing Paget's infant welfare centre in Czechoslovakia travelled to Turzovka, in north-western Slovakia and spent ten days 'inspecting' living conditions in the Kysuca river valley region, before establishing a central clinic in the town of Zilina in September 1920. In November of that year, the supervisory sister of the clinic, Muriel Payne reported to Muriel Paget that in the first month, registered attendances totalled nearly 700.[131] Qualitative data was also sought, and indeed, as we will see, became a critical tool for the wider cultural narratives that Paget would go on to disseminate.[132] Humanitarian practice, as these examples show, nonetheless, worked initially through a social scientific authority derived from data collection and social classification. For example, Muriel Payne's report included a 'Notice to Parents' that had been distributed to the doctors in charge of local clinics and local priests informing mothers that clinics were specified for particular 'types of cases': children up to the age of six for fortnightly check-ups and weighing; children with chronic illnesses and disease; mothers having difficulty feeding babies; and expectant mothers.[133] The social science expertise in mothercraft that was drawn here is significant also when it is remembered that Muriel Paget was herself the mother of four children – the youngest, John, was six years old in 1920. This family context, the personal expectations of which Paget had to battle at times in order to justify her commitment to the humanitarian field, moreover helps to underscore how philanthropy functioned as an intellectual practice rather than an emotional or 'feminine' one.[134]

The broader educative work associated with medical intervention that had been an important part of British missionary projects in the nineteenth century remained a vital source in the 1920s for the developing practice of healthcare and the cultural politics of humanitarian governance.[135] The system by which data was channelled upwards in relief organizations can be seen in the processes by which the senior British sisters at welfare centres in Czechoslovakia, Romania and the Baltic States submitted monthly reports both about the immediate medical needs of those who used the clinics and the broader health and living conditions of local populations, which were filed by Muriel Paget's Mission and the SCF.[136] Moreover, Paget's relief programmes harboured ambitions for wider and more culturally-embedded forms of health education. In 1920, under the auspices of her Mission to Russia and in conjunction with the LORCS, Paget sponsored an international nursing scholarship for students enrolled at King's College for Women, London, who it was hoped when they returned to their countries of origin would 'carry on educational propaganda' in social medicine.[137] The humanitarian field in the newly created European States proved more fertile ground for experiments in the cultural dissemination of social and medical knowledge in this period than did the terrain of revolutionary Russia (and as we will see, later Soviet Russia), as the closure of the children's hospital in Sebastopol in 1920 highlights. However, in each case there remained the need to stress humanitarian actors' legitimizing routes of access: it was through personal channels of influence that the frameworks of imperial social knowledge, and humanitarian workers' claims to access to models of 'modern' healthcare, were reinforced. In June 1920 Muriel Paget reported to a representative of the London-based Official Committee for Relief in Europe on her own recent 'inspection' of Czechoslovakia and Romania as having cemented her conviction that education centres were essential for the effective institution of relief and to combat the 'total ignorance in matters concerning general health and infant welfare'.[138] The connection drawn between ideas about new health policy and community work emerges clearly as shaping the direction of Paget's international initiatives in this period. Writing to Paget from the Volga region that had been devastated by famine, in the autumn of 1922 Muriel Payne advised a system that would more fully integrate medical training within community structures and extend the practice of the earlier work of inspection and knowledge dissemination yet further. The plan would see Russian public health and child welfare nurses living in the towns and villages specifically for the purpose of educating mothers in childcare and the prevention of disease and unsanitary living conditions.[139]

Therapeutic practice

Public rhetoric of Muriel Paget's humanitarian interventions in the 1920s needs to be understood within the contemporary vogue for asserting the cultural meanings of clinical practice, and Paget's own goal to position her work within the intellectual contours of new scientific fields.[140] In her work in Russia in the later 1920s, the aims of medical practice and health policy were joined to her developing interest in psychology in relation both to children's policy, the policy of displaced and homeless populations and food assistance. Paget found a receptive space within mainstream British media commentary upon the Soviet Union in this period to promote her international projects within the contemporary language of psychoanalytic and therapeutic child welfare work.[141] In 1927, the *Daily Telegraph* published a series of articles authored by Muriel Paget on conditions in contemporary Russia, in which she claimed scientific, social and political knowledge for her interventions in her role as participant observer.[142] Her article published in February 1927 focused on the problem of homeless children in Russia, estimated at one time to total two million and in autumn 1926 to total 300,000 (the majority were boys between the ages of eight and sixteen), around 80,000 of whom were based in Moscow. The wide age range of the boys that Paget was concerned for fitted with the findings of contemporary psychologists that developmental stage was more significant than calendar age in defining childhood.[143] Muriel Paget identified homes in around eighty districts in Russia that were accommodating these children, though maintained there needed to be more. She wrote that the issue of obtaining personnel trained in psychotherapy to support young people was equally as urgent to that of building homes, where '[g]reat tact and patience and a knowledge of psycho-therapeutics are necessary in order to tempt them back to ordinary civilised life'.[144] The language of tact and social finesse that scholars have claimed continued to define elite women's philanthropic practice up to the period of the Second World War was evidently still part of Muriel Paget's public vocabulary (and notably shaded here into her construction of professional social work).[145] But it was tied to an equally strong claim for the contributions of her work to the fields of modern psychology and juvenile policy. Her description signalled how female philanthropists were shaping the interpretation of theories of therapeutic research in child welfare work through concrete evidence gained from philanthropic practice.[146] The authority which Muriel Paget claimed in the work of juvenile policy was evidenced in 1931 when she and Lady Baring organized a seminar on 'Mind and Health and Children of the Juvenile Court' in connection with the newly proposed Institute of Medical Psychology.[147]

In 1927 Muriel Paget was also thinking strategically about how to present the work of the London-based charity, the IKL, within the vocabulary of new medical research. That year the IKL registered a deficit of £597.14s.0d., a figure that would rise by late 1928 to £1159. 1s.10d.[148] Organizational literature packaged the charity's financial difficulties as evidence of the ongoing demand for its work and the imperative for continued public support. However, over and above the focus on social need, the fundraising drive in the late 1920s projected the IKL's food assistance work as motivated by the active production of medical knowledge. Thus, the annual report of 1927–8 appealed for funding to enable the charity's application of new research:

The nation has created a MEDICAL RESEARCH COUNCIL for the express purpose of wringing more of the secrets of health and happiness out of silent uncommunicative Nature. That Council led by Sir Walter Fletcher is a most indefatigable body, and they have got some news for us.

FOOD,

They are telling us, if better selected and better prepared could change the whole aspect of life for us. This they have proved by a series of remarkable experiments.[149]

Scholars have argued that the MR (Medical Research Council) constructed the public rhetoric of scientifically 'controlled' therapeutic trials in the interwar period, and by the 1930s had consolidated its leading position in the scientific policy that influenced government and pharmaceutical companies.[150] The focus of the work was not unique however, and in fact it extended a much longer-established domestic science movement, in which women had played a central role, evidenced for example in American women's work at the Boston Cooking School from the late 1870s.[151] As the IKL's publicity shows, by the late 1920s the public authority attributed to the MR functioned as a useful institutional vehicle for women's philanthropic ventures to claim a stake in modern scientific research. The IKL's statement in 1927–8 positioned the charity's work as validating medical research in the ongoing debate not only about the science of hunger but also about the epistemologies of social action; as the annual report's wording stressed, this was to be a framework for claiming the charity's contribution to the development of scientific knowledge that could show truths kept hidden in 'nature'. In the context of earlier international domestic science projects that centred women's influence, the charity's puff that it was the only organization 'attempting to bring the fruits of these discoveries into the homes of those that need them most' needs to be critiqued. However, the emphasis was significant in indicating the ideas of Muriel Paget, and those around her, about the relationship between the practice of food assistance and welfare policy. In making explicit the connection – '[w]on't you support your own Medical Research Council by assisting the Kitchens and so giving us fewer invalids, and more healthy nursing mothers and more healthy babies' – the IKL claimed an important galvanizing role in moving between the spheres of medical research and social experience that used theoretical engagement to extend its practical ends.[152]

Conclusion

It has become better understood that women's philanthropic contributions in the nineteenth and early-twentieth centuries, while often framed in public rhetoric that foregrounded women's moral and domestic authority, actively shaped the construction of modern social scientific and scientific principles.

Florence Nightingale, whose altruistic motivations were famously re-evaluated in Lytton Strachey's critique, *Eminent Victorians* (1918), is now recognized as pioneering important examples of data visualization in her Coxcomb charts illustrating mortality rates amongst soldiers in the Scutari Hospitals during the Crimean War. Historians have argued that although social and cultural resistances to women's contributions to the development of academic social science proved strong into the first decades of the twentieth century, public opportunities for women in this sphere were in fact forthcoming along alternative directions.[153] The interwar careers of Evangeline Booth, Lettice Fisher and Muriel Paget point to a more complex situation still, in which the authority of the social sciences and medical sciences was both simultaneously embraced and complicated in the presentation of the epistemological contributions of women's philanthropic projects. Evangeline Booth's claims that the Salvation Army reduced theory to action and applied faith to deeds was reminiscent of the sorts of language that Lettice Fisher would use to configure the praxes of economics and social policy, but the women's construction of the value of social scientific knowledge differed substantially. By contrast, Booth's emphasis upon the revelation of God through the natural world was in tension with the 1920s rhetoric of Muriel Paget's charity, the IKL, which presented the findings of scientific research and new models of scientific psychology as necessary precisely to overcome the 'silences' of nature. Paying attention to these conceptual differences provides another way into exploring questions about the 'mixed economies' of welfare provision and humanitarianism.[154] It also sheds new light upon the multifaceted contributions of female philanthropy to the conceptual development of a number of intellectual fields. In this respect, the significant forms of divergence, as well as parallels, between individual women's constructions of their commitments reflect more than the distinct sites in which female philanthropists worked; they show their contributions to the interwar search for the connection between theory and action.

Contemporary understandings of women's professionalization in the interwar period, alongside women's contested relationship to the social sciences, opened up particular opportunities for female philanthropists to marshal composite theories of social work. It was these opportunities that explained Elizabeth Macadam's decision to frame her book *The New Philanthropy* in terms of both embedded social relationships and the science of observation, and her argument for the continuing vitality of philanthropy in and alongside the expanding interwar state. When Macadam chose the 'social servant' for the title of her revised textbook on social work published in 1945, she alluded to a related debate well underway in the interwar period addressing the epistemologies of philanthropy and social work.[155] The term 'social servant', used by international commentators in the war years, was less well-known in Britain in the interwar period than 'civil servant' or 'public servant', both of which connoted forms of public and professional practices that were undertaken primarily for the common good. The opening up of the Civil Service formally to women was one of the critical measures of women's professionalization in the nineteenth and early-twentieth centuries, but one which remained bound precisely by gendered constructions of women's work.[156] Equally, if not more fundamentally, in the years after the end of the First World War, the Civil Service was recognized as a space for experimental social engagement: in *The Social Worker* (1920), Clement Attlee wrote of a 'realisation of the possibilities of adventure in breaking new ground, that is offered to the civil servant'.[157] Within the context of these wider debates, Elizabeth Macadam's use of the term social servant signalled the fluid and expansive possibilities of women's social work and philanthropic contributions. But individual women performed and interpreted different calibrations of the role. In stretching public commitment between concept and practice and theory and action, female philanthropy tested both the bases and production of social knowledge and how that knowledge was to be understood.

3

Identity

In 1935 the UK YWCA celebrated eighty years of social work with young women.[1] In March of that year the organization's members' magazine, the *Blue Triangle Gazette* showcased a new cover image that had been commissioned for the anniversary. The black and white print, depicting a woman in a crinoline dress handing a lamp to a young woman dressed in a contemporary tunic, signalled the organization's motivating principles of social connection and spiritual revelation in a resonant image of women's active service (see Fig. 10). The metaphor would have been familiar to YWCA members and supporters. Emily Kinnaird had explained the rationale for writing her autobiography, *Reminiscences*, by using the imagery of a line of torchbearers passing on the spirit of earlier exemplars of practical Christian work.[2] A short history produced for the eightieth anniversary used another variation of the conceit on its front cover to pick out the YWCA's motto, 'By love serve one another', in a drawing that intertwined the 'Lamp of Service', the Rose of England, Thistle of Scotland and Leek of Wales.[3] As the eightieth anniversary gala celebrations drew closer, in June 1935 Emily Kinnaird rallied support for a fundraising jubilee by using once again the idiom of participation as a mode of collective connection and implored members to pray for a 'fellowship in giving', building 'an ever widening chain of demand: "[a]sk and ye shall receive" . . . gather ye together the links, i.e. the bonds of comradeship, old family ties, eighty years of unexhausted life'.[4]

The interwar years saw a reconfiguration of the social contract between individuals and the state that focused new questions about the nature of modern identity. In the wake of the psychological and social ruptures of the First World War and the gradual achievement of universal enfranchisement, many commentators explored what individuals were giving up, and what they should demand, in the new democracy that connected the governing classes and citizens. The Representation of the People Act of 1918, which introduced the entirely new elements to the franchise of the military and naval voter as well as the woman voter over thirty who met minimum property qualifications, registered an

Figure 10. The YWCA's eightieth anniversary image, *The Blue Triangle Gazette*, March 1935. Reproduced with the permission of the Young Women's Trust (formerly the YWCA) and The Modern Records Centre, University of Warwick, MSS 243/1/2/3 (Young Women's Christian Association Records).

urgency to the debate about what was to be the contribution and responsibilities of new citizens that was further extended by the widening provisions of the Representation of the People (Equal Franchise) Act of 1928.[5] The 'voluntary citizen' emerged as a category in its own right in the interwar period, discussed by experts as a linchpin of the modern, moderate state.[6] Voluntary engagement was understood to be a central attribute of democratic behaviour through which individuals expressed their active relationship to the state: for the social worker Elizabeth Macadam in the 1930s, voluntary effort represented a 'powerful safeguard ... against the interference with freedom and personal liberty that has overtaken other lands' – she meant the Soviet Union – while Constance Braithwaite observed in 1938 the interdependency of the state, that existed to serve 'human purposes', and the voluntary activity undertaken by citizens.[7]

Questions about the identities that were embodied in citizens' participatory engagement emerged internally within voluntary organizations in the interwar period in ways that indicated the further complexities of contemporary understandings of democratic subjectivity. Working outwards from particular social needs and responses, individual organizations explored a range of relational and categorical models of social identity. The YWCA's *Blue Triangle Gazette*'s eightieth anniversary image illustrated one set of models. It would be easy to read the image of the flame passing between women as a pious idiom, illuminating principally spiritual enlightenment, but this would be overly reductive of its meaning and the YWCA's social contribution. Here, the visual impact of the change in the women's dress is particularly important: modern dress signals an agency that could denote the need to forge new kinds of intimate, emotional relationships outside the family – precisely the sorts of affiliations the YWCA had been concerned to address and foster with young women since its first programmes of work in the mid-nineteenth century. As we will see, these relationships were configured in the interwar years often to explore women's capacities for participation in relation to the practices and spaces of home life. Partly as a consequence, such relationships were not necessarily equal, and although allowing for the demonstration of individual agency, they might uphold multiple transactions of power.[8] The YWCA's symbolism expressed a particular concern to apprehend modern identities in terms of the interdependency of individual and social selfhood. The point of the anniversary image was to underscore the potential for the construction of new forms of personal freedoms in terms of the mutuality of individual and community development; individual agency was only to be fully achieved as part of a wider project of social connection.

My interest in this chapter is in the metaphors that female philanthropists used within their social projects to explore the reconfiguration of inter-class subjectivities for a regime of the new post-war social contract. Put another way, this chapter explores what female philanthropists wrote and said about the formulations of individual and collective identity in the context of the new mass democracy of the interwar years. Evangeline Booth's, Lettice Fisher's and Emily Kinnaird's contributions to debates about individual agency and democracy that are traced on the following pages sit on an influential faultline with contemporary feminist perspectives that called for the fuller development of women's (and men's) self-identity. Voluntary women's organizations in these years were part of a broad and influential 'women's movement' encouraging members to participate in local and national politics in ways that addressed traditional domestic contexts as part of new constructions of citizenship.[9] Female philanthropists and those who lead voluntary women's organizations in this period, in conversation with their organizations and membership, actively reformulated the central imagery of women's domestic influence in an idiom of outward-facing democratic subjectivity, in which women's citizenship was defined through a series of relationships, practices and acts, as much as a designated 'status'.[10] There were direct links between this work, itself connected rhetorically and explicitly to maternalist traditions of women's activism, and the activism of interwar feminist organizations that expanded the scope and meanings of democratic selfhood.[11] Lettice Fisher's work both for the NCUMC and the NFWI notably complemented, and was supported by, her involvement with feminist organizations, the Six Point Group and the NUSEC. But the ideas driving female philanthropists also reached beyond feminist ambitions. What I see as distinctive about the campaigns of the interwar period is the concern amongst female philanthropists to expand the rhetoric of domestic maternalism for new expressions of freedoms that were rooted in cross-class and cross-cultural identities. As I argue in this chapter, female philanthropists were fundamentally concerned between the wars with understanding the place of the individual human actor in relation to shifting forms of social affiliations and as part of the politics of community development. They explored the principles of self-determination as personal as well as structural concerns and understood individual freedom as embedded within social, economic and political structures working in conformity with markers of individual identity. In examining this conjunction, they moved between economic, sociological, cultural and religious explanations of society and community and developed important contributions to interwar debates about the meanings of democracy.

Self-development in a Christian democracy

It had become by the interwar years something of a cliché to label pejoratively those women, who were committed like their male counterparts to supporting the public administration of social and political bodies, 'committee women'. Requiring investment of time as an unpaid occupation, women's committee work was dismissed in the interwar period as falling short either of 'modern' feminist principles,[12] or (from a male perspective) the traditions by which educated women, like men, ought to be engaged in intellectual work, rather than administrative 'spade work'.[13] As the NUSEC observed in an ironic poem in their magazine the *Woman's Leader* in 1920, committee work was one avenue (the poem suggested there were many) in which women's domestic and public contributions were undervalued, if not overlooked.[14] Scholars, too, have paid women's committee work little attention beyond assessments of the legal contractual obligations of voluntary agencies, and largely have been unconcerned with its broader conceptual and practical significance to the shaping of the idea of community and the role the individual was to play within society.[15] The wider historical significance of committee work needs to be reassessed. Committees were an essential feature of the voluntary impulse and a pivotal mechanism of the 'desire to cooperate' that contemporaries argued distinguished the voluntary motive in the first decades of the twentieth century.[16]

Emily Kinnaird understood that – at the level of public perception at least – committee work was a gendered practice of voluntary engagement. As well as her many executive roles within the YWCA, Kinnaird was co-founder and a long-serving committee member of the British Council of Women Workers, later the NCW.[17] In *Reminiscences*, she contrasted her approach to committee work with the example of her late brother, Arthur Kinnaird's 'associated' roles as 'president or treasurer of twenty-eight different societies', and the family friend and fellow philanthropist, Quintin Hogg, whose Polytechnic in Regent Street, London for the education of boys and girls of artisan and lower-middle-class families (opened in 1882) she described as an 'individualistic' mode of voluntary commitment.[18] Associational principles of 'fellowship for mutual service' underpinned all of these models, but Emily Kinnaird saw a gendered distinction in the 'degree' of her work compared to her brother's and Hogg's; whereas male relations and friends had additional public outlets in business, she claimed a greater personal responsibility as a woman to dedicate her time and energy to the causes for which she held executive committee positions.[19]

Although there was an emphasis upon the gendered terms of this community engagement, Emily Kinnaird's reflections on committee work further revealed her understanding of the practice as an expression of both civic and Christian community and the proper fulfilment of an individual's collective duties and obligations. She configured the commitment as carrying out Biblical precepts: '[i]n the multitude of counsellors there is wisdom' (a committee), and '[a] threefold cord who shall break?' (a sub-committee) (Mark 2:3 and Ecc. 4:12).[20] The concept and practice of participatory democracy were formulated here as an essentially Christian method. Committee work was to be a mechanism for collective participation on the widest scale: Kinnaird maintained that if people believed in the principle of organization as 'Divine method' then 'nearly everyone can be a useful member'.[21] Emily Kinnaird was drawing here on the arguments of her friend, Lilian Duff who, in the first years of the twentieth century, oversaw the YWCA training centre for student secretaries in Finsbury Square, London.[22] Biblical study was central to the training programme (Kinnaird herself taught on the subjects of the Prophets and the Gospels), alongside personal religious devotion.[23] Kinnaird recalled that Lilian Duff required students to keep an hourly diary, in the spirit of a much older evangelical practice, to record their daily activities in a disciplined manner; 'an index of her [Duff's] own methodical mind, and how resolutely she kept, and would have them keep, the hour of solitude with God'.[24] Efficiency in administrative work was therefore to support, rather than hinder, reflexive spiritual practice. And in combining the two, women could explore a purposeful relationship between individual action and community development.

Committee work was one articulation of the wider Christian ideal of mutuality in individual relationships, inspired by the guidance of God, that had been expanded formally as an organizational principle of the World's YWCA in 1914. As discussed at that year's World's YWCA Conference at Stockholm, encouraging women to perform service for other women required YWCA leaders actively to foster social channels for the modelling of interpersonal and spiritual development. In 1916, Emily Kinnaird had written an article about committee work for the YWCA leaders' magazine, the *News Letter* in which she argued that a committee was a vehicle for securing social ties and 'the best way in which we can serve our Master and our generation'.[25] Although there were some in the YWCA at this point who remained convinced that true service was best performed as individuals, Kinnaird argued that such people 'should have the courage to leave Committee work to others', or else learn a deeper reason for collective service: '[u]nless you believe that it is the very constitution which God has implanted in human nature – family, tribe, city, State – that it is a Divine attribute to "set the solitary in families", that a city, not a wilderness, is the ideal of the Kingdom of Heaven', she wrote, 'your presence will not be conducive to good work'.[26] The imperative of collective participation once again reaffirmed the YWCA's historical practice of supporting young women working and living in towns away from their family homes and friends. Emily Kinnaird defined the issue in terms of looking beyond families, communities, nations and states as agglomerations of individual actors, to an understanding of the development of men's and women's social natures, and the natural groupings in which men and women were joined together. This focus complicated the conceptualization of individual service as a self-denying practice and stressed instead how Christian *sociability* configured the mutuality of personal and collective development. It was an emphasis that would shape the YWCA's motto, 'By love, serve one another', around providential explanations of human experience. As Kinnaird argued in relation to committees, human sociability should be encouraged and expanded for 'the communion of souls not only as a matter of spiritual fellowship, but a necessity for the right appreciation of the Divine possibilities of ordinary work'.[27]

The conference as a democratic space

The YWCA's commitment to a model of democratic agency in which young women were helped to develop confidence through coming into active contact with forms of collective expression was further visible in the importance the organization attached to conferences as a space for discussion and debate.[28] Along with other lay voluntary movements, the YMCA and the Student Christian Movement, the YWCA developed the conference format specifically for Christian democratic participation.[29] Emily Kinnaird attended the first UK YWCA Conference in 1894; in 1898, she began keeping a diary during the first World's YWCA Conference, held in London, which she continued to use until 1926 to record conference themes and delegate attendance.[30] Defending the criticism that conferences were a waste of time, Kinnaird wrote in *Reminiscences* that they were the most effective means of 'drawing nations and individuals together in a fellowship'.[31] Themselves models of collective authority, conferences provided vital stimulus to democratic participation in theory and practice: 'the mind of the membership must be ascertained, its voice be heard, it must express itself,' Kinnaird wrote, '[t]he power of thought is as great as that of action ... a corporate mind is not only the sum of individual minds, but has itself a separate consciousness'.[32] Kinnaird's language here was reminiscent of the wider reflections upon the purpose of the conference format that had come out of COPEC the previous year where, in the context both of the divisions within evangelical groups in the post-war years and the search for ecumenical approaches, 'Christian deliberation', rather than inculcation, was to be the central purpose.[33] The desire to combine voices (and minds), in one respect, was holding out against a shifting direction undertaken by other bodies of collective organization away from the encompassing ideal of cooperation; for example, by the 1930s British trades unions were broadly running out of steam with the effectiveness of cross-class methods.[34] Furthermore, conferences were understood in the YWCA as a vehicle for the expression of religious faith as democratic practice. They were such effective fora because they provided a safe space for women to engage in reflexive thinking within the creative context of a permeating spiritual influence. Prayer sessions were thus central features of conference schedules and the work of the Holy Spirit was channelled for corporate guidance and direction in 'commonplace duty'.[35]

Self-determination through collective participation

As we have seen, in the years before the First World War the UK YWCA's policy for addressing the changing needs and expressions of the 'modern girl' aimed fundamentally at encouraging young women's capacities for self-development. YWCA campaigns in the 1920s, notably those to improve the status of domestic service, as Selina Todd has argued, addressed 'young [working] women's own (limited) choices', as well as changes in labour demand.[36] While, as will be discussed below, the organization critically examined the scope of young women's choices in the interwar decades, in fact organizational goals were closely focused upon questions of self-realization and the relationship between service and self-fulfilment *within* structural contexts. YWCA wartime and interwar discussions repeatedly debated the fulfilment of 'woman's personality' for the common good.[37] In October 1922, the UK YWCA's Biennial Conference met under the theme of 'A World Fellowship of Young Women' to consider the development of 'Christian personality for service'. In preparation for the conference, members were asked what opportunities for young women's self-government were offered in their own branch or club and how membership amongst younger members could be increased.[38]

The focus upon fostering self-determination took a particular direction in the years following the First World War as part of the YWCA's impetus to increase its recruitment of younger members. Inroads had been made in this direction during wartime when the organization augmented the extension of its campaigns to support WAAC members and women munitions workers by the formation of Blue Triangle Clubs for younger members (in 1914 the UK YWCA adopted the blue triangle as its logo). These developments focused a new urgency to consider the practical organization of groups and clubs to support this young membership. The *nature* of girls' and younger women's participation within the organization was a particular concern throughout the 1920s.[39] In *Reminiscences* Kinnaird wrote of the danger of the attachment of 'old workers and members', of which she acknowledged she was one, and regretted that there was not a comparable trend in the UK YWCA, as there was in America, where older secretaries were in middle life moving into business careers 'in order not to remain in and hinder the younger generation'.[40] The worry that young women's emerging capacities of independence and leadership might be compromised by the continued influence of older members also framed a discussion on 'Social Service' in the association's eightieth anniversary commemorative pamphlet. The final analysis in that pamphlet was more upbeat than Kinnaird had been, however, and concluded that the YWCA's success in remoulding its engagements for young women had enabled the evolution of the work through a number of societies for related and specific objects.[41] The ambition was to broaden young women's participation within a sphere of interconnected social and political life.

Politics of cooperation

The emphasis the YWCA continued to place in the interwar years upon cooperative exchange – the working with and alongside organizations for 'allied objects' – should be understood as part of the contemporary vogue for the ideas of corporatism and cooperatism that diffused widely in interwar Britain. Corporatist ideals have typically been interpreted in respect of evolving governing and economic systems designed around a centrifugal state.[42] Developing further both the influential late-nineteenth- and early-twentieth-century organicist philosophy and the developing strands of industrial politics, however, the ideas stretched in the years following the First World War from industry, to business, social policy and voluntary organizations.[43] The YWCA is a good example of how voluntarist traditions were also extended and revived in the interwar period as part of the vogue for cooperative and corporatist systems. In the early 1920s, YWCA leaders' recommendation for cooperation between associational groups and bodies, 'who have in common the desire for social righteousness' and who searched for the 'permeation of the democratic movements and political bodies in every country with Christian ideals',[44] spoke to the institutional memory of federation that celebrated the merger in 1877 of Mary Jane Kinnaird's London-based welfare work and Emma Robarts' women's payer union. Building upon this collective memory, in the 1930s, the YWCA was one of five national organizations through which the work of the confederal body, the National Council of Girls' Clubs (established in 1911) was coordinated.[45]

Nonetheless, voluntary organizations needed to address principles of cooperation in the light of the additional social and political affiliations that individual members of non-partisan organizations might hold. The scope for members' diverse and varying ideological commitments also needed to be acknowledged in this context, and wider common ground established. Rhetorically, this challenge could provide an opportunity for a voluntary organization to define its public identity in distinction from competitor organizations. In the mid-1920s Emily Kinnaird maintained the need to distinguish the YWCA's work from the most popular women's voluntary organizations of the day, notably the Women's Institutes, which she thought unhelpfully 'shut out' the vital subjects of religion and politics, and from Christian organizations that she regarded as narrower than hers in their outlook, such as the Anglican Girls' Friendly Society.[46] Furthermore, leading YWCA figures, including Kinnaird herself, were members of the Labour Party and for some, the party political route became of central importance to the development of the organization's (and wider) advocacy and policy work. Edith Picton-Turbervill, Foreign Secretary of the UK YWCA (from 1909) and then Vice-President (1914–20 and 1922–8) came to realize that 'fundamental changes in law were necessary to obtain better conditions of life for the people'.[47] Having joined the Labour Party in 1919, in 1922 Picton-Turbervill stood for the first time as a Labour parliamentary candidate for North Islington, and was elected Labour MP for the Wrekin Division of Shropshire in 1929.[48]

Where young women could practice civic cooperation was also a question of concern to YWCA leaders and precipitated a related discussion within the organization about the social sites of democratic participation. At the Biennial Conference of the UK YWCA in October 1922, delegates were asked to prepare for discussion on the place of the organization in community, town life and the life of the neighbourhood, and to consider how far branches were cooperating with churches, religious movements and other women's organizations, including Girls' Clubs and women's trades unions.[49] The distinction drawn between community, town and neighbourhood demonstrated a broader awareness of how both class and gender functioned to ascribe women's modern social affiliations. The idea that neighbourhoods were a site of distinctively 'female social solidarity' and female influence was widely held amongst working-class communities in this period.[50] YWCA leaders recognized that the organization's presence in individual neighbourhoods should be extended to provide fellowship not only for members of the organization but in fact for 'the largest possible number of girls'.[51] The question, connected to the post-war debates within the organization about the relationship between the individual and the 'mass', was a broad one, but it also signalled once again a particular concern to widen the scope for girls' personal development. This focus propelled the preoccupation with the unit of neighbourhood life; as Emily Kinnaird cautioned in 1925: some YWCA branches, dominated by older women, were incapable of making an impression on neighbourhood life, and had become 'totally out of touch with young life'.[52]

The YWCA's emphasis in the first half of the 1920s upon the values of fellowship and federation was premised upon sustained scrutiny of the ways in which the terms of the new post-war social contract would allow for the effective expression of Christian community. What emerges from the organization's records is a deep awareness of the various registers impacting upon women's democratic subjectivity. The debate was an international one, and members' and leaders' discussions moved between imagining young women across global contexts as social and political actors and economic units, and the psychological and spiritual influences upon them. Preparatory materials produced for the World's YWCA Commission in Salzburg in 1922 showed leaders' assumptions of the 'restlessness and the defiance of convention and revolt against accepted standards' of the current generation of young women, although they recognized the complexity in identifying the causes of this restlessness that might arise variously from the spread of democratic ideas, the 'breakdown of convention', women's new economic status, and 'an exaggerated sense of independence and need of distraction due to the upheaval of recent years'.[53] This summing up of the collective psychology of young women fits in part with Susan Kingsley Kent's argument for the fundamental impact of the trauma of the First World War upon society and politics in the 1920s,[54] but it also shows how organizations such as the YWCA developed a conception of trauma as experienced collectively alongside the complex negotiation of newfound freedoms for social groups that had been previously marginalized in the national political system. The imperative to uncover what young women were 'thinking about', 'what they are feeling' and 'working for' required YWCA leaders to consider the interdependencies of individual and community needs, immediate personal considerations and social concerns of the future. Questions surpassed answers at this moment in the spirit of collective deliberation. For example, at the 1922 World's YWCA Commission delegates were asked: '[i]n demanding bigger wages do you find a girl is thinking more of social status, family claims, provision for old age, better living conditions or of spending money?'[55] YWCA leaders recognized that class feeling; ideals of marriage and friendship with men; the pattern for 'exclusive friendships between women'; and young women's economic concerns were each potentially aspects of the new choices young women might have to make in the modern conditions of democracy, and the contexts for which Christian organizations needed to provide support.[56] Tracing the multiple and varied influences upon young women's lives – those which spanned material, psychological and spiritual experience – was therefore vital to meeting the ambitions for Christian community and for the full and effective bases of women's social and political participation.

A democracy for women

Defining the terms of women's civic rights was a critical aspect of many female activists' work in the interwar years which explored, from the ground up, how society would move beyond a property-owning electorate. In the years immediately following the end of the First World War it remained imperative for second-generation suffragists to claim public spaces, such as those in local and national newspapers, to challenge the denial of women's civil rights to work in chosen occupations and the restrictions upon women's collective political voice.[57] Lettice Fisher emerged as an authority in these debates. In 1921 she wrote a letter for the *Times'* editorial page critiquing the limitations of recent franchise and employment legislation so far as women were concerned. The Franchise Act (1918) and the Sex Disqualification Act (1919), Fisher wrote, had removed some of the barriers against women's employment and public status, but left in place others, and the room for still more to be 're-erected'. Furthermore, although opportunities in many professions had been opened up to educated women, Fisher found that business and industry remained largely closed.[58]

Second-generation suffragists like Fisher continued to argue in the years following 1918 that economic and structural inequalities between the sexes needed to be a central target of attack for the expanding mass democracy, but these factors needed to be addressed equally as a concern for the fulfilment of women's subjective experience. In 1924 Lettice Fisher explored these themes in a lecture for University of London students on 'The Economic Position of the Married Woman', in which she critiqued the ban on married women's paid employment and insisted that a married woman's work in the home was essential to support a married man's paid labour or public work.[59] Fisher had argued similarly for the need to value the interconnections (alongside the distinctions) between paid and unpaid labour in her textbook, *Getting and Spending*, where she maintained that a woman, like a man, ought 'to earn enough to pay some one else to cook and clean and wash for her', in order to be fully efficient.[60] Lettice Fisher was supported in her own public and domestic work by Kate Smith, who acted as 'housekeeper, cook, and nanny' rolled into one.[61] The relationships underpinning the economy of domestic service, of course, reinforced structural inequalities across social classes; Kate Smith was never present at the many dinner parties that the Fishers hosted, although she played a crucial role in organizing the household for these occasions. But the servant-employer relationship also contained the possibility for mutual psychological support, in particular between women, and the possibility to articulate meaningfully vital exchanges across class divisions; as Lettice Fisher's daughter, Mary Bennett would recall in later life, Kate Smith and her mother forged a mutually reinforcing relationship respectively out of 'devot[ion]' and the building of 'confidence'.[62]

The NCUMC as a connecting agency

In her early work with the NCUMC, Lettice Fisher was engaged centrally in the projection of the civic identity of unmarried mothers and their children as a question of both structural and subjective experience. Early NCUMC publications, for example advocating the reform of the Affiliation Laws, appeared under the auspices of the feminist Six Point Group, established by Lady Rhondda in 1921, and its publication *Time and Tide*.[63] Assured of the sympathy of a feminist readership, these communications were overtly critical of the structural inequalities of social and legal frameworks which meant, as Lettice Fisher stated with regard to the Affiliation Laws, '[n]ot to put too fine a point upon it, the laws, having been evolved entirely by men, are inevitably a little one-sided'.[64] Although such emphases were pointed sharply in literature aimed at feminist audiences, in wider publicity, the NCUMC advanced the practical implementation of an organicist philosophy, which configured the problem of the illegitimate child and the unmarried mother in respect of the broader question of the interrelationship between individual and social efficiency. It was this emphasis, rather than a feminist concern for women's capacities for law-making, that framed a NCUMC notice about the Bastardy Bill (1920) which imagined objections to the proposals to discourage mothers from concealing illegitimate pregnancies: '[s]uch interference', it was stated, 'will be for the **ultimate benefit** of the **mother**, of the **child** and of the **State**. Concealment leads to death, disease and suffering for both mother and child, and to loss or damage of future citizens by the State. It is no more defensible than concealment of infectious diseases'.[65]

The argument in the 1920 notice about the Bastardy Bill developed the sorts of emphases reformers of medical and public health had placed upon social interconnectedness from the turn of the twentieth century in campaigns for national health insurance, notably in respect of the provision of sanatorial benefit for the insured as a means to seek treatment for tuberculosis rather than to be hidden (in ill health) in plain sight.[66] As the NCUMC developed its profile in the early 1920s, it cast the work for community development around a particular anxiety about the unmarried mother and the illegitimate child as detached social units. The unmarried mother emerged in early publicity as integrated insufficiently into social life. In 1922 Fisher authored an NCUMC appeal in the *Times* describing that, although in the eyes of the law the unmarried mother was the sole legal parent of her child, 'in actual fact she is usually its sole means of support'; and wider community intervention was needed to support her economic position as a response to her own 'physical and mental agonies' and the 'appalling death-rate among children born out of wedlock, and the still more appalling damage rate among those who survive'.[67] Notwithstanding the stated concern about the deaths of illegitimate babies,[68] the rhetorical construction of the unmarried mother as a lonely, isolated social unit was not necessarily the reality of experience within local communities; in working-class communities, unmarried mothers were frequently supported by family, kith and kin or cohabited in unmarried relationships.[69] Furthermore, the shift from Edwardian to wartime and post-war society registered the growth of state services and income support for groups including unmarried mothers, an ideological commitment to supporting a minimum standard of life that marked a distinct move away from mid-nineteenth-century principles that were anathema to the provision to these social groups of 'outdoor relief'.[70]

Perhaps in recognition of the need to acknowledge these conditions, and the opportunity to shape the shifting priorities of public policy, in the mid-1920s, NCUMC publicity shifted its focus also towards the illegitimate child and the representation of the organization as a mechanism for supporting the child's social connection as a vehicle for a model of citizenship that was linked but, nevertheless, independent of his/her mother's. In an appeal in the *Times* in 1924

Lettice Fisher argued for the need to support the illegitimate child to become a citizen in the same sort of terms she had used to define education in *Getting and Spending* (1922) – 'healthy in mind and body' – and for the organization to function as a nationwide coordinating body, though lacking government funding, to 'economize' the effort of local provision.[71] There are two further things worth noting here. Firstly, Fisher's emphasis upon the illegitimate child's citizen status pointed to the contribution of voluntary organizations such as the NCUMC to the development of discourses of futurity that by the 1930s would have much broader influence in discussions of children's citizenship.[72] In 1925 Fisher spoke of 'do[ing] what we can to help these helpless creatures, not only in their own interest, but in the interest of our own children who will be their future citizens'; to support the 'unhappy children' to make as much of themselves as they were able 'in the interests of the whole community', and 'in the interest of society as a whole we must do what we can to enable it, and its parents, to make good as far as possible'.[73] Secondly, her emphasis upon the NCUMC as a coordinating body consciously located the organization within an important stream of post-war voluntary engagement, evident also in the example of the NCSS (founded in 1919).[74] Although this rhetorical emphasis foregrounded the NCUMC's non-partisan commitment – in 1925 Fisher described the NCUMC on a BBC wireless radio charity appeal as 'a correlating and connecting agency', providing support to women and illegitimate children across the whole country – it nevertheless was performed through a clear political voice.[75] Lettice Fisher began the radio appeal by celebrating the 'splendid edifice' of public support that was in place for English children in language that echoed the public rhetoric of Edwardian New Liberalism, notably in David Lloyd George's arguments in 1912 for the aim of the new National Insurance legislation to establish a 'parapet' between the people and the poverty that comes from sickness and unemployment (Lloyd George, a close friend of the Fishers, would in 1925 write an introduction to Lettice Fisher's book *Then and Now*).[76] In the 1920s it was precisely the hole in the edifice of statutory welfare provision – that which discarded the illegitimate child – that Lettice Fisher advocated now needed to be filled through the effective coordination of voluntary and statutory provision.

Democracy and the 'social sin of sloth'

It is becoming better understood that the concepts and practices of the 'individual' and 'community' have not always (if ever) been opposed. While much scholarship has invoked a binary paradigm that sets the language of individual rights against the shared values of community, historians now argue that the individual was not imagined in distinction from the community in the past, but rather the two were fundamentally interdependent.[77] It is historically significant that Lettice Fisher framed the needs of unmarried mothers and their children in the interwar years as those of both the individual and the community: it was precisely the challenges raised by addressing the place of the individual *within* the community that she, like other liberal reformers of the period, argued needed to be readdressed in the era of universal suffrage. Fisher explored these opportunities in *The Citizen: A Simple Account of How We Manage Our National and Local Affairs* (1927), a text published for the Home University Library series on the eve of the passing of the 1928 Representation of the People (Equal Franchise) Act that extended the participatory franchise to women on the same terms as men. In 1927 *The Citizen* was already in many respects a post-suffrage book; the caption of the frontispiece photograph of MP Lady Astor's introduction to the House of Commons highlighted the separate galleries for peers, 'Distinguished strangers' and ordinary 'strangers' in the background of the image, 'formerly for men only, now open to both sexes'.[78] Moreover, *The Citizen* can be read as one of many books, articles and commentaries written after 1918 that illuminated the preoccupation with the future of democracy, centred typically around debates about civic status.[79] The evidence of the educationalist William Henry Hadow, a family friend of the Fishers, writing the foreword to the text seemed to confirm this focus. Hadow had himself authored an influential text, *Citizenship*, which was published in 1923.[80]

The new interwar citizen was to have political and cultural bargaining power. Where does democracy come from? In *The Citizen*, Lettice Fisher prescribed democracy not primarily as the assignation of individual rights but rather the acceptance by men and women for taking 'a share of the responsibility for working the machine of *self*-government' [my italics].[81] It was a model of community life, evolving after 1918 as a central understanding of the work of the new voluntary social services and expanding in conformity with the growth of state services.[82] Fisher discussed the modern system of social organization as characterized by a shared belief in 'co-operation in organised methods', where both state and local authorities assumed roles that historically 'we used to do for ourselves or do without'.[83] She maintained that in contemporary society there was an unsatisfied demand for voluntary workers but a risk that the over-systematization of informal human responsiveness through centralization would undervalue reciprocal economic activity. What needed to be avoided was the removal of the impetus to do things with, as well as for, each other and the total subsuming of the economic, moral and social purpose of service and voluntary commitment by the new social services.

In his history of the social politics of medieval guilds, Gervase Rosser defined community as 'a conception of shared obligation to meet human debt' that could involve individuals giving up privileges, as well as widening personal experiences,[84] and Lettice Fisher's elaboration of active citizenship seems to come very close to this model. She wrote that '[e]normous numbers of people are wanted to serve upon endless committees, to do the steady, regular work that must be done if our needs are to be adequately met . . . A community which is unable to produce an adequate supply of loyal, responsible service, is a community which is doomed to failure.'[85] Re-routing an emphasis upon individual gain to shared obligation was not necessarily easy, or done willingly, and Lettice Fisher's point here was that although some freedoms were gained in mass democracy, others might be lost. She argued that it was right to work hard 'for ourselves and our families, that we should keep their needs always in mind', but the necessity of working collectively for the benefit of the community always had to be addressed: 'we have to combine all that with a more difficult habit of thought, that which considers our own needs and desires, or those of the class to which we belong, in relation to the needs and desires of the community as a whole.'[86] Ensuring that this was achieved would not be easy, and Fisher mused on how people might be 'made' to vote, and the need to 'combat the social sin of sloth'; she bemoaned laziness about social responsibility and a failure of 'imagination' to consider how individual actions, such as littering the countryside, affected the wider community.[87] The model for which Fisher sought public appreciation was that of the organic community – '[w]e are all so much mixed up together, so dependent upon one another, that pure selfishness may easily lead to disaster' – which required continuous instruction and motivation in the principles of active social engagement.[88] In this respect, while the achievement of universal suffrage was a highpoint of Fisher's reformist politics, it was not to be the endpoint. The nature and force of community now needed to be fundamentally readdressed in the post-suffrage world.

Revisiting the citizen housewife

Because of the rhetorical and real connections between women, neighbourhood and community action in the late-nineteenth and early-twentieth centuries, the emphases placed upon democratic subjectivity in the interwar years were well-suited to a message of the extension of women's influence in local spheres. Elite women's political influence since the mid-nineteenth century and earlier had been tied to the local community, performed by those who were enfranchised in local elections and who sat on local government, school and Poor Law boards.[89] Philanthropic and social work, itself, harnessed a wider ambit of local female energy in the nineteenth century that scholars have shown drew upon rich traditions of women's involvement in informal and formal politics.[90] The extension of the parliamentary franchise in 1918 and 1928, whilst a symbolic designation of women's national citizenship, in practice was presented in terms that celebrated an expanded series of everyday opportunities made available distinctively to women through participation in local political life and activism.[91] Many female philanthropists and women involved in community work in this period continued to privilege local praxes in social projects, but found localism easier to explore in some contexts than others. Village communities, rather than towns, frequently seemed more apposite to women for the exploration of opportunities for democratic participation. Specifically, the marked and rapid growth in the number of voluntary organizations in country areas was observed as a key development of the interwar period in its own right, but also of pivotal importance in illuminating the contribution of voluntary social services to understandings of social connectivity and participation. Anne Bourdillon, who would play a central role in the Nuffield Social Reconstruction Survey during the Second World War, argued in the early 1940s that the village, understood as a unit where historically people of different classes and 'kinds' learned how to live together, exemplified the social gains that were to be achieved through democracy. Her experiences in interwar rural projects meant she understood precisely why those who worked to set up voluntary organizations in country districts felt aggrieved at plans for the implementation of centralized social services, which 'would imply a serious social loss in country districts'.[92]

The quotidian bases of women's local activism were central to the evolution of interwar representative democracy. As scholars including Caitríona Beaumont, Karen Hunt and June Hannam have shown, the image of the housewife in particular emerged as a critical resource for women's social and political influence in this period.[93] The emphasis was not an entirely new development in the interwar period: good housekeeping, if not the housewife, had been configured as pivotal to the prevention of working-class poverty in late-Victorian and Edwardian society.[94] The housewife, herself, had emerged centrally in Edwardian tariff reform campaigns as well as socialist women's wartime campaigns about consumption,[95] and would go on to feature centrally in Beveridgean planning in the 1940s. However, the potential political force of the housewife was much more widely recognized in the 1920s and 1930s than it had been previously, and the authority of the housewife became attached to a wider range of political messages linked to the everyday and local experiences of women's family and social labour. The political agency of the citizen housewife was projected in diverse cultural outputs in this period, ranging from social commentaries, such as the secretary of the London Charity Organization Society, John Christian Pringle's publication *The Nation's Appeal to the Housewife and Her Response* (1933), to middlebrow literature and popular magazines.[96] The widespread anxiety of the *neuroses* of the (suburban) housewife, struggling to adjust to the realities of keeping home without servants, further illuminates just how central the housewife's participatory agency was understood to be in interwar social and cultural discussion.[97]

As a cultural, economic and social identity, the housewife could cut across the politics of class and stand for women's common experiences, expertise and sensibilities. The 'thorny class problems' that scholars have identified which women social workers often struggled to address in the nineteenth century, however, continued to pose challenges in the interwar years in the formulation of the housewife as a cross-class identity.[98] It has been argued that in negotiating class divides, elite women, such as those working for the Women's Institutes, launched a conservative politics of deference that attempted to counter Labour women campaigners' claims that only working women could speak to other working women.[99] Certainly, as a rapidly expanding movement in the 1930s and without sustained government funding, the NFWI was compelled to further links with other voluntary organizations in aid of its cultural educational agenda.[100] Notwithstanding this necessary work, the NFWI demonstrated a commitment to extending the process of interpersonal identification as a vehicle for women's emancipation. In a series of BBC broadcasts and publications in the early-to-mid-1930s in connection with the NFWI, Lettice Fisher appropriated the identity of the housewife to claim commonalities of experience with working women with relevance to issues including women's contributions to local government, the causes and impact of the economic depression and, separately, motherhood.[101] Establishing a *relational* orientation between herself and the working women, she addressed the central component of inter-class subjectivity in the project of individual and community development.

Family photographs from the early 1920s at Sheffield record Lettice Fisher happy in family life with pet goats and chickens, which her daughter, Mary Bennett remembered both her mother and Kate Smith feeding and milking.[102] This sort of practical country living, that Fisher would also enjoy in the family home in Thursley, Surrey from the mid-1920s onwards, spoke both to a personal temperament and to her conviction in the central role of pastoral traditions in civic life. In *The Housewife and the Townhall*, Fisher emphasized the rewards brought to women by opportunities for bee, poultry and other animal keeping and fruit growing, whilst stressing the responsibilities women should undertake in local administration.[103] The rhetorical juxtaposition of town life is interesting in the light of the wider argument that it was precisely the *rural* setting that was easier for the development of community; as Grace Hadow, the Vice-Chairman of the NFWI had argued in her essay, 'The Adult Education Movement and Rural Local Government', traditions of English village unity, supplemented not overtaken by the modernizing forces of communication and education, ought to stand as a pillar of modern democracy.[104] However, the scale of civic action Fisher imagined in her talk was widely encompassing, moving between the ecological, the scientific, the legislative and the moral: Fisher argued that it was up to housewives 'to enforce the existing laws about pollution, to do what we can at home ... to keep public opinion alive on what we think matters, whether it is the cinema, or unclean food or unclean smoke'.[105] Understanding the role of agency is central to recognizing people as responsible persons; as scholars have observed, we act and choose to act in one way rather than another.[106] What was needed in the interwar period, as Fisher stressed repeatedly in her BBC talks, was for women to look outwards from domestic experience to collective knowledge of their local environment and beyond to national and international concerns. It was the sort of work that had been explored in the village surveys undertaken by Fisher's former student C. V. Butler and others in the 1920s.[107] Lettice Fisher appropriated the contemporary vogue for rural culture as an additionally resonant device for explaining women's social participation that illuminated the movement from the local to the global within civic action with relation to questions of the natural environment and community.[108] In this model, good housewives were good homemakers, pro-active members of society and careful custodians of the environment.

The mechanisms of identification that Fisher used in order to galvanize women for democratic participation are thus, in themselves, significant. In the NFWI talks, broadcast in the morning to reach 'those listeners mostly women (working!) in their own homes',[109] Fisher stressed women's expertise in domestic economy as a route for participation not only in local administration, but moreover in national and international economy. The medium of the wireless radio had a specific importance in the project of cross-class identification. 'Listening in' was a collective endeavour, every bit as much as it could be a private one; this was not only symbolized by the early BBC ideal of a family audience, at the fireside, tuned in and attentive to the wireless radio, it was also *performed* by many men and women in the interwar years who listened to the wireless at village clubs, schools, or in listening groups set up by voluntary organizations.[110] Talks based upon Lettice Fisher's BBC broadcasts for the NFWI happened, for example, in local Women's Guilds and MU branches in the 1930s and thus the practice of listening, just as much as the content of the talks, was part of women's associations' broad educative programme in democratic participation.[111] In this respect, broadcasting can be seen to work in a complementary way to the modern (as distinct from Modernist) novels of the late 1920s and 1930s that David Trotter has argued imagined 'an informal social solidarity', working through 'a certain kind of space, neither wholly public nor wholly private, [and] primed for a certain kind of talk'.[112] This formulation of sociability, evident also in the proliferation of community centres, village and travelling libraries and youth clubs in the interwar period, was an important challenge to the 'mobile privatization' increasingly coming to the fore in the period through the popularization of connective technologies that seemed to speak as much, if not more, to individualized preoccupations. Social solidarity continued to be structured in these devices through the values of cultural and moral uplift that was common to the interwar BBC and to many voluntary organizations of the period.[113] The sorts of identities that were envisaged, however, were renewed in relation to the idea of community that was coming to be understood as central to the new types of social service at the heart of the post-1918 social project. As G. D. H. Cole would recall of the period in the 1940s, '[i]t was no accident that the new social service fixed upon the equipment of Community Centers and the founding of Community Councils as its most vital activities'.[114]

In *The Housewife and the Townhall*, Fisher argued that '[w]hat mattered for housewives [was] getting *our* money's worth' and it was 'not spending, but wise spending, that is the heart of the problem' [my italics].[115] In one respect, the idea of women's shared expertise in domestic experience challenged masculine constructions of civic identity that were focused upon the theatres of work and state, but not on the home and family. Fisher's language, part of a wider feminist critique of the inequalities of structural forces that foregrounded concepts of gender difference,[116] addressed women's minority position in local government by calling for an alternative local economy of women's political action: '[a]s a practical housewife', she wrote, 'I have an instinctive distrust of the man who wants to get on to the local council simply in order to cut down the rates, and of the other one who tries to get on by lavish promises of spending other people's money'.[117] This emphasis upon women's domestic understanding echoed the sorts of discourses to which Fisher had been exposed and developed in the Edwardian years when she visited poor families in their homes in East Oxford.[118] But here there was a conscious effort to stress identification between women across classes. In this respect, the NFWI's model of the citizen housewife was directly connected to the sorts of initiatives middle-class and elite women undertook with groups of working women during the First World War, in Lettice Fisher's case the local thrift meetings that she led with female munitions workers and others in Sheffield.[119] This context of women-centred political communities allowed for the development of more intricate metaphors of democratic agency to emerge. In *The Facts Behind the Crisis*, Fisher used the imagery of the flow of water to expand the point about the need for women to appreciate the forces of economy: housewives needed to avoid wasteful spending that was comparable to 'water flowing out of the stream into the sand', and ensure instead that 'water flow[ed] out of the stream into irrigation channels which produce more and more goods and services'.[120] The housewife's influence did not end either within the walls of the home or in the local community. The message consciously framed women's agency within projects of creating and sustaining the whole of economic and human life.

Global kinship and the universalism of mankind

When Evangeline Booth wrote in her pamphlet about female emancipation, *Woman* (1930) that women's political and economic opportunities had exceeded those that might have confined women previously to domesticity, she did not denounce expertise in domestic economy as a collective force in modern society. The 'task ahead', Booth argued, was that of 'changing the world into a home': '[t]he housekeeping that we have now to undertake, is housekeeping on the grand scale; it must include all nations, all people in a nation, the rich and the poor, the saints and the sinners'.[121] Evangeline Booth's message in *Woman* spoke to the shared concern of many interwar female social activists to project the wide significance of domesticity and the household economy for shaping individual and community development, but it was rooted in a particular construction of Christian community as both expansionist and inclusive. Within this wider epistemological project, Booth imagined female activism, archetypally, as developing a shared identity through its commitment to working for others: she wrote that 'in every age the woman who lives for herself has been overcome by the woman who lives for others ... Sarah, following the patriarch ... the mother of Moses defended her son from mortality; Deborah [the prophetess], Ruth, Hannah, Anna, Mary'. 'Glance over the scroll of history', Booth wrote, 'stained on every page with the shedding of blood and tears, and you will be amazed by the dynasty of sainthood, which women have maintained unbroken. They have been the heroines of home'.[122]

Evangeline Booth's emphasis upon the Christian meanings of housekeeping moved the argument about female solidarity and common identity in a different direction from Lettice Fisher's. Firstly, Booth emphasized the movement between temporal and spiritual experience to be critical to the advancement of women's political selfhood. In part this was the difference between suffragism and Christian suffragism: in *Woman*, Booth praised the expansion of women's opportunities in social and professional spheres and defined the 'woman's movement' [sic] as much more than a struggle for material and personal gain, and rather for the possibility for a fuller spiritual connection through 'the direct fulfilment of the gospel of the Redeemer'.[123] Secondly, although like Lettice Fisher, Evangeline Booth examined women's household roles as constructing habits of cooperation for the achievement of individual and community development, Fisher framed the discussion around the context of women's particular local engagement and civic agency, whereas Booth foregrounded a religious ideal of cultural universalism. She used the Christian language of redemption to move the argument about the significance of the home towards constructions of the community of mankind marked by the concept of the 'undividedness' of human experience of '[a]ll nations [and] all people in a nation'.[124]

The imagery of the home had been stretched onto the Salvation Army's theological canvas in the nineteenth century in the organization's shaping of the experience of individual regeneration in relation to the rhetoric of women's authority in housekeeping. While the emergence of the Salvation Army as a body employing women, as well as men, in the public work of salvation and preaching appropriated and critiqued the ideology of men's and women's separate spheres, nevertheless in its organizational structure it underscored the belief that women were largely responsible for creating the everyday climate for regeneration around the home.[125] These principles were institutionalized within the organization in 1907 in the establishment of the Home League, which became a highly successful international programme for women's training in domestic management and childcare.[126] As has been discussed previously in further depth, the emphases upon domesticity were used in the Salvation Army in the years following the First World War to advance claims for women's expertise in the psychological proximity of personal service, but they were also linked, crucially, to the organization's ambitions for international expansion.[127] In *The War Romance of the Salvation Army* (1919), which explored on the one hand the social and spiritual growth that could be achieved within Christian domestic settings, Evangeline Booth described the organization's universalist aims forcefully as an 'empire geographically unlike any other', lacking a frontier, and 'composed of a tangle of races, tongues, and colors [sic] and types of civilization and enlightened barbarism such as never before in all human history gathered together under one flag'.[128] By 1920 the Salvation Army was represented in seventy-one countries worldwide within Europe, America, Australasia, Africa, South and East Asia.[129]

Homecraft as an internationalist creed

As Evangeline Booth's use in the 1920s of the language of empire infers, social and cultural inequalities were far from absent in the Salvation Army's programme of international expansion in the early-twentieth century. The ethical superiority and the assumed stronger sense of self of those who had been won for the organization than those who had not were continually stressed in publicity literature. In 1920 Booth explored this theme in an article for the American *National Geographic Magazine* in which she was reported to have stated that as the Salvation Army had grown, 'it has become increasingly apparent that the faith which regenerates men recognizes no barrier of nationality or geographical limitation'.[130] The statement advertised specifically the Salvation Army's expansion in the years following the end of the First World War in the institution of projects in Japan, where the Emperor Taishō had granted an annual fund to support the Salvation Army's work, and amongst the poor in India. Cultural inequalities were embedded in the organization's representation of universalism. In the 1920s, imperialist language of enlightened Christian mission continued to be favoured as a vehicle for communicating the vision of the implementation of Christian citizenship upon other religious communities. One photograph reproduced in the article in the *National Geographic Magazine* captured a long line of Hindu girls in India standing outside a newly opened Salvation Army home for girls and depicted the organization as 'working to destroy idols of wood and stone, and to convert temples into such homes as this'.[131] The image of the Christian home as a site for civilization and for spiritual and moral renewal was contrasted to the Hindu temple that was projected as a site of idolatry. It was one example of a wider and resurfacing narrative in Salvation Army publicity in the 1920s and 1930s that continued to centre the home as a space for personal and social transformation. A 1937 charity appeal, *Will You Help*, noted the 147 Salvation Army Homes and Institutes in the UK – for the elderly, boys, girls, holiday homes, children's homes and maternity homes – in which the organization's officers interpreted evidence of residents' self-growth. For example, at the Children's Home in Southend, Essex, 'Barbara' was claimed to be 'winning many victories over self ... "I used to fight other girls, especially if they was [sic] pretty", remarked she thoughtfully, "but now I am a Soldier of Jesus, most of the things I want to fight are inside my own heart."'[132] The pamphlet promoted how 'the years spent in the Children's Homes are not merely a happy interlude', but in fact a resource for future life, 'a time when the secrets of happiness are mastered. The Army's children bloom into unselfish womanhood and become home-makers in the truest sense.'[133]

Evangeline Booth's casting of the Salvation Army's interventions as global kinship was connected via this imagery to an older and international 'cult of womanhood', which was expanded here to signal interconnected spiritual and material identities and found resonance internationally, the more so in the global political climate of the 1930s.[134] The concept of a world of peoples joined through Christian love and values that transcended race and creed resonated with broader teachings in this decade of the collective social responsibility accompanying the ideals of international cultural community. Calls for the articulation of citizenship across national borders were advanced with increasing urgency in the mid-to-late 1930s against the rising threat posed by ideological nationalisms on both the political right and the left. In 1937 the UK Salvation Army distilled these ideals into its international appeal, *This Brotherhood Of Nations*, which called upon British men and women to uphold the imperatives of global citizenship, 'both in the Homeland and throughout the world', through supporting the 'personal service' of Salvationists.[135] In one respect, the appeal sought to advertise the 'world-wide influence' of the Salvation Army's Home League programme for 'promoting the sanctity of marriage and family life and helping women to excel in home-making' through homecraft and other training.[136] But it went further. The appeal pamphlet included photographs of deprivation in Korean opium dens, amongst Indonesian children and prisoners, and blind people in Jamaica, where the Salvation Army continued to expand residential provision in organizational homes and hostels. The construction of social and cultural difference between the potential (British) donor and (international) subject was a key conceit, fashioned through the sorts of emotionally-affective, visual representations of poverty, ill health and distress used by humanitarian organizations that historians have critiqued.[137] This was cross-cut, however, by the message of religious universalism and the collectively-embodied nature of humanity. The front cover of the appeal booklet thus repurposed the ubiquitous interwar motif of comradeship and collectivization in an image of cross-national fellowship of a group of men and women standing side by side in national costume (see Fig. 11). The message explicitly stretched the call for the Home League's work of homecraft onto an

Figure 11. Front cover of the 1937 UK Salvation Army international appeal, *This Brotherhood of Nations*. Reproduced with the permission of the Salvation Army International Heritage Centre, London, UK.

image of identification beyond the boundaries of kin; it called for the building of community around respect for national and ethnic difference that extended traditional and bounded networks of reciprocity.[138] The message advanced the implications of the responsibilities of a Christian global kinship that specifically connoted the opportunities of an expansive language of housekeeping and the development of distinctive inter-class subjectivities.

Cosmopolitan subjectivity

The question of global citizenship was one that Evangeline Booth returned to often throughout the interwar period to claim the Salvation Army's vision of social and spiritual expansiveness and connection. In the 1920 issue of the *National Geographic Magazine*, Booth had experimented with a language of global citizenship as cosmopolitan, writing that '[t]he Salvation Army maintains that, as suffering recognizes neither race nor creed nor clime, human service should be equally cosmopolitan'.[139] In one respect, her emphasis repurposed a mode of thought developed in the 1880s by her father, William Booth in schemes for the global diversification and expansion of the Salvation Army. Tanya Agathocleous has argued that William Booth's *In Darkest England and the Way Out* (1890), a scheme developed in response to the difficulties the organization had faced in its initial decades in establishing an evangelical presence in London's slums, exemplified the 'cosmopolitan realism' of late-Victorian city writing, that addressed both the growing size and diversity of the city (especially London), and Britain's changing global fortunes. It specifically sought to understand the plural cultures of London's poor.[140] William Booth proposed a model for ending the destitution of the 'submerged tenth' of England's urban poor that sought to improve the health of participants in interconnected City stations, Farms and Overseas Colonies – the latter conceived as communities where English city-dwellers might eventually move to seek employment. The concept of cosmopolitanism was developed at this point by means of an imperialist vision, and the scheme's successful publicity was in part attributed to it having capitalized on the public interest in Henry Morton Stanley's *In Darkest Africa* (1890).[141] In its exploration of a vision of global interchange, however, William Booth's *In Darkest England* also appropriated a broader-minded 'Arnoldian cosmopolitanism' in the search for overcoming cultural provinciality and the conviction that the best ideas from one nation would be exchanged with others.[142]

The cosmopolitan idea of citizenship developed in a different direction within the Salvation Army in the interwar years in response to the redrawing of international politics from the 1920s into the 1930s. The direct challenge to the language of cosmopolitanism posed by the idea of the absolute state, which seemed in most European countries by the 1930s to be framing claims for nationalism and racial superiority, was also a challenge specifically to the work of the Salvation Army. Evangeline Booth argued, in common with many other church leaders in the 1930s, that nationalist discourse worked fundamentally against the ideal of a universal Christian community because it placed a higher value on political expediency than upon religious duty and faith, and it was thus a non-political, spiritual model of cosmopolitan identification that was needed.[143] 'Divine illumination' was to be the directing force that would move individuals beyond consideration of the self towards recognition of the cosmopolitanism of peoples. In this respect, salvationism was envisaged as potentially further levelling social and cultural difference through practices which transcended both place and time.[144]

Exploring what the Gospel of redemption meant for the interrelationship of personal and collective identity in this context was a question Evangeline Booth addressed in the 1930s in a talk to the IMC (International Missionary Council), an international organization seeking to facilitate the achievement of shared missionary goals. Established in 1921 as an outgrowth of the World Missionary Conference in Edinburgh in 1910, the IMC was part of a late-nineteenth- and early-twentieth-century ecumenical movement growing in significance internationally in the interwar years.[145] Interwar ecumenical thinking was both a theological and a political project, in which the prioritization of Christian unity went hand-in-hand with commitment to the universal applicability of social and moral codes and the political mobilization of the churches.[146] The IMC wrote to Evangeline Booth in the 1930s asking her to prepare a speech addressing the Salvation Army's understanding of evangelism and the contemporary relevance of the Gospels. Booth was critical of the terms of the question. Addressing the contemporary international forces of nationalism, she began her talk by challenging any prescription of the political mobilization of churches through arguing that the Salvation Army was 'non-political'.[147] She used the emphasis here, similarly to in *Woman* where she wrote of the development of female identity 'across the scrolls of history', to argue for common human identity, rooted neither solely in material nor political experience but in spiritual engagement that spanned temporal metres. She explained evangelism as the acceptance of Christ as the Incarnation of God, a principle she believed needed to be recognized as 'infinite in time and space' and 'embrac[ing] all peoples, at all periods in history, whatever their race, religion and culture, in one continuous mission to seek and to save those who are lost'. The concern for what aspects of the Christian Gospel were the most applicable to the conditions of contemporary experiences, however, seemed to Booth a misguided preoccupation that 'might be taken, at first sight, to suggest that the Gospel is a kind of statesmanship to be adapted, like legislation, to circumstances and tendencies'.[148]

Evangeline Booth's point was not that material or political experience were, or ought to be, divorced from the spiritual, so much as spiritual experience should be looked for in all aspects of life. She made the argument about the intersections between these levels of experience more boldly in a future speech delivered in America on 'Communism and Christianity', in which she critiqued the Communist judgement of history and society for 'forbid[ding] a transcendent judgment' on human action.[149] Exhorting Christian universalism in this regard involved not only challenging the prioritization of the values of political expediency by nation states or churches, but also a conception of the individual in society that subsumed the spiritual beneath the material. In presenting the Gospel as a text to which a cosmopolitan civilization should adapt itself, not the other way around, Booth conveyed the message that however much social, political and material circumstances changed, it was the Christian response through the theology of salvation that provided the path to the fulfilment of both personal and social identity.

The tension that existed between the strengthened expression of self and the work of social connection through the model of Divine imminence and the search for salvation, however, remained always to be addressed. In a speech at the Commissioners' Conference in the summer of 1939, Evangeline Booth implored Salvationists to emulate Christ's example to 'strengthen the bonds that bind them to their comrades in any and every part of the world'.[150] Her message positioned once again the theology of salvation as a force for the regeneration of individual believers and for unification in a world perilously threatened by virulent nationalisms. But there was a risk that the work of social service could become all encompassing, and Booth recognized, too, the need to support the active process of men's and women's self-development. In 1938 she addressed a group of Salvation Army Officers where she argued there was not only 'universality' but also 'monotony – in "living for others"', and a risk that spiritual commitment and social work could rob men and women of individuality and interest, who would become 'but "part of a machine"' in a 'humdrum round of irksome activity', with no outlet for relief or relaxation.[151] Such monotony of service to others was to be eschewed in the search for the principles of constructive identification. Building communities of Christian engagement and identity across cultures, places and times, Salvation Army members could be confident in celebrating difference, Booth maintained, whilst seeing 'God in common things ... and in common tasks'.[152]

Conclusion

Assessing the behaviours and orientations of philanthropists towards those individuals and groups whom they sought to represent has been a central preoccupation of historians. Scholarship treating female philanthropy as a project of social control or for the development of women's civic agency has provided critical insights into the sorts of social identities embodied in the philanthropic project.[153] But it leaves questions about philanthropy's shaping of concepts of democratic and wider social identities unasked. Women's philanthropic projects were at the heart of debates about the principles of freedom and the role of the democratic subject in the interwar world. In interwar Britain, the new relationship between state and citizen that was encoded in the parliamentary franchise legislation of the period seemed to hold the key to a potentially more inclusive political culture, and one that brought with it more extensive demands upon citizens for active social participation. The sorts of opportunities outlined independently by Evangeline Booth, Lettice Fisher and Emily Kinnaird for effecting individual enrichment within social life reveal female philanthropists' critical concern with the elaboration of the new social contract in the interwar years that reached from the home and the locality to global spheres. Moral exhortations to the responsibilities of service as well as participation formed part of the argument for individuals to fully demonstrate the freedoms that were to be associated with modern democracy. Thinking in terms of collectivities did not preclude a concern for individual expression; in fact, personal freedom was central to the project of participation as these women saw it. The selfhoods that were explored through these projects were outward-facing ones, whether established through the mutuality of partnerships, local community work or global Christian mission.[154]

In the interwar period, female philanthropists shaped understandings of individual freedom as inhabiting spaces in which the outward-looking logics of social and subjective fulfilment were interleaved, and where 'individual freedom [w]as [always] social commitment'.[155] While, fundamentally, the arguments of female philanthropists for social engagement that have been explored in this chapter were linked to the ambition to foster women's confidence for citizenship, the implications of the expansive forms of collective identity that Booth, Fisher and Kinnaird each explored reached beyond a gendered frame. As we have seen, the women defined collective endeavour within various traditions of Christian community, cooperation, confederation and cosmopolitanism. The critical issue was how to link subjective experience with the obligations of collective and organized participation. There were strains as well as creative tensions within this search for the reconciliation of individual agency and collective participation. In the interwar period, female philanthropists were already articulating what would become a central critique in Britain in the 1940s of centralization in terms of the stifling of voluntary organizations' contribution to social life:[156] in *The Citizen*, Lettice Fisher warned that Britons needed to take heed of an international commentator's remark that 'as a people we are rather tending to lose our instincts of independence, our enterprise, our powers of helping ourselves through the difficulties of life'; she worried that in the modern 'organised' capacity of doing so much for each other, individuals had rather forgotten 'how to deal with difficulties'.[157] In this respect, the optimism female philanthropists showed towards the expanded scales of social solidarity and connectedness that seemed to be promised by interwar democratic cultures was cross-cut by an anxiety that older practices of everyday engagement might be usurped. Female philanthropists understood that the acquisition of citizen rights was not the same as the effective demonstration of those rights: the modern world could hamper as much as harness individual agency. Individuals' effective engagement within the world meant reviewing existing models of social organization as much as formulating new ones.

4

Culture

In February 1937, Muriel Paget wrote home to her husband from Leningrad that 'I love this crazy country & am v[ery] happy in the garden & planning & arranging impossible things for impossible but v[ery] nice people.'[1] Paget was in Russia at this time working with her charity, the BSRRA, formally established in 1930, for British-born subjects who were unable, due to illness, old age or other difficulties, to leave Russia under the British government's schemes of the early 1920s to repatriate British citizens. It was in fact to be her last visit to Russia; Muriel Paget died in 1938 following a long battle with cancer. In 1937 the writer Una Pope-Hennessy had found Paget, however, in a vivacious mood. Pope-Hennessy had travelled to Leningrad that year with her husband to research a historical biography of Paul I, the Russian Emperor (1796–1801) on an itinerary organized by VOKS, a key organizational vehicle for Soviet cultural diplomacy. Wanting to explore the city as it was, and had been, lived in and from the 'point of view of the ordinary citizen', Pope-Hennessy delighted in Leningrad's architecture, infrastructure and cultural life, including opera, film and theatre. As the itinerary indicated, the point of view from which she explored the city was a privileged one; it allowed for an elite interpretation of elite international culture. As part of her trip, Una Pope-Hennessy visited Muriel Paget's Relief Centre for the ageing British nationals in the Krasnaia Ulitsa, where she found Paget personifying sympathy with Russian people and culture. In her memoirs of the visit, *The Closed City: Impressions of a Visit to Leningrad* (1938), Una Pope-Hennessy described how Paget 'loved Russia and the Russians . . . with an almost fantastic indulgence' and how she would speak of the 'inexpressible feeling', after having been with her family in England or travelling elsewhere, of returning to a country 'in which she had left part of herself [that was] really her spiritual home'.[2] There was a large degree of stereotyping and essentialization in the portrait of both Muriel Paget and 'the Russians' here, but the positive treatment of Paget's personal encounters in Russia bore out the sentiments that Paget herself had wanted to affirm both in public and private narratives.

The sorts of assessments Muriel Paget, and those who came close to her, made about her feelings towards Russian society illuminate a broad enterprise that female philanthropists engaged in between the wars to document models of inter-cultural exchange. I am interested in this chapter in the stories and texts female philanthropists produced in this period to imagine cross-cultural encounters. Although by the early-twentieth century there was a rich heritage of European women's relationship to international culture across key moments in modernity in the evidence of women's travel writings,[3] it was still relatively unusual in this period for women to have personal opportunities to explore cultures other than those into which they were born: international travel remained largely the preserve of the educated and elite classes (and thus a bias in this endeavour towards emphasizing elite culture is probably to be expected). Yet for those women who had the time, money and opportunity for international travel, geographical and cultural mobility afforded insights into a range of societies and the chance to consider comparative questions about human existence and the possibilities for cross-fertilizations between cultures. Having experienced and learned about inter-cultural exchanges themselves, female philanthropists moved towards representing these encounters to their publics. In paying attention to what they specifically had to say, as Patricia Lorcin has argued with reference to European women's narratives of colonial Africa, we need to listen critically to women's voices to gauge what women feel and think, or more specifically, 'what they think listeners should know about why they do or do not feel and think';[4] to hear, in other words, with a critical ear, their strategies and responses to political and social situations on the ground. My particular interest is in the narratives that female philanthropists produced in a range of international contexts as *interpreters* of national and transnational cultural modes and as authors of inter-cultural dialogues. This focus connects to scholarship on the role played by humanitarian actors in interwar systems of international exchange. There is now a large body of work exploring these dynamics in relation to the histories of globalization, aid and development. To date this work has been particularly concerned with the role of non-state actors in processes of governmentality and in the formulation of social and (geo)political expertise.[5]

My focus is different: female philanthropists were concerned in the interwar years with cultural identity and the search for interpretations of, and interconnections between, cultures and peoples as exemplifying comparative method. In this respect, while I am interested in the narratives female philanthropists composed in response to their experiences of international travel (both specifically in connection with their philanthropic projects and more widely), I am also interested in how they approached international exchange through the imaginative practices of research, writing and curating. Their engagements with modes of comparative thinking indicate various intellectual, ideological and political ambitions which funnelled their understandings of cultural forms in particular directions. The work of comparison was a vehicle for cultural brokering and gatekeeping that grew out of philanthropists' ambitions to put cultures, as well as peoples, 'in dialogue' in ways that sought deeper understanding.[6] At a collective level, the geopolitical context of the interwar years focused a particular urgency and resonance to women philanthropists' projects. Against the backdrop of the movement from the 1920s into the 1930s that saw overly-firm and insistent worldviews dominate channels of formal international relations, female philanthropists addressed the personal, political and social opportunities and tensions that revolved around delineations of national culture, and the similarities and differences that comparison illuminated. This dynamic revealed and expanded the peace-building momentum begun in the years after the First World War, when the *realpolitik* of transnational thinking sharpened what Glenda Sluga has described as the ideological shift towards 'a new international age of nationalism', expressed both by national policy makers and new federated institutions such as the League of Nations.[7] Philanthropic activity offered women routes towards comparative understandings of national traditions directly, or through the networks and wider fora they participated in, as part of their charitable and wider intellectual projects.

The comparative thinking female philanthropists engaged in in their search for cultural interpretation shows how women used the authenticity derived from access to cross-cultural, transnational spheres to disclaim parochial models of nationalism whilst reaffirming the significance of national culture. My finding here is that, once again, female philanthropists constructed direct personal experience as the means for authentic cultural understanding, but in this chapter it is the identity of the *inhabitant* that surfaces as a critical vehicle for their claims to insights through comparison. I turn again to Muriel Paget's, Lettice Fisher's and Emily Kinnaird's stories to discuss three expressions of this thinking. I consider, first, Muriel Paget's engagement with transnational possibilities through the cultivation of Anglo-Russian relations; second, I examine how Lettice Fisher explored the opportunities for, and limitations of, inter-European thinking in historical and philanthropic practice; third, I trace Emily Kinnaird's contribution to Christian missionary work in forging real and imagined bonds between 'Eastern' and 'Western' cultures. In exploring the interrelations and interdependencies between different cultures, the women composed narratives that stretched between and beyond the philanthropic realm in their assessments of culture, history and place. A key focus here is on the consciousness of historicization that animated the comparative thinking in their narratives as well as the social and the cultural capital the women acquired through their storytelling. Interpreting contemporary evidence as a product of historical development was a powerful tool for the communication of these women's public authority and expertise within the field of transnational cultural understanding, and it was also crucial to the way philanthropists shaped stories about different societies in relational terms.

Aesthetics and politics in Anglo-Russian relations

Images of Russia and the Russian people were pivotal to the British cultural imagination of the early-twentieth century. While memories of the antagonism of the Crimean War still lingered in the national memory, Russian identity and the character of the Russian people emerged as subjects for revived and positive interest amongst intellectuals and cultural elites in this period. Stimulated by the cult of Dostoevsky, the publicity accorded to Russian artists by Roger Fry's second Post-Impressionist exhibition in London (1912–13), and the performances of the Ballets Russes in Europe (1909–14), a wide range of international commentators in this period sought out the discovery of the 'real' or 'old' Russia of Orthodox Muscovy and peasant villages. In Britain, cultural outputs produced by novelists, artists and musicians, ranging from Maurice Baring, to Stephen Graham and Rosa Newmarch, sought to delineate the 'Russian soul', and in the process helped to create a new, positive 'English "Russian myth"'.[8] Calibrating Russian identity through cultural experience also became a past time of those who took up the calls for international relief work programmes in the period. Storytelling about Russian people emerged at the Scottish Women's Hospitals in Russia in 1916–17 as an important part of the women doctors' and nurses' perceptions of their work.[9] At the Anglo-Russian Hospital in Petrograd – Muriel Paget's first intervention in Russia – the personal writings of the doctor Lyndall Pocock show how medical professionals placed the evidence of cultural and literary products in dialogue with lived experience. Pocock reflected in 1916 upon Stephen Graham's model of the simple and superstitious character of the Russian in *With the Russian Pilgrims to Jerusalem* (1913) in the face of the characters of those Russians fighting on the eastern front who were coming before him for X-rays and surgery.[10]

Visions of a free Russia

The spectre of the Russian Revolution of 1917 focused a new urgency for sympathetic British commentators to reimagine the 'real' Russian identity. In the immediate aftermath of 1917, commentators who were keen to re-route critical perspectives on the Anglo-Russian relationship adopted a programme of positive education amongst British audiences, including public talks, writings and other events.[11] Even amongst supporters, constructive emphases were needed to depict this cross-cultural engagement, as Muriel Paget found when addressing the London-based committee for her international missions. Speaking to that group she described Russia, 'though nominally in Europe[,] still in heart largely Asiatic and though nominally in the 20th century is largely mediaeval'. Paget imagined Anglo-Russian exchanges as an intellectual encounter akin to that between contemporary England and the England of the sixteenth century: '[y]ou must therefore judge', she exhorted, 'of Russian actions and events as if you yourself were living in the time of Queen Elizabeth. You would then have found in England great love of art, great developments of literature and music but coupled with a very low standard of humanity and a low valuation of human life'.[12] This sort of assessment underpinned, implicitly at least, the case Paget would make in 1920 for the work of her charity, the Women and Children of Russian Relief Fund, to attend to the distress and deprivation suffered by those mothers and children who, she claimed, had been forced by the Soviet authorities to give up their infants three months after they had given birth, to be brought up in public institutions.[13] Muriel Paget's projection of Russian identity, channelled through such interpretations, fitted the terms of a wider European 'Orientalizing' project, in which the non-Western 'Asian' characteristics of Russian identity was the foundation for the development of the trope of backwardness (although her thinking developed over time and in the 1930s she would critique more generally the Orientalist binary of 'west' and 'non-west').[14] But Paget's delineation of Russian identity to the committee members was also more specific. In romanticizing English historical cultural superiority as a foil for apprehending the complexities of life in contemporary Russia, she posed the questions – how should Russian identity be conceived publicly and what role would it play when 'the Russian Empire is dead' and the federated republics that had replaced it after 1917, each with their own language seeking a distinctive identity? – as crucial not only for the formal avenues of high politics or high culture, but for the sorts of practical and wide-ranging engagements with social, political and cultural life that international non-state actors were undertaking. It was through her own traversing of a 'mixed economy' of social engagement, experienced not only through the blending of voluntary and state traditions in humanitarian projects, but by means of her involvements with commerce and culture, that Muriel Paget claimed to have perceived the political and cultural complexities of the new Russia, as she described it: a combination of idealism, sacrifice, appreciation of music and the arts, developments in applied science and 'brutality and indifference to human life'.[15]

The visions of Russian society and culture with which Muriel Paget claimed expertise in this period were rooted in broader ideological engagements that romanticized a specific model of Russian life as a vehicle for a very particular set of freedoms. As the Russian Provisional Government lurched towards Bolshevism, Muriel Paget, like other Russian sympathizers, held onto the early-twentieth-century progressive ambition for a 'Russia [that] is free'. Her developing perspective takes more specific shape when viewed through her friendship with the British-born historian of Russia, Bernard Pares. Pares, who became a leading figure in the British school of Russian studies, was both celebrant of the exoticism of Russian culture and champion of the constitutional experiments of early-twentieth-century governance of the Duma, a subject he addressed in his first book, *Russia and Reform* (1907).[16] In the first decade of the twentieth century, Muriel Paget formed part of an international circle supporting Russian democratic progress, joining the Anglo-Russian committee in London (for which Pares became Secretary) that arranged parliamentary exchanges between London and St Petersburg.[17] It was Bernard Pares, as we have seen, in his capacity as the official correspondent with the Russian army on the eastern front, who wrote to Muriel Paget in 1915 urging the need for medical provision to support Russian peasant soldiers, which prompted Paget to begin fundraising and organizing for the Anglo-Russian Hospital.[18]

We have seen how publicity about Muriel Paget's international missions consciously appropriated 'the language of medicine' to claim social and scientific knowledge for the humanitarian project. However, individuals setting up the Anglo-Russian Hospital, including Bernard Pares, intended it to be more than a resource of modern healthcare and to function as a symbol of cross-cultural cooperation between allied powers.[19] In this respect, the Anglo-Russian Hospital was a distinctively elite cultural project. Materially, this is indicated by the establishment of the hospital in the Grand Duke Dmitri Pavlovich's palace that was loaned for the duration of the war. Furthermore, Muriel Paget's own social activities in Russia during this period reinforce the positioning of her interventions within the circles of the international political and cultural elites. During the revolutionary fervour of the summer of 1917 Paget socialized with the Russian aristocracy, including Prince Yusupov, and remained resolute against the revolutionaries: she remembered going home from the Prince's palace on the River Moika in July 1917 and confronting a revolutionary mob in the evening streets of Kiev where she overcame 'a fierce Russian' holding a revolver; she pushed the gun away, she recalled and, laughing at him, he let her pass.[20] Such recollections – which were highly romanticized – themselves formed part of the early-twentieth-century Russophile narrative that sought to construct the 'real' Russian identity around a cordial cultural temper (in contrast to the image of the revolutionary Russian). Muriel Paget, herself, was to be instrumentalized in this project, partly as her friendship with Bernard Pares illustrates, through the strategic fluidity that was applied to her philanthropic, intellectual and political aims. In 1931 Pares wrote to Paget that he would like to meet to discuss her latest work in Russia and offered to show her the Russian library at King's College, London, where he was Director of the School of Slavonic and East European Studies.[21] The invitation deliberately configured Muriel Paget's public contributions as embedded within scholarship on Russian life and culture. This was to be a model Pares extended further after Paget's death. In his obituary of Muriel Paget for *The Slavonic and East European Review*, Pares described her very 'likeness' for 'a Russian in her unfailing good nature and the charm of her simple friendliness'.[22] Muriel Paget had herself become the personification of the 'English "Russian myth"'.

Art and cultural heritage

Art was a particularly important platform for Muriel Paget's cross-cultural storytelling and its mediation of cultural and political meaning. There was, of course, nothing new about the relationship between art and philanthropy: the model of the philanthropist as cultural patron has a very long history.[23] In the early-twentieth century, along with other Society figures, Muriel Paget lent her patronage to English artists and cultural figures in the organization of a number of charity balls, including two at the Albert Hall, London; in May 1912 in aid of the Soldiers' and Sailors' Help Society and in December 1913 a 'Picture Ball' in aid of the IKL, which showcased a tableau of Futurist costumes designed by the artist and writer Wyndham Lewis.[24] Lewis, who would go on in 1914 to establish the short-lived but influential avant-garde experiment of Vorticism, benefitted in the pre-war years both from the funding and public exposure that came from the Picture Ball; Christopher Nevinson encouraged Lewis to take the commission in the knowledge that Muriel Paget was one of the important wealthy, aristocratic female 'buyer[s]' of modern art.[25] The significance of the relationship between Lewis, Nevinson and Paget, however, lies not simply in the dynamics of female patrons of fashionable art. It reveals the connection between specific artistic *method* (avant-garde) and the cultural ambitions of Muriel Paget's philanthropy. In the first decades of the twentieth century, avant-garde artists explored a complex set of questions about the interrelationship between history, art and modernity. Michael Saler has discussed how this practice – social as well as aesthetic – was legitimated by interwar English artists through the appropriation of the cultural standards of the medieval past constructed by nineteenth-century intellectual movements.[26] As well as providing patronage to artists, Muriel Paget seemed at times to speak the sorts of broad interpretative language used by avant-gardists to apprehend the cultural influence of the past, whilst claiming her own authority in the field of personal service and philanthropy. Indeed, her focus on the highpoint of English cultural life in the sixteenth century in the narrative to her committee where she projected the 'Asiatic' basis of Russian culture is striking in its depiction of Elizabethan English cultural heritage, a cultural past that Lewis and others had venerated in the Vorticists' 1914 manifesto for modern English art.[27]

Muriel Paget's role, not only as patron and collector, but fundamentally as cultural broker was on display explicitly in May 1917, when she organized an exhibition at the Grafton Galleries, Bond Street, London in aid of the Anglo-Russian Hospital. Publicity for the exhibition stated the rationale to educate British publics of the work of the hospital since the February Revolution, and Anthony Cross has described the 1917 exhibition as a 'quixotic gesture' in its interest in promoting the new 'free Russia' thought to have been brought into being by the revolution.[28] Echoing the language used originally to promote the hospital, the 1917 exhibition was conceived as a vehicle for cross-cultural friendship and public education about the 'real' Russia.[29] This sort of cultural fundraising was widely in vogue at the time: Winifred Stephens' book *The Soul of Russia* (1916) was sold in aid of the Fund for Russian Refugees;[30] and a range of literary personalities supported the organizing committee for the 1917 exhibition, including Rosa Newmarch (who concluded her 1916 book *The Russian Arts* with a description of 'the beauty of the Russian soul'[31]) and John Galsworthy.[32] Moreover, the idea of an exhibition on Russian culture had, itself, been in progress for a number of years amongst sympathetic groups: in 1911, the Anglo-Russian committee, with which Bernard Pares and Muriel Paget were involved, began drawing up plans to hold an exhibition in London not merely to showcase commercial ties, but 'to show in a picturesque way as much as possible of the life of Russia and to be an education in the subject'.[33]

The exhibition catalogue gives an insight into how Muriel Paget and other organizers of the 1917 event wanted to educate the British public in this period in a particular historical vision of Russia. It records the seven sections that were featured at the exhibition, incorporating photographic displays of wartime and revolutionary Russia; paintings, costumes, jewellery and *objets d'art*; peasant handicrafts; religious icons; literature; a commercial intelligence bureau, alongside a Russian restaurant, musical concerts, dramatic performances and lectures.[34] The diversity of cultural products on show represented the range of sources from which exhibits were borrowed from both private individuals and families, including the Bennett and Cazalet collections. Historical sensibility alongside sociology defined the version of Russian identity on display. For example, rather than being chronologically arranged, icons (numbering 168), together with church vestments and ornaments, featured in the exhibition's section on '[p]easant industries'.[35] Some concession to the regional and cultural diversity of the Russian population was acknowledged in the catalogue in discussion of the distinct material culture of the peasantries of North and South Russia. However, the homogenizing prescriptions of the 'English "Russian myth"' surfaced in a number of catalogue descriptions, from John Galsworthy's portrait of 'the great and magnanimous Russian people', to N. Peacock's definition of the 'intricate simplicity' of peasant handicrafts and Muriel Paget's own description of the Russian restaurant as exemplifying an 'open-handed welcome which is so universal in Russia'.[36]

The 1917 Russian exhibition fitted into a longer trajectory in which sympathetic commentators defined Russian life and history to British publics and in the process sought to encourage a cultural broad-mindedness. Although the work was promoted as anti-political, it steered a determinedly political course. In the development of this praxis, Muriel Paget's philanthropy was located within the principles of a burgeoning transnational associational culture. By the mid-1920s, in the context of Soviet Union politics, groups such as the Society for Cultural Relations between the Peoples of the British Commonwealth and the Union of Socialist Soviet Republics (founded in 1924), in which Paget was active, aimed to forge and retain links between Britain and Russia though sociology and art, in a method the group promoted as 'outside the sphere of politics altogether'.[37] Of particular importance to the educative programme was the construction of the 'myth' of Russian Orthodox Christianity. Positive representations of Russia (and Russians) to British audiences had long treated Orthodoxy as indicative of an authentic national sensibility that stood in contrast to the British but showed a spiritual vigour that was worthy of admiration.[38]

From the mid-nineteenth century onwards, British commentators interested in the free democracy of Russia celebrated the surviving relics of Orthodox civilization. Muriel Paget's interest in Orthodoxy is illustrated through a number of sources dating from the war years to the periods of the Soviet administrations of the 1920s and early 1930s. In May 1916 she wrote to her husband after the ritual of the formal blessing of the Anglo-Russian field hospitals and motor ambulances describing the candles, icons and gold, bejewelled clothing of the priest.[39] Paget also documented the spaces and architecture of Orthodoxy in a lantern slide collection of photographs of Orthodox churches she had taken during visits to Russia and the Baltic States in the early 1920s.[40] These depictions of Russian spiritual heritage, intended to be shown to family members and donors and supporters of her work, functioned as relics that imagined transnational cultural practice as transcending political system. Arguably, therefore it was the greater urgency to educate the British public in the *myths* of Russian Orthodoxy, notwithstanding the specific politics or regime of the time, that motivated Muriel Paget to organize another exhibition at the Bloomsbury Gallery, London, in 1931 to display seventeenth-century icons and paintings by Russian artists, including examples from her private collection.[41] Here it was not the contrast drawn between the historical and contemporary culture of Russia (as in the 1917 exhibition), but the *convergence* of cultural form that is interesting, and was evident in the aesthetic parallel of the event with the Soviet government-sponsored 'Russian Ikon exhibition' at the Victoria and Albert museum two years earlier, and the subsequent publication of a book in response to the exhibition, *Masterpieces of Russian Painting*.[42]

Distressed British subjects

In 1924 Muriel Paget began fundraising for what would become her last private charitable venture in Russia: the BSRRA. That year she met the British ambassador to Moscow, Sir Robert Hodgson at a Health Conference, who informed her about a group of infirm and elderly British men and women who had been living and working in Leningrad and Moscow and who were unable to leave the country under British repatriation schemes.[43] The plight of these British-born subjects, many of whom had been attached to wealthy Russian families divested during the revolution or British-based companies that had ceased trading in the country, had been precarious since late 1917. Initially supported by the British consul, they were dispossessed in 1924 following the severance of diplomatic relations between the British and Soviet governments.[44]

This context signalled unprecedented practical and political difficulties for Paget. In her humanitarian projects in 1922 she recorded her regular meetings in Moscow with the Soviet ministers of Education and Health that proffered constructive discussions, including about ideas for establishing a scheme for training Russian nurses in Moscow.[45] In contrast, by 1924 Muriel Paget's work on the ground was limited to the supply of clothing and food on the few occasions in which the Soviet authorities permitted her to enter Moscow and Leningrad. Assessing the work of Paget's Mission over a number of years, Robert Hodgson perceived in 1927 that the need of the British subjects had been met and he wrote to Paget doubting that in reality the men and women still needed financial support or the donations of food and clothes.[46] But Paget carried on the work. Organizational literature specified that the charity supported between 70 and 120 men and women, typically of the middle-classes, though one British press report of the summer of 1931 claimed that Paget's philanthropy was supporting '300 English people'.[47] Returning to Leningrad in the early 1930s, Muriel Paget formally instituted the BSRRA, initially setting up temporary headquarters in the flat in the Krasnaia Ulitsa that Una Pope-Hennessy would visit in 1937.

The form and content of Muriel Paget's work for the 'Distressed British subjects' met with criticism from the British diplomatic establishment in the 1930s. Unsurprisingly, Paget's model of social action was ripe for critique within these circles precisely because it circumvented the formal bureaucratic channels of an exclusively masculine profession.[48] The Consul General in Moscow and later Leningrad, Reader Bullard who came into close contact with Paget in the course of the work in the early 1930s, found her approach hugely frustrating, recording in his diary her presence as 'Lady Bountiful', distributing onions from the garden of the flat when the men and women supported by her charity came for their monthly pensions.[49] The critique – an instrumentalized depiction of elite women's philanthropy – in fact belied the much wider and more dynamic forms of assistance that the BSRRA provided. As well as financial support, the charity offered medical provision for the elderly men and women, and during the course of its work recognized the need also to provide dental services.[50] In June 1934, after several years of planning, a purpose-built residential home in Sosnovka, south-east of Leningrad, was completed.[51]

That the BSRRA came to embody a particular cultural imagination, and one that was juxtaposed consciously against Soviet public policy in the 1930s, is evidenced through a number of channels of reporting in Britain. Against the background of the reality of collective living in Soviet Russia, in which in the early-to-mid-1930s the populations of Moscow and Leningrad faced a severe housing shortage,[52] the provisions at the Home (*dacha*) in Sosnovka were highly politicized. The British tabloid, the *Daily Sketch* in October 1936 projected a romantic sensibility onto the work of Anglo-Russian collective living in the *dacha* 'in a forest glade', in photographs of Muriel Paget surrounded by vegetables grown in the garden; an image of sociability, nurturing and contentment that complemented Paget's own romantic imagination in a pair of watercolour paintings of the *dacha* and the garden produce, and also local journalism in England that described the 'romantic work' (see Fig. 12).[53] Other sympathetic commentaries illuminate how the work was appropriated to reinforce the perceived relative national sensibility of English hospitality and civility. Una Pope-Hennessy signalled such possibilities when describing 'the easy comfort' of the sitting room in the Relief Centre in the Krasnaia Ulitsa and Paget's approach of keeping 'open house' for British nationals. Pope-Hennessy imagined the project as mandating inter-cultural dialogue and an openness to others that befitted late-nineteenth-century models of hospitality. In doing so, her account projected the work as an informal diplomatic mode which addressed conflicting cross-cultural expectations about the provision of food and homely support

Figure 12. Watercolour painting of the *dacha* in Sosnovka, painted by Muriel Paget, 1936. Copyright, Sir Richard Paget. Reproduced with the permission of Sir Richard Paget and Special Collections, Leeds University Library, Box 25, LRA/MS 1405 (Lady Muriel Paget Papers).

explicitly in the context of Soviet cultural practice: she contrasted the 'open[ness]' of accommodation for the 'Distressed British subjects' with the 'closed[ness]' of the city of Leningrad.[54]

In distinction to the disclaiming of political motivations that we have seen characterized attempts to build the 'English "Russian myth"', these narratives that were sympathetic to Muriel Paget's interventions framed the inter-cultural endeavour of her charity the BSRRA as a fundamentally cultural-political project. Through its presentation of a distinctive pastoral model of social engagement, the enterprise was understood as registering a deliberate critique of the Soviet state. It highlighted a supposedly higher form of civility in the model of elite English hospitality. But the cultural triumph, if it was one, was not to last. That the Soviet government, as well as British commentators, also recognized in Paget's work a mechanism for international critique at this moment is clear: in 1938, as the government began to cement its policy to close off Leningrad to foreigners, the *dacha* in Sosnovka would be shut and its residents forced to leave in an evacuation to Estonia. The cultural dialogue between England and Russia that had been narrated via Muriel Paget's charitable work for over twenty years as a diplomatic and a philanthropic tool had come to an end.

European imaginations and reformist practice

In April 1882, Courtenay Peregrine Ilbert embarked on a nineteen-day sea voyage to Bombay, and then on by train and cart to Simla, North India to take up the appointment as Legal Member of Council under the Viceroy of India, Lord Ripon. In early October of that year, his wife Jessie, four daughters (Lettice, Olive, Jessie and Mora), governess, nurse and maid, Jeanetta, set sail from Tilbury Docks, Essex, finally reaching Calcutta on 22 November, from where they travelled on to the new family home: no. 2 Middleton Street, Simla.[55] The four and a half years the family spent in North India were formative especially upon the children's developing cultural experience: on arrival, Jessie Ilbert added to her domestic staff the services of an ayah to help look after her youngest children, and friends made in India remained visitors to the family's London home after their return in the 1890s.[56] In 1936 Lettice Fisher was commissioned to write a short article, 'Indian Memories', for the *Cornhill Magazine* in celebration of Rudyard Kipling's life in which she rehearsed her own imagination of the encounters she had experienced as a child in 1880s Imperial India. As well as remembering parties with the Kiplings (who had first visited the Ilberts in 1884 as a relatively unremarked family), and with the Anglo-Indian Council families,[57] Fisher recalled the geography and the people she had seen. She remembered exploring the mountainous terrain of Mashobra, near the Himalayan woods and thought she could recall 'caravans of camels, laden ponies . . . strange Mongolian faces, and fair, blue-eyed hillmen'.[58]

Lettice Fisher's recollections of her childhood time in India privileged a Eurocentric imagination. Hers was a European's impression of the people and places that she remembered in the 1880s and differences that existed between European culture and the 'strange[ness]' of the Mashobran. This framework of course bounded the degree to which she was able (or wanted) to 'know' the Mashobran and other peoples. However, her recollections of these childhood experiences projected her own sense of immersion in transnational cultural experience that went beyond merely the observation of difference; they were located in a repertoire of developing selfhood that included her memory of being unwell in bed clutching an alabaster elephant-headed-god Ganesh, a present to the family;[59] and of learning Hindustani (it was claimed her sister, Mora grew up fluent in the language).[60] There were evidently limits to the extent and depth of the imaginative explorations of other societies and peoples that female philanthropists undertook, even while they accorded intellectual and subjective perspectives on inter-cultural exchanges. Fisher did not profess in the 1936 article to have understood India, but her focus on culture and ecology, albeit inflected with romanticism, was an attempt to comprehend the 'conditions' of local culture. Lettice Fisher's remembered perspective, from the point of view of an *inhabitant* of Indian society, meant that the inter-cultural encounter for her was a more personally-embedded experience than the typically more transitory set of observational practices in which travellers engaged.

Seeing and knowing other cultures

The significance of the distinction between inhabitant and traveller is not a moot point. It can be appreciated further in this context through comparing Fisher's husband, H. A. L.'s recollections of the couple's travels to Canada in 1909 and 1924.[61] The visits, like those the Fishers made to South Africa in 1908 and 1923, to India in 1913 and North America in 1909, 1930 and 1934, were arranged around H. A. L.'s academic and political commitments and lecture invitations, and planned to build upon and expand the couple's intellectual networks. Additionally, they provided opportunities for assessing the practice of inter-cultural encounter. For H. A. L., foreign travel confirmed the difficulty of mediating distinct vernacular traditions: reflecting on the visit to Canada in 1909, he recalled being struck by how in Quebec the 'English and the French then lived entirely apart, sharply divided by race, speech, and religion', a fracturing confounded by a Canadian press that was 'thoroughly American'.[62] H. A. L. Fisher's observations, gleaned through the experiences of the traveller, addressed the process of interaction between populations and environment through focusing upon relational cultural distance and proximity between societies and peoples. The perspective differed from the sorts of engagements achieved by the inhabitant – the identity that Lettice Fisher would assume in her recollections of Imperial India – in that it was derived from the perspective of the tourist interpreting difference through the lens of the familiar. The project of tourism, as we have seen in the example of Una Pope-Hennessy's reflections on Leningrad and 'Russians', risked reductionism of cultural identity. H. A. L. Fisher interpreted often stark comparisons between ecologies and societies, describing, for example, how 'South Africa, haunted by its colour problem, tortured by drought and cursed by gold', stood in contrast to 'Canada a land of corn, forest, and mountains, watered by majestic rivers and peopled by the two white races whose conflicts have made one of the chief strands of European history'.[63] Returning his narrative to a 'European' perspective, H. A. L. Fisher measured difference less on its own terms than in juxtaposition with the dominance of the familiar.

The particular cultural identities privileged in Lettice Fisher's comparative narratives, themselves, shifted according to the intended reader. There were often quite conscious slippages between national, imperial and transnational vectors of exchange in her writings. In contrast to her recollections of Imperial India, in her educational texts, Lettice Fisher tended to infer greater cultural determinism by introducing the topic of inter-cultural encounter deliberately within frames of reference she assumed her readers would recognize. For example, in *A Brief Survey of the British Empire* (1932), targeted at a workers' education readership, Fisher argued for self-government for the 'white colonies', at once culturally similar to each other, 'all more or less of one kind, thinking in the same way'. Her emphasis presented cultural (and racial) difference within a shared colonial framework of kinship: she wrote that 'for though any one from Britain feels at once that Canada is full of relations and friends and is very British, yet it is American-British, and Canadian ways are not ours'; she went on to define Canadians as a distinctively 'vigorous race: hardened by cold and strengthened by splendid sunshine'.[64] Beyond Eurocentricism, it seemed an Anglocentric perspective was privileged in her interpretation, through which American cultural codes were contrasted to the assumed Britishness of the readers' experience.

Lettice Fisher used this framework again in her *Introductory History of England and Europe from the Earliest Times to the Present* (1935) to position the integrity of English models of citizenship and representative democracy (there was a slippage between 'English' and 'British' identities in her writing), romanticizing a discourse of British cultural supremacy in the struggle for colonial independence whereby American colonies and 'other dominions overseas have all adopted for themselves the British plan of representative government'.[65] Here, Fisher consciously re-evaluated the heritage of British imperial history in order to stress a form of inter-cultural connectivity that valued the expression of national traditions of democracy, writing that the 'Commonwealth of nations ... made us realise something of what a free union of free self-governing peoples, bound not by formal ties, but by common beliefs and traditions, might mean to the world'.[66] Although there was a great deal of essentializing of cultural meaning here, such interpretation pivoted upon an acknowledged need for a relational knowledge of countries and cultures other than one's own that might hold the promise of commonality and here, the essential political goal of democratic freedoms. It was an approach that again stretched beyond the sorts of transitory knowledge gained through the experience of the traveller as tourist. Lettice Fisher was convinced that acquiring such knowledge was an intellectual and subjective challenge, but one which ought to be readily achievable in the communications infrastructure of contemporary society. Thus in *The Citizen* she wrote of the imperative of knowing 'something' of people in other parts of the world with 'whom in these days of swift and easy communication we are brought into such close contact', and if not a deep knowledge then at least 'some idea of what there is to know, some realisation of perspective, some vision which enables us to guard against narrowness, and sectionalism, and insularity'.[67]

European histories and European historians

Lettice Fisher appropriated historical imagination as an influential tool for addressing cultural change. It was an approach we have seen that Muriel Paget used, but it was focused with a sharper conceptual edge through Fisher's sensibility as a professional historian. The ever-quickening and expanding communications and encounters that characterized the new global economy of the interwar years was a phenomenon she understood through her scholarship as unprecedented in scale, though one which was deeply rooted in much older, evolving traditions.[68] Beyond an interest, specifically, in the centuries-long development of global economy, Lettice Fisher contributed to wider methodological developments amongst interwar historians who were committed to developing comparative historical practice. She shared an interest in understanding national historical stories through comparative perspective with her husband, especially in respect of the history of Europe. As well as writing her own European histories for a student readership, in the early 1930s H. A. L. Fisher was writing his three-volume *History of Europe* (1936), a contribution that would sit alongside other titles by European scholars including Henri Pirenne's, *Historie de l'Europe* (1936), Oswald Spengler's, *Decline of the West* (1919–22), and the first six volumes of Arnold Toynbee's, *A Study of History* (1934–9).[69] Maxine Berg has discussed the seminal influence of the First World War upon the economic and political histories produced in the interwar period: comparative and world history, along with economic and social history approaches, developed as they did in response to the military, political and nationalist histories that predominated in the years before and during the war.[70] However, some influential historians believed the opportunities for educating a broad readership in *international thinking* were going largely unrecognized within the discipline. The medieval historian, Eileen Power, for example, registered her anger with nationalist histories for schoolchildren written during the First World War and her disappointment over the Eurocentric focus of the major global histories begun just after the war.[71]

The Eurocentric preoccupations that surfaced in major international histories written in the period reflected the conviction, shared by a wide range of interwar intellectuals and politicians, that the 'European idea' was in crisis. Thinkers across Europe in these years bemoaned the Great War as having marshalled, if not stimulated, the decay of Europe.[72] Such anxiety, which had preoccupied scholars during the First World War and would do so again during the Second World War, developed a particular urgency during the 1930s as fascist regimes forced the pace of international political and cultural debate.[73] Richard Overy has argued that the pessimism amongst European intellectuals and thinkers in the 1930s, closely linked to the discoveries of human and natural sciences, was wider still, and articulated the fear that Western civilization, itself, was in crisis.[74] H. A. L. Fisher acknowledged such pessimism as a driver for his writing of the *History of Europe*, recording in the preface that 'the tides of liberty have now suddenly receded over wide tracts of Europe … the spread of servitude' threatening progress.[75] Intellectual responses to the crisis differed, however, between those who called for the reimagining of creeds of historic unity, and those who sought reinforcement of the integrity of distinct national identities.[76] Lettice Fisher, like another popular British-born historian of the period, Esme Wingfield-Stratford, responded to the fear of a second twentieth-century European war by combining the warning bell of the threat to

Western civilization with affirmation that national strength and values could yet be reinvigorated.[77] Fisher concluded her *An Introductory History of England and Europe* observing that the traditions of English national 'experiment ... and good will' needed to be revived in order to overcome the responses of human fear, ignorance and hatred that if left unchecked would cost the nation the attributes of progressive civilization that had been built up over centuries.[78]

Lettice Fisher's reassertion of national perspective within the interwar European project embodied a specific set of understandings about the progress towards mass democracy and citizenship as both a universal and particular goal. The European idea was not anathema to national identity in this reading, but rather was strengthened by the determined display of, and respect for, national sensibility. Fisher understood that the writing of history, itself, played a vital role in this practice and she furthered this line of thought in the second half of the 1930s in her professional engagements with other scholars. She proofread Isaiah Berlin's manuscript on Karl Marx that her husband had commissioned in 1933 for the Home University Library as a text on the history of European thought,[79] and reviewed the French-born historian and philosopher Élie Halévy's *History of the English People in the Nineteenth Century* (1924–34). Her response to Élie Halévy's work was particularly revealing of the development of her own thinking on European approaches to national history and her perception of both the opportunities for transnational exchange and the limits to which the markers of national identity could be grasped by people from cultures other than one's own. Halévy, himself, was defensive about being a 'Frenchman' writing about 'English' identity. Reviews of his history, which would go on to be published in 1937 as one of the first British Pelican paperbacks, identified Halévy's pioneering research methods that explored the concept of Englishness as captured through political, economic and religious life: the English social psychologist, Graham Wallas, notably identified in Halévy's writing, a new attention to the 'social phenomenon' of ideas and feelings, as much as 'structural' mechanisms.[80] Lettice Fisher was sympathetic to the approach and to Halévy's argument about national democratic freedoms being an essential part of an authentic liberalism: in *An Introductory History of England and Europe* she made a complementary argument for national distinctiveness when observing that 'England had discovered that her future lay not in France but in the development of her own liberties.'[81] However, she departed from Halévy's conception of English liberal democracy as a form of individualism to infer a more complex picture of national social action that accounted for the diversity of lived experience including in provincial and rural England, where quiet commitment to social service continued to be vital.[82] As we have seen, such privileging of the pastoral narrative was more broadly in vogue in the interwar years amongst British thinkers and writers interested in the socially-embedded progression of an authentic British participatory democracy, but Fisher's analysis points additionally to the consciously comparative bases of these ideas as a method of cultural understanding.[83] She diverged from Halévy principally over the interpretation of the *form* of participatory democracy, but this in turn pointed to her conviction of the limitations of historical imagination that was divorced from lived cultural experience. Fisher's constructive criticisms of her friend's work reasserted the value of lived experience both to the historical project and for understanding the compatibility of national sensibility with the interwar European idea.

Comparative research and welfare politics

A related creative tension about respecting both the particularities of national identity and the commonality of traditions across cultures emerged in the work for the reformulation of the political status of unmarried mothers in Britain that the NCUMC undertook from 1918 onwards, with Lettice Fisher as Chair. The evidence of high mortality rates amongst infants born illegitimate in Britain, which had precipitated the establishment of the organization, prompted a series of comparative studies of conditions in Britain and elsewhere, focusing initially on researching the legal provision for the welfare of children born outside of marriage in Central and Northern Europe.[84] Beginning in March 1918, leading NCUMC personnel exploited intellectual networks amongst state and voluntary actors across these territories. In autumn 1919, the NCUMC's secretary reported on discussions with the LORCS about provision for unmarried mothers and children in Holland and Italy.[85] Talks given at formal meetings in the early 1920s included 'Status of the Illegitimate Child in Germany', delivered in November 1922 by the German Minister and former member of the national sex reform movement, Adele Schreiber, which praised the passing earlier in 1922 of the National Child Welfare Act in Weimar Germany and spoke of the hope that in the next sitting of the Reichstag an act would be passed giving illegitimate children a claim on paternal inheritance.[86] At a meeting in February 1923 the talk, 'Illegitimacy in Norway: The Castberg Laws', addressing the 1915 provision that granted rights for parental name and inheritance to children born outside marriage in Norway, was read on behalf of its author, the British magistrate and member of the NCUMC's Legal Subcommittee, Mrs Edwin Gray.[87] Gray's paper criticized the degree of centralization in Norwegian child welfare policy, arguing that, while in theory, the Norwegian state offered support to groups including unmarried mothers, the model disclaimed women's capacity for active citizenship through its appropriation of all aspects of the legal processes of affiliation and guardianship of illegitimate children.[88] Building on this discussion, in 1924 the NCUMC executive studied the Norwegian Illegitimacy Act, the Act for the Protection of Illegitimate Children in Sweden (1917), and a translation of the provisions of the Norwegian Marriage Laws (1918).[89]

The models of citizenship and methods of research that reformers such as Adele Schreiber and Mrs Edwin Gray appropriated directly influenced the formulation of the NCUMC's policy for political lobbying in the 1920s. For example, there were parallels in Schreiber's proposal for illegitimate children's claim on paternal inheritance in Weimar Germany and the NCUMC's pressure in the early 1920s for fathers of illegitimate children to pay maintenance in the campaigns to reform the Bastardy Act (achieved in 1923), which included provision to raise the top limit for affiliation orders from the ten shillings to which it had been raised by the Affiliation Orders Act (1918) to one pound. Both Adele Schreiber and Mrs Edwin Gray framed responses to illegitimacy in terms of the need to encourage the active participation of women, including unmarried mothers, within society, and like Lettice Fisher, both had had long careers in infant welfare work and public health and in suffrage and feminist activism.[90] These reformers' commitments to understanding and improving women's political and legal status were focused as much upon questions of women's dignity and identity as they were upon the rights gained via national enfranchisement; between them they wrote books on the subjects of women's work and wages, women's friendly societies, women on juries and motherhood.[91] Here, what is interesting is that the models of citizenship they constructed in their narratives about illegitimacy bridged European, North American and imperial contexts, drawing attention both to the European bases of transnational political and communication exchanges, as well as transatlantic fields of interconnection.[92] For example, Mrs Edwin Gray's study of the Norwegian Castberg Laws incorporated research on American, Dutch, Finnish and Swedish models of state provision (previously, in 1919, she had studied the New York State Bill on adoption, for comparison with the NCUMC's research on the West Australia, New Zealand and Queensland Acts).[93] Comparative research models continued to be favoured by the NCUMC in its lobbying work throughout the interwar period: in 1936, the executive committee heard about reforming drives in the Netherlands (including the unsuccessful 1929 National Health Insurance Bill which proposed maternity benefit and sick benefit should be payable before and after confinement to unmarried as well as to married mothers) and plans for an Argentinian Council for unmarried mothers.[94]

In developing an international framework for their analysis, reformers did not suggest there could or should be a neat transfer of the legislative and operational systems towards illegitimacy used by one nation upon another. Some NCUMC committee members were staunch critics of the value of the comparisons between policies towards unmarried mothers and their infants constructed respectively by British and German administrations and argued that the analytical framework of mature 'civilisation' did not leave enough room for national distinctiveness.[95] Mrs Edwin Gray, herself, pointed out that it was neither feasible, nor worthwhile, simply to explore whether the laws of one country could be applied in another; for example it was arguably Norway's relatively small population (not replicated in Britain) that had facilitated the implementation of the Castberg Laws, though she was convinced that further study should be undertaken, including of the laws obtaining to unmarried mothers and their children in Denmark, Sweden and Finland.[96] Such evidence points to the importance of comparative research in the policy work of organizations such as the NCUMC, but also to historical actors' recognition that ideals of citizenship – whilst at the broadest level amongst 'progressive' thinkers cross-cutting national traditions – were mediated in practice by national vectors of understanding. Still, the debates illuminate the critical way in which inter-European approaches, framed notably around the model of civilization and democratic perspective working through codes of law and bolstered by standards of social justice and conscience, were appropriated as vehicles for a deepening appreciation of cross-national conditions and response. At the level of imagination, if not always practice, this demanded comparative modes of thinking. As the conclusions of Mrs Edwin Gray and Adele Schreiber were want to stress, at the very least it ought to be the *common obligation* of democratic societies to strive for mechanisms of reform appropriate for their distinctive national structures and cultures.

Between 'East' and 'West': narratives of inter-cultural discovery

Looking at the notice boards in UK YWCA clubs in the autumn of 1935, members would have seen an advertisement for the forthcoming World Fellowship Week. Under the title 'Relayed from the World', the poster included details of YWCA projects in Burma, Denmark, Finland, India, Jamaica, Japan and Korea, as well as short articles on water collection in West Africa and transatlantic commerce (see Fig. 13). The range of subjects refracted the twofold

RELAYED FROM THE WORLD

SPECIAL SUPPLEMENT TO THE BLUE TRIANGLE
Published by the Y.W.C.A. of Great Britain,
Great Russell Street, London, W.C.I.

Y.W.C.A. WEEK OF PRAYER AND WORLD
FELLOWSHIP. NOVEMBER 10th—16th, 1935.

GREENLAND

The beautifully decorated costumes are designed for warmth. Note the stove behind.

MRS. KIM OF KOREA

says the most popular activities at Seoul Y.W.C.A. are day classes in cooking and sewing. Evening classes were attended by forty older women. When they had a recreational evening the room was crowded. Of course! We know how mothers like to play! Two Korean Y.W.C.A. members have been visiting their progressive next-door neighbour, Japan.

DENMARK
World's Y.W.C.A. President in a Cathedral.

The audience at a Y.W.C.A. meeting in Roskilde grew so large that the meeting was moved into the famous Cathedral where Miss Van Asch Van Wych gave her address.

TEDDY USK UNG

This is the address in Pennsylvania from which Miss Mary Dingman wrote the inspiring article in the October BLUE TRIANGLE called "Turning towards the Dawn"—don't miss it.

DR. KAGAWA VISITS MELBOURNE.

The Y.W.C.A. presented Dr. Kagawa with Australian lantern slides for use in Japan. He made a speech describing conditions in Japan, and, says the reporter, "made us wish to live more simply and truly, that thereby the great work of God might be furthered."

INDIAN GIRLS HAVE THEIR EYES WIDE OPEN

for everything that can be done for their country. In hospitals, factories, and schools, Indian women are working as doctors, teachers and social workers.

The Y.W.C.A. in India has been a pioneer in social work for women and children.

In the big cities it opened the first commercial training schools for Anglo-Indian business girls.

HOUSES IN JAMAICA.

The Jamaican Y.W.C.A. had a "perfect house" lent to them for two week-ends. It was on the Blue Mountains looking over the bluff of Blue Bay beyond the fascinating peaks and curves of hills.

Kingston Y.W.C.A. members are grouped in four "houses." They call them "Kinnaird" and "Robarts" after the British founders, and "Probyn" and "Heath" after the founders of the Jamaican Association.

A BURMESE BIRTHDAY

Rangoon Y.W.C.A. members give a birthday present to their Association each year. It was 35 this year! Part of the gift went to the equipment of their Prayer Room and part to the Quetta Earthquake Fund.

Rangoon Y.W.C.A. members have vivid memories of the earthquake that shook down part of their building a few years ago.

GIRLS CLIMB A MOUNTAIN BEFORE DAWN.

Members of the Auckland Association make their way in twos and threes up the winding paths of Mount Eden to the summit. It is early morning, the first day of the Week of Prayer and World Fellowship. The nearby hills with their farms are wrapped in mist. Far below the city lies dreaming on the strip of land between the two harbours.

A sunrise service of worship is held, with thanksgiving that God has called our Association to the Week of World Friendship together with the Y.M.C.A. and the World's Student Christian Federation. As the sun moves on its way sunrise services follow in Japan, and so throughout the day and week, one gathering after another, country by country makes its special contribution of thanksgiving and prayer, of pageant or of festive meal in common.

"SO THE ROUND WORLD IS EVERY WAY BOUND BY GOLD CHAINS ABOUT THE FEET OF GOD."

REMEMBER TO PRAY

that the creeping shadow of war may be withdrawn from the homes of Italy and Abyssinia.

FINLAND

It was one of those perfectly lovely evenings, which one only gets in the far North when sunset and dawn nearly touch each other, that the Norwegian and Danish delegates to the Northern Conference arrived at Savonlinna, a small town with about 5,000 inhabitants built on islands in the Saimaa lake. We had been about nine hours on the lake on a rather crowded boat and we were growing at last a bit tired, but this was quickly brushed away by the hearty welcome of the Finnish General Secretary and her helpers. It took some time before we all reached our quarters as we were to be in tiny cottages on small islands, and it was broad daylight before we got to bed. The hospitality and kindness of the Finnish people is something quite extraordinary. Already on arrival at Helsingfors we had been received in their beautiful Hospiz in the most perfect way.

The meeting began the next afternoon when the Swedish delegates also had arrived and we were about 300 in all. The gathering was held in the village church. Many hands had been working hard on yards of garlands made of juniper which decorated the Church. These and the many birch trees and lovely flowers on the altar and in the choir gave an impression of being partly in a wood and partly in a garden. The flags of the four countries, so alike and yet so different, gave a lovely touch of colouring. The Finnish people are very musical and the beautiful singing by the choir, made up of members of the Y.W.C.A., was something wonderful; it filled the church with joy and praise.

DO YOU DRAW YOUR WATER FROM A WELL?

These West African teachers are doing so. An American Negress Miss Celestine Smith has been working for a year in the new Lagos Y.W.C.A. A new British worker goes there this Autumn.

THE SHUTTLES OF COMMERCE

(Tune—"Come to the Fair"—Easthope Martin.)

The shuttles of commerce are threading the sky,
Oh, oh, wings o'er the world,
They're binding the world into one as they fly,
Oh, oh, wings o'er the world,
Oh, the web they are weaving,
It flows through our hands,
Our lives are enmeshed
In its swift gleaming strands
And we work with the girls of all lands
As we fashion the fabric of commerce,
So into the loom we will weave our goodwill
Oh, oh, . . . wings o'er the world.

The quivering currents, tho' silent as light,
Oh, oh, sing round the world,
They blossom with sound when we harness their flight,
Oh, oh, sing round the world.
Oh, the words we send out
Toward the east at the dawn
We hear from the west
Ere the daylight has gone
And the world is girdled with song
As it sways with the rhythm of commerce.
So each in our own tongue we'll breathe our goodwill
Oh, oh, . . . sing round the world.

This song is a very popular one among Association members in U.S.A. The tune is a familiar one; why not try it out in your Club?

THESE JAPANESE WOMEN

are wearing kimonas to entertain Miss Niven to tea.

But Japanese girls leave their kimonas at home with their grandmothers nowadays.

They are great at games and make extremely smart lift-girls and telephone clerks.

A Japanese gramophone record and some jolly pictures of modern Japan can be borrowed from Headquarters. Many things and pictures from other countries may be borrowed too.

Figure 13. 'Relayed from the World'. Poster produced for the UK YWCA's World Fellowship Week, 1935. Published in a supplement to *The Blue Triangle Gazette*, Oct. 1935. Reproduced with the permission of the Young Women's Trust (formerly the YWCA) and The Modern Records Centre, University of Warwick, MSS 243/1/2/10a (Young Women's Christian Association Records).

aims of World Fellowship Week: to educate members in the YWCA's work worldwide and in the methods of cross-cultural encounter that the organization approached more broadly. Various mechanisms were used to support these goals, including travel bureau posters, newspaper clippings of international news stories, language study groups, wireless talks and trips to local collections of international art.[97] Film showings were thought to be a particularly useful educative medium. Suggested titles for the 1935 Fellowship Week included the GPO (General Post Office) Film Unit productions, *The Great St. Lawrence, Canada's Metropolis, People and Products of India, Tea Leaves, African Trails* and Gaumont British titles, *Secrets of India, Bikaner, Katmandu,* and from their miniature series, *A Friesland Wedding, The Hague* and *Dutch Cheese.*[98] The wide geographical and cultural content of the films illuminates the organization's active attempts to encourage international-mindedness amongst branch leaders and members.[99] Social and spiritual unity, core teachings of the YWCA, required the creative stimulation of an outward-facing imagination.

While as we have seen, in the interwar years YWCA leaders exhorted the unit of the nation as one representation of community,[100] the Christian principles the organization fostered consciously looked beyond national borders. There was an imperative for YWCA leaders to think internationally and to engage members in the exploration of social issues on as broad a basis as possible. In 1894 the World's YWCA had been established as an umbrella body by the national organizations of Britain, Norway, Sweden and the United States.[101] Beginning in 1898, the UK YWCA held an annual Week of Prayer every November, in part to fundraise for the headquarters of the World's YWCA. By 1904 the Week of Prayer was combined with World Fellowship Week, which sought to extend exploration and study of the interdependencies of peoples in the contemporary world through the conscious encouragement of international thinking. The aim was to imagine YWCA members into proximity with young women in other countries and cultures whilst also acknowledging cultural difference. The wider goal was the extension of Christian mission, so that a foreign country's religious beliefs – and scope for Christianization – mattered vitally to the outreach work the YWCA chose to undertake over time. However, in 1935 the UK YWCA executive lamented members' disinterest in the organization's 'overseas' work, and wrote of the need for branches to educate in international affairs beyond interest in stories about 'the epic of Everest', travel news and 'exploration parties'.[102] It was the interrelationship between societies, cultures and nations that needed to be grasped, but communicating this sort of connection was precisely the challenge. As one leading YWCA member put it: 'it is not possible for any country to live sufficient unto itself [even though] it may die sufficient unto itself'.[103] Although the inter-cultural vision seemed incontrovertible in institutional narratives, YWCA members were not necessarily receptive to this emphasis, and there is evidence that the interest of young women remained, more realistically, in the excitement of international travel.

Travel writings

For many YWCA leaders, comparative thinking was an essential aspect of working for a worldwide organization, but it was to be the particularities and modes of comparisons drawn that mattered. In April 1926, Emily Kinnaird travelled to Oporto, Portugal to visit YWCA Blue Triangle Clubs running leisure and social activities for young Portuguese girls. Recording her trip in an article for the UK YWCA members' magazine, Kinnaird observed the popularity of the clubs as places for local girls to meet friends and to explore educational resources, including foreign language classes and a library service. She reflected that there was still much work for the YWCA to do in Portugal with older girls and young women: the association did not yet tackle the sorts of structural issues the organization was addressing in Britain, notably the inequalities that women industrial workers faced, or, more generally, the lack of provisions of maternity leave for many working women.[104] International travel, here again, was a starting point for addressing inter-cultural exchange and the potential for comparative approaches towards understanding both national and universal principles. Emily Kinnaird had visited Portugal for the first time in the autumn of 1923 when she had attended YWCA clubs in Lisbon and met Baroness Olga Meyendorff, a secretary of the World's YWCA. Conveying that visit to members, Kinnaird registered her surprise that the religious work of YWCA visitations began in Lisbon at 8.30 p.m. (much later than she was used to in Britain), with tea taken between 11.00 p.m. and midnight, and continued into the early hours of the morning.[105] Her reflections invoked a series of additional comparisons; between the Portuguese capital and her home city of London as a former shipping power-turned-industrial centre and seat of government; between Lisbon and Berlin, a city Kinnaird understood to be strictly ordered by civic law; and between Portugal, America and India, where she had delighted in each country at passing fields of 'Indian corn'.[106] The examples enabled Emily Kinnaird to make the broader observation that religious experience was embedded within distinct ecologies, national habits and traditions of sociability but fundamentally illuminated wider commonalities of human expression. It was precisely the sort of international thinking the YWCA looked to encourage, and Kinnaird's article was recommended to YWCA secretaries and branch leaders as a useful stimulus for discussion during the 1923 World Fellowship Week.[107]

Travel writing was a popular genre in the YWCA's programme for the social and spiritual education of young women in the interwar years. In one respect this should not be surprising. A popular genre from the nineteenth century onwards, scholars have argued that travel writing reached its highpoint in the interwar period in an international travel context that followed imperial exploration but preceded mass tourism.[108] There was a commercial value to the revelatory promise of this literature, and voluntary organizations such as the YWCA saw it as part of their role to be particularly attuned to the consumer tastes of young women. Emily Kinnaird contributed short travel reflections for the YWCA's members' magazine *Our Own Gazette* between 1906 and the 1940s, and she also re-used and re-worked parts of these articles in her autobiographical writings. Some writings recorded her European travels; however, most explored her visits to India and South East Asia, which she undertook alone or with her sister, Gertrude from the late 1880s onwards. In 1906 Emily and Gertrude wrote an article recalling their first visit to India as part of a mission organized by the American Presbyterian preacher, George Frederick Pentecost that Emily Kinnaird would narrate again in her autobiography, *Reminiscences* as having involved a five-week sea voyage on board the *Hedive*, from London docks to Calcutta, from where the sisters explored Patna, Simla and Mussoorie, working with local women to set up YWCA centres.[109] In *Reminiscences*, Emily Kinnaird recalled the visit both as pivotal to her and her sister's personal development (they visited Karachi, Hyderabad (Sindh), Ajmere, Lahore, Abu Road and Calcutta), and as a milestone in the YWCA's history in India. By 1891 work with young women in towns including Bombay, Calcutta and Lahore had begun in an 'incidental way', with the years between 1890 and 1896 seeing further expansion of branches in close link to British 'mother' branches.[110] In 1892 the YWCA began work in Bangalore, and in 1900 Emily Kinnaird founded the Madras YWCA, in a year that would see the establishment of the National YWCA of India, Burma and Ceylon. In 1909 she was delegated to Ceylon where, in Colombo, she established Bible classes, organized a tennis club, and moonlight picnics.[111] By the late 1920s the work in Ceylon was focused around supporting young Anglo-Indian women training for teaching, nursing, business or commercial posts in the growing service economy; Kinnaird reported that in Colombo in 1929 the new YWCA Hostel in Union Place housed thirty-four girls who had moved there to study and to take up training opportunities, a development she saw as necessary both for advancing women's social status and addressing family poverty in South India.[112]

For literary scholars, tracing the 'thrill' of the journey, as perceived by the travel writer, is especially revealing. It points to the psychological and intellectual drivers of the author, and uncovers insights into the broader social and cultural parameters framing their stories.[113] In Emily Kinnaird's writings, the 'thrill' of her travels manifests moments of personal and spiritual education. An example occurred in her notes from a week's travel from Poona to Calcutta, published in *Our Own Gazette* in 1922, which documented her first day's journey over the ghats and on to Allahabad and then via a shuttle train to the YWCA National Office in Calcutta. The 'thrill' of visiting the pilgrimage site of Nazik on that first day of travelling, 'one of the twelve sacred spots of India', was enriched by Kinnaird's travelling to the spot across a landscape 'bursting with verdure after the rains', and in the company of 'two pretty Parsi girls'.[114] Furthermore, the experience facilitated her examination of the coalescing of everyday spiritual experience with social, cultural and technological developments. Just as she would report from Portugal in 1923, Kinnaird identified the significance of the shifting experiences allowed by new transport technologies at this moment; in recollecting the custom of Buffalo Day in Nazik, she juxtaposed an image of poor pilgrims travelling on bullock carts and the 'motor-cars decorated with marigolds and other offerings to the gods' that transported wealthy citizens to the holy temple on the hill.[115]

In transit

Notwithstanding her imaginative engagement with the journeys she undertook, Emily Kinnaird's writings come closer, I argue, to a form of 'transit writing' that scholars have described as a vehicle for exploring not solely the experience of travelling but the *mechanisms* of inter-cultural connectivity.[116] Transit, encompassing the movement of information as much as the movement of people and goods, was at root concerned with both personal and social transformation.[117] It was the sort of sensibility that Emily Kinnaird displayed in her writings about her visit to Lisbon, when musing on the extent to which national customs would be levelled through the impact of aeroplane travel.[118] The sentiment of transit was evident again in Kinnaird's published notes for British YWCA readers on her visit to Ceylon in 1929, in which she described the global economy of tea drinking, beginning with the 'thousands of deft little Ceylon girls' fingers ... in picking, sorting and packing the tea leaves which you put into the pot so gladly and so frequently'.[119] The emphases placed upon connectivity in transit writing were cross-cut in this example with the logic of the missionary narrative. Emily Kinnaird represented the opportunities of global economic activity in language that highlighted the outwardly expansionist ambitions of Christian missionary work; she asked readers when they next poured a cup of tea to think about 'this island of five million people which has been in touch with the West for several hundred years and is not yet Christianized'.[120] An instructive comparison of this juxtaposition emerges in the GPO Film Unit's documentary film, *The Song of Ceylon* (1934), sponsored by the Ceylon Tea Propaganda Bureau and the Empire Tea Marketing Board, which explored the global connecting lines of Sinhalese commerce, stretching from the work and industry of local populations to the wireless communications networks of imperial organizations. In the film, religious life was used as a central conceit for national identity, notably in the footage of Sinhalese Buddhism, shot by Basil Wright.[121] Emily Kinnaird, similarly, captured the Sunday evening Buddhist procession towards the site of the sacred Bo Tree, with 'gaily dressed boys and girls' singing and carrying pink and green nosegays. For Kinnaird, however, the significance of such scenes lay in what they revealed about the possibility (and limitations) of Christian mission. Unlike in South India, where she celebrated the influence upon local populations of the London Missionary Society and CMS workers in the area between Trivandrum and Neyoor, Emily Kinnaird observed 'an anti-Christian movement' in Ceylon.[122] In Ceylon she feared the revivalism of Buddhism, not only out of interest in the transformations brought by transit, but specifically because it would challenge the fervour of Christian mission.

Missionary work

Emily Kinnaird did not always consciously foreground the enterprise of transit in her writings. Nevertheless, her writings consistently interrogated moments and contexts for the exchange of ideas, customs and cultures. In *Reminiscences*, she had captured the YWCA's ambitions for inter-cultural exchange as part of a wider ambition for cultural, social and spiritual connectedness in her description of the organization's approach as 'interdenominational ... international and ... inter-class'.[123] Implementing this methodology in practice, however, was challenging. It involved the YWCA sometimes in contested dialogue with the deeply-rooted social, cultural and religious sensibilities and traditions of local communities. In 1929, Emily Kinnaird described the difficulties of bringing together young women of 'ancient Syrian Churches with their multiform differences' in South India, and she emphasized again the importance of the study programmes organized by World Fellowship Week and YWCA Bible circles for this enterprise, for example with groups in Neyoor and Trivandrum.[124] Kinnaird had addressed opportunities to encourage pan-Christian practice over a long period of time. In 1908, on a visit to South Africa as Vice-President of the World's Executive of the YWCA, she spoke at the Transvaal YWCA branch at a pan-Anglican thank-offering meeting for fundraising that had been undertaken for the worldwide needs of the Anglian church, where she called for the extension of city-based work for students and schoolgirls, and the establishment of branches 'for coloured girls'.[125] Yet there remained tensions within the YWCA's missionary ambitions for pan-Christian engagement and the practice of inter-cultural interactions. The ambitions did not necessarily preclude the racial segregation of the work, as Kinnaird's talk at the Transvaal branch underscored. Indeed, as Nancy Marie Robertson has shown with respect to the American YWCA, there remained a wider disconnect in the organization's work throughout the first half of the twentieth century between the rhetoric of interracial integration and Christian sisterhood and the implementation on the ground of racially-segregated activities.[126]

Emily Kinnaird's commitment to personal spiritual development for wider missionary ambitions did demand reflection upon the dialogic praxis of inter-cultural integration, nonetheless. In this context, it is her articulation (once again) of female activism proceeding through ideas about domesticity in and outside of the *home* that is striking. Kinnaird's ambitions for spiritual connectedness across cultures were rooted in this expansive sphere; as she wrote in her autobiography, *My Adopted Country*, it was this more than travel per se that caught her imagination: 'I am not a traveller, or a sightseer by instinct, and I always take a return ticket'.[127] What attentiveness to the vehicle of domesticity allowed for, and required, was constructive dialogue between everyday 'Eastern' and 'Western' cultures, and the potential to locate the linkages within and between cultural difference. Reflecting on her 1921–2 visit to India, Kinnaird recalled, that in contrast to the Prince of Wales' empire tour of the same year, characterized by public performances of set piece 'tamashas', she and her sister, Gertrude, sought to 'get into closer touch with its people'.[128] Emily Kinnaird's language signalled specifically the principles of cultural, social and spiritual interchange that drove missionaries to reach out to local communities and the interpersonal methods that we have seen continued to animate women's philanthropic practice in the interwar years. Kinnaird claimed that local populations across India looked on YWCA secretaries as 'friends'; she herself recalled staying as a guest in the homes of 18 Hindu and Christian Indian families on the visit.[129] In one respect this was a celebration of the reciprocal exchange of hospitality that had been enjoyed also by Indian families in Emily Kinnaird's childhood home in London, which Edith Picton-Turbervill remembered if not a 'home for Indians [was] certainly a social centre for them'.[130] Yet Kinnaird recalled of her own experience the opportunities provided not only to live a different way of life, but to learn at first-hand the sorts of social and political interventions that local communities admired and resisted; she observed the hardships her hosts recalled in response to British imperial policy including Queen Victoria's proclamation of 1858, the Amritsar affair and the continuation of the Rowlatt Acts.[131] It was the possibility that these cross-cultural encounters provided for a more profound understanding that Kinnaird perceived as critical to spiritual and political life, and made her a sharp critic of the wider degree of separation that endured between the European and educated Indian communities.

Like both Lettice Fisher and Muriel Paget, being an inhabitant – of homes both in her own and her 'adopted country' – was a central conceit of Kinnaird's inter-cultural understanding. In her 1921–2 tour of India, she sought an authentic sense of everyday life as part of the broader project of developing real understanding of Indian culture, even if this knowledge was used ultimately for the purpose of re-articulating Western perspectives.[132] In 1891, Kinnaird had written about the YWCA initiative, the Loving Service League, that funded missionaries' medical and dispensary provisions to local populations in Indian towns, as a way of forging the 'link' between 'England's and Indian women'.[133] Yet she continued to acknowledge the limitations to this practice. As Lettice and H. A. L. Fisher had observed, Emily Kinnaird also stressed the challenges to inter-cultural dialogue posed by the strictures of vernacular traditions: in *Reminiscences*, she reflected on the difficulties of effecting cross-cultural communication in the work in India in the 1890s when most local women spoke vernacular languages. On her first visit she had stayed, with her sister Gertrude, with the first female Indian lawyer, Cornelia Sorabji at Poona and the Indian social reformer, Pandita Ramabai at Mukti: both were unusually highly educated women. In retrospect Kinnaird recognized how imperative had been the opportunities for cultural interchange provided by the women's hospitality and shared understanding; she wrote that '[t]he lack of knowledge of the East among the people of the West' was as much the result of 'preconceived notions and prejudice as of a general unwillingness to learn'.[134] The time Kinnaird spent in Poona and Mukti therefore revealed to her the limitations to the project of

cultural exchange, expressed not only by embedded divisions between the Indian
and British communities, but also between both and the 'Eurasian community'
that exposed deeper racial and gender inequalities.[135] Thus, in 1930, addressing
British women who had relocated to India as part of imperial families, she
cautioned strongly against the criticism of local customs that could come
through well-meaning attempts at social work. She encouraged instead a deeper
cultural understanding that might be achieved through learning vernacular
languages and finding ways for education in national customs.[136]

Progressive nationalism

Emily Kinnaird's work in India is a further example of how female philanthropists'
projects in the interwar years considered and illuminated various vectors of
cultural exchange. Her outreach work was, like Paget's and Fisher's philanthropy,
a political project. Kinnaird's interest in the movement from vernacular to
international idioms with respect to Indian society developed in an important
direction through her engagement with schools of progressive nationalist
thought rooted in early-twentieth-century Indian movements for independence.
Associational culture provided distinctive opportunities for her personal
education in progressive national politics, both in Britain and internationally.
The establishment in London in 1920 by the Indian National Council of the
YMCA of an Indian Students' Union and Hostel near Russell Square afforded
Emily Kinnaird and her sister Gertrude opportunities to talk with the male
students, and meet leaders of the Indian National Movement including
Rabindranath Tagore, Mahatma Gandhi and Jawaharlal Nehru.[137] In *My Adopted
Country*, Kinnaird pledged her support for the Indian hostel as a space for inter-
cultural intercourse alongside East and West Societies and 'the Labour Party
Clubs for knowledge of the English working man's life', but she regretted that
Indian students continued to form exclusive Ceylon Societies, Pars Hostels,
Hindu groups and Travancorian groups.[138] Her work with the YWCA in India
facilitated the extension of her personal and political connections: during her
1921–2 Indian tour, Tagore's son-in-law, Professor Ganguli took her to visit
Bolepur, and she also visited Gandhi and his wife in Bombay, following his
imprisonment in 1920 for sedition.[139]

Emily Kinnaird's friendship with the Mahatma would become a celebrated
thread of her personal narrative in later life, when she recalled visiting him in
Bombay, and living there 'in his adopted simply way'.[140] As thinkers, Kinnaird
and Gandhi differed markedly on theological grounds. Emily Kinnaird's spiritual

affiliation to India was one expression of her conviction of the need for a pan-Christian world that stood in contrast to the aspirations for religious pluralism for which Gandhi campaigned. But Kinnaird and Gandhi shared – along with a broad range of progressive thinkers – a conviction in obtaining dialogue between nations, whilst reinvigorating a form of tolerant nationalism.[141] In *Reminiscences*, Kinnaird reflected on how the rise of nationalist sensibility in the post-war period had altered not only the map of Europe but extended much further, with a more fundamental impact, in respect to the implementation of ambitions for the interdependencies between peoples and cultures. She posited that the 'clash of colour', felt on every continent, was 'not disloyalty or hate, but a natural instinct for independence which actuates Eastern and African as much as European races': '[w]hen the principles of the Kingdom of God prevail, and a sense of superiority and pride of race are banished for ever', she wrote, 'I believe we shall see a still greater unity in which each race and colour will make its own contribution'.[142] Emily Kinnaird's imagination of political independence across the globe, although not freed from the assumptions of superiority underpinning cultural and racial hierarchies, did contribute to an important developing vocabulary of inter-cultural engagement in the interwar years. Much as we have seen with respect to the way that women's personal freedoms were understood to be central to the achievement of democratic citizenship, so the celebration of the distinct participation of different nations and societies, in this reading, was pivotal for the sorts of cultural exchanges the YWCA sought out through Christian mission at home and abroad. Recognizing and celebrating difference in this project was thus an integral aspect of the search to put cultures in dialogue.

Conclusion

The philanthropic encounter was an encounter between cultures. Alongside the motors of social and welfare principles, in the interwar years philanthropy involved the negotiation of national, imperial and transnational vectors of exchange. Seeing female philanthropy in this period as a site where cultures met requires a reorientation of the way we approach the philanthropic project. Female philanthropists were themselves the products of rich cultural heritages and they were also deeply aware and reflexive of those heritages, and the heritage of those nations and societies with which they came into contact. As the three examples explored in this chapter have shown, putting culture at the heart of the philanthropic project (and philanthropy at the heart of culture), was, in one respect, political, whether channelled through international relations, ambitions for the development of state policy, or for national independence movements or religious missions. But it was also a much more subtle and complex exercise. The romanticization, for example, of Muriel Paget's work in Russia both sought affirmation of cultural identities within an exclusively elite register and was personally effecting. In this respect it is Paget's commitment to the work and the sensibilities with which it seemed to evoke in her – not least when she had a young family 'at home' in Britain herself – that tells us more about the relationship between philanthropy and culture; we can only imagine the sorts of pleasure she experienced in 1920 when receiving a miniature set of children's clothing (in the style of traditional Russian costume) that had been made up from donations of material, an example of those being distributed to Russian child refugees through her Mission to Eastern Europe.[143] Equally, if in the 'state of civilisation' debate with which Lettice Fisher engaged, the re-pointing of the national idiom was a political refrain, it was also intertwined with the examinations of how culture worked, and could be made to work, which was equally significant for the development of subjective experience. Thus, in *Life and Work in England*, Fisher compared the cultural change brought about by the wireless radio and the aeroplane in the contemporary world to the period of cultural revolution of 'our Tudor ancestors' – both were periods of excitement about discovery and anxiety about the implications of change; and her historical reflections seemed to support her own sense of grappling with the puzzlement of the modern world.[144]

The narratives that women philanthropists told about inter-cultural exchange show that in the interwar years female philanthropy was on the front line of the interpretation of culture that has typically been defined in terms of anthropological expertise. The commonplace narrative highlights the broad influence of anthropology in the transatlantic world from the late-nineteenth century onwards in disseminating understandings of cultural relativism that ranked populations according to racial characteristics and cultural status. Variation between individuals and cultures was seen to be a living reality, modelled via hierarchical scales of social, cultural and racial status.[145] Peter Mandler has argued it would take the ruptures of the Second World War for important developments in transatlantic schools of anthropology to advance new understandings of positive inter-cultural relations that could make the world 'safe for differences'.[146] This interpretation, pivoting on the shifting contexts and priorities of the Cold War era, prioritizes the paradigm of public policy, exploring the influence of anthropologists' advancing ideas of cultural universalism upon international politics. Yet the social activism of female philanthropists in the interwar period – operating outside of, if in dialogue with, disciplinary fields and formal structures – enabled experimentation in advance of, and tangentially to, academic and social research and policy developments with new thinking about inter-cultural relations that might value difference in conformity with commonality. The narratives of people, places and culture that women philanthropists composed, as we have seen, could be culturally determinist, but their framing as part of a broader philanthropic sensibility focused an understanding of the building of communities in accordance with difference. This was itself both a project distinct to the terms of cultural exploration of the interwar period and would be part of a longer trajectory in the evolving practice of social development.

5

Communication

Towards the end of November 1939, one month after she officially retired as World General of the Salvation Army, Evangeline Booth boarded a British liner at Liverpool to return to her home in Hartsdale, New York. She arrived in New York on 5 December.[1] On 20 December, Booth wrote a letter to the British portrait artist, Frank O. Salisbury recalling the anxiety of the journey, which she noted included an eleven-day black-out and several overnight submarine chases.[2] The whole voyage, Booth wrote, was deeply stressful to all passengers, but she thought in particular to herself, in having responsibility for the wellbeing of others.[3] Evangeline Booth was psychologically shaken, but spiritually reassured by this episode; the letter reinforced her sense of public responsibility in harnessing social relationships and the authority she derived from God to do so. In writing the letter, Booth positioned her sense of self to complement the sorts of qualities that Salisbury, a specialist in religious subjects, had painted in a portrait of her earlier in 1939. The full-length portrait featured Evangeline Booth standing upright in a military-style black jacket and skirt, holding a red and gold flag (see Fig. 14). It is an arresting image, but in a revealingly self-effacing phrase Booth wrote after the bad sea-crossing that 'the form and the comeliness' of her portrait was created solely by the artist's 'genius'.[4] Three years later, in the autumn of 1942, Evangeline Booth made another argument for the interrelationship between her public image as a religious leader and the need for, and value of, social connectedness, in a letter to the Women's Commentator on the Cincinnati radio station, WCKY on which she was to feature in a forthcoming programme in the series, 'Famous Women'. In this letter, Booth modelled her self-image around an ideal of public worthiness and depth of religious conviction that stressed both the extraordinary moral and social responsibilities that came with her public role, and her humility in the recognition that, before God, she was no different to anyone else. Booth framed this message within a collectivist idiom which chimed well with American wartime rhetoric of the early 1940s and the Salvation Army's characteristic emphasis upon quotidian experience: '[y]ou

Figure 14. Photograph of Evangeline Booth with Frank O. Salisbury inspecting her portrait by Salisbury at the Royal Institute Gallery in Piccadilly, London, 17 November 1939. Photograph by Reg Speller. Copyright, Getty Images. Reproduced with the permission of the Hulton Archive, Getty Images.

need not climb onto a platform in order to be famous with God', she wrote, '[y]ou can be famous in His sight when you are in the home, in the kitchen or doing your bit in the defense [sic] factory, canteen and hospital'.[5]

Evangeline Booth's correspondence here with a well-known artist and a radio station employee respectively draws attention to the communication practices used in women's philanthropic projects with which this chapter is interested. In part, this chapter is about the development and dissemination of the public image of the female philanthropist as a celebrity in the interwar period. Evangeline Booth's transatlantic celebrity, understood in the sense of Charles Ponce de Leon's definition of a 'particular kind of public visibility',[6] was certainly confirmed by the time she wrote the letters to Frank O. Salisbury and the radio presenter. As World General of the Salvation Army, in the mid-to-late 1930s stories about her featured regularly in the international press, attesting to the commodification of both her own public persona and the organization's public reputation.[7] Her letters, however, illustrate how Booth deployed her celebrity status to claim forms of selfhood that explored public legitimacy for broader educative ends.

Moving outwards from Evangeline Booth's letters, this chapter addresses the ways in which female philanthropists worked to combine celebrity and social activism and negotiated the logic of the consumer marketplace and wider models of the expert. Female philanthropists' engagement with models of communication that were used in commercial practice emerge here in conformity, and some tension, with wider public narrative devices of expertise and affect. Interwar publicity about Evangeline Booth, for example, presented often only very fine distinctions between religious frames of reference and those that spoke more obviously to the marketplace of consumerism, including the commodification of her celebrity personality. These nuances could be mediated by emphasizing different aspects of the relationship between the philanthropist and her audience, and by the recognition of the creative opportunities through which an individual's self- and public images, together with their social message, could be shaped to reach multiple constituencies. The shifting insights about personal service that we have seen coalesced around female philanthropy in the interwar period allowed for the development of varied communication practices that targeted different audiences flexibly. Thus, while Evangeline Booth constructed an image of self-effacing femininity in conversation with Frank O. Salisbury, she explored the possibility of *multiple* expressions of the feminine self and authority, in relationship with God, for the broader audience of WCKY listeners. Furthermore, in consciously casting her public reputation in these letters, Booth appropriated a range of narrative registers. She constructed her persona through written textuality that worked both to connect up her public visualization in the image that was celebrated in Frank O. Salisbury's formal portrait and the sorts of mediated personal exchange that could be achieved through the power of broadcasting.

From one point of view, the interwar years marked the emergence of a 'media age', characterized by the expanding range and speed of communications that fostered new sorts of social relationships. David Trotter has argued that this period can be defined as the 'first media age' not simply because of the proliferation of mass media, but because of the wide contemporary awareness of the coexistence of multiple media forms and the evidence that communication technologies accrued around them particular rituals, values, behaviours and narratives.[8] New media technologies were frequently discussed by British writers between the wars as either building up or breaking down social and community ties. Alongside cinematography and photography ('new media' of the nineteenth century), Trotter suggests that beginning in the 1920s writers observed the development of 'connective' media, including the telegraph, telephone and teleprinter allowing for the exploration of modes of interactive 'communication at a distance' and 'politics of connectivity' that crossed over time and space.[9] There was not, as Trotter insightfully shows, a definite progression from 'old' to 'new' cultural forms in this period, either in terms of the popularity of particular media technologies, or in the social values the media was thought to uphold: for instance, the industries around existing technologies, including the newspaper and periodical press and film expanded markedly whilst such media forms were also used to develop and support emerging media innovations (consider, for example, the role of the *Radio Times* in supporting the early innovations of BBC broadcasting). While commentators might celebrate the social effects of connective media, some British writers lamented the challenge these media posed to traditional forms of community and asserted the need for the reassertion of social relationships through face-to-face encounters. In the 1920s and 1930s, writers who lamented the shift used devices and narrative plots to reassert collective rather than individual identity, and to privilege informal forms of social connection which might become the basis for more established modes of political solidarity.[10]

This chapter looks once more at Evangeline Booth's, Lettice Fisher's and Muriel Paget's stories, and examines how each woman worked with and through various forms of technology to develop their philanthropic practice as modes of connective communication in the interwar period. I argue that these women's engagement with technological systems went further than appropriation solely for the purposes of fundraising:[11] it actively shaped new models of communication practice that bridged the logics of information and affect for a range of public ends. As this chapter discusses, media and mass culture were sites for the creative exploration of the social possibilities of philanthropy and civic participation between the wars. My interest, in particular, is in the devices through which women's philanthropy functioned as a mode of public communication that moved between the spheres of social activism and commercialism, as well as the way in which female philanthropists communicated shifting idioms of social intervention and expertise in this period. Female philanthropists used both 'old' and 'new' technologies of communication in the interwar period. They conceived their presentational strategies between the textuality of the printed press and literature, film and the radio. Also they explored a range of generic developments of the period, including those in which existing forms of media repackaged new forms of documentation and new media fashioned imaginative and fictive frameworks.[12] In charting the various models of public communication Booth, Fisher and Paget each developed in the various roles of broadcaster, journalist, public speaker and performer, I trace how in the interwar years, female philanthropists' politics of communication expanded public understandings of their competencies significantly beyond the association of philanthropy with perceptions of the feminine or the emotional. Women's philanthropic practice emerged in this period as a communicative practice of central significance to understanding the developing information age.

Opinion-forming and the politics of unmarried mothers

In the summer of 1939, Lettice Fisher wrote a short institutional history of the NCUMC. *Twenty-one Years, 1918–39* (1939) began by outlining the organization's foundation in the context of wartime concerns about rising illegitimacy rates and public support for child welfare workers, and went on to list the charity's early key achievements in law reform and enactment, including the laws around affiliation orders and the Bastardy Act (1923).[13] The NCUMC's political lobbying projects aimed, as we have seen, both at education for citizenship and the amelioration of public health.[14] The organization's social ambition was also larger and more fundamental than these economic, political and social goals, however. In consciously confronting negative attitudes towards illegitimacy and the unmarried mother, NCUMC personnel worked as 'opinion former[s]' to challenge the social isolation faced by unmarried mothers and their children through a programme of public education.[15] Fisher explained in *Twenty-one Years*, 'The first task of the Council was to educate public opinion':

> Measures for the benefit of the unmarried mother were honestly regarded as a challenge to the accepted standards of morality, and the difficulty of getting workers or indeed subscribers to accept a constructive rather than a deterrent policy was considerable. Much energy had to be expended in the production of newspaper and magazine articles, leaflets, addresses to every sort of meeting,

and in getting editors to accept and audiences to hear the articles and addresses
... We circularised, we wrote, we spoke, and before long we came to feel that we
were meeting with sympathy and response.[16]

As Fisher recalled, this early work was as much about organizing the
NCUMC's lobbying profile and establishing accommodation and support for
unmarried mothers and their children, as it was about reformulating the critical
public image of the early-twentieth-century unmarried mother. Indeed, the two
were intertwined. The NCUMC was not alone in this period in suggesting a
constructive approach towards the support of unmarried mothers, but the
organization represented a minority position, and many British men and women
objected to unmarried mothers being 'helped', just as they objected to what was
perceived to be the subversion of public morals through campaigns run by
bodies such as the National Children Adoption Association (founded in 1917).[17]
Certainly, the ideal that the unmarried mother and her baby should be kept
together, for which the NCUMC campaigned strongly from its beginnings, ran
counter to the principle of deterrent encoded under nineteenth-century Poor
Law legislation which provided for the institutionalization of unmarried mothers
and their babies in workhouses in separate accommodation.[18] The necessity of
keeping mother and baby together was stressed originally by organizations such
as the Child Welfare Council of the Social Welfare Association for London as a
wartime expedient in response to the limited numbers of foster mothers, and in
the social and moral outrage against 'baby-farming' – the practice of taking in
babies to nurse them for a fee, in which conditions varied greatly and which
from the late 1860s onwards was reported widely by medical practitioners, social
scientists and the press to be a source of a large number of infant deaths.[19] The
NCUMC lobbied for the policy to keep babies with mothers to be instituted
generally in the post-war years alongside recognition of the multiple and varied
circumstances of 'unmarried' mothers: the organization worked to secure funds
for waiting and maternity homes for expectant unmarried mothers; residential
accommodation for mothers and babies; and for adoption homes for babies in
cases where mothers were unable to keep their infants.[20]

Developing press experience

In fact, in *Twenty-one Years*, Fisher discussed the most *challenging* early work of
the organization's practice as that of informing and shaping public opinion.
'Educat[ing] public opinion' did not simply involve the dissemination of
information, but required energy and commitment appropriate for the

achievement of attitudinal, as well as social, change. It is instructive to consider the form in which this energy was expressed, and what issues were emphasized. Lettice Fisher's language of 'circularizing, writing and speaking' was reminiscent of the vocabulary used by suffrage campaigners before the war, with whom she worked, that levelled challenges to the limitations of women's political, economic and social roles.[21] The NCUMC configured provision for unmarried mothers as a public health concern and, as we have seen, organizational literature immediately after the war emphasized the problem of rising infant mortality, both of illegitimate and 'legitimate' babies. The charity's presentational work in this area was morally freighted. In one respect it was part of a broader shift made visible in wartime when media, political and social elites channelled older rhetorical labelling of the problem of women's sexuality into a renewed object of social and moral concern, linked to the evidence of women's newfound economic independence.[22] NCUMC leaders challenged consistently the definition of illegitimacy as a moral failing of women: media interventions in the years immediately following the war asserted a moral currency for the work, typically clarifying the distinction between sex outside marriage (which was regarded as a moral and social problem) and the unmarried mother, who was capable of personal reformation and could be educated in the full responsibilities of positive and active citizenship.[23] In an article in the *Times* in the autumn of 1922, Lettice Fisher defended unmarried mothers against criticisms that they were 'abandoned or depraved' as instead 'the victims of folly and ignorance'. While the NCUMC did not condone 'the sin' of illegitimacy, Fisher stressed its concern was to prevent 'suffering' by innocent infants and the further social and psychological isolation of those women who had children outside of marriage who, under existing legislation, were denied full citizen status.[24]

Much of the NCUMC's early work was organized around the management of information that sought to elicit positive public responses to the 'problem' of illegitimacy. The NCUMC Press and Publications committee, which was established soon after the organization was founded, met for the first time in May 1918, chaired by the writer and eugenicist Caleb Saleeby, with the aim of securing a 'convergence' of newspaper articles on relevant subjects. Writers considered for the work included Fru Anker (the Norwegian representative at the Conference of the British Dominions' Women's Suffrage Union), Mr Harold Begbie, Mr Arthur Lee, Mrs H. B. Irving (Dorothea Baird) and Saleeby himself. Not all of these distinguished figures took up the invitation to endorse the NCUMC: the actress Mrs Irving, who had scripted and starred as a health visitor in the British National Baby Week's film, *Motherhood: A Living Picture of*

Life Today (1917), diverged with the organization and the writer and journalist Harold Begbie pleaded lack of time.[25] However, while the identification of sympathetic authors was critical to an effective media strategy, NCUMC personnel also recognized the necessity for knowledge of the functioning of the newspaper industry. In this respect, in *Twenty-one Years* Lettice Fisher reflected on the benefit to the Council of the 'press experience' of the NCUMC's second secretary Mrs Trounson, and the public support of the Lord Mayor of London, Sir Edward Cooper.[26] Cooper's endorsement helped to ensure the organization's work was framed in the press in terms that emphasized the reform of, rather than disregard for, conventional moral codes of Christian understanding: an article in the *Times* which reported on a meeting chaired by Cooper to promote the NCUMC at the Mayoral residence, the Mansion House in January 1919 thus included extracts from an interview with the Bishop of Birmingham, Henry Russell Wakefield, discussing the 'temptation' that unmarried men and women should resist, the 'sin' that was committed in conceiving a child outside of marriage, and, the severest trial of all, the 'remorse' that was to be shown for these actions. The culpability, the bishop argued, should not be apportioned to the unmarried couple: he suggested that illegitimacy was as much the fault of the *couple's* poor parentage; of the state, for allowing them to be brought up in 'evil' environments; the limitations of religious teachings; and the 'low class of public opinion'.[27] In this example, NCUMC publicity can be seen to have capitalized on public platforms for reformist debates to liberalize attitudes to marriage, sex and family life that were rooted in progressive Christian thinking. Contemporary media outputs such as the silent film, *A Bill of Divorcement* (1922), an attempt to reform marriage laws and liberalize attitudes toward divorce, illustrated the wider recognition of the utility of playing up this conjunction. Furthermore, the Bishop of Birmingham, himself, had previously advanced a liberal position on the politics of sex in 1919 in publicizing his role as chairman of the National Birth Rate commission and his support for the wider dissemination of birth control.[28]

Radio appeals

In 1925, the NCUMC was one of the first organizations to be given airspace on BBC national wireless radio to broadcast a charity appeal. Following a national appeal in 1923 on behalf of the Winter Distress League that supported homeless First World War veterans, BBC charity appeals were broadcast on an extraordinary basis, notably for charities for those who had served in the war or in times of national emergency, until 1927, when *The Week's Good Cause* charity appeal was established as a weekly broadcast. Charity appeals were part of the BBC's educative programming schedule: *The Week's Good Cause* was produced by the education and religious department, and managed by an advisory committee of seven outside experts, chaired by the BBC's Director General, John Reith.[29] Once the broadcast became a regular feature, the committee used a classificatory system that grouped charities around particular types of causes and within distinct social spheres: Health, The Services, Children, Social Services, Women's Charities, and Miscellaneous.[30] The delineation of these categories points to why the BBC was receptive in 1925 to the early approach by the NCUMC, a charity that worked for both children and women and was concerned with public health. Lettice Fisher broadcast the NCUMC's 1925 appeal herself. Indeed, Fisher's profile as a public intellectual in this period developed substantially as a consequence of her broadcasting experience. It was a new space for the sorts of opinion-forming work that she undertook in the press and in popular publications and, as we have seen, she went on to broadcast regularly in the late 1920s and early 1930s in the BBC's 'Talks' programme, in connection with her work for the NFWI.[31]

Mirroring discussions in American broadcasting about the importance of the regulated personality of broadcasters,[32] by the 1930s, BBC conventions of charity appeals came to place a particular emphasis upon the broadcasting experience of the 'personality' making the appeal. The model of the 'microphone personality' was acknowledged as integral to the construction of mediated personal engagement between the broadcaster ('speaking to') and the listener ('at home').[33] The importance attached both by charities and the BBC to celebrity endorsement, additionally, expanded a much older tradition amongst charitable organizations which stressed the need for a 'figurehead' in order to frame their activities and fundraising within a personal dimension. Advertisements for charities in both the mainstream printed press and the BBC press deployed this approach widely between the wars. The association of a celebrity figure and charitable causes could be fluid, nonetheless. Some well-known personalities were associated with multiple 'Good Causes': Christopher Stone, who was first employed by the BBC in 1927 to present a weekly programme on popular music, was the most sought-after name to broadcast appeals in the 1930s, and the appeals which he made were always in the top three annual revenue-raisers.[34]

Building on the NCUMC's earlier press publicity, and in line with the ambitions of the early BBC for an integrated and national reach,[35] Lettice Fisher spoke in the 1925 appeal about the need for an active response to the problem of illegitimacy by men and women across the country and in order to address the evidence that 40,000 illegitimate babies were born every year in Britain, and one in seven died before their first birthday. The use of statistics supported the informational logic of the NCUMC's campaign for the legitimation of children born to unmarried parents, which was achieved under the Legitimacy Act (1926).[36] The storytelling that Fisher used in the appeal narrative, however, was arguably more important to the sorts of integrative effects at which her broadcast was aimed. Fisher spoke of the reconstruction of families who had been socially and psychologically broken, giving the example of a mother in Devon writing to the charity about her daughter 'who has got into trouble somewhere in the north'.[37] This emphasis upon the values of conventional domestic life and maternal care imagined a nationwide moral landscape upon which to construct identification between donors and those in receipt of the NCUMC's support and spoke to a broader cultural resistance to the break-up of traditional communities advocated by cultural commentators in this period.[38] It also indicated the charity's vision for the reconfiguration of civil society, in which support and provision for the 'deserving' unmarried mother would garner the right sort of social solidarity.

Imagining the unmarried mother

In conceiving of a community of interdependent social relationships, the five-minute broadcast included a detailed portrait of an 'unmarried mother'. 'Let us try to imagine for a moment', Fisher announced, 'the position of a girl who becomes an unmarried mother':

> She may be only young, ignorant, or irresponsible. She may have been deceived by the child's father. She may be a girl of warm feelings and ill trained, through no fault of her own, but through the fault of all of us, who have built up this imperfect civilisation. She may be capable of infinite devotion, and indeed nothing is more remarkable than the way in which so many of these mothers pull themselves together, if only they can be given the chance, and become splendid mothers and self-respecting citizens.
>
> The girl has almost certainly lost her work, and probably has lost it for some little time before the birth of her child. She has used up her savings, she has suffered in health, she has suffered terribly in other ways. Every woman with the least particle of imagination can realise something of what such a girl must have endured, if she comes, as she often does, of decent people. Her child is born in a maternity ward or hospital. When it is but ten days or perhaps a fortnight old, she has to go back to the world, with this helpless, exacting little creature in her

arms, knowing but little of how to care for it, and faced with the problem of earning its living and her own, while she nurses and rears it. What chance has either of them? Is it any wonder that the babies die?[39]

The emphasis at the end of this section of Fisher's talk reinforced how, centrally, the philanthropic practice of the NCUMC was concerned with keeping babies alive. Since 1920, the Infant Life Protection Act (1905) provisions had been implemented with increasing effectiveness, and by 1922 it was regarded as a triumph that most local authority Infant Protection Visitors (instructed under the provisions of the 1908 Children's Act) were women.[40] Yet the language Fisher used continued to stress the urgency of infant life preservation of illegitimate children. Within this context, the organization's communication programme was designed as both a culturally-interventionist and culturally-unifying project. It incorporated the public transfer of knowledge about illegitimacy and the representation of a constructive image of the 'unmarried mother' that could be used to support the goals of infant life preservation within the wider project of social connectedness.

Positive characterizations of the unmarried mother had been attempted before by the NCUMC's press committee, notably in the film *Unmarried*. A melodrama about two unmarried mothers in Derbyshire in the First World War, the film was commissioned and produced by Grangers' Executive in 1920 and featured members of the NCUMC executive committee alongside the star, Gerald du Maurier and up-and-coming actors including American Malvina Longfellow, Mary Glynne, Edmund Gwenn and Constance Backner, wife of the co-writer Arthur Backner (see Fig. 15).[41] Yet tensions remained between the media configuration of the NCUMC's work within the popular innovations of 'dramatic human interest journalism' and melodrama and the organization's claim to facilitate rational and scientific social intervention.[42] In the 1925 BBC appeal, Lettice Fisher evoked the sense of dignity and self-respect of democratic selfhood ('self-respecting citizens') that we have seen was featured widely in the period in the renewed emphasis amongst philanthropists and social commentators upon projects of assisted self-help. Interpreting this practice as primarily an economic one, Fisher directed her appeal to the 'imagina[tive]' identification of a particular group of 'decent' women: the unmarried mother was construed as having been gainfully employed and prudent (she previously had savings), and her child was born in a clean, modern and respectable environment.[43] This storytelling – notable for its emphasis upon domestic economy – deliberately sought an imagined connection between the unmarried mother and the 'respectable' female listener, whilst always appealing to the listener's (self-)perceived social difference. The domestic metaphor

Figure 15. 'A scene from the propaganda film *Unmarried*: Lady Greenwood (wife of Sir Hamar Greenwood), Lord Henry Cavendish Bentinck (in the chair), Mr Gerald du Maurier', reproduced in *The Sketch*, 11 Feb.1920, 227. Copyright, Illustrated London News Ltd/Mary Evans Picture Library. Reproduced with the permission of the Mary Evans Picture Library.

was developed in the plot of *Unmarried*, which followed the heroine, Mary Myles, making the personal, social and moral journey from unmarried mother to her work as an orderly nurse. Viewed from one perspective, the NCUMC's messages applied a reformulated framework of personal 'deservingness' that had framed the policy of poverty relief in the nineteenth century and which continued to direct popular notions of charitable support.[44] They also suggested the comparatively privileged social status of those listeners who donated to the appeals, building on the technique of constructing identification with difference that framed the ambitions for cultural interconnectedness of early broadcasters more generally in this period.[45] Lettice Fisher played further with the vocabulary of identification in a February 1931 BBC talk, 'The baby's point of view', which inaugurated a new NFWI wireless series, entitled 'Other people's standpoints'.[46]

The gendered constituency of the radio audience emerged as an issue for especial consideration in the interwar period in the construction of identification between the broadcaster and listener of charity broadcasts. In one respect, the NCUMC's work offered a subtle challenge to the established perspectives of advertisers and psychologists whom Elspeth Brown has observed in late-nineteenth- and early-twentieth-century America 'shifted their model of the typical consumer from "rational man" to "emotional woman"'.[47] In placing the emphasis upon the perceived rationalism of women listeners' engagement, the NCUMC's 1925 broadcast aligned with the feminist politics that Lettice Fisher advanced more broadly in her journalism and writing of the period. However, subsequent charity appeals framed the subject of identification differently in order to stretch to a wider audience. In a *Week's Good Cause* broadcast in May 1930, the NCUMC Vice-President and future Prime Minister, Neville Chamberlain appealed to women listeners to compare the opportunities they had (as children and mothers) with those of the unmarried mother and her illegitimate child, but urged men to donate out of a communal sense of responsibility for selfish behaviour.[48] Here, female listeners were encouraged to identify with the unmarried mother, whereas male listeners were appealed to through a sense of difference (individual and collective) to men who had fathered illegitimate children. Neville Chamberlain's broadcast was the most successful national appeal at that point in the NCUMC's history, and raised £463.[49] Yet it was nowhere near as successful as the charity's BBC radio appeal of autumn 1936, broadcast by the theatre and film actor, Cyril Maude.[50] Adopting a similar tone to early press publicity defending the NCUMC's policy, Maude stressed that contrary to the high-minded assumptions of some commentators, 'we are not encouraging immorality!'[51] The appeal raised £1,502.10.6.[52] It is unclear whether the results of these appeals point to the limitations of a gendered segregated marketing policy; to a public that was simply more willing to donate to the cause in 1936 (than 1930) amidst signs of economic recovery following the Slump; the rhetoric of the NCUMC's moral work; or to the particular 'microphone personality' making the appeal. But NCUMC personnel continued to engage, and experiment, with the terms of the celebrity and broadcasting markets throughout the interwar period. Educating the public in the necessity and value of a constructive approach to unmarried mothers and their children demanded a strategic communication policy. It involved addressing the public as both rational and emotional beings.

Cultural diplomacy: communicating international expertise

The interwar period witnessed the emergence of public relations in Britain in the increasingly systemized attempts of private and public sector organizations to manage the media. The demands initiated by the First World War had provided one important impetus, as an infrastructure of public information services was expanded to facilitate communication to national and imperial citizens.[53] Taking hold first in the Civil Service, public relations was initiated in this period also under the alternative names of 'personal relations' and salesmanship to formulate the expanding bases of state social provision and interventionism which it was felt were too harshly bureaucratized to be expanded.[54] Scott Anthony has argued that public servants pioneered a distinctively British form of public relations (itself rooted in a 'Victorian philanthropic ethos') that diffused useful knowledge to the public, as well as favourable images of a diverse yet united nation. In this interpretation, early public relations in Britain was a form of activism opposed to the corporatist mentality of American public relations, and can be seen itself as an educative mode that combined philanthropic principles with a belief in the efficacy of managing scientific and cultural knowledge.[55] A central controversy within interwar public relations was how to distil the ethics of social responsibility. One aspect of this debate emerged around the discussion between the vocabularies of 'projection' and 'propaganda'.[56] In the interwar years, the term propaganda became increasingly morally and politically freighted against the backdrop of European fascism and communism and in the light of revelations about the distortions of publicity during the First World War, for example over the issue of America's entry into the war. Internationally, this was a period which saw the development of alternative propaganda formats for cultivating informational influence, ranging from formal policy settings, media outputs and wider scholarship.[57] In Britain, the 1930s, specifically, as scholars have argued, was a critical decade in the development of the idea of 'national projection', itself a tool of political and cultural diplomacy.[58] The debates centred around the governing elites' recognition of a new model of active citizenship that was maturing between the wars, in which the nature of the relationship between citizen and state needed to be reconfigured along with its form.

In the interwar years, the term 'propaganda' was also used to describe examples of philanthropic enterprise. In 1938 Constance Braithwaite discussed the range of 'international philanthropy' activities, from 'voluntary financial contributions and voluntary personal service to propaganda activities [which] should be regarded as types of philanthropy'.[59] Other commentators in this period maintained the potential for international philanthropic projects, including those led by women, to be recognized, themselves, as a mode of propaganda. The feminist Ray Strachey described the Fight the Famine Council (established in 1919), the organization that would become the SCF, as 'an organization for investigation and propaganda'.[60] Strachey framed Fight the Famine's work in a similar narrative to the one Lettice Fisher had used to discuss the early communication work of the NCUMC, as having faced 'much prejudice and opposition' in its first years, and women like Eglantyne Jebb had to find the energy to press on and formulate a more attractive, or at least publicly palatable, message about the cause.[61] The conjunction of philanthropy, politics and cultural diplomacy was critical to these communication practices; during the First World War, Jebb helped her sister, Dorothy Buxton, in editing her weekly column, 'Notes from the Foreign Press' in the *Cambridge Magazine*.[62] Ray Strachey identified nationalistic propaganda was a key driver of SCF communications in the interwar years, which pivoted on a particular vision of social responsibility: an imperialist humanitarian project, spearheaded by a self-consciously British citizenry.[63] Strachey observed that press campaigns were vital to the effectiveness of the SCF's early work, but the challenge of retaining public interest increased following the resolution of the initial crises: she wrote that once 'the sensational period of horrors and emergencies was over ... the task was very hard'.[64]

The foreign policy expert

Muriel Paget's connection with the SCF is interesting in relation to the developing formulations of philanthropic practice around contemporary communications expertise and understandings of propaganda. Although as we have seen, the SCF initially provided substantive funding for Paget's Mission to Eastern Europe,[65] the organization cut off its support in 1922 amidst the perception of the 'political' drivers of Paget's relief work.[66] It is possible that Paget's personal friendships, for example, with the Masaryk family in Czechoslovakia, were deemed to compromise the integrity of humanitarian agencies' independence in these geographical and political fields. But it is instructive to consider the ways in which the break might also have reflected a divergence in the SCF's and Muriel Paget's respective communication policies. As leader of the SCF, Eglantyne Jebb was reported to have said that she dedicated all her time in the organization giving public talks for fundraising campaigns; though also as a marker of a particular sort of femininity, she reported that friends told her she was very poor at doing so.[67] By contrast, in the interwar years Muriel Paget's reputation was developed through her public authority on international relations on various public stages. Although the work was not necessarily vitally different from Jebb's, Paget actively embraced opportunities for the political extension of the philanthropic realm far beyond the practices of fundraising and the immediate marshalling of support for a cause. She was not self-effacing in the process.

In the late 1920s a series of experts recognized Muriel Paget's role in cultural diplomacy as a tool for the developing study of foreign policy in Anglo-Soviet relations. In 1929 Paget was invited to give talks at the IDC (Imperial Defence College) and in 1930 at Chatham House. Paget used these platforms to develop arguments about the commercial and political bases of relations between Britain and the Soviet Union. The notes for her talk to the IDC in 1929 included a schema of recent political and economic developments that cut across the chronologies of elite opinion of Soviet history.[68] Paget went on to discuss the growth of 'Soviet patriotism' that had been building since 1922 and the 'nascent nationalism' in Poland, Finland, Georgia and the Ukraine as economic strategies, rather than ideological separatism. Her argument was focused on commercial and trading relations between Britain and Russia since the ending of the Anglo-Soviet Trade Agreement in 1921 and the monopoly of foreign trade held by the Soviet government. Muriel Paget intended to make three claims in the talk for the future success of British trade with the Soviet Union: firstly, it was possible for a country to trade with Soviet Russia without its national government having accorded recognition to the Soviet government; secondly, recognition of the Soviet government would not guarantee foreign trade; and finally if diplomatic relations were established between a nation and the Soviet Union any subsequent rupture of those relations would entail the loss of a large proportion of, if not its total, trade arrangements.[69] Despite a number of authorities disputing Muriel Paget's diplomatic effectiveness, what is of interest here is precisely the acknowledgement of her public authority for making these statements by organizations such as the IDC.[70] The IDC legitimated within the field of international relations the translation and extension of Paget's expertise from her philanthropic practice on the ground to the wider political and diplomatic experience that she herself continued to seek out within the philanthropic realm. Emphasizing once more the importance of this process, in November 1932 Paget would visit Leningrad again in connection with work for the BSRRA and recorded for her London committee her observations of 'temporary anti-British feeling' on the termination of the Anglo-Soviet Trade Agreement of 1930.[71]

The notes for Muriel Paget's talk at Chatham House in 1930 illuminate further her appropriation of the field of international relations and foreign policy as a vehicle for shaping her reputation as an expert upon Russian politics.[72] Emphasizing the economic hardships of the Russian population, she tackled critical perspectives on Russia, stating that the country was at war 'against principles rather than nationalities', and that the Russian youth were committed to developing a new nationality no more or less than young people in the recently formed states in Central and Eastern Europe.[73] In discussing her relationship to the Soviet authorities, Paget also deliberately inferred her knowledge from the inside of the Soviet regime. It is notable that she only stressed the most constructive parts of that working relationship (and not the more restrictive ones). She talked about the amicable relations she had enjoyed in her 'direct dealings' with Soviet ministers, including the Minister of Health, Nikolai Semashko in her work for child welfare, and the support of the Soviet government over the building of the *dacha* in Sosnovka for the BSRRA. She did not note her own feelings that at various points she had been suspect with the Soviet authorities: she thought this was likely in 1922 when, following her communications with the acting Commissar of Education, V. Maximovsky about the potential plans to establish a Child Welfare Unit in Bzuluk in the Volga region that had been hit hard by famine, her proposals were refused.[74] In late 1932, during her visit to Russia in connection with the BSRRA, Muriel Paget would become convinced that she was being tracked by the Soviet intelligence service.[75] In her emphases upon her positive relations with Soviet authorities, Paget's political presentation in the Chatham House talk modified the notion that the propagandist model of international philanthropy was characterized by *circumvention* of the ideologies of state governance, and the formulation of an alternative international-mindedness framed by the sympathetic social convictions of individuals that spanned geographical or cultural boundaries.[76] The route that Paget laid out here was a much more direct and proactive one. Propaganda work, as a form of international-mindedness, for Paget meant actively cooperating with, if not infiltrating, state systems. Her argument, set out through practical example, was for the sorts of extensive political influence that were made possible through the 'mixed economy of humanitarianism'.

A lecture tour

As we have seen, in the early-twentieth century Muriel Paget was a celebrated figure in brokering a romanticized and historicized notion of Russian identity to British audiences.[77] This work was, itself, international in its reach. In early January 1927 it took her to New York to begin a three-month lecture tour, where she would give nineteen lectures in fourteen American cities across the East Coast and Midwest with the aim of reanimating American interest in Russian society and politics.[78] Muriel Paget steered clear of offering overt political critiques in this tour. Rather she sought to reorientate discussion away from wholly negative portraits of Sovietization; as she explained to the agents of the

Foreign Press Service, Paul Kennaday and Arthur Livingstone in 1927 in a resonant biblical idiom, she intended her media interventions to educate the American public in a portrait of Russia as a 'land of promise'.[79] This sort of cultural diplomacy, working to educate audiences in a constructive social and political message, had parallels with the media engagements undertaken by Lettice Fisher in Britain in connection with the NCUMC in challenging social attitudes towards unmarried mothers. Like Fisher, Muriel Paget combined imaginative characterizations of Russian people and society with claims for her acquisition of scientific data about life in contemporary Russia. For example, in a talk to expatriate American women at the American Women's Club in London in December 1930, Paget argued that deteriorating food conditions in Russia was the outcome of Soviet government policy (the first Five Year Plan), which classified citizens via dietary requirements.[80] Discussing nutrition – a subject she had not addressed in the formal international relations talks in Britain – was doubly purposeful for this audience: it played to a gendered discourse which configured women as managers of family nutrition within the domestic economy and it reaffirmed Paget's particular authority in establishing international feeding programmes. More than this, such a practical, political project was a way of advancing a more subtle form of propaganda against the Soviets that rethought the popular critique of 'cut throats' in a message about the sincerity of the government's aims, no matter how ruthless the means.

Constructing celebrity

Muriel Paget hired the services of the lecture agent, William Feakins to coordinate her lecture tour in America. Feakins, who specialized in promoting writers of non-fiction, history, education, music and poetry was contracted by a range of distinguished international figures in the 1920s to develop and extend their public profile.[81] Certainly, William Feakins' publicity for Paget's tour affirmed her celebrity status within the commercial literary marketplace. The brochure for his winter 1925–6 programme advertised Paget as the star speaker in an international line-up including author, Mary Agnes Hamilton, Congregationalist minister, Dr. Charles F. Aked, poets DuBose Heyward and Joseph Auslander, and wife of the Estonian Minister to London, Madame Aino Kallas. It described Paget as a 'fascinating speaker' with 'experiences [that] are as exciting as romance'.[82] The 'romance' genre was particularly well suited to the processes of commodification used to develop celebrity persona in the interwar period. On the one hand, it embodied the sort of blending of fact and fiction that Michael Saler has described as amounting to the 'spectacularization of culture'.[83] Moreover, Alison Light has argued that, while romance writing was traditionally gendered female, the genre was repurposed between the wars to become more closely associated with the sorts of sentimental femininity of the 1920s Hollywood film industry, and thus critiqued by consciously 'progressive' female writers and their middle-class readers.[84] Light observes that at stake in these debates over 'romance' were the gendered and social codes against which women in the public sphere were to be categorized and their status measured. William Feakins' publicity fitted Paget within the mould of a 'modern' kind of romance that once again complicated a straightforward reading of philanthropy as feminine and emotional. Shown in her portrait photograph in the brochure as a glamorous but serious-minded looking woman, dressed in a chiffon blouse and pearls, audiences were promised that Muriel Paget would address them based upon extraordinary personal experience rather than emotionality.

Muriel Paget's hiring of a literary publicist indicates her recognition of the role of media and literary professionals in mediating distinctive vernacular emphases of cultural diplomacy in the post-war years. It also points to the significance of her public reputation in the developing international discourses of wartime memory. The formulation of American memory of women's war work at this point was a central component of Paget's transatlantic cultural authority and celebrity. William Feakins' advertising literature painted a commercial gloss over the veil of public authority that was confirmed in the apparently informational logic of Muriel Paget's talks within this context of war work: 'Women's work in war and reconstruction', 'Episodes of the Russian debacle and revolution' and 'Russia and Central Europe'.[85] The titles of the talks demonstrate a conscious positioning of Paget's interventions within the sphere of foreign affairs: Muriel Paget had been to Leningrad and Moscow again in the summer of 1926, when she had done work, and gained more publicity, on behalf of the BSRRA. When Muriel Paget's biographer Wilfrid Blunt wrote about her 1927 American lecture tour he described it as a 'failure' because Paget was unwilling to meet the demands of her audiences for gossip about the British royal family and high society.[86] Publicity about Muriel Paget in the American press suggests, however, that her expertise and experience in wartime were foregrounded in this period as a vehicle for the articulation of English exceptionalism as a marker of her celebrity, defined in terms of the sorts of civilized interventionism she carried out as an elite Englishwoman. In March 1927, the *New York Herald Tribune* described Paget as 'a far sighted, tolerant, intelligent citizen of the world, such as old England produces so successfully'.[87] Future First Lady Eleanor Roosevelt was by 1927 being proclaimed a public champion of Muriel Paget's and lent her weight to organizing Paget's American trip.[88] It is arguable, therefore, that by 1927 William Feakins was more confident of the viability of claiming Paget's expertise for an American public as exemplification of English women's war work and felt it less imperative to position her within the parameters of an explicitly commercial model as emphatically as he had done the previous year. Her talks were by then advertised more stringently within the model of experiential authority; as the brochure read, Muriel Paget would address her audience 'based on her experiences in founding and operating the Anglo-Russian Hospitals and the Lady Muriel Paget Missions in Estonia, Latvia, Lithuania, Czecho-Slovakia and Roumania [sic]'.[89]

Human-interest journalism

Back in Britain in 1927, Muriel Paget further experimented with the blending of celebrity status and the cultural authority derived from her humanitarian work in Russia in the series of newspaper articles she was commissioned to write for the *Daily Telegraph*. Her visit to Leningrad in 1926, together with her fundraising drive for the BSRRA (which raised £2,000), provided the immediate contexts for this journalism.[90] In the articles, entitled 'Some Pictures of Russia', Paget assumed the role of participant journalist in reports about the Russian Revolution; life in 1920s Moscow and Leningrad; schooling; healthcare; and homelessness amongst children. Some articles seemed to be written primarily with a political purpose: in the first in the series, Paget wrote that revolution could never be justified, but '[a]t the same time, one can have great sympathy with the nation to whom these things have happened'.[91] Others were more explicitly geared to elicit the reader's psychological response, if not rhetorically geared to shock; thus as well as discovering a trend for Russian school leavers' desires to go to university, Muriel Paget reported evidence about child drug use in Moscow. 'Anitpieff, a boy of 14, was asked why he had started snuffing [cocaine]', and Paget interpreted through a language of psychology: 'he said, "It is our habit – everyone snuffs, so why should not I? We always want to do what others do. If one of us is eating a cake the others must also go and get a cake. We always imitate each other"'.[92] This story was not a media scoop: fiction in the 1920s portrayed drug use (most commonly cocaine and opium) amongst Russian students, the intelligentsia and gangs of homeless children.[93] Rather, in making these claims to knowledge about Russian children's drug addictions, Muriel Paget was tapping into a popular narrative of the period for a British audience, whilst also claiming authority for a modern philanthropic project that was rooted in the logic of personal relationships in combination with scientific expertise.[94] In this respect, the veracity of these comments was not as important as the publicity that they generated. Muriel Paget's selection of both the subjects for the narrative and the styles of reporting channelled a journalistic mode through which she self-consciously commodified her own philanthropy.

The interwar popularity of the human-interest genre explains to a large extent the particular development of Muriel Paget's communication strategies in these articles. In coming to dominate the British popular press in the period, human-interest journalism was typically associated with sensationalism and with a collapsing of the boundaries between public and private life.[95] The media interest in Muriel Paget's sensational storytelling is shown in 1927 in a *Manchester Guardian* report of a talk that she had given at a London meeting of the Societies for Cultural Relations.[96] The journalist began by reporting Paget's description of the relief work she had done in Russia since 1922 and outlined her aims to maintain cultural links between Britain and Russia. His main focus, however, was upon the tone of Muriel Paget's talk (which he described as 'full of human touches'), reporting her story about a Russian maternity hospital where a baby had been killed by a rat, and evoking a heart-rending portrait of the 3,000 'wild children' who were orphaned in the 'revolutionary war'.[97] The emphasis placed in the report upon the 'heart-felt' aspects of Paget's talk suggests her success in relating both her public image and philanthropy to the sorts of narrative techniques of human-interest journalism. This mode of journalism, specifically, held the scope to marshal public communication strategies both for the purposes of garnering individual celebrity status and for extending social effects.[98] The *Manchester Guardian* article positioned a critical link between reporter and celebrity: the journalist recognized that the readership would be moved by the representation of Muriel Paget's emotive speech.[99] In this regard, the two functions of the human-interest device came together to extend the significance of Paget's philanthropic practice as a combination of celebrity and social activism. While this publicity reinforced her status around the terms of sensational public interest, it also therefore played a critical role in modelling her public communication within the philanthropic goal for social connectedness.

The visceral logic of public communication

In integrating celebrity and social activism in their public personae, female philanthropists were themselves important figures in the interwar communications economy. As developments and techniques in mass culture and other forms of popular cultural production proliferated in the interwar period, philanthropists saw both an opportunity to appropriate communication models that were being successfully applied in consumer contexts and the need to refine these models in conformity with more explicitly social goals. In some cases, the synergies of their performances with the sorts of strategies developed in public relations that manoeuvered around the logics of the market and managerialism, were foregrounded. However, female philanthropists continued to develop broader and more varied forms of dramatic storytelling and performance to position their practice within popular realms of affect. Melodrama, in particular, was established from the mid-nineteenth century as a dramatic form that could enable societies to confront social and moral questions, presenting what Lynn Williams has defined as recognition of the virtue of 'victim-heroes'.[100] It was a favoured mechanism of philanthropists' affective work.

Giving as self-denial

The conjunction of such devices of storytelling and publicity can be seen in the Salvation Army UK's appeal in 1937 for which Evangeline Booth was the figurehead. The *Will You Help?* appeal campaigned to raise £75,000 for the forthcoming year's social work amongst children and poor mothers, the elderly, homeless and unemployed. Publicity literature contained statistics of the scale of deprivation which the Salvation Army was addressing in Britain in its 147 Homes and Institutes and 44 'Slum Posts'; in 1936 Salvation Army Motor Kitchens distributed 19,433 hot meals and 28,925 gallons of soup; 55,065 subsidized meals; tea and coffee were freely distributed to 8,956 people waiting outside Labour Exchanges; and over one million free or farthing meals were served up in poor areas in North England and Wales.[101] Statistics were only the starting point for this appeal, however, which was framed explicitly around a call for affective response. The quantitative evidence of need (and demand) was given a human face in the literature through a series of 'success stories' of the Salvation Army's interventions in which the affective pull of the story fell back upon the organization's established models of communications. In 'Homes are crashing every moment', readers learnt of an 'exemplary wife' who, through grief at her husband's hanging for murder, tried to kill herself and her two children, but with the assistance provided by accommodation in Salvation Army hostels and holiday homes, restored herself to health and happiness and established a new family home on a farm.[102] The extension of the familial and domestic idiom, in this example through the use of the melodramatic mode, was a central framing device of the organization's public message.

The factual or representational accuracy of the 'Homes crashing every moment' story is not verifiable, but I suggest that in any case its significance for the historical record lies elsewhere. It raises critical questions about the visceral effects of communication for philanthropic organizations. How did philanthropists make people feel, rather than simply desire? How did they connect up the project of psychological transformation and social connectedness? The focus on the affective dimensions of donors' experiences of giving remains a central feature of charity fundraising campaigns, and already by the early-twentieth century many organizations were using well-developed mechanisms aiming to achieve such response.[103] An established vehicle for this project within the Salvation Army was what became known early on as 'self-denial' activities. The Salvation Army organized its first 'Self-denying week' in September 1886, when members were asked to give up something for seven days and give the money they saved to the organization; the device became a publicity tool and a key annual fundraising drive. Deborah Cohen has argued that the 'self-denial week', introduced in the 1860s by Thomas Barnardo to raise money for his orphanages, inaugurated a new fundraising approach which popularized the notion that self-denial could be contained within a week, rather than the lifetime's work that a strict personal faith required.[104] By the late-nineteenth and early-twentieth century, public practices of self-denial were closely associated with gendered models of campaigning. Historians have noted the influence of the practice upon the Edwardian suffrage movement's fundraising activities: the Women's Social and Political Union organized a Self-Denial Week scheme beginning in February 1908. Furthermore, self-denial would become a broader critical register of the public campaigning of the suffrage movement in the years leading up to the First World War through the reports of the hunger-striking and force-feeding of imprisoned suffragettes.[105]

Salvation Army publicity continued to imagine the direct association of women and self-sacrifice throughout the interwar period as a mechanism for galvanizing collective social behaviour. An article in the *Daily Mirror* in February 1935 promoting the Salvation Army's annual self-denial appeal reimagined the connection under the light-hearted heading, 'Salvation in a poke bonnet'.[106] Written by the *Daily Mirror*'s feature editor, Basil Nicholson, the article used the gendered conceit of self-sacrifice as a vehicle to envisage a wider set of interconnected social relations. The ideal of self-sacrifice, originally conceived as part of a well-spent Christian life, was refined as a model of inter-class relations that encouraged readers to respect 'the poor's' knowledge and experience (in subheadings such as 'The poor know best'), and to view their own compassion as a marker of social solidarity. As we have seen in many examples throughout this book, identities of difference were not eradicated in the message of philanthropic connection. In this example, self-sacrifice was to be the basis for social connectedness that worked precisely because of the assumed sense of social and cultural distance between the newspaper's lower-to-middle-class readership and the poor as well as the reader and the Salvation Army men and women: '[w]e can all smile', Nicholson wrote, 'if realities seem distant enough to us, at the crudities of the Banner and the tambourines and the poke-bonnets of Salvation … But when we look into our own hearts we will give – or hold back – according to how much good will we find there!'[107] The Salvation Army's campaign was framed in the popular press to engage potential donors in a *moral* encounter with the poor that configured psychological proximity as compatible with social and cultural distance and judgement about the donor's self-perceived 'goodness'. In this respect, the newspaper acknowledged the coexistence of practices of consumption and giving by focusing the message of the appeal on whether the reader deserved his or her money more than the poor and the Salvation Army did. Evidently having some fun in playing with these themes, alongside Nicholson's article, the *Daily Mirror* inset an advertisement for Brand's A1 sauce next to an anecdote about a man who had gone without pudding for a year in order to give to the self-denial appeal.[108]

Performance and personality

Within Salvation Army traditions women played a distinctive, if controversial, role in the drama of public communications, and not only the self-denial schemes. Pamela Walker has observed that the organization's encouragement of women preachers dressed in uniforms, singing and playing musical instruments was 'shocking' to a nineteenth-century public.[109] However, in common with other nineteenth-century nonconformist denominations that allowed women to preach, Salvation Army leaders capitalized upon the perceived physical attractiveness of women preachers.[110] Evangeline Booth was no exception, and throughout her career her physical appearance was accorded a central place in her renown for a dramatic style of oratory. She herself frequently rehearsed the story that as a young woman her parents had worried she would leave the Salvation Army in favour of a career on the stage, because of her 'good looks' and 'gift for speaking'.[111] One of her most celebrated public performances was the 'Commander in Rags', when, dressed as her younger self visiting the East London slums in 1880, she enacted the Salvation Army's work with the poor and disadvantaged; when she performed this for a fundraising drive in 1924 it was said to have reduced the audience at the Metropolitan Opera House in New York to tears.[112] Diane Winston has argued that, in translating her work amongst the late-Victorian London poor for a post-war American audience, Booth gave a studied performance of her public persona.[113] The 'Commander in Rags' performance, however, did not simply affirm Evangeline Booth's accommodation to the end products of a celebrity system, focused on the symbolic significance of the commoditized individual. It personified the sort of visceral public preaching around which the Salvation Army constructed the theatre of the charitable encounter for affective response.[114] As Booth emphasized in a talk in 1921 accepting an honorary MA at Tufts University, dressing in rags as she did as a young woman preaching in the East End slums, enabled her to reach the 'bodies and souls of men' in the 'lowest and darkest places'.[115]

Contemporary writers reported Evangeline Booth's repertoire of visceral public expression as a mix of gendered performance styles. Muriel Harris, who wrote a book in 1935 on the preaching styles of popular religious figures, observed Booth's oratory as 'partly muscular'; during addresses her hand would sometimes quiver, other times she would strike her breast with her fist.[116] Other commentators acknowledged the tension in Booth's presentational style between natural and contrived performance. One critique, which focused on the didacticism of her interventions, emerged in a feature on her retirement in autumn 1939 in the British patriotic magazine, *John Bull*. Journalist Hannen Swaffer wrote about Booth in his 'Who's Who' column as 'eloquent' in platform speeches, but 'histrionic' in rehearsed performances.[117] Swaffer expressed admiration for the 'phrase after phrase [that] falls naturally from [Booth's] lips' in speeches but critiqued her 'wisecracks', her overstressed performances like the 'Commander in Rags', and set-pieces like the World's Romance. (Booth used the same title for a popular talk she first gave in 1922. In a later wireless version she elaborated the literary qualities of the description of the Salvation Army as '[t]he world's greatest romance' as a 'bold and startling statement', but one which conveyed its history as 'a wondrous, chivalrous, adventurous, and mysterious tale'.[118]) It is notable that in the interwar years Salvation Army leaders tended to be characterized as 'an interesting group of religious personalities', but British journalists in this period singled out Evangeline Booth's unusually 'magnetic personality' as a religious preacher.[119] Swaffer considered the distinctive emotional impact of Evangeline Booth's performances: he wrote that she had 'much more personality' than her predecessors, Bramwell Booth or General Higgins (whom she succeeded); '[e]ven when chatting to one man she can be as dramatic and compelling with her words as when she is swaying an audience'.[120]

It was precisely the recognition of Evangeline Booth's efficacy in these methods, framed both by the unequal distortions in the psychological power of her communication as we have seen, and the dramatic emphases of her performance, that Hannen Swaffer criticized. Contrasting the Salvation Army's praxis to trades unions' campaigns for higher wages for East London workers and the late 1930s Labour Party's commitment to a programme of slum clearance, he wrote: 'I told her [Booth] that I believed more in a New London than in an Old London with a bun, a cup of coffee and a hymn – that, in my view, people should have food and shelter as a right and not because of charity'.[121] Hymn singing and refreshments – the 'crudities' of the work that Basil Nicholson had described in the *Daily Mirror* feature on the 1935 'Self-denial' campaign – were a carefully choreographed part of the Salvation Army's social work from its foundation in the 1860s and 1870s, and a means of reaching out to poor city men and women, who in non-work time sought avenues for popular entertainment.[122] Hannen Swaffer's rhetoric configured the Salvation Army's brand of social work between the wars as little changed from the missionary and geographical framework of this early activity, and thus at odds with the models of social engagement that the emerging interwar social democratic discourse claimed was appropriate for a model of mass representation: one that was to be supported effectively not by charity but friendship.[123] Yet Salvation Army literature of the period reveals the organization shaping the shifting idiom of social welfare in these political directions, too. Its interwar practices of communication show how the repurposing of older messages of moral uplift and support remained an audible voice in this discussion. In the pamphlet for the 1937 *Will You Help?* appeal, Booth specified that she wanted to see a 'Home-to-save – homes' established in every large town, in which mothers and children could be provided shelter and support 'without questions' that smacked too much of social and moral investigation. Contrary to Swaffer's critique, organizational literature presented this practice as wholly compatible with the sorts of inspiration that had animated the organization's work since its mid-nineteenth-century beginnings. As the pamphlet maintained, in the modes of non-judgemental welfare provision the Salvation Army claimed to offer, men and women would be supported to rebuild family life by '[r]oad-makers, experienced and filled with the practical compassion of Jesus Christ'.[124]

Embodying competence

As the first woman leader of the Salvation Army, Evangeline Booth contributed seminally to the shifting public idiom of female social activism between the wars in ways that both played upon her talents for performance and the authenticity that could be derived from the example of her personality. Evangeline Booth's *body* (and voice) was also recognized as a vital aspect of the organization's public communication strategy in this period, and a focus upon the ways her body was discussed opens up further complexities in the terms through which the competencies of female philanthropists were projected in the era. Specifically, the public discussion that centred around Booth's body shows how her appropriation of public authority as World General tested the association of women's philanthropic practice with commonplace feminine codes. The very moment of her accession as General highlighted the difficulty. A front-page article in the *Daily Mirror* in September 1934 featured a photograph of Booth shaking the hand of Commissioner Larson, the President of the High Council of the Salvation Army in front of a group of (all male) members of the High Council. The article went on to describe Booth's 'hatless' appearance and 'her light brown hair'; '[s]he stood as erect as a solider on parade while she spoke in a voice vibrating with emotion and shook hands with the journalists nearest her and said to them: "God bless you"'.[125] The *Daily Mirror* article fitted Evangeline Booth into the modes of 'set-drama' that Hannen Swaffer would later critique and the modes of delivery Muriel Harris would observe. However, it also contained her within additionally gendered models of communication through emphasizing her physicality, including her hands and hair. The focus on Evangeline Booth's physical characteristics in the article worked in part to legitimize her public authority as World General, but this in subtle ways also positioned the work as radicalizing the traditions of female social activism within the organization. Evangeline Booth's light brown hair, emphasized by her being hatless, was in sharp relief both against the fashion within the organization for women members to wear hats as a way to better identify with poor women and against the article's description of the 'grey-headed leaders of the Army', the male High Council members who had elected her.[126]

In Victorian and Edwardian Britain, the fragility of women's bodily strength was a familiar conceit that assigned moral strength to women in the public sphere. Gendered ideals of social service presented the social work commitments of notable figures such as Josephine Butler and Florence Nightingale as embodying a concern for others that extended a supererogatory sublimation of personal physical needs.[127] An article in the *Manchester Guardian* in November 1936 focused attention on this theme in a report of Evangeline Booth's forthcoming world tour. Listing the extensive five-month itinerary, which would see Booth visiting China, India, Japan, Korea, Malay and the United States, the article observed that she was 'thinner and rather more frail' than when she had been elected World General in late 1934, but that 'she did not look a day older', and she 'talked energetically about her plans for the future'.[128] The emphasis placed upon Evangeline Booth's physical appearance represented a strategic opportunity within which to claim gendered forms of public dedication, expertise and fitness, framed specifically around the image of Booth's ageing and over-worked body as a sign of spiritual strength. Indeed, it seemed at times in the mid-to-late 1930s that Evangeline Booth was in the news as often for being ill – and sometimes only for the suspicion of illness – as for her robust activism. Yet the attention given to Evangeline Booth's body as a symbol for affective response was also configured in terms that challenged older rhetorical emphases upon feminine frailty. In his sympathetic biography, P. W. Wilson described Evangeline Booth at victory parades in France following the First World War in terms which focused attention upon the movement and position of her body as she marched alongside Marshal Foch, General Pershing and Earl Haig, 'a soldier amid the soldiers – as erect, as correct in her military bearing as they were'. Here was an attempt to convey Booth's status through an alternative image to feminine frailty, one that came closer to the traditions of male affective power through focusing upon bodily demeanour, though it would not be sustained. Just two pages later, Wilson reverted to using the domestic imagery of 'the angel of the slums' to characterize Evangeline Booth's work in reaching out to the public, where she 'first won millions of hearts'.[129] Moreover, Booth's letter to Frank O. Salisbury about the 'comeliness' of her portrait continued to suggest the significance of her attractive physical embodiment of religious authority to her own sense of self.

Religious selfhood, for women, retained a central tension between ideas of attractiveness, beauty and spiritual commitment and this, too, was a model used in publicity by and about Evangeline Booth to explore and challenge gendered codes of competency. In *Woman* (1930), Booth wrote that beauty was not about the 'lottery' of outer appearance but rather reflected the 'inner' qualities of love.[130] This comment, in part invoking historical Christian teaching about vanity, was also rooted within specific historical contexts and was a critique in the interwar period, specifically, of consumption and the burgeoning mass market in which young women were increasingly using cosmetics.[131] Evangeline Booth justified wearing make-up and a wig at this stage in life because of illness and age. Young women, whose inner grace she insisted was reflected outwardly, had no need to fall for the allure of the market. Yet, there was yet another twist within her communication strategy. Her comments were not meant to dismiss Salvation Army women's attractiveness. Indeed, being attractive was a marker of the effectiveness of her own performance, signalled by the apparent fear of her parents that as a younger woman she would leave the organization for the stage. More generally it was attested in the many media advertisements for Salvation Army campaigns that typically featured imagery of modestly dressed, attractive young women.[132] As the evidence underscores, social activists, like other media and cultural institutions, exploited the commercial power of women's attractiveness in their interwar communication strategies. Even if attractiveness was not to be an explanatory device of women's competency in itself, it was, still, a critical vehicle for public consumption.

Conclusion

Where and how female philanthropists communicated to the public mattered significantly to the calibration of philanthropy in the interwar period. The eighteenth and nineteenth centuries had witnessed the expanding influence of female philanthropy in fields that spanned the public and private and the social and political. By the nineteenth century, the symbiotic relationship between public space and commercial space was also well established, and middle- and upper-class women had come to occupy forms of influence and prestige through the commoditized worlds of fashion and shopping, as well as those of benevolence.[133] Women's autonomy and agency in these spaces was always contested, however, whether through forms of consumer exploitation, or through the rhetorical emphases that positioned philanthropic engagement as domestic occupations as much as public work. In the interwar period, as the mechanisms for the development of celebrity status expanded, female philanthropists combined narratives used in the consumer marketplace with the logics of information and affect. They inhabited public fields spanning the press, the wireless radio, film, politics, policy and the urban centre. Each of these spaces incurred a different set of implications for how, both as women and public figures, female philanthropists communicated with their publics. They actively chose to position themselves and their causes alongside a range of communicative discourses that moved between the spheres of political expertise, popular and media cultures and visceral message.

Evangeline Booth, Lettice Fisher and Muriel Paget provide powerful evidence of the interwar interest in treating philanthropy as a project of communication. Female philanthropists worked in proximity to a range of models of public communication: public relations; diplomacy and international relations; the popular literary market; and the spheres of advertising and publicity. Examining Booth's, Fisher's and Paget's contributions to these cultural realms reveals that female philanthropists were an influential group both enacting and evaluating the impact of technologies for the development of 'connective sociability'.[134] It is not incidental that Evangeline Booth was photographed for Salvation Army publicity sat at a well-appointed desk using the telephone, or that reports of her motorcade tours homed in on imagery not only of the motorcar, but also the loudspeaker – both indicators of the interwar sense in which technology was increasing the speed (and volume) of everyday life.[135] Yet still Evangeline Booth saw the public effectiveness of the drama of envisaging face-to-face encounters between the East London poor and Salvation Army women. The tensions between the sorts of communications practices that were made possible either through personal encounters or the interactivity at a distance that was channelled through new communication technologies placed women's philanthropic practice at the forefront of the developing interwar information economy and the related debates about contemporary vehicles for social connection. As the various examples of Evangeline Booth's publicity infer, female philanthropy was made to invoke forms of moral and political authority that were reincorporated into the modelling of powerfully affective social relationships for which women's expertise continued to be fêted. In this respect, the evidence of female philanthropists' practice once again complicates interpretations of the shaping of modern identity around consumer and individualist cultures. Their communication strategies involved an understanding of the coexistence of cross-class cooperation and community that worked not to counter the logics of the commodity and consumer markets, but to advance the resonance of female social activism and philanthropic practice in conformity with them.

Conclusion

This book has drilled down deeply into the histories of philanthropic practice. The interconnected threads of material action, theoretical engagement and self-reflection that have been examined in this study show how intertwined celebrated philanthropists were in the interwar period with the conflicts of modernity. Philanthropists' contributions as thinkers, as well as practitioners, expanded outwards from their own and varied conceptions of the socially-embedded nature of personal life and within conceptual geographies that moved flexibly between the sites of the local, the national and the global. Appreciating both the trends and idiosyncrasies of these endeavours has required close attention to the registers of language through which the individual philanthropist addressed her publics and herself. My decision to approach the historical record to listen closely to what female philanthropists said, in relation to what they actually were doing, is in constructive dialogue with the paradigm of the 'new' history of welfare that discerns the interactions between poor people and ameliorating institutions as the most significant encounter of the charitable relationship.[1] I agree entirely that '[i]t has been surprisingly easy to forget what the poor say' and that scholarship working to restore the voices of the poor and working classes into the histories of welfare is vital.[2] My book has suggested a pathway for another new history of charity and welfare, one that as importantly seeks to open up discussion about the multiple and varied contributions of 'givers' in the philanthropic relationship. For it has also been far too easy to instrumentalize the contributions of individuals who had the resources – money, time, political, religious or other sorts of conviction – to dedicate to philanthropic work and who chose to do so. I wanted to look at the reflexivity of the philanthropist, her intellectual approach and her philanthropic practice, hoping to find a new way to challenge the stereotyping of the 'Lady Bountiful' or the 'Do-Gooder'. Illuminating female philanthropists' contributions in particular to the interwar politics of social connection, I have hoped to show how the cultural repertoires of philanthropy offered critical models for confronting the social, moral and psychological challenges of a transforming world.

The four women whose stories have been at the heart of this book illustrate how the transformations that were generated and mediated through philanthropic practice were *responses* to interwar modernity not reactions to it. Such responses, of course, took various shapes. In the late-nineteenth century and early-twentieth century public observations of the innovations of modern life ranged from astonishment and wonder to fear.[3] Philanthropists who worked, themselves, within the conditions of modernity, and in the light of its effects, also approached the shifting affiliations and relationships of contemporary society ambivalently but constructively. They recognized in these modern identities and forms opportunities to repurpose and extend earlier methods of charitable effort and benevolence which could be reconfigured for their wider theory work. We have seen, for example, how Muriel Paget advanced the reanimated principle of assisted self-help, first through international humanitarian projects addressing populations displaced by the European conflicts of the Great War and then her London-based charity the IKL, in dialogue with the models of relational behaviour that were appropriated from the new psychological thought into contemporary medical and social discourse. At a wider conceptual level, Lettice Fisher wrote frequently of the principle of the 'elasticity' of voluntary action in the historical and contemporary world. 'Elasticity' (Fisher paired the term with the word 'experimental') indicated the intention for voluntary practice to address the needs and manifestations of social and political change, to remould itself around the shifting shape of social life whilst retaining its essential value.[4] The approach, in other words, was to be a proactive response to debates and ideas of the day.

Philanthropy's responsiveness to the evidence of individuals' shifting relationships to society in the conditions of interwar modernity is also illustrated by female philanthropists' elaboration of methods of political discussion. The women studied in this book legitimized critical examination of interpersonal experience as an approach to understanding the shifting expressions of social and cultural ties that seemed to contemporaries to characterize the period. A striking example is drawn from the archives of the UK YWCA. In the autumn of 1936, an article in the organization's *Blue Triangle Gazette*'s 'Pioneers' page' for young members launched what its authors hoped would become a nationwide discussion in the organization about 'Skin-colour'. The article began by asking readers what World Fellowship Week, practiced since 1904, meant to their group. Encouraging them to see it as a time for 'intelligent thinking about international affairs', it went on to list nine questions that could form the basis for debate, including: '2. What is prejudice? Where do we get our prejudices?'; '4. Can wrong ideas continue when they are contrary to personal experience?'; '6. Why are coloured people often treated so badly in this country? Have you ever met or had anything to do with coloured people? Would you like them to come to your home or to be seen walking in the street with them?'[5] The article was contextualized in the light of recent political episodes and interwar debates about race, whereby allusions to the Japanese Christian pacifist and reformer, Toyohiko Kagawa signalled the YWCA's intellectual positioning within the wider attacks on racism levelled by missionary and Christian groups' writings and activism.[6] The evidence of philanthropy's response to modernity emerges here in the conscious work YWCA leaders were undertaking to facilitate young women's self-development through the encouragement of curiosity and self-questioning in relation to events of the political world. Asking eleven to sixteen year olds about what constituted the sources and actions of their own openness or prejudice prompted questions not only about the cultural forms and educational principles with which young people were familiar, but also how they reflected upon personal feelings and reached out from their interior selves towards engagement in social and political spheres. The expectation that an individual *would* play an active role in society is undoubted in this example; the logic of individual reflexive experience, channelled through the YWCA's practice of group discussion, was to be a critical motor for social action.

My intention in this book has not been primarily to map out the different ways in which female philanthropy did or did not function as a symbol of modernity in the interwar years. Rather I have been interested to trace how individual philanthropists *lived through* the conflicts of modernity. The threads of political, cultural, ethical, social and religious thought that have been followed through Evangeline Booth's, Lettice Fisher's, Emily Kinnaird's and Muriel Paget's stories reveal how the personal and social identities that philanthropists imagined were the product of integrated and socially applied thinking. This process has emerged in the book partly in the evidence of the dialogue between the philanthropic realm and realms beyond philanthropy in which philanthropists claimed experience and expertise. Writing in *Life and Work in England* (1934), Lettice Fisher suggested how her own thinking about community was constituted through her inhabiting simultaneously of the worlds of economic theory, history and philanthropy. She used the conceit of an 'African chief caught by Portuguese explorers' in the sixteenth century – who, transposed into contemporary England (or Britain) exchanged 'neither things nor services, and needs therefore no money' – to debate the meanings of community in relation to the global market economy. This historical character, Fisher wrote, would be as bemused by modern transformations in communications and transport technologies that characterized the contemporary world as he would by how reliant interwar communities were on consuming goods and services that had been produced elsewhere.[7] Fisher's attention to the economic forces of production and consumption was one aspect of her intellectual interest in the functioning of contemporary (and historical) economic and social relationships that she addressed materially through her own voluntary social work enterprises. Other women drew upon alternative theoretical models. As Booth's and Kinnaird's activism has shown, Christian faith continued to provide a critical framework for the development of action and reflexive practice in which the philanthropic realm was a central, though not all-encompassing, aspect of individuals' religious lives.

If Booth's, Fisher's, Kinnaird's and Paget's access to various sites of intellectual, political, social and spiritual authority looks to have been challenged in a British context by the systematization of state administration from the 1940s onwards, this is a reflection of the dominance of interpretative emphases in the history of the politics of welfare which have focused too narrowly upon the question of the shifting national landscape of the voluntary and statutory sectors to the neglect of the consideration of philanthropy and philanthropists' influence upon cultural, ideational and subjective movements.[8] Having revised scholars' earlier concentration upon the fields of the state's influence, historians now emphasize the adaptability of the voluntary sector and voluntary bodies in relation to the growth of the welfare state, and its later rolling back and dismantling, in the twentieth century.[9] The four women's stories have interesting things to say about this evolving, symbiotic relationship. For example, the IKL, for which Muriel Paget worked from its foundation in 1905 until her death, was one of a number of voluntary agencies that gave evidence to William Beveridge's enquiry into voluntary action, published in 1949 as a supplement to his *Report on Voluntary Action as a Means of Social Advance* (Beveridge had submitted his seminal report, *Social Insurance and Allied Services* to the wartime government in 1942).[10] While the IKL, continuing in the mid-twentieth century found its public support waning, its vision of inter-class community relations that sought to secure mutual independence, having been recalibrated in the 1920s, was itself recognized as an important model for community life within shifting political and policy frameworks. In the 1950s the charity received a grant from the LCC to partly fund its work. By 1960, the enterprise, administered by the LCC, would take to the streets to supply meals to the elderly and infirm in their own homes as a meals on wheels service.[11]

This book has explicitly sought to shift the interpretative lens beyond the question of the state/voluntary divide, however, in order to address the depth and breadth of philanthropy's influence upon interwar practices of thought. The wide permeation in the interwar years of the idea of the 'philanthropic relationship' in the media, educational and political discussion offered up distinctive public models for the shaping and interpellating of modern identity and affiliations. The broad contemporary significance of the 'philanthropic relationship' lay in its revelatory power. Ideals of friendship and women's personal service provided in the interwar years routes to the apprehension of personal transformation, social connection and identification across classes and societies in ways that opened up questions about the purpose of interpersonal relationships, the construction of knowledge, new thinking about democracy, the meanings of culture and the project of building public opinion. This is not to say that the material (or the imagined) encounters between the 'giver' and 'receiver' in the philanthropic relationship, or between the philanthropist and her audiences, were free from social and cultural inequalities in this period. Indeed, as has been traced in this book, the behavioural models that contemporaries extrapolated from the examples of female philanthropists' encounters with varied publics show how philanthropy developed currency in fields that stretched far beyond the ethical motors of compassionate response in part because it seemed to offer lessons about the exploitation of differentials of everyday power relationships. Paying attention to interwar critiques of the inequalities that were harboured within the philanthropic exchange can further sharpen our understandings of the historical debates around which philanthropy was accredited meaning and significance. In this period philanthropists' visions for social connectedness were always contested. Many on the political Left remained convinced that inter-class political aspirations could not escape the chauvinism associated with some models of charity, nor reach the principles of solidarity that were perceived to have been achieved authentically only amongst the comradeship and fraternity of the working classes. Women's philanthropy remained for these critics throughout the period an imposition of social and moral capital upon the working class and the poor.[12]

A broad finding of this book has been that philanthropic practice operates as a marker of social and historical change; that philanthropic practice is indicative of wider and shifting historical forces. Operationally, this was illuminated through the gradual, evolving nature of women's philanthropic praxes: female philanthropy was both much more interleaved with, and reflexive of, the forces of (women's) professionalization in nineteenth- and twentieth-century society than is often accepted, notably in its relationship to the specialization of the fields of the social sciences, social work and medicine.[13] Equally, if not more fundamentally, the extra-professional dimensions of the work, and the flexibility with which philanthropy could move beyond the occupational and rhetorical constraints of professions and institutions, rooted its engagement within the spheres of everyday life and individual behaviour; there was no linear shift between amateur and professional practice in this period. The meanings of interwar philanthropy were further drawn in relation to the wider scale of its (geo)political practice. When Evangeline Booth addressed the Lord Mayor's Grocers' Lunch in London in early 1939 against the growing threat of world conflict, she claimed rhetorically that '[t]he Salvation Army took no part in politics'.[14] It was exactly the sort of language that Muriel Paget had used to justify her relief work with children in North Russia in 1920;[15] yet despite the claim to the apolitical stance, Paget's humanitarianism was a deeply politicized project as we have seen in the context of the energy she expended mediating the policies of the Soviet authorities in the 1920s and 1930s. Only two years before the Lord Mayor's event in London, the UK Salvation Army had developed publicity literature for its international appeal, *This Brotherhood of Nations* that re-routed the recognizable imagery of Soviet collectivization to project the pluralism of national traditions and customs that could be brought together in common cause.[16] Studying the language and imagery philanthropists chose to use at various moments and to various audiences – both to claim and disclaim ideological meaning – is therefore critical. Philanthropy was indicative of historical and social change as often when it sought distance from governmental and other expressions of political behaviour as when it embraced them.

The point I think Evangeline Booth was seeking to make in these instances of publicity in the late 1930s was that Christian philanthropy was to be an anchor for the extension of meaningful human relationships within the ideological and social ruptures of the interwar world, and beyond. As I have argued in this book, religious selfhood continued to play a pivotal role in the construction of the meaning of philanthropic practice in the interwar era. Religious thought provided important reference points for the interpretation of philanthropy in a changing world that spoke to the contemporary project of revitalizing enduring social traditions and community work that was pursued both within and beyond a Christian frame. One of the recurring motifs I have been most struck by in the archives and publicity of the women studied in this book was the flame glowing in a lamp or torch. An iteration emerged on Muriel Paget's death in 1938 in her obituary in the *Times*. Paget was commemorated in the article in the still resonant image of Florence Nightingale, as 'the second lady of the lamp', whose qualities would be carried on by others after her death so 'the lamp is always kept burning'.[17] The remit of this publicity, to underscore Muriel Paget's reputation in the field of international female philanthropy, is obvious but is complicated not least through the choice to commemorate her in relation to Nightingale's reputation (including in her work in the Crimea), which by the interwar years had exceeded that of solely 'philanthropist'.[18] What interests me, specifically, is how the metaphor of the lamp was used to imagine philanthropy's revelatory power through the perceived lasting effects of women's philanthropic expression. The YWCA's eightieth anniversary image of the woman in Victorian dress passing a lamp to a young woman of the 1930s placed a similar, multifaceted emphasis. This image signalled how philanthropic practice was used to project ideals of social and psychological connection, here depicted across generations: the lamp was to be passed on from one woman to another.[19] Philanthropy, in this representational logic, was both of the self (a route to individual freedom and self-development) and for the other (symbolizing the practice of rebuilding social ties). The imagery challenges the interpretation of the interwar period as characterized by the popular preoccupation with the interiority of the self.[20] Indeed, in other examples of YWCA literature, the flame and lamp were powerful metaphors of the ideals of interconnection that imagined a distinctive model of social engagement and active citizenship moving outwards from a critically engaged selfhood in a vision of global community. A wartime pamphlet of 1918 produced by the organization made the latter point of integration explicit: '[m]any lamps are stronger than one', it was written: '[o]f course they are! Your small light, flickering and feeble in itself, joined with that of thousands of other girls would become a beacon'.[21]

Philanthropy was a historically-specific endeavour in the interwar years in large part because it was a practice of negotiation between the language of tradition and modernity. The models of philanthropy traced in this book built upon, but redesigned, those of the Edwardian campaigns of women social activists with which scholars are more familiar.[22] The emphases used to illuminate this practice would be disrupted in the middle of the twentieth century through the reconfiguration of social and administrative institutions from the 1940s onwards (though as Beveridge's writings indicate, the reconfiguration was never intended to be a total one). In many ways, the specific conflicts of modernity negotiated by Booth, Fisher, Kinnaird and Paget highlight what were to become the very significant tensions that have accompanied changing approaches to the 'work of care' in the twentieth and twenty-first centuries; changes that have professionalized and to various extents bureaucratized and depersonalized that work. However, the frameworks of social and cultural understanding that female philanthropists shaped in the interwar period, which foregrounded the interpersonal logic of constructive human relationships, appear again highly relevant. Social workers today talk of a 'lost generation' of practitioners who, since the 1980s and 1990s, have been hampered from enacting the methods of relationship-led practice because of the rising demands of case-loads and the pulls of technology.[23] Equally, the trends of globalization, interconnectedness and ready access to information that now influence alternative methods of giving were expressed no less vitally in interwar debates about philanthropy. And cross-sector collaboration, whether a mechanism of the current politics of cost-shifting governments or broader cultural dialogue, requires a decided, and political, willingness to blur the lines between institutions and sectors in a response to society that once again, in a different idiom, calls upon the vital contribution of individual commitment. In looking back upon a period before the cementing, rolling back and now the dismantling of the welfare state in Britain, when models of social action were conceived as moving between self and other and across local, national and transnational fields, we can perceive the threads of a conversation still ongoing about the interrelationship between civic and personal agency. It is most vitally the range and depth of the conversations female philanthropists encouraged in this debate, not only between the voluntary and statutory sectors, but between cultures and peoples and across time and place, that need to be heard.

Notes

Introduction

1 Hyde Park was closed to the public during the General Strike when it was used as a milk distributing centre for London, see *Daily Mail*, 3 May 1926, 8.

2 The British Broadcasting Company (established in 1922) was dissolved on 31 December 1926 and the British Broadcasting Corporation was formed with a royal charter in January 1927. On the role of the BBC in the General Strike see '"100 Voices": History of the BBC, Interview with John Snagge, Part 1', http://www.bbc.co.uk/historyofthebbc/bbc-memories/john-snagge [accessed 28 Mar. 2017].

3 Charles Ferrall and Dougal McNeill, *Writing the 1926 General Strike: Literature, Culture, Politics* (Cambridge: Cambridge University Press, 2015), 43.

4 See e.g. Patricia B. Ardley, 'A Man's Job: They Used To Call It, But Today—', *Woman's Own*, 7 Jan. 1933, 448–9.

5 M. E. Marshall, 'The Health Services', *Our Own Gazette*, May 1926, 7.

6 Seth Koven, *Slumming: Sexual and Social Politics in Victorian Britain* (Princeton: Princeton University Press, 2004); Mark Peel, *Miss Cutler and the Case of the Resurrected Horse: Social Work and the Story of Poverty in America, Australia, and Britain* (Chicago: University of Chicago Press, 2012).

7 My approach therefore differs from studies that have addressed the 'language of charity' primarily to trace philanthropy's influence upon women's civic agency, e.g. Margaret H. Preston, *Charitable Words: Women, Philanthropy and the Language of Charity in Nineteenth-century Dublin* (Westport, CT: Praeger, 2004).

8 Emily Kinnaird, *Reminiscences* (London: Murray, 1925), 114. See also 'Filling Our Purses: by the Hon. Emily Kinnaird – A Wizard At It!', *Blue Triangle Gazette*, June 1935, 89.

9 Patricia Clavin, 'Defining Transnationalism', *Contemporary European History, special issue on 'Transnational Communities in European History, 1920–1970'* 14, no. 4 (2005): 421–39.

10 On domestic service in twentieth-century Britain see e.g. Lucy Delap, *Knowing Their Place: Domestic Service in Twentieth-Century Britain* (Oxford: Oxford University Press, 2011); Alison Light, *Mrs Woolf and the Servants: The Hidden Heart of Domestic Service* (London: Fig Tree, 2007); Selina Todd, 'Domestic Service and Class Relations in Britain, c. 1900–1950', *Past and Present* 203, no. 1 (2009): 181–204. On the relationship between anthropology and imperialism in this period see e.g. Annie

Coombes, *Reinventing Africa: Museums, Material Culture and Popular Imagination in Late Victorian and Edwardian England* (New Haven, CT: Yale University Press, 1994).

11 James Hinton, 'Voluntarism and the Welfare/Warfare State: Women's Voluntary Services in the 1940s', *Twentieth Century British History* 9, no. 2 (1998): 283. See also F. K. Prochaska, *Women and Philanthropy in Nineteenth-century England* (Oxford: Clarendon Press, 1980), 133–4; 223; Jane Lewis, *Women and Social Action in Victorian and Edwardian England* (Aldershot: Elgar, 1991), 24–82; Martha Vicinus, *Independent Women: Work and Community for Single Women, 1850–1920* (Chicago: Chicago University Press, 1985), 215.

12 Peter Brooker has offered one definition of Modernism as a response to these manifold changes: Peter Brooker, 'Afterword: "Newness" in Modernisms, Early and Late', in *The Oxford Handbook of Modernisms* ed. Peter Brooker *et al.* (Oxford: Oxford University Press, 2010), 1031.

13 Anne Olivier Bell ed., *The Diary of Virginia Woolf* (London: The Hogarth Press, 1982) 4:192; 191.

14 Bell, *The Diary of Virginia Woolf*, 4:250.

15 Andreas Huyssen, *After the Great Divide: Modernism, Mass Culture, Postmodernism* (Bloomington: Indiana University Press, 1986), vii–viii.

16 T. J. Jackson Lears, *No Place of Grace: Antimodernism and the Transformation of American Culture 1880–1920* (Chicago: University of Chicago Press, 1994), xvii; 118.

17 Huyssen, *After the Great Divide*, vii.

18 David Trotter discusses the transition from an interest in the sciences of energy to the sciences of information during the interwar years: see *Literature in the First Media Age: Britain Between the Wars* (Cambridge, MA: Harvard University Press, 2013), 22–32.

19 Clare Wightman, *More Than Munitions: Women, Work and the Engineering Industries, 1900–1950* (London: Longman, 1999), 49. On the development of welfare policy and social work practice at the Ministry of Munitions, see George Smith, Elizabeth Peretz and Teresa Smith, *Social Enquiry, Social Reform and Social Action: One Hundred Years of Barnett House* (Oxford: University of Oxford Department of Social Policy and Intervention, 2014), 33–5.

20 Susan Pedersen, 'Macadam, Elizabeth (1871–1948)', *Oxford Dictionary of National Biography*, Oxford University Press, 2004, http://www.oxforddnb.com/view/article/53582 [accessed 22 Apr. 2017].

21 As well as lecturing on the methods and practice of social work on the University of Liverpool's programmes, in the 1920s and 1930s Elizabeth Macadam advised leading figures at centres such as Barnett House, Oxford, founded in 1914 to combine social enquiry, policy debate and social work training: see Smith, Peretz and Smith, *Social Enquiry*, 193; 198.

22 Smith, Peretz and Smith, *Social Enquiry*, 194–5.

23 Peter Grant, *Philanthropy and Voluntary Action in the First World War: Mobilizing Charity* (London: Routledge, 2014), 3.

24 Grant, *Philanthropy and Voluntary Action*, 7; 17.

25 Grant, *Philanthropy and Voluntary Action*, 17. Grant was drawing on the findings of Jacqueline de Vries in her introductory essays to the microfilm collection, *A Change in Attitude: Women, War and Society*, ed. Susan R. Grayzel (Woodbridge, CT: Thomson Gale, 2005).

26 Elizabeth Macadam, *The New Philanthrophy: A Study of the Relations Between ithe Statutory and Voluntary Social Services* (London: G. Allen and Unwin Ltd., 1934), 27–33.

27 Constance Braithwaite, *The Voluntary Citizen: An Enquiry into the Place of Philanthropy in the Community* (London: Methuen & Co. Ltd., 1938), 2.

28 Braithwaite, *The Voluntary Citizen*, ch. 2.

29 Braithwaite, *The Voluntary Citizen*, 8; Macadam, *New Philanthropy*, 21.

30 C. R. Attlee, *The Social Worker* (London: G. Bell, 1920), 5.

31 'Social Service: Address delivered at the Annual Meeting of the Union of Girls' Schools, 27 Oct. 1927', in Stanley Baldwin, *Our Inheritance: Speeches and Addresses* (London: Hodder and Stoughton Ltd., 1928), 202.

32 Lettice Fisher, 'The Liberal Party's Woman Power', *The Manchester Guardian*, 28 Feb. 1928, 20.

33 Winifred Holtby, 'Feminism Divided', *Yorkshire Post*, 26 Jul. 1926 (reprinted by *Time and Tide*, 6 Aug. 1926), in *Testament of a Generation: The Journalism of Vera Brittain and Winifred Holtby*, ed. Paul Berry and Alan Bishop (London: Virago, 1985), 48.

34 David Edgerton, *The Shock of the Old: Technology and Global History Since 1900* (London: Profile Books, 2006).

35 On time-space compression as a constitutive experience of the new communications media of interwar modernity see Trotter, *Literature in the First Media Age*, 219.

36 See e.g. Vicinus, *Independent Women*; Lewis, *Women and Social Action; The Voluntary Sector, the State and Social Work in Britain: The Charity Organisation Society/Family Welfare Association since 1869* (Aldershot: Elgar, 1995); Anne Summers, 'A Home from Home – Women's Philanthropic Work in the Nineteenth Century', in *Fit Work For Women*, ed. Sandra Burman (London: Croom Helm, 1979), 33–63. On upper-class women's philanthropy, see K. D. Reynolds, *Aristocratic Women and Political Society in Victorian Britain* (Oxford: Clarendon Press, 1998), ch. 3.

37 Prochaska, *Women and Philanthropy*.

38 Seth Koven and Sonya Michel eds., *Mothers of a New World: Maternalist Politics and the Origins of Welfare States* (New York: Routledge, 1990).

39 Genevieve Lloyd, *The Man of Reason: 'Male' and 'Female' in Western Philosophy* (London: Methuen, 1984).

40 In late-nineteenth- and early-twentieth-century British examples, this is borne out by comparison of the content of biographies of male and female subjects in the *DNB* (*Dictionary of National Biography*).

41 For a novelistic interpretation see Henry James, *The Princess Casamassima* (1886; repr., Harmondsworth: Penguin, 1987). See also the arguments of early-twentieth-century eugenicists and sexologists, e.g. Arabella Kenealy, *Feminism and Sex-Extinction* (London: T. Fisher Unwin Ltd., 1920), 101–2; Charlotte Haldane, *Motherhood and its Enemies* (London: Chatto & Windus, 1927), 156.

42 James Hinton, *Women, Social Leadership and the Second World War: Continuities of Class* (Oxford: Oxford University Press, 2002), 9.

43 See e.g. Alison Twells, 'Missionary Domesticity, Global Reform and "Woman's Sphere" in Early Nineteenth-Century England', *Gender & History* 18, no. 2 (2006): 267; 279.

44 Susan Mumm, 'Women and Philanthropic Cultures', in *Women, Gender and Religious Cultures in Britain, 1800–1940*, eds. Sue Morgan and Jacqueline de Vries (London: Routledge, 2010), 54.

45 Jane Garnett, 'At Home in the Metropolis: Gender and Ideals of Social Service', in *'Nobler Imaginings and Mightier Struggles': Octavia Hill, Social Activism and the Remaking of British Society*, eds. Elizabeth Baigent and Ben Cowell (London: Institute of Historical Research, 2016), 243–54; Julie Melnyk, 'Women, Writing and the Creation of Theological Cultures', in *Women, Gender and Religious Cultures in Britain*, eds. Morgan and de Vries, 32–53. The argument for the reformulation of theology in dialogue with women's experiences is Ann Braude's: 'Women's History *Is* American Religious History', in *Retelling U.S. Religious History*, ed. Thomas A. Tweed (Berkeley: University of California Press, 1997), 97.

46 Jessica Gerard, '"Lady Bountiful": Women of the Landed Classes and Rural Philanthropy', *Victorian Studies* 30, no. 2 (1987): 183–210; Melanie Oppenheimer, '"We All Did Voluntary Work of Some Kind": Voluntary Work and Labour History', *Labour History* 81 (Nov. 2001): 4–5; 8.

47 Kathleen D. McCarthy ed., *Lady Bountiful Revisited: Women, Philanthropy and Power* (New Brunswick, NJ: Rutgers University Press, 1990), ix.

48 Seth Koven, *The Match Girl and the Heiress* (Princeton: Princeton University Press, 2015), 2.

49 Koven, *Slumming*; Ellen Ross ed., *Slum Travelers: Ladies and London Poverty, 1860–1920* (Berkeley: University of California Press, 2007).

50 Peel, *Miss Cutler*, 6–7. Peel's work is part of a rich literature on 'charity writing': see e.g. Karen Tice, *Tales of Wayward Girls and Immoral Women: Case Records and the Professionalization of Social Work* (Urbana: University of Illinois Press, 1998); Daniel Walkowitz, *Working With Class: Social Workers and the Politics of Middle-Class Identity* (Chapel Hill: University of North Carolina Press, 1999); Ellen Ross, *Slum Travelers*; Koven, *Slumming*. There was scope for the working classes to subvert the messages that social workers 'saw', see Koven, *Slumming*, 193–4.

51 Mumm, 'Women and Philanthropic Cultures', 61. Mumm writes of the challenge for the historian of discerning where women's philanthropy ended and more radical

activism – that might call into question social structures – began, giving the example of Emily Kinnaird and other YWCA women such as Mary Morehead '[who] were convinced that they were creating a better world and working towards a more just society': 62.

52 James Vernon, *Hunger: A Modern History* (Cambridge, MA: The Belknap Press of Harvard University Press, 2007), 182. For interpretations that stress the shift from amateur to professional see Carrie Howse, 'From Lady Bountiful to Lady Administrator: Women and the Administration of Rural District Nursing in England, 1880–1925', *Women's History Review* 15, no. 3 (2006): 423–41. On the idea of the 'Lady Bountiful' being replaced by the voluntary citizen see Jos Sheard, 'From Lady Bountiful to Active Citizen: Volunteering and the Voluntary Sector', in *An Introduction to the Voluntary Sector*, eds. Justin Davis Smith, Colin Rochester and Rodney Hedley (London: Routledge, 1995), 114–27. On the secularization of twentieth-century philanthropy see Frank Prochaska, *Christianity and Social Service in Modern Britain: The Disinherited Spirit* (Oxford: Oxford University Press, 2006).

53 Koven, *Match Girl*, 19.

54 'The Zenana Bible and Medical Mission', *The Times*, 6 Nov. 1903, 8.

55 'The World's Work', *Our Own Gazette*, Nov. 1923, 15. On suffrage imagery see Lisa Tickner, *The Spectacle of Women: Imagery of the Suffrage Campaign, 1907–1914* (Chicago: University of Chicago Press, 1988).

56 Natalie Zemon Davis, 'Conclusion', in *Poverty and Charity in Middle Eastern Contexts*, eds. Michael Bonner, Mine Ener and Amy Singer (Albany: State University of New York Press, 2003), 324.

57 Leela Gandhi, *Affective Communities: Anticolonial Thought, Fin-de-Siècle Radicalism, and the Politics of Friendship* (Durham, NC: Duke University Press, 2006).

58 Sigmund A. Lavine, *Evangeline Booth: Daughter of Salvation* (New York: Dodd, Mead and Co., 1970). Evangeline Booth emerges in a number of histories of the Salvation Army: Pamela J. Walker, *Pulling the Devil's Kingdom Down: The Salvation Army in Victorian Britain* (Berkeley: University of California Press, 2001); Andrew Mark Eason, *Women in God's Army: Gender and Equality in the Early Salvation Army* (Waterloo, Ont.: Wilfrid Laurier University Press, 2003); Diane Winston, *Red Hot and Righteous: The Urban Religion of the Salvation Army* (Cambridge, MA: Harvard University Press, 1999); Lillian Taiz, *Hallelujah Lads and Lasses: Remaking the Salvation Army in America, 1880–1930* (Chapel Hill: University of North Carolina Press, 2001).

59 The two women to have held the position of Salvation Army General since Evangeline Booth are Eva Burrows (1986–93) and Linda Bond (2011–13).

60 'Salvation Army General-Elect video newsreel film', 5 September 1934, http://www.britishpathe.com/record.php?id=5051 [accessed 2 Mar. 2017].

61 Evangeline Booth was awarded the American Distinguished Service Medal (for wartime services); honorary degrees from Tufts College, Massachusetts (1921), and

the University of Columbia (1939); the Fairfax medal for eminent patriotic service (1928); Vasa gold medal (Swedish, 1933); the gold medal of the American National Institute of Social Sciences (1933) and of the Humanitarian Society (1945).

62 Margaret Troutt, *The General Was a Lady: The Story of Evangeline Booth* (Nashville: A. J. Holman, 1980), 192–3.

63 Pearl Hamilton held positions in the American Salvation Army Women's Social Service department and within the executive office before becoming secretary of a divisional Home League on her marriage in 1922 to Salvation Army captain, Arthur Woodruff.

64 Emily Kinnaird, *My Adopted Country 1889–1944* (Lucknow: E. Kinnaird), 16.

65 Kinnaird, *Reminiscences*, 19–20.

66 Susan Mumm, 'Women and Philanthropic Cultures'; Angela Woollacott, 'From Moral to Professional Authority: Secularism, Social Work, and Middle-Class Women's Self-Construction in World War I Britain', *Journal of Women's History* 10, no. 2 (1998): 85–111. Emily Kinnaird emerges fleetingly in Catriona Parratt's article-length discussion of female recreations in the late-nineteenth and early-twentieth centuries, though her interventions in debates about young women's leisure in the post-First World War period have not been traced: Catriona M. Parratt, 'Making Leisure Work: Women's Rational Recreation in Late-Victorian and Edwardian England', *Journal of Sport History* 26, no. 3 (1999): 481. For an important treatment of Kinnaird in relation to her mother's life see Jane Garnett's *ODNB* entry on Mary Jane Kinnaird: 'Kinnaird, Mary Jane, Lady Kinnaird (1816–1888)', *Oxford Dictionary of National Biography*, Oxford University Press, 2004; online edn, May 2006, http://ezproxy.ouls.ox.ac.uk:2117/view/article/15636 [accessed 22 Apr. 2017].

67 Emily Kinnaird, 'The Young Women's Christian Association', in *Woman's Mission: A Series of Congress Papers on the Philanthropic Work of Women*, ed. Angela Burdett-Coutts (London, 1893), 386; *Our Eighty Years: Historical Sketches of the YWCA of Great Britain* (London: YWCA, 1935), MSS 243/15/4, Young Women's Christian Association Records, Modern Records Centre, University of Warwick (hereafter cited as YWCA Records, MRC).

68 Edith Picton-Turbervill, *Life is Good: An Autobiography* (London: Frederick Muller, 1939), 308.

69 Kinnaird, *Adopted Country*, 23.

70 'Mrs H. A. L. Fisher', *The Times*, 16 Feb. 1956, 12.

71 On Courtenay Peregrine's career see Mary Bennett, *The Ilberts in India, 1882–1886: An Imperial Miniature* (London: BACSA, 1995); R. C. J. Cocks, 'Ilbert, Sir Courtenay Peregrine (1841–1924)', *Oxford Dictionary of National Biography*, Oxford University Press, 2004; online edn, Jan 2008, http://ezproxy.ouls.ox.ac.uk:2117/view/article/34090 [accessed 2 Mar. 2017].

72 Olive Heseltine, *Lost Content* (London: Spottiswoode, Ballantyne and Co., 1953), 55.

73 Interview, Brian Harrison with Christina Violet Butler, 7 October 1974, 8 SUF/B/014, Oral Evidence on the Suffrage and Suffragette Movements, the Brian Harrison Interviews, London School of Economics Library, The Women's Library Collection, London (hereafter cited as TWL).

74 Interview, Brian Harrison with Mary Bennett, 9 Oct. 1974, 8 SUF/B/016, TWL.

75 Interview, Brian Harrison with Mary Bennett, 9 Oct.

76 Wilfrid Blunt, *Lady Muriel: Lady Muriel Paget, Her Husband, and Her Philanthropic Work in Central and Eastern Europe* (London: Methuen, 1962), ch. 1.

77 Paget was the 'first lady passenger' to fly from Paris to London on the Arico 4A in August 1919: *Flight: The Aircraft Engineer,* 4 Sept. 1919, 1188. See also 'Air travel and transport', *Aeroplane,* 30 Aug. 1933, 375–6.

78 Muriel Paget's father, Murray Edward Gordon Finch-Hatton, 12th Earl of Winchilsea and 7th Earl of Nottingham (1851–1898) was a Conservative MP for the constituencies of Lincolnshire South (1884) and Spalding (1885–1887) and subsequently a Conservative peer in the House of Lords.

79 David Mitchell, *Women on the Warpath: The Story of the Women of the First World War* (London: Cape, 1966), 90–1.

80 Sybil Oldfield, *Women Humanitarians: A Biographical Dictionary of British Women Active Between 1900 and 1950* (London: Continuum, 2001), 160–3; Caroline Moorehead, *Dunant's Dream: War, Switzerland and the History of the Red Cross* (London: HarperCollins, 1998), ch. 9; James Muckle, 'Saving the Russian Children: Materials in the Archive of the Save the Children Fund Relating to Eastern Europe in 1920–23', *The Slavonic and East European Review* 68, no. 3 (1990): 507–11. Muriel Paget appears as one of the characters in Helen Rappaport's recent book on the Russian Revolution of 1917: *Caught in the Revolution: Petrograd 1917* (London: Hutchinson, 2016).

81 Marcel Mauss, *The Gift: The Form and Reason for Exchange in Archaic Societies,* trans. W. D. Halls (1950; repr., London: Routledge, 1990).

82 Maurice Glasman, 'Politics, Employment Policies and the Young Generation', *Economia Politica* / a. xxx, n. 2 August 2013. On social entrepreneurship see e.g. Andrew Mawson, *The Social Entrepreneur: Making Communities Work* (London: Atlantic Books, 2008).

83 Susan Pedersen, *Eleanor Rathbone and the Politics of Conscience* (New Haven, CT: Yale University Press, 2004).

1 Relationships

1 Vera Brittain, 'The Whole Duty of Woman', *Time and Tide,* 23 Feb. 1923, in *Testament of a Generation,* eds. Berry and Bishop, 121–2.

2   Koven, *Slumming*; Garnett, 'At Home in the Metropolis'.

3   Winifred Holtby, 'Feminism Divided', *Yorkshire Post*, 26 Jul. 1926 (reprinted in *Time and Tide*, 6 Aug. 1926), in *Testament of a Generation*, eds. Berry and Bishop, 48–9.

4   M. D. S., 'Social Work as a Career', *The Woman's Leader*, 3 Oct. 1924, 287–8.

5   Macadam, *New Philanthropy*, 30.

6   Beatrice Webb, *My Apprenticeship* (1926; repr., Cambridge: Cambridge University Press, 1979), 207.

7   Braithwaite, *Voluntary Citizen*, 26.

8   Mathew Thomson, *Psychological Subjects: Identity, Culture, and Health in Twentieth-century Britain* (Oxford: Oxford University Press, 2006), 43.

9   As has been noted, Muriel Paget was seen publicly in philanthropic settings before this, see Introduction, note 54.

10 'A Woman's Enterprise', *The Queen, the Lady's Newspaper and Court Chronicle*, 5 Jan. 1901, 43.

11 'The Invalid Kitchens of London', *The Times*, 15 Feb. 1911, 6.

12 Vicinus, *Independent Women*, 212.

13 'The Invalid Kitchens of London', *The Times*, 15 Feb. 1911, 6.

14 Peel, *Miss Cutler*, 9–11.

15 Yuriko Akiyama, *Feeding the Nation: Nutrition and Health in Britain Before World War One* (London: Tauris Academic Studies, 2008), 112.

16 'Dudley Guild of Help: Lady Muriel Paget on Social Reform', *Birmingham Mail*, 19 Jan. 1911, 2.

17 On national efficiency see G. R. Searle, *The Quest for National Efficiency: A Study in Politics and Political Thought, 1899–1914* (Oxford: Basil Blackwell, 1971).

18 'Dudley Guild of Help', *Birmingham Mail*, 19 Jan. 1911, 2.

19 Jane Lewis, 'Women, Social Work and Social Welfare in Twentieth-century Britain: From (Unpaid) Influence to (Paid) Oblivion', in *Charity, Self-interest and Welfare in the English Past*, ed. Martin Daunton (London: UCL Press, 1996), 212–13; Keith Laybourn, 'The Guild of Help and the Changing Face of Edwardian Philanthropy', *Urban History* 20, no. 1 (1993): 44.

20 On the history of guilds in constructing relationships between the individual and the community see Gervase Rosser, *The Art of Solidarity in the Middle Ages: Guilds in England, 1250–1550* (Oxford: Oxford University Press, 2015).

21 H. H., 'The Invalid Kitchens of London', *The British Journal of Nursing*, 22 Apr. 1916, 366.

22 'The Week's Good Cause: Appeal on Behalf of the Invalid Kitchens of London by Lady Muriel Paget', *The Radio Times*, 11 Oct. 1929, 96.

23 Eleanor T. Kelly, 'Welfare Work', in *The Woman's Year Book 1923–1924*, ed. Evelyn G. Gates (London: Women Publishers Ltd., 1924), 557.

24 'The Invalid Kitchens of London Subscription List and Balance Sheet for 1926', 16, Box 1, Lady Muriel Paget Papers, Special Collections, Leeds University Library, LRA/MS 1405 (hereafter cited as LRA/MS 1405).

25 Kelly, 'Welfare Work', 557.

26 Amy Barnard, 'Invalid Kitchens', *The Quiver*, Mar. 1916, 482.

27 Elizabeth Macadam, 'Introduction: Social Work', *Woman's Year Book 1923–1924*, 531. For a critical commentary contrasting the formal training required for professional social work with 'untutored' philanthropic practice see Vera Brittain, *Women's Work in Modern England* (London: Douglas, 1928), 137.

28 'The Invalid Kitchens of London Report and Accounts, 1 October 1929 to 30 September 1930', 1; 'The Invalid Kitchens of London Annual Report, 1927–1928', 1, Box 1, LRA/MS 1405.

29 'The Week's Good Cause: Appeal on Behalf of the Invalid Kitchens of London by Lady Muriel Paget', *Radio Times*, 11 Oct. 1929, 96.

30 Antoine Capet, 'Photographs of the British Unemployed in the Inter-war Years: Representation or Manipulation?', in *The Representation of the Working People in Britain and France: New Perspectives*, ed. Antoine Capet (Newcastle-upon-Tyne: Cambridge Scholars Publishing, 2009), 93–105.

31 Pamphlet, 'Invalid Kitchens of London, 1930', Box 1, LRA/MS 1405.

32 Dan LeMahieu, *A Culture for Democracy: Mass Communication and the Cultivated Mind in Britain Between the Wars* (Oxford: Clarendon Press, 1988), ch. 3.

33 'The Week's Good Cause: Appeal on Behalf of the Invalid Kitchens of London', *Radio Times*, 11 Oct. 1929, 96.

34 On Helen Bosanquet's thinking see e.g. *Rich and Poor* (London, 1898).

35 Mrs Alec Tweedie, 'The Children's Order of Chivalry', *The Queen, the Lady's Newspaper and Court Chronicle*, 29 June 1895, 1160.

36 *In the Garb of a Beggar. A Letter Urging the Claims of the Children's Order of Chivalry: Addressed to Parents and All Others Who Wish to See their Children Take an Active and Sympathetic Interest in the Welfare of the Poor and Needy*, by the Children's Editor of 'The Cable', n.d., Box 33, LRA/MS 1405.

37 S. P. B. Mais, 'Wanted! Work – Not Charity', *The Listener*, 25 Jan. 1933, 118.

38 S. P. B. Mais, *The Listener*, 25 Jan. 1933, 119.

39 Bruno Cabanes, *The Great War and the Origins of Humanitarianism, 1918–1924* (New York: Cambridge University Press, 2014).

40 Tara Zahra, *The Lost Children: Reconstructing Europe's Families After World War II* (Cambridge, MA: Harvard University Press, 2011), 25–30; 36–46; Michelle Tusan, 'Crimes Against Humanity: Human Rights, the British Empire, and the Origins of the Response to the Armenian Genocide', *American Historical Review* 119, no. 1 (2014): 47–77. Cabanes has argued for the turning point of the 'transnationalization of humanitarianism' during the post-First World War era: *The Great War*, 4–5.

41 Muriel Paget, 'Child Welfare Work in the New States of Europe', *The Record of the Save the Children Fund* 3, no. 1 (1922): 21.

42 'News from the Stricken Lands', *The Record of the Save the Children Fund* 1, no. 2 (Nov. 1920): 25.

43 On the feeding kitchen in Kiev see Rappaport, *Caught in the Revolution*, 327.

44 Eugene Michail, *The British and the Balkans: Forming Images of Foreign Lands, 1900–1950* (London: Continuum, 2011), 60; Zahra, *Lost Children*, 27–8.

45 Paul Weindling, *Epidemics and Genocide in Eastern Europe, 1890–1945* (Oxford: Oxford University Press, 2000), 149.

46 Meeting of London Committee of Lady Muriel Paget's Mission to Eastern Europe, 17 Jan. 1922, Box 4, LRA/MS 1405.

47 The work began in Modra, Slovakia, in July 1919 with the establishment of a home for undernourished children: Blunt, *Muriel Paget*, 139.

48 *The Record of the Save the Children Fund*, 1 Oct. 1920, 3.

49 See e.g. Heide Fehrenbach and Davide Rodogno, eds., *Humanitarian Photography: A History* (Cambridge: Cambridge University Press, 2015).

50 *The Record of the Save the Children Fund*, 1 Oct. 1920, 3.

51 Dorothy Buxton and Edward Fuller, *The White Flame: The Story of the Save the Children Fund* (London: Longmans, Green & Co., 1931), 23; 22.

52 Report No. 1 from Mr L. Webster to Muriel Paget, 19 Mar. 1920, Box 4, LRA/MS 1405.

53 *Red Cross World* (Oct-Dec. 1920), 525.

54 Lady Muriel Paget, 'Child Welfare Work in the New States of Europe', *The Record of the Save the Children Fund* 3, no. 1 (1922): 21.

55 Tehila Sasson, 'From Empire to Humanity: The Russian Famine and the Imperial Origins of International Humanitarianism', *Journal of British Studies* 55, no. 3 (2016): 519–37.

56 Sasson, 'From Empire to Humanity': 521.

57 See, e.g., documentation in relation to the establishment of clinics in the Baltic States under Lady Muriel Paget's Mission to Eastern Europe: L. B. Golden to Lieut. Col. Crossfield, 25 Feb. 1921, Box 4, LRA/MS 1405.

58 Proposals by Lady Muriel Paget and L. Webster for Missions in the Baltic States, 5 Apr. 1921, Box 4, LRA/MS 1405.

59 William Booth to Evangeline Booth, 22 Oct. 1904, Box 30, Evangeline Booth Papers, The Salvation Army National Archives and Research Center, Alexandria, VA (hereafter cited as Booth Papers, SAA).

60 William Booth to Evangeline Booth, 22 Oct. 1904, Box 30, Booth Papers, SAA.

61 William Booth to Evangeline Booth, 22 Oct. 1904, Box 30, Booth Papers, SAA.

62 William Booth to Evangeline Booth, 4 Sept. 1897, Box 30, Booth Papers, SAA.

63 Ann R. Higginbotham, 'Respectable Sinners: Salvation Army Rescue Work With Unmarried Mothers, 1884–1914', in *Religion in the Lives of English Women,*

1760–1930, ed. Gail Malmgreem (Bloomington: Indiana Press, 1986), 216–33; Jenty Fairbank, *Booth's Boots: The Beginnings of Salvation Army Social Work* (London: International Headquarters of the Salvation Army, 1983).

64 Frank Mort, *Dangerous Sexualities: Medico-Moral Politics in England Since 1830* (London: Routledge & Kegan Paul, 1987), 103–4; Paula Bartley, *Prostitution: Prevention and Reform in England, 1860–1914* (London: Routledge, 2000), 26; Judith R. Walkowitz, *City of Dreadful Delight: Narratives of Sexual Danger in Late-Victorian London* (London: Virago, 1992).

65 W. T. Stead, 'The Maiden Tribute of Modern Babylon', *Pall Mall Gazette*, 6 Jul. 1885, 1–6; 7 Jul. 1885, 1–6; 8 Jul. 1885, 1–5; 10 Jul. 1885, 1–6.

66 Walker, *Pulling the Devil's Kingdom Down*, 239.

67 Walker, *Pulling the Devil's Kingdom Down*, 241.

68 'Evangeline Booth Speech to The Woman's Club, Jersey City', 2/3 Feb. 1912, Speeches II, 313/3, Booth Papers, SAA.

69 William Bramwell Booth to Evangeline Booth, 18 Mar. 1918, Box 28, Booth Papers, SAA. See also Cassandra Tate, *Cigarette Wars: The Triumph of the Little White Slaver* (New York: Oxford University Press, 1999), 79–80. The Salvation Army's wartime work sat somewhat awkwardly with its earlier social campaigns. For example, while in the early 1900s the organization ran a campaign against smoking as socially destructive, during wartime it was sending an estimated 15 million tons of cigarettes and smoking tobacco to France.

70 Evangeline Booth, 'What the $13,000,000 Will Be Used For', *The War Cry* (US), 14 June 1919, 8. See also Sabine Noelle Marsh, 'Religious Women in Modern American Social Reform: Evangeline Booth, Aimee Semple McPherson, Dorothy Day, and the Rhetorical Invention of Humanitarian Authority' (PhD diss., Graduate College of the University of Illinois at Urbana-Champaign, 2012), ch. 1.

71 Evangeline Booth to Herbert Booth, 4 May 1925, Box 29, 29/13, Booth Papers, SAA.

72 Evangeline Booth and Grace Livingstone Hill, *The War Romance of the Salvation Army* (Philadelphia: J. B. Lippincott Co., 1919), 10–11.

73 Booth and Livingstone Hill, *War Romance*, 18.

74 Booth and Livingstone Hill, *War Romance*, 11.

75 Booth and Livingstone Hill, *War Romance*, 11.

76 Booth and Livingstone Hill, *War Romance*, 23.

77 Booth and Livingstone Hill, *War Romance*, 258–9.

78 Joanna Bourke, *Dismembering the Male: Men's Bodies, Britain and the Great War* (London: Reaktion, 1996), 124–70.

79 Booth and Livingstone Hill, *War Romance*, 60.

80 Henry Gribble, 'Salvationists in the Trenches', *Times Literary Supplement*, 20 Nov. 1919, 667.

81 Kathleen W. Jones, *Taming the Troublesome Child: American Families, Child Guidance, and the Limits of Psychiatric Authority* (Cambridge, MA: Harvard University Press, 1999).

82 Booth and Livingstone Hill, *War Romance*, 283–4.

83 On the public debate about the American Sallies, gender and sexuality see Winston, *Red Hot and Righteous*, 189–90. For discussion of the dominance of middle-class women in Salvation Army rescue work see Walker, *Pulling the Devil's Kingdom Down*, 154–5.

84 Booth and Livingstone Hill, *War Romance*, 284.

85 Walker, *Pulling the Devil's Kingdom Down*, 2; 5–6; 56–60.

86 Booth and Livingstone Hill, *War Romance*, 7.

87 'Miss Booth Tells Women Her Secret: Personal Contact Explains Why the Salvation Army Has Grown So Great. Needs $250, 000 More', *Toronto Star*, 31 Jan. 1913, 9.

88 Booth and Livingstone Hill, *War Romance*, 7.

89 Ella A. Fanning, 'Evangeline Booth Goes on Tour', *The New York Times*, 26 May 1924, reprinted in Agnes Lizzie Page Palmer, *1904–1926. The Time Between: Reviewing the Progress of the Salvation Army in the United States Under the Leadership of Commander Evangeline Booth* (New York: Salvation Army Printers, 1926), 43. John Larsson, *1929: A Crisis that Shaped the Salvation Army's Future* (London: Salvation Army, 2009).

90 Fanning, 'Evangeline Booth Goes on Tour'.

91 Gustav LeBon, *The Crowd: A Study of the Popular Mind* (London, 1896).

92 Dale Carnegie, *Five Minute Biographies* (1937; repr. Surrey: The World's Work, 1946), 98.

93 Carnegie, *Five Minute Biographies*, 98–100.

94 Walker, *Pulling the Devil's Kingdom Down*, 67–8; 88–9.

95 Advertisement, *The New York Times*, 8 Mar. 1931, 75.

96 Homer N. Calver, 'Strategy in Handling People', *Journal of Public Health* 21, no. 4 (1931): 459. The review in *The Rotarian* gendered the characters exclusively male: 'Like a "Bomb-Shell",' *The Rotarian*, November 1931, 1.

97 On the links between advertising, religious and psychological cultures that stressed self-realization see T. J. Jackson Lears, 'From Salvation to Self-Realization: Advertising and the Therapeutic Roots of the Consumer Culture, 1880–1930', in *The Culture of Consumption: Critical Essays in American History, 1880–1980*, ed. Richard Wightman Fox and T. J. Jackson Lears (New York: Pantheon Books, 1983), 1–38.

98 Ewing T. Webb and John B. Morgan, *Strategy in Handling People* (New York: Garden City Publishing Co., 1930), 32.

99 David W. Bebbington, *Evangelicalism in Modern Britain: A History from the 1730s to the 1980s* (London: Unwin Hyman, 1989), ch. 6.

100 Mumm, 'Women and Philanthropic Cultures', 63. Caitríona Beaumont notes that these internal divisions saw a fall in the membership of the YWCA in England and Wales from 80,000 women in 1918 to 33,800 in 1926: Caitríona Beaumont, 'Fighting for the "Privileges of Citizenship": The Young Women's Christian Association (YWCA), Feminism and the Women's Movement, 1928–1945', *Women's History Review*, 23, no. 3 (2014): 463–79.

101 Kinnaird, *Reminiscences*, 2.

102 Mumm, 'Women and Philanthropic Cultures', 63; 61.

103 Peter J. Bowler, *Reconciling Science and Religion: The Debate in Early-Twentieth Century Britain* (Chicago: Chicago University Press, 2001), 211–12. For discussion of the debate in an American context see Andrew S. Finstuen, *Original Sin and Everyday Protestants: The Theology of Reinhold Niebuhr, Billy Graham, and Paul Tillich in an Age of Anxiety* (Chapel Hill: University of North Carolina Press, 2009), 48–9.

104 Kinnaird, *Reminiscences*, 85.

105 Kinnaird, *Reminiscences*, 93.

106 Circular Letter in Response to Accusations of 'Worldly Methods', 24 Jul. 1918, MSS 243/42/2/5, YWCA Records, MRC.

107 Religious Work Committee, 1918–19, MSS 243/105/3, YWCA Records, MRC.

108 Emily Kinnaird, 'YWCA', *Our Own Gazette*, Jan. 1884, 12. See also 'Monthly Letter by the Editor, M. Jane Menzies', *Our Own Gazette*, Jan. 1884, 2. The figure for membership in 1900 is quoted in Beaumont, 'Fighting for the "Privileges of Citizenship"', 467.

109 Emily Kinnaird, 'Fifty Years of Christian Work', *The Gentlewoman*, 4 Feb. 1905, 160.

110 'Girls of Yesterday and To-day. The Romance of the YWCA', by Lucy M. Moor c.1913, foreword by W.H.M.H. Aitken, 3–4, MSS 243/15/2, YWCA Records, MRC.

111 'Girls of Yesterday and To-day', foreword by W.H.M.H. Aitken, 5.

112 'Girls of Yesterday and To-day' (see Emily Kinnaird's foreword). On the YWCA's longer concern with the health of girls and young women working in factories see Hilary Marland, *Health and Girlhood in Britain, 1874–1920* (Basingstoke: Palgrave Macmillan, 2013), ch. 5. Marland identifies the emphasis upon young women's contribution to the future health of the nation as a wartime idiom of medical advice literature: 186.

113 Brian Stanley, *The World Missionary Conference, Edinburgh 1910* (Grand Rapids, MI: William B. Eerdmans Pub. Co., 2009), 88.

114 'Girls of Yesterday and To-day' (see Emily Kinnaird's foreword).

115 World's Young Women's Christian Association, *A Study of the World's Young Women's Christian Association* (London: World's Young Women's Christian Association, 1924), 16.

116 Circular letter from H. M. Proctor and K. J. Wood, May 1915 regarding the UK YWCA autumn 1915/spring 1916 campaign, MSS 243/64/22, YWCA Records, MRC.

117 Eve Colpus, 'Women, Service and Self-actualization in Inter-war Britain', *Past and Present* (forthcoming, 2018).

118 Programme of YWCA Secretaries' Conference, 7–14 Apr. 1916, filed in Emily Kinnaird's Conference Diaries, MSS 243/24, YWCA Records, MRC.

119 'The Interpretation of Christ in a World Fellowship: A Study for Members of the British YWCA in Preparation for their Biennial Conference, Oct. 1922', MSS 243/40/3, YWCA Records, MRC.

120 Discussion paper, 'The Interpretation of Christ to Young Women To-day': World's YWCA Commission, Salzburg, 10–16 June 1922, MSS 243/40/3, YWCA Records, MRC.

121 *Our Eighty Years*, 3 (see Introduction, note 67).

122 Lucy Delap, 'Conservative Values, Anglicans, and the Gender Order in Inter-war Britain', in *Brave New World: Imperial and Democratic Nation-Building in Britain Between the Wars*, eds. Laura Beers and Geraint Thomas (London: Institute of Historical Research, 2012), 158.

123 Minna C. Gollock, 'The YWCA and the New Situation' (1919), 6–8, MSS 243/14/5/19, YWCA Records, MRC.

124 Gollock, 'The YWCA and the New Situation', 6–8; 10–11.

125 Kinnaird, *Reminiscences*, 68.

126 Kinnaird, *Reminiscences*, 67; 54.

127 Stanley, *World Missionary Conference*, 7; William Richey Hogg, *Ecumenical Foundations: A History of the International Missionary Council and its Nineteenth-century Background* (New York: Harper and Brothers, 1952); John Maiden, 'Evangelical and Anglo-Catholic Relations, 1928–1983', in *Evangelicalism and the Church of England in the Twentieth Century: Reform, Resistance and Renewal*, eds. Andrew Atherstone and John Maiden (London: The Boydell Press, 2014), 142.

128 Kinnaird, *Reminiscences*, 16.

129 Emily Kinnaird, 'In Touch With the Unseen', *Our Own Gazette*, May 1927, 18; 'Seeing the Invisible', *Our Own Gazette*, June 1927, 17.

130 'The YWCA Today: A Review' (1931), 1, MSS 243/2/1/16, YWCA Records, MRC.

131 Prochaska, *Women and Philanthropy*.

132 Braithwaite, *Voluntary Citizen*, 9–12; 10.

133 Kinnaird, *Reminiscences*, 90–1.

2 Knowledge

1 Macadam, *New Philanthropy*, 9.

2 Macadam, *New Philanthropy*, front page.

3 Ronald G. Walton, *Women in Social Work* (London: Routledge & Kegan Paul, 1975), 158–60.

4 Rodney Lowe, 'Welfare's Moving Frontier', *Twentieth Century British History* 6, no. 3 (1995): 372.

5 For interpretations of Elizabeth Macadam's contribution to conceptualizing interwar philanthropy, see Bernard Harris, 'Health by Association', *International Journal of Epidemiology* 34, no. 2 (2005): 489. See also Jane Lewis, 'Reviewing the Relationship Between the Voluntary Sector and the State in Britain in the 1990s', *Voluntas: International Journal of Voluntary and Nonprofit Organizations* 10, no. 3

(1999): 260; Frank Prochaska, *The Voluntary Impulse: Philanthropy in Modern Britain* (London: Faber and Faber, 1988), 80. Although Prochaska argues that Macadam's views were not representative of interwar philanthropy, but rather that they anticipated post-Second World War developments.

6   Elizabeth Macadam, 'The Universities and the Training of the Social Worker', *Hibbert Journal: A Quarterly Review of Religion, Theology, and Philosophy* 12, no. 2 (1914): 292.

7   Elizabeth Macadam, *The Equipment of the Social Worker* (London: G. Allen and Unwin, 1925), 5.

8   Lawrence Goldman, 'Victorian Social Science: From Singular to Plural', in *The Organization of Knowledge in Victorian Britain*, ed. Martin Daunton (Oxford: Published for the British Academy by Oxford University Press, 2005), 87–114.

9   Eileen Janes Yeo, *The Contest for Social Science: Relations and Representations of Gender and Class* (London: Rivers Oram Press, 1996), chs. 9–10.

10 Lears, *No Place of Grace*, 41; Garnett, 'At Home in the Metropolis'; Melnyk, 'Women, Writing and the Creation of Theological Cultures'.

11 Mrs S. A. Barnett, 'The Beginnings of Toynbee Hall' (1903), reprinted in Canon and Mrs S. A. Barnett, *Practicable Socialism*, new ser. (London: Longmans, Green and Co., 1915), 119.

12 Yeo, *Contest for Social Science*, 288. See also M. C. Curthoys and Janet Howarth, 'Origins and Destinations: The Social Mobility of Oxford Men and Women', in *The History of the University of Oxford*. Vol. 7: *Nineteenth-Century Oxford Part 2*, eds. M. J. Brock and M. C. Curthoys (Oxford: Clarendon Press, 2000), 594; Gillian Sutherland, *In Search of the New Woman: Middle-Class Women and Work in Britain 1870–1914* (Cambridge: Cambridge University Press, 2015), 38.

13 Yeo, *Contest for Social Science*, x; 288.

14 See 79.

15 Macadam, 'The Universities and the Training of the Social Worker': 291.

16 A. H. S. C., 'Charity', *The Queen, The Lady's Newspaper and Court Chronicle*, 1 Jan. 1921, 13; 'The Editor's Letter', *Mothers' Union Journal*, June 1932, 30.

17 Charlotte Ward, *Lending a Hand, or Help for the Working Classes* (London, 1866). For discussion of Ward see Kathryn Gleadle, *Borderline Citizens: Women, Gender and Political Culture in Britain, 1815–1867* (Oxford: Oxford University Press for the British Academy, 2009), 48–9.

18 Julia Bush's work on women's imperialist associations in the Edwardian period offers one model for writing about these interrelated forces with respect to the construction of women's gendered expertise within an imperial context: Julia Bush, *Edwardian Ladies and Imperial Power* (London: Leicester University Press, 2000).

19 I am engaging with Thomasina Borkman's concept, see her 'Experiential Knowledge: A New Concept for the Analysis of Self-Help Groups', *Social Service Review* 50, no. 3 (1976): 445–56.

20 P. W. Wilson, *The General. The Story of Evangeline Booth* (London: Hodder and Stoughton Ltd., 1935), 39.

21 On training practices in the Salvation Army see Eason, *Women in God's Army*, 48; Walker, *Pulling the Kingdom Down*, 113–7.

22 A. M. N., 'How the Commander Prepares Her Addresses', *The Field Officer*, May 1906, 403.

23 Wilson, *The General*, 37.

24 Evangeline Booth Miscellaneous folder 3, Booth Papers, SAA. The list included the titles *Encyclopedia Britannica* (11th edition); *Works of Shakespeare*; *Works of Hawthorne*; William M. Sloane, *Life of Napoleon Bonaparte*; J. G. Nicolay and John Hay, *Abraham Lincoln*; *Works of Lord Byron*; *The Works of Thomas Carlyle*; *Charles Kingsley, His Letters and Memoirs of His Life*; Herman Grimm, *Life of Michael Angelo*; *The Writings of George Eliot*.

25 Evangeline Booth, *Woman*, (1930; repr., London: Salvationist Publishing and Supplies, 1936), 10; 22.

26 Martha C. Nussbaum, *Political Emotions: Why Love Matters for Justice* (Cambridge, MA: The Belknap Press of Harvard University, 2013), 2.

27 Evangeline Booth, 'Around the World With the Salvation Army', *The National Geographic Magazine* 37, no. 4 (1920): 347.

28 Evangeline Booth, *Toward a Better World* (London: Salvationist Publishing and Supplies, 1929), 13.

29 'Home League Meeting', 17 Sept. 1935, Speeches II, 312/1, Booth Papers, SAA.

30 'Institute of Social Sciences', 11 May 1933, Speeches II, 312/4, Booth Papers SAA.

31 'Speech on the Receipt of the Humanitarian Award', 18 May 1945, Speeches II, 312/2, Booth Papers, SAA.

32 Yeo, *Contest for Social Science*, ch. 5. On maternalism see Koven and Michel eds., *Mothers of a New World*; Gisela Bock and Pat Thane, eds., *Maternity and Gender Policies: Women and the Rise of the European Welfare States 1880s–1950s* (London: Routledge, 1991).

33 Booth, *Woman*, 21–2.

34 Deborah M. Valenze, *Prophetic Sons and Daughters: Female Preaching and Popular Religion in Industrial England* (Princeton, NJ: Princeton University Press, 1985), 35; Walker, *Pulling the Devil's Kingdom Down*, 80; Judith Smart, 'Modernity and Mother-heartedness: Spirituality and Religious Meaning in Australian Women's Suffrage and Citizenship Movements, 1890s–1920s', in *Women's Suffrage in the British Empire: Citizenship, Nation and Race*, eds. Ian Christopher Fletcher, Philippa Levine, Laura E. Nym Mayhall (London: Routledge, 2000), 57.

35 Walker, *Pulling the Devil's Kingdom Down*, 131.

36 The ceremony was cancelled due to the outbreak of war.

37 'The Home League', Earls Court, 2 Sept. 1939, Speeches II, 312/1, Booth Papers, SAA.

38 'Address to Women's Clubs in Tokyo', 25 Nov. 1929, Speeches I, 313/3, Booth Papers, SAA.

39 Peel, *Miss Cutler*, 8.

40 Walker, *Pulling the Devil's Kingdom Down*, 155.

41 John Read, *Catherine Booth: Laying the Theological Foundations of a Radical Movement* (Cambridge, UK: The Lutterworth Press, 2013); Walker, *Pulling the Devil's Kingdom Down*, 8–17.

42 Harold Begbie, 'Booth, William (1829–1912)', *Dictionary of National Biography, 1912–1921*, eds. H. W. C. Davis and J. R. H. Weaver (London: Oxford University Press, 1927), 50.

43 Booth, *Toward a Better World*, 194.

44 Booth, *Toward a Better World*, 191–2.

45 Booth, *Woman*, 25.

46 Eve Colpus, 'Landscapes of Welfare: Concepts and Cultures of British Women's Philanthropy, 1918–1939' (DPhil thesis, University of Oxford, 2011), 126–32. The practice built upon the popularity of collective biographies of famous and exemplary women in the nineteenth century that Alison Booth argues encoded epistemological values in representational forms that reduced difference to a single message: see *How to Make It As A Woman: Collective Biographical History from Victoria to the Present* (Chicago: University of Chicago Press, 2004), 8.

47 'Home League Meeting', 17 Sept. 1935, Speeches II, 312/1, Booth Papers, SAA.

48 'The Home League', Earls Court, 2 Sept. 1939, Speeches II, 312/1, Booth Papers, SAA.

49 Eason, *Women in God's Army*, 121–2.

50 Wilson, *The General*, 8–9.

51 Mrs Booth, *Papers on Practical Religion* (London, 1879), 130.

52 Mrs Booth, *Papers on Aggressive Christianity* (London, 1880), 9.

53 Evangeline Booth, *Love Is All* (London: Marshall, Morgan and Scott, 1935), 40.

54 See e.g. Arnold Gesell, 'Scientific Approaches to the Study of the Human Mind', *Science* 88, no. 2280 (1938): 225–30.

55 'Home League Meeting', 17 Sept. 1935 (see note 47).

56 'London School of Economics and Political Science, Papers 1898–99: Arrangements for the Session 1898–99', 4, LSE/Unregistered/27/2/1A (Year Books 1895–1903), London School of Economics Library (hereafter cited as LSE Library).

57 Maxine Berg, *A Woman in History: Eileen Power, 1889–1940* (Cambridge: Cambridge University Press, 1996), 8–9; Maxine Berg, 'The First Women Economic Historians', *The Economic History Review* 45, no. 2 (1992): 309–11.

58 Ralf Dahrendorf, *LSE: A History of the London School of Economics and Political Science 1895–1995* (Oxford: Oxford University Press, 1995), 20.

59 Elizabeth Macadam, 'Social Work', *Woman's Year Book 1923–1924*, 409.

60 Berg, *Woman in History*, 10.

61 Lettice Fisher, 'Labourer's Dwellings', *The Economic Journal* 9, no. 36 (1899): 609–10;
'Local Authorities and the Housing Problem in 1901', *The Economic Journal* 12,
no. 46 (1902): 263–71; 'The Town Housing Problem', *The Economic Journal* 15,
no. 57 (1905): 23–36. See also Lettice Ibert, 'Pioneers in Housing', *Economic Review* 9
(1899): 450–62. Fisher also contributed to the Palgrave *Dictionary of Political
Economy* an article on old age pensions: Robert W. Dimand, 'Women Economists in
the 1890s: Journals, Books and the Old *Palgrave*', *Journal of the History of Economic
Thought* 21, no. 3 (1999): 273. Lettice Fisher published under a number of names: her
first article was published under Lettice Ilbert, as noted above and in the
Bibliography. From the early 1920s she published usually under the name 'Mrs
H. A. L. Fisher'. For ease, in the Bibliographic references, I have standardized the
author name to Lettice Fisher.
62 Mrs Courtenay Ilbert, *Six Lectures on Practical Nursing* (Calcutta: Superintendent of
Government Printing India, 1885).
63 Elizabeth Peretz, 'Infant Welfare Between the Wars', in *Oxford: Studies in the History
of a University Town Since 1800*, ed. R. C. Whiting (Manchester: Manchester
University Press, 1993), 139. Peretz has discussed how in the interwar period, the
Oxford Health and Housing Association pressed for publicly funded health visitors,
general practitioner medical advisors and a supervised maternity home to augment
the local voluntary provision.
64 Lettice Fisher, 'Review of C. J. Stewart, "The Housing Question in London"', *The
Economic Journal* 11, no. 41 (1901): 57.
65 A. J. R., ed., *The Suffrage Annual and Women's Who's Who* (London: Stanley, Paul and
Co., 1913), 239.
66 Yeo, *Contest for Social Science*.
67 H. A. L. Fisher, *An Unfinished Biography* (London: Oxford University Press, 1940), 86.
68 Fernanda Perrone, 'Women Academics in England, 1870–1930', *History of
Universities* XII (1993), 360. Perrone states that 79–85% of women academics
between 1884 and 1904 and 67% by 1924 remained lifelong spinsters.
69 Carol Dyhouse, *No Distinction Of Sex? Women in British Universities, 1870–1939*
(London: UCL Press, 1995), 147–8; 151.
70 Lettice Fisher, *Getting and Spending: An Introduction to Economics* (London: Collins
Clear-Type Press, 1922), 19.
71 Fisher, *Getting and Spending*, 37.
72 Fisher, *Getting and Spending*, 34–8.
73 Fisher, *Getting and Spending*, 18.
74 Interviews, Brian Harrison with Christina Violet Butler, 16 Sept. 1974 and 7 Oct.
1974, 8 SUF/B/012 and 8 SUF/B/014, TWL. C. V. Butler authored a social survey of
Oxford which she attributed to the mentorship of Lettice Fisher amongst other
women: *Social Conditions in Oxford* (London: Sidgwick & Jackson, 1912).

75 C. V. Butler, 'Review: *Getting and Spending: An Introduction to Economics*, by Lettice Fisher', *The Economic Journal* 32, no. 127 (1922): 394; 393.

76 E. St John Brooks, 'Getting & Spending', *Times Literary Supplement*, 1 June 1922, 361.

77 Brooks, 'Getting & Spending', *Times Literary Supplement*, 361.

78 Jane Garnett, 'Political and Domestic Economy in Victorian Social Thought: Ruskin and Xenophon', in *Economy, Polity and Society: British Intellectual History 1750–1950*, eds. Stefan Collini, Richard Whatmore and Brian Young (Cambridge: Cambridge University Press, 2000), 205.

79 Lettice Fisher described the works of J. M. Keynes, whilst 'brilliant' as 'wayward': *Earning and Spending: An Introduction to Economics* (London: Collins Clear-Type Press, 1938), 182.

80 Fisher, *Earning and Spending*, 16.

81 G. D. H. Cole, 'A Retrospect of the History of Voluntary Social Service', in *Voluntary Social Services: Their Place in the Modern State*, ed. A. F. C. Bourdillon (London: Methuen & Co., 1945), 25. For a useful history of the policy work of the NCUMC (later renamed The National Council for One Parent Families, and now Gingerbread) see Pat Thane and Tanya Evans, *Sinners? Scroungers? Saints? Unmarried Motherhood in Twentieth-Century England* (Oxford: Oxford University Press, 2012).

82 'National Council for the Unmarried Mother and Her Child, Preliminary Constitution of the National Council', 5OPF/01/2, NCUMC Papers, TWL.

83 First Council Meeting, 15 Apr. 1918, 5OPF/01/4/1, NCUMC Papers, TWL. There were thirty-six organizations listed as represented at the meeting along with individual delegates.

84 Lettice Fisher, *Twenty-one Years: 1918–1939* [A history of the National Council for the Unmarried Mother and her Child] (London: National Council for the Unmarried Mother and her Child, 1939), 5. See also Thane and Evans *Sinners? Scroungers? Saints?*, 15.

85 Pat Thane, 'Voluntary Action in the "Welfare State": The National Council for the Unmarried Mother and her Child', in *People, Places and Identities: Themes in British Social and Cultural History 1700s–1980s*, ed. Alan Kidd and Melanie Tebbutt (Manchester: Manchester University Press, 2017), 132–51.

86 Anna Davin, 'Imperialism and Motherhood', *History Workshop Journal* 5, no. 1 (1978): 10–11.

87 NCUMC Pamphlet, 'The Bastardy Bill, 1920', Special Collections Pamphlets, 346.017 BAS, TWL.

88 Legal Subcommittee Minutes, inserted in Minutes of Meeting of Legal Subcommittee of the Child Welfare Council, Thursday 22 Nov. 1917, 5OPF/2/12/b, NCUMC Papers, TWL.

89 NCUMC Pamphlet, 'The Bastardy Bill, 1920'.

90 Chairman's Report, 22 Oct. 1918, 5OPF/01/4/1, NCUMC Papers, TWL.

91 Simon Szreter, *Fertility, Class and Gender in Britain, 1860–1940* (Cambridge: Cambridge University Press, 1996), 76–128.

92 Jenny Keating, *A Child for Keeps: The History of Adoption in England, 1918–45* (Basingstoke: Palgrave Macmillan, 2009), 31; Kathleen Kiernan, Hilary Land and Jane Lewis, *Lone Motherhood in Twentieth-Century Britain: From Footnote to Front Page* (Oxford: Clarendon Press, 1998), 98.

93 Ninth Quarterly Meeting, 3 Nov. 1920, 5OPF/1/4/1, NCUMC Papers, TWL. Data from the NCUMC's Individual Case Department for the period Oct. 1919-Sept. 1920 categorized unmarried mothers by age (youngest 14, oldest 46) and occupation: 'clerical, domestic, miscellaneous or unknown'.

94 'Provision for Unmarried Mothers and Their Children': Policy adopted by a Conference held at Mansion House, London, 14 Feb. 1918: Findings of the Special Committee, 5OPF/01/1, NCUMC Papers, TWL.

95 Second Council meeting, 3 Jul. 1918, 5OPF/01/4/1, NCUMC Papers, TWL.

96 Lettice Fisher, 'Preface', in Fisher, *Unfinished Autobiography*, x.

97 Fisher, *Unfinished Autobiography*, x; Mary Bennett, *An Autobiography* (Privately published, 1997), 21.

98 Draft seating plans, MS Eng.d.3780, ff. 1–99, Additional Papers of H. A. L. Fisher, BL (Bodleian Libraries).

99 Edward Armstrong to Lettice Fisher, 22 Dec. 1916, MS Fisher 219, fols. 263–4, Papers of H. A. L. Fisher, BL.

100 Bennett, *Ilberts of India*, 193; 195.

101 See e.g. Virginia Woolf's essay, 'A Modern Salon' (1909), in Virginia Woolf, *Carlyle's House and Other Sketches*, ed. David Bradshaw (London: Hesperus, 2003), 12–13.

102 Deborah Simonton, *Women in European Culture and Society: Gender, Skill and Identity from 1700* (London: Routledge, 2011), 88–90.

103 Olive Heseltine, *Conversation* (London: Methuen, 1927), 228.

104 Lettice Fisher to Frances Stevenson, 3 June n.d., FCG2/7, Frances Stevenson Papers, National Library of Wales. Guests were not always convinced that these occasions did work out smoothly: for a critical perspective see the reflections of Isaiah Berlin in Henry Hardy, ed., *Isaiah Berlin: Letters 1928–1946* (Cambridge: Cambridge University Press, 2004), 70.

105 Élie Halévy to Lettice Fisher, 26 Jul. 1934, MS Fisher 70, fol. 7, Papers of H. A. L. Fisher, BL; John L. Hammond, 'Life & Work in England', *Times Literary Supplement*, 31 June 1934, 420.

106 Hilary Callan and Shirley Ardener, eds., *The Incorporated Wife* (London: Croom Helm, 1984), ch. 2.

107 Visitors' Book, New College Warden's Lodgings, 1925–43, MS Eng.d.3779, Additional Papers of H. A. L. Fisher, BL.

108 For example, in July 1934 Lettice Fisher was invited to Mrs Cyril Bailey's teatime 'At Home' at the King's Mound, Mansfield Road to meet Deaconess Beatrice Creighton,

MS Eng.d.3780, f.49, Additional Papers of H. A. L. Fisher, BL. The Fishers were also invited to an 'At Home' by the Viscountess Gladstone in support of the League of Nations Union: MS Eng.d.3780, f.36, BL.

109 Hardy, *Isaiah Berlin: Letters*, 70; Interview, Brian Harrison with Michael Crum, 30 Nov. 1974, 8 SUF/B/027, TWL.

110 Bernard Pares, *My Russian Memoirs* (London: Jonathan Cape, 1931), 289.

111 For a detailed discussion of the Anglo-Russian Hospital see Michael H. Harmer, *The Forgotten Hospital: An Essay* (Chichester, Springwood Books, 1982). Muriel Paget's early international work needs to be distinguished from that of Lady Leila Paget. Leila Paget had opened a hospital in Skopje, Serbia under the Serbian Relief Fund in 1914, following her nursing in the country during the typhus epidemic of 1912–13: see Louise Margaret Leila Wemyss Paget, *With Our Serbian Allies* (London: Serbian Relief Fund, 1915).

112 'Notes: Anglo-Russian Hospital', *British Medical Journal*, 12 Feb. 1916, 252.

113 Manuscript diary of L. C. Pocock, Sunday 15 May 1916 (also labelled 28 May 1916); 14 Aug. 1916 (also labelled 27 Aug. 1916); L. C. Pocock's MS diary: 'The X Ray Car: Anglo-Russian Hospital', Documents. 3648, Papers of G. M. and L. C. Pocock, Imperial War Museum, London (hereafter cited as IWM).

114 'Relief for Slovakia', *Christian World*, 16 Oct. 1919, 6.

115 Isabel Emslie Hutton, *Memories of a Doctor in War and Peace* (London: Heinemann, 1960), 188–91.

116 Isabel Emslie Hutton, *With a Woman's Unit in Serbia, Salonika and Sebastopol* (London: Williams and Norgate, 1928).

117 Hutton, *Memories of a Doctor*, 203; Louise Westwood, 'Explorations of Scottish, German and American Psychiatry: The Work of Helen Boyle and Isabel Hutton in the Treatment of Noncertifiable Mental Disorders in England, 1899–1939,' in *International Relations in Psychiatry: Britain, Germany, and the United States to World War II*, eds. Volker Rolecke, Paul J. Wiendling and Louise Westwood (Rochester, NY: University of Rochester Press, 2010), 185–6.

118 Hutton, *Memories of a Doctor*, 224–5.

119 Yeo, *The Contest for Social Science*, 287.

120 W. C. Cullis, 'Scharlieb, Dame Mary Ann Dacomb (1845–1930)', *Dictionary of National Biography, 1922–1930*, ed. J. R. H. Weaver (London: Oxford University Press, 1937), 749–51.

121 Muriel Paget to Eglantyne Jebb, 19 Aug. 1920, SCF/A401/EJ68, Papers of Eglantyne Jebb, Save the Children Fund Papers, Cadbury Research Library: Special Collections, University of Birmingham (hereafter cited as Jebb Papers, CRL).

122 Muriel Paget to Dr Emslie, 7 Sept. 1920; Dr Emslie to Muriel Paget, 9 Sept. 1920; Report from Dr Emslie from Sebastopol, 22 Sept. 1920 ('Winter's Work'); Dr Emslie to Muriel Paget, 20 Dec. 1920, Box 12, LRA/MS 1405.

123 Muriel Paget to Dr Emslie, 21 Jul. 1920, Box 12, LRA/MS 1405.

124 Lady Muriel Paget, 'Report on Visit to Moscow and need for Child Welfare Programme in Russia' [1922], Box 13, LRA/MS 1405.

125 'Impressions on Visit to Moscow for my Committee' (Memorandum by Lady Muriel Paget [1922]), Box 14, LRA/MS 1405.

126 Vernon, *Hunger*, 22; 27–8.

127 'Welfare Work in the Baltic States', *The Manchester Guardian*, 22 Apr. 1922, 10.

128 Dr Emslie, Report ('Winter's Work'), 22 Sept. 1920, Box 12, LRA/MS 1405.

129 L. B. Golden to Miss Jameson, 9 Jul. 1921, SCF/A401/EJ68, Jebb Papers, CRL.

130 For evidence of this process in respect of the international humanitarian response to the Russian famine of 1921–22 see Sasson, 'From Empire to Humanity', 532.

131 Muriel Payne, 'Report of the Infant Welfare Work to 1 Nov. 1920', Box 18, LRA/MS 1405.

132 See ch. 4.

133 'Notice to Parents', in Muriel Payne's 'Report of the Infant Welfare Work to 1 Nov. 1920'.

134 In 1916 when Muriel Paget was based in Petrograd at the Anglo-Russian Hospital her husband had written asking her to come home: see (Richard) Artie Paget to Muriel Paget, July 1916, Correspondence Box Z, LRA/MS 1405.

135 Ruth Compton Brouwer, *Modern Women Modernizing Men: The Changing Missions of Three Professional Women in Asia and Africa* (Vancouver: UBC Press, 2002), 18; Helen Sweet and Sue Hawkins, 'Introduction: Contextualising Colonial and Post-colonial Nursing', in *Colonial Caring: A History of Colonial and Post-colonial Nursing*, eds. Helen Sweet and Sue Hawkins (Manchester: Manchester University Press, 2015), 7.

136 See e.g. 'Paget Mission Estonia Monthly Report of Reval Welfare Clinic' (Oct. 1921), SCF/A401/EJ72, Jebb Papers, CRL.

137 'International Nursing Students', *The British Journal of Nursing*, 9 Oct. 1920, 199. On the establishment of the LORCS in 1919 see Peter Macalister-Smith, *International Humanitarian Assistance: Disaster Relief Actions in International Law and Organization* (Dordrecht: Martinus Nijhoff Publishers, 1985), 77.

138 Muriel Paget to Mrs Brooke, 21 June 1920, Box 17, LRA/MS 1405. An article in 1921 in the *North American Review* identified Muriel Paget's work in connection with the LORCS' child welfare division for the establishment of child welfare and maternity centres in Romania and Czechoslovakia as initiatives seeking to combat the spread of disease in Central and Eastern Europe: Richard P. Strong, 'International Public Health Problems', *The North American Review* 213, no. 784 (1921): 327.

139 Muriel Payne, 'Memorandum Scheme for the Establishment of Public Health and Child Welfare Training in Connection with Medical Relief for Russian Children', 1 Sept. 1922, Box 15, LRA/MS 1405.

140 On the social and cultural authority of the medical sciences in the interwar period see Christopher Lawrence, *Rockefeller Money, the Laboratory, and Medicine in Edinburgh 1919–1930: New Science in an Old Country* (Rochester, NY: University of Rochester Press, 2005), 17; 26; Steve Sturdy and Roger Cooter, 'Science, Scientific Management, and the Transformation of Medicine in Britain c. 1870–1950', *History of Science* 36, no. 4 (1998): 347; 449.

141 On the influence of clinical psychological vocabulary upon interwar and mid-twentieth-century child welfare work see John Stewart, *Child Guidance in Britain, 1918–55: The Dangerous Age of Childhood* (London: Pickering & Chatto, 2013).

142 Muriel Paget's access to Soviet Russia, like all international travellers, was dependent upon the Soviet authorities issuing her a visa, and there were periods in the later 1920s, notably 1929, where she was unable to travel because she was refused one: see Muriel Paget, 'Personal Relations with the Soviet Government': Address given to the Institute of International Affairs, 13 Nov. 1930, Box 28, LRA/MS 1405.

143 Cyril Burt, *The Yong Delinquent* (New York: D. Appleton and Co., 1925), 17.

144 Muriel Paget, 'Some Pictures of Soviet Russia III: The Wild Children', *The Daily Telegraph*, 3 Feb. 1927, 9.

145 Hinton, *Continuities of Class*, 93.

146 Alice Smuts notes the practice with reference to social justice reformers and social scientists in North America in the early-twentieth century: see Alice Boardman Smuts, *Science in the Service of Children, 1893–1935* (New Haven, CT: Yale University Press, 2006), 65–8.

147 'Medical Psychology', *The Sunday Times*, 22 Mar. 1931, 17.

148 'The Invalid Kitchens of London Annual Report, 1927–1928', 1. Box 1, LRA/MS1405.

149 Notice, 'The Next Big Step Forward': 'The Invalid Kitchens of London Annual Report, 1927–1928'.

150 Martin Edwards, *Control and the Therapeutic Trial: Rhetoric and Experimentation in Britain, 1918–1948* (Amsterdam: Editions Rodopi B.V., 2007), 9–10.

151 Laura Shapiro, *Perfection Salad: Women and Cooking at the Turn of the Century*, 2nd edn (Berkeley: University of California Press, 2009).

152 Notice, 'The Next Big Step Forward'.

153 Yeo, *Contest for Social Science*, 196.

154 John Stewart, 'The Mixed Economy of Welfare in Historical Perspective', in *Understanding the Mixed Economy of Welfare*, ed. Martin Powell (Bristol: The Policy Press, 2007), 23–40; Sasson, 'From Empire to Humanity'.

155 Elizabeth Macadam, *The Social Servant in the Making: A Review of the Provision of Training for the Social Services* (London: G. Allen and Unwin Ltd., 1945).

156 Helen Glew, *Gender, Rhetoric and Regulation: Women's Work in the Civil Service and the London County Council, 1900–55* (Manchester: Manchester University Press, 2016).

157 Attlee, *Social Worker*, 112; 252.

3 Identity

1 *The Times*, 11 Nov. 1935, 16. The highpoint of formal celebrations was planned for November 1935, including gala festivities at the Royal Albert Hall.

2 Kinnaird, *Reminiscences*, 3.

3 *Our Eighty Years*, MSS 243/15/4, YWCA Records, MRC.

4 'Filling Our Purses: by the Hon. Emily Kinnaird – A Wizard At It!', *Blue Triangle Gazette*, June 1935, 89.

5 Julie V. Gottlieb and Richard Toye, 'Introduction', in *The Aftermath of Suffrage: Women, Gender and Politics in Britain, 1918–1945*, ed. Julie V. Gottlieb and Richard Toye (Basingstoke: Palgrave Macmillan, 2013), 1.

6 Braithwaite, *The Voluntary Citizen*.

7 Macadam, *New Philanthropy*, 303; Braithwaite, *The Voluntary Citizen*, 81.

8 Amartya Sen, *Development As Freedom* (Oxford: Oxford University Press, 1999), xi–xii.

9 Caitríona Beaumont, *Housewives and Citizens: Domesticity and the Women's Movement in England, 1928–64* (Manchester: Manchester University Press, 2013), 2–3; 48. For further reading on voluntary women's organizations see: S. Clements, 'Feminism, Citizenship and Social Activity: The Role and Importance of Local Women's Organisations, Nottingham, 1918–1969' (PhD diss., University of Nottingham, 2008); Lorna Gibson, *Beyond Jerusalem: Music in the Women's Institute, 1919–1969* (Aldershot: Ashgate, 2008), 42–8; Maggie Andrews, *The Acceptable Face of Feminism: The Women's Institute as a Social Movement* (London: Lawrence and Wishart, 1997); Cordelia Moyse, *A History of the Mothers' Union: Women, Anglicanism and Globalization* (London: The Boydell Press, 2009); Caitríona Beaumont, 'Citizens Not Feminists: The Boundary Negotiated Between Citizenship and Feminism by Mainstream Women's Organisations in England, 1928–39', *Women's History Review* 9, no. 2 (2000): 411–29; Helen McCarthy, 'Service Clubs, Citizenship and Equality: Gender Relations and Middle-class Associations in Britain Between the Wars', *Historical Research* 81, no. 213 (2008): 531–52; Linda Perriton, 'The Education of Women for Citizenship: The National Federation of Women's Institutes and the British Federation of Business and Professional Women 1930–1959', *Gender and Education*, 12 no. 1 (2009): 81–95. On the growth of women's organizations especially in the 1920s see Helen McCarthy and Pat Thane, 'The Politics of Association in Industrial Society', *Twentieth Century British History* 22, no. 2 (2011): 225.

10 I am drawing on the following work in this definition of citizenship: Ruth Lister, *Citizenship: Feminist Perspectives* (Basingstoke: Macmillan, 1997); Adrian Oldfield, *Citizenship and Community: Civic Republicanism and the Modern World* (London: Routledge, 1990); Will Kymlicka and Wayne Norman, 'Return of the Citizen: A

Survey of Recent Work on Citizenship Theory', *Ethics* 104, no. 2 (1994): 352–81; Chantal Mouffe, 'Democratic Citizenship and Political Community', in *Dimensions of Radical Democracy: Pluralism, Citizenship, Community*, ed. Chantal Mouffe (London: Verso, 1992), 225–39; Lynn Staeheli, 'Political Geography: Where's Citizenship?', *Progress in Human Geography* 35, no. 3 (2010): 393–400.

11 On the significance of maternalist traditions of women's activism in welfare politics see Koven and Michel eds., *Mothers of a New World*; Bock and Thane eds., *Maternity and Gender Policies.*

12 Vera Brittain, 'Committee Versus Professions' (previously unpublished, 1929), in *Testament of a Generation*, eds. Berry and Bishop, 105–108; Letter from Vera Brittain to Winifred Holtby, 10 Jan. 1926, published in *Selected Letters of Winifred Holtby and Vera Brittain, 1920–1935*, eds. Vera Brittain and Geoffrey Handley-Taylor (London: A. Brown, 1960), 77.

13 H. A. L. Fisher to Lettice Fisher, 1 Nov. 1918, MS Fisher 205, fol. 44, Papers of H. A. L. Fisher, BL.

14 'One Of The Idle Rich', *The Woman's Leader*, 13 August 1920, 624. The journal noted acknowledgement for the poem to the *Association Monthly* (U.S.A.). The NUSEC discussed indepth women's committee work: see e.g. H. Reynard, 'Committee Procedure', *Woman's Year Book 1923–1924*, 206–10.

15 Tim Darlington, 'Trustees, Committees and Boards', in *Introduction to the Voluntary Sector*, eds. Rodney Hedley, Colin Rochester and Justin Davis-Smith (London: Routledge, 1995), 211–26.

16 A. F. C. Bourdillon, 'Introduction' and 'Voluntary Organizations to Facilitate Co-operation and Co-ordination', in *Voluntary Social Services*, 1; 192.

17 Emily Kinnaird declined invitations to sit on committees of some additional organizations, see e.g. Emily Kinnaird to Olga Nethersole, 20 June 1918, PLH/1, Papers of the People's League of Health, LSE Library.

18 Kinnaird, *Reminiscences*, 116.

19 Kinnaird, *Reminiscences*, 116; 105; 81.

20 Kinnaird, *Reminiscences*, 117.

21 Kinnaird, *Reminiscences*, 117.

22 Kinnaird, *Reminiscences*, 102–3; 116–7.

23 Kinnaird, *Reminiscences*, 103.

24 Kinnaird, *Reminiscences*, 103. On the traditions of evangelical autobiographical record-keeping see e.g. Christopher Tolley, *Domestic Biography: The Legacy of Evangelicalism in Four Nineteenth-Century Families* (Oxford: Clarendon Press, 1997); D. Bruce Hindmarsh, *The Evangelical Conversion Narrative: Spiritual Autobiography in Early Modern England* (Oxford: Oxford University Press, 2005).

25 Emily Kinnaird, 'Committee Work in the YWCA', *The News Letter*, Oct. 1916, 107, MSS 243/14/22/12, YWCA Records, MRC.

26 Kinnaird, 'Committee Work in the YWCA', 107.

27 Kinnaird, 'Committee Work in the YWCA', 107.

28 Kinnaird, *Reminiscences*, 105–8.

29 Ruth Rouse and Stephen Charles Neill eds., *A History of the Ecumenical Movement 1517–1948*, 2nd edn (London: SPCK, 1954; 1967), 602–4; 328. Citations refer to the 1967 version.

30 Emily Kinnaird's Conference Diaries (see ch. 1, note 118).

31 Kinnaird, *Reminiscences*, 106.

32 Kinnaird, *Reminiscences*, 107–8.

33 C.O.P.E.C. Commission Report, *The Social Function of the Church* (London: C.O.P.E.C. Continuation Committee, 1924), 7.

34 Smith, Peretz and Smith, *Social Enquiry*, 52.

35 Kinnaird, *Reminiscences*, 107–8.

36 Selina Todd, *Young Women, Work, and Family in England 1918–1950* (Oxford: Oxford University Press, 2005), 35.

37 See 59.

38 'The Interpretation of Christ in a World Fellowship: A Study for Members of the British YWCA in Preparation for their Biennial Conference, Oct. 1922', Questions 11–17 (see ch. 1, note 119).

39 Memorandum, 'The Secession Period of the YWCA' (Papers Relating to The Secession Period of the YWCA), MSS 243/80/1, YWCA Records, MRC; Kinnaird, *Reminiscences*, 61.

40 Kinnaird, *Reminiscences*, 118–19.

41 *Our Eighty Years*, 14 (see Introduction, note 67).

42 Keith Middlemas, *Politics in Industrial Society: The Experience of the British System Since 1911* (London: A. Deutsch, 1979); Alan Booth, 'Corporatism, Capitalism and Depression in Interwar Britain', *The British Journal of Sociology* 33, no. 2 (1982): 200–23. An exception is José Harris, 'Political Thought and the Welfare State 1870–1940: An Intellectual Framework For British Social Policy', in *Before Beveridge: Welfare Before the Welfare State*, ed. David Gladstone (London: Institute of Economic Affairs, 1999), 46.

43 Leslie Hannah, *The Rise of the Corporate Economy* (London: Methuen, 1979); B. R. Cheffins, *Corporate Ownership and Control: British Business Transformed* (Oxford: Oxford University Press, 2008); Harris, 'Political Thought and the Welfare State 1870–1940', 46.

44 'The Interpretation of Christ in a World Fellowship: A Study for Members of the British YWCA in Preparation for their Biennial Conference, Oct. 1922', Question 8, Recommendation 2, Champery Findings, 1920.

45 David Doughan and Peter Gordon, *Women, Clubs and Associations in Britain* (Abingdon: Routledge, 2006), 100.

46 Kinnaird, *Reminiscences*, 33; 65. On the popularity of the Women's Institutes by the mid-1920s see Pat Thane, 'Women of the British Labour Party and Feminism, 1906–45', in *British Feminism in the Twentieth Century*, ed. Harold Smith (Aldershot: Elgar, 1990), 70; Brittain, *Women's Work in Modern England*, 165.

47 Picton-Turbervill, *Life is Good*, 154.

48 Picton-Turbervill, *Life is Good*, 155–6; 170.

49 'The Interpretation of Christ in a World Fellowship': Questions: 8c) and d). The encouragement to YWCA branches to forge relationships with women's trades unions signals how the organization extended the purpose of voluntary organizations beyond what Ross McKibbin argues was the primary aim to reinforce the 'informal Conservative hold on bourgeois associational life': Ross McKibbin, *Classes and Cultures: England 1918–1951* (Oxford: Oxford University Press, 2000), 96–8.

50 Elizabeth Roberts, *A Woman's Place: An Oral History of Working-Class Women 1890–1940* (Oxford: Basil Blackwell, 1984), 169.

51 'The Interpretation of Christ in a World Fellowship': 2a ('The place of the Association in the locality').

52 Kinnaird, *Reminiscences*, 119.

53 'The Interpretation of Christ to Young Women To-day', Questionnaire: 5 (see ch. 1, note 120).

54 Susan Kingsley Kent, *Aftershocks: Politics and Trauma in Britain, 1918–1931* (Basingstoke: Palgrave Macmillan, 2009).

55 'The Interpretation of Christ to Young Women To-day', Questionnaire: 8 (see above, note 53).

56 'The Interpretation of Christ to Young Women To-day', Questionnaire: 6.

57 I am drawing on the insights of Sylvia Walby, who has argued that citizenship is about a transition from private to public patriarchy, and that political citizenship for women destabilizes private patriarchy: Sylvia Walby, 'Is Citizenship Gendered?', *Sociology* 28, no. 2 (1994): 379–95.

58 Lettice Fisher and T. C. Elder, 'Woman's Place in the New Order', *The Times*, 29 Apr. 1921, 13.

59 Lettice Fisher, 'The Economic Position of the Married Woman', The Stansfield Trust Lecture, University of London, 1924 (London: Oxford University Press, 1924), 8.

60 Fisher, *Getting and Spending*, 112.

61 Bennett, *Autobiography*, 2.

62 Bennett, *Autobiography*, 2.

63 See e.g. Lettice Fisher, 'The Unmarried Mother', issued by The Six Point Group (Women's Printing Society, Brick Street, Piccadilly, n.d.), reprinted from *Time and Tide*, 21 Jan. 1921.

64 Fisher, 'The Unmarried Mother'.

65 'The Bastardy Bill, 1920' (see ch. 2, note 87).

66 Bentley B. Gilbert, *The Evolution of National Insurance in Great Britain: The Origins of the Welfare State* (London: Michael Joseph, 1966), 349.

67 Lettice Fisher, 'Unmarried Mothers', *The Times*, 24 Oct. 1922, 8.

68 See 81.

69 Thane and Evans, *Sinners? Scroungers? Saints?*, 8–13; Vicky Holmes, 'Finding a Bed: The Experiences of Unmarried Mothers in Working-Class Victorian Society', paper presented at the Women's History Network Conference, Leeds Trinity, September 2016. I am very grateful to the author for letting me cite this paper.

70 G. D. H. Cole, 'A Retrospect of the History of Voluntary Social Service', in *Voluntary Social Services*, 24.

71 Lettice Fisher, 'An Appeal to Humanity', *The Times*, 22 Sept. 1924, 8.

72 Laura King, 'Future Citizens: Cultural and Political Conceptions of Children in Britain, 1930s–1950s', *Twentieth Century British History* 27, no. 3 (2016): 389–411.

73 Speech of broadcast NCUMC appeal, Lettice Fisher, 'The Unwanted Child', 1925, 5OPF/2/2/7/1, NCUMC Papers, TWL.

74 Cole, 'A Retrospect', in *Voluntary Social Services*, 25.

75 Fisher, 'An Appeal to Humanity', *The Times*, 22 Sept. 1924, 8; Fisher, 'The Unwanted Child', 1925.

76 David Lloyd George, 'The National Insurance Act', Speech delivered at Kennington Theatre, 13 Jul. 1912, quoted in Herbert du Parcq, *Life of Lloyd George* (London: Caxton Publishing Company, 1912–13), 4:792.

77 See e.g. Rosser, *Art of Solidarity*, 13.

78 Lettice Fisher, *The Citizen: A Simple Account of How We Manage our National and Local Affairs* (London: W. & R. Chambers, Ltd., 1927), frontispiece.

79 José Harris, 'Political Thought and the State', in *Boundaries of the State in Modern Britain*, eds. S. J. D. Green and R. J. Whiting (Cambridge: Cambridge University Press, 1996), 16; 20.

80 William Henry Hadow, *Citizenship* (Oxford: Clarendon Press, 1923). William Hadow succeeded H. A. L. Fisher as Chancellor of Sheffield University in 1916; his sister Grace Hadow was the Vice-Chair of the NFWI and would have been well known to Lettice Fisher.

81 Fisher, *Citizen*, 30–1.

82 Cole, 'A Retrospect', in *Voluntary Social Services*, 24.

83 Fisher, *Citizen*, 195; 268.

84 Rosser, *Art of Solidarity*, 191.

85 Fisher, *Citizen*, 246.

86 Fisher, *Citizen*, 259.

87 Fisher, *Citizen*, 257.

88 Fisher, *Citizen*, 259.

89 Patricia Hollis, *Ladies Elect: Women in English Local Government 1865–1914* (Oxford: Clarendon Press, 1987).

90 See e.g. Gleadle, *Borderline Citizens*.

91 Karen Hunt and June Hannam, 'Towards an Archaeology of Interwar Women's Politics: The Local and the Everyday', in *The Aftermath of Suffrage*, eds. Gottlieb and Toye, 124–41.

92 A. F. C. Bourdillon, 'Voluntary Organizations to Meet the Needs of the Countryman', in *Voluntary Social Services*, 234.

93 Beaumont, *Housewives and Citizens*; Hunt and Hannam, 'Towards an Archaeology of Interwar Women's Politics', 133.

94 See e.g. Mrs M. S. Pember Reeves, *Round About a Pound a Week* (London: G. Bell and Sons Ltd., 1913).

95 David Thackeray, 'From Prudent Housewife to Empire Shopper: Party Appeals to the Female Voter, 1918–1928', in *Aftermath of Suffrage*, eds. Gottlieb and Toye, 47; Hunt and June Hannam, 'Towards an Archaeology of Interwar Women's Politics', 134.

96 John Christian Pringle, *The Nation's Appeal to the Housewife and Her Response* (London: Longmans, Green and Co. and [London] Charity Organization Society, 1933). On the targeting of advertising of new household appliances to the middle-class housewife see Nicola Humble, *The Feminine Middlebrow Novel, 1920s to 1950s: Class, Domesticity and Bohemianism* (Oxford: Oxford University Press, 2001), 118.

97 See e.g. Rhodri Hayward, 'Desperate Housewives and Model Amoebae: The Invention of Suburban Neurosis in Inter-war Britain', in *Health and the Modern Home*, ed. M. Jackson (New York: Routledge, 2007), 42–62.

98 Yeo, *Contest for Social Science*, 271.

99 Thackeray, 'From Prudent Housewife to Empire Shopper', 48.

100 On the NFWI's work with the Horace Plunkett Foundation see Lynne Thompson, 'Agricultural Education in the Interwar Years', in Paul Brassley, Jeremy Burchardt and Lynne Thompson, eds. *The English Countryside Between the Wars: Regeneration or Decline?* (Woodbridge: Boydell, 2006), 59–60.

101 The talks were subsequently published as Lettice Fisher, *The Housewife and the Townhall* (London: Ivor Nicholson and Watson Ltd., 1934); *The Facts Behind the Crisis* (London: Oxford University Press, 1931); *Mothers and Families* (London: Ernest Benn Ltd., 1932).

102 Photographs in the Ilbert Family Papers, Photographs and Press Cuttings, Private collection, Sophie Ilbert Decaudaveine (and the late Robert Ilbert); Bennett, *Autobiography*, 5.

103 Fisher, *Housewife*, 100.

104 Helena Deneke, *Grace Hadow* (London: Oxford University Press, 1946), 102–7.

105 Fisher, *Housewife*, 111–12.

106 Sen, *Development As Freedom*, 190.

107 Smith, Peretz and Smith, *Social Enquiry*, 49–50.

108 Brassley, Burchardt, Thompson, eds. *The English Countryside Between the Wars*. See also Jeremy Burchardt, *Paradise Lost: Rural Idyll and Social Change in England Since 1800* (London: Tauris, 2002), chs. 11–12.

109 Fisher, *Facts Behind the Crisis*, foreword.

110 Maggie Andrews, *Domesticating the Airwaves: Broadcasting, Domesticity and Femininity* (London: Continuum, 2012), 1. Andrews notes that initially the cost of wireless radios and licenses were prohibitive to many individual listeners and that group listening was an important early experience.

111 L. Hill, 'Advertising Local Government in England', *Public Opinion Quarterly* 1, no. 2 (1937): 65.

112 Trotter, *Literature in the First Media Age*, 29.

113 On the BBC see LeMahieu, *Culture for Democracy*, 138–54.

114 Cole, 'A Retrospect', in *Voluntary Social Services*, 24.

115 Fisher, *Housewife*, 109.

116 Holtby, 'Feminism Divided', in *Testament of a Generation*, eds. Berry and Bishop, 47–8.

117 Fisher, *Housewife*, 108. On women's minority position in local government as a specific campaigning issue that was pursued by non-party women's groups see Hunt and Hannam, 'Towards an Archaeology of Interwar Women's Politics', 132.

118 Peretz, 'Infant Welfare Between the Wars', 137. On the rhetoric of middle-class and lady visitors see Ross McKibbin, 'Social Class and Social Observation in Edwardian England', *Transactions of the Royal Historical Society* 5th series, 28 (1978): 175–99.

119 H. A. L. Fisher to Lettice Fisher, Nov. 1915, MS Fisher 202, fol. 167, Papers of H. A. L. Fisher, BL.

120 Fisher, *Facts Behind the Crisis*, 36.

121 Booth, *Woman*, 33.

122 Booth, *Woman*, 14; 22.

123 Booth, *Woman*, 15–16.

124 Booth, *Woman*, 33.

125 Eason, *Women in God's Army*, 121.

126 Eason, *Women in God's Army*, 122; 145.

127 See 49–50.

128 Booth and Livingston Hill, *War Romance*, 20–1.

129 Evangeline Booth, 'Around the World with the Salvation Army', *National Geographic Magazine* 37, no. 4 (1920): 351.

130 Booth, 'Around the World with the Salvation Army': 351.

131 Booth, 'Around the World with the Salvation Army': 349.

132 Evangeline Booth, *Will You Help? A Call From Evangeline Booth* (London: The Salvation Army, 1937).

133 Booth, *Will You Help?*

134 On the late-nineteenth and early-twentieth-century American 'cult of womanhood' see Beryl Satter, *Each Mind a Kingdom: American Women, Sexual Purity, and the New Thought Movement, 1875–1920* (Berkeley: University of California Press, 1999).

135 Evangeline Booth, *This Brotherhood of Nations* (St. Albans: The Campfield Press, 1937), 3.

136 Booth, *This Brotherhood of Nations.*

137 See e.g. Stanley Cohen, *States of Denial: Knowing About Atrocities and Suffering* (Cambridge, UK: Polity, 2001), ch. 7; Susan D. Moeller, *Compassion Fatigue: How the Media Sell Disease, Famine, War and Death* (New York: Routledge, 1999).

138 I am engaging here with Jonathan Sacks' metaphor in *The Dignity of Difference: How to Avoid the Clash of Civilizations* (London: Bloomsbury, 2002).

139 Booth, 'Around the World with the Salvation Army', 358. On Christian universalism as both a discursive construct and a symbol of the practical necessity of Christian mission organizations working together with groups and peoples across racial lines see Jeffrey Cox, 'From the Empire of Christ to the Third World: Religion and the Experience of Empire in the Twentieth Century', in *Britain's Experience of Empire in the Twentieth Century*, ed. Andrew Thompson (Oxford: Oxford University Press, 2012), 94–5.

140 Tanya Agathocleous, *Urban Realism and the Cosmopolitan Imagination in the Nineteenth Century: Visible City, Invisible World* (Cambridge: Cambridge University Press, 2011), 147; 150.

141 Walker, *Pulling the Devil's Kingdom Down*, 240.

142 Agathocleous, *Urban Realism and the Cosmopolitan Imagination*, 164.

143 Martin Erdmann, *Building the Kingdom of God on Earth: The Churches' Contribution to Marshal Public Support for World Order and World Peace, 1919–1945* (Eugene, OR: Wipf and Stock, 2005), 67.

144 A concept noted of religion more broadly by Henrietta L. Moore, *Still Life: Hopes, Desires and Satisfactions* (Cambridge, UK: Polity Press, 2011), 62.

145 Compton Brouwer, *Modern Women Modernizing Men*, 12–14; William Richey Hogg, *Ecumenical Foundations: A History of the International Missionary Council and its Nineteenth-Century Background* (New York: Harper and Brothers, 1952).

146 Jörg Mathias, 'Unity in Christ or Pan-Europeanism? Nathan Söderblom and the Ecumenical Peace Movement in the Interwar Period', *Religion, State and Society* 42, no. 1 (2014): 12.

147 Evangeline Booth's manuscript in response to questions by the IMC, Speeches II, 312/7, Booth Papers, SAA.

148 Booth's manuscript in response to questions by the IMC.

149 'Communism and Christianity', n.d., Speeches I, 298/18, Booth Papers, SAA.

150 'Internationalism', Commissioners' Conference, Aug. 1939, Speeches I, 298/18, Booth Papers, SAA.

151 'Build You Up', Speech to Officers at the Associate Headquarters, Congress Hall, 13 Jan. 1938, Speeches I, 311/5, Booth Papers, SAA.

152 'Build You Up'.

153 E.g. Lewis, *Women and Social Action*; *The Voluntary Sector, the State and Social Work in Britain*; Summers, 'A Home from Home'; Prochaska, *Women and Philanthropy*.

154 This outward-facing model of selfhood cross-cuts that of the inward-looking 'conservative modernity' that Alison Light argued defined women's subjective experience in the interwar years: see *Forever England: Femininity, Literature and Conservatism Between the Wars* (London: Routledge, 1995).

155 Sen, *Development As Freedom*, xii.

156 Bourdillon, 'Voluntary Organizations to Meet the Needs of the Countryman', in *Voluntary Social Services*, 233.

157 Fisher, *Citizen*, 199.

4 Culture

1 Muriel Paget to (Richard) Artie Paget, 9 Feb. 1937, Correspondence Box H, LRA/MS 1405.

2 Una Pope-Hennessy, *The Closed City: Impressions of a Visit to Leningrad* (London: Hutchinson & Co., 1938), 44.

3 The scholarly literature on women's travel writings is vast. Key interventions include: Ali Behdad, *Belated Travelers. Orientalism in the Age of Colonial Dissolution* (Durham, NC: Duke University Press, 1994); Alison Blunt, *Travel, Gender, and Imperialism: Mary Kingsley and West Africa* (New York: Guilford Press, 1994); Jane Fletcher Geniesse, *Passionate Nomad: The Life of Freya Stark* (New York: Modern Library, 2001); Indira Ghose, *Women Travellers in Colonial India: The Power of the Female Gaze* (Delhi: Oxford University Press, 1998); Cheryl McEwan, *Gender, Geography and Empire: Victorian Women Travellers in West Africa* (Aldershot: Ashgate, 2000); Sara Mills, *Discourses of Difference: An Analysis of Women's Travel Writing and Colonialism* (London: Routledge, 1991).

4 Patricia M. E. Lorcin, *Historicizing Colonial Nostalgia: European Women's Narratives of Algeria and Kenya 1900–Present* (New York: Palgrave Macmillan, 2012), 6–7.

5 For studies addressing humanitarian governance and transnational exchange see Barbara Metzger, 'Towards An International Human Rights Regime During the Inter-war Years: the League of Nations' Combat of Traffic in Women and Children', in *Beyond Sovereignty: Britain, Empire and Transnationalism, c.1880–1950*, eds. Kevin Grant, Philippa Levine and Frank Trentmann (Basingstoke: Palgrave Macmillan, 2007), 54–79; John F. Hutchinson, '"Custodians of the Sacred Fire": The

ICRC and the Postwar Reorganisation of the International Red Cross', in *International Health Organisations and Movements 1918-1939*, ed. Paul Weindling (Cambridge: Cambridge University Press, 1995), 17–35; Bridget Towers, 'Red Cross Organisational Politics, 1918–1922: Relations of Dominance and the Influence of the United States', in *International Health Organisations*, ed. Weindling, 36–55; Helen McCarthy, 'The Lifeblood of the League? Voluntary Associations and League of Nations Activism in Britain', in *Internationalism Reconfigured: Transnational Ideas and Movements Between the Wars*, ed. Daniel Laqua (London: I. B. Tauris, 2011), 187–208. On women's international humanitarianism see especially Carol Miller, 'Women in International Relations? The Debate in Inter-war Britain', in *Gender and International Relations*, eds. Rebecca Grant and Kathleen Newland (Milton Keynes: Open University, 1991), 64–82; Carol Miller, 'Lobbying the League: Women's International Organisations and the League of Nations' (DPhil thesis, University of Oxford, 1992); '"Geneva – The Key to Equality": Inter-war Feminists and the League of Nations', *Women's History Review* 3, no. 2 (1994): 219–45; Susan Pedersen, 'Metaphors of the Schoolroom: Women Working the Mandates System of the League of Nations', *History Workshop Journal* 66, no. 1 (2008): 188–207.

6 On cultural brokering as inter-cultural dialogue, explored in an early American context, see Nancy L. Hagedorn, '"A Friend to Go Between Them": The Interpreter as Cultural Broker During Anglo-Iroquois Councils, 1740–70', *Ethnohistory* 35, no. 1 (1988): 60–80.

7 Glenda Sluga, *The Nation, Psychology, and International Politics, 1870-1919* (Basingstoke: Palgrave Macmillan, 2006), 1–2.

8 On the 'English "Russian myth"' see Anthony Cross, ed., *A People Passing Rude: British Responses to Russian Culture* (Cambridge, UK: Open Book Publishers, 2012).

9 Jane McDermid, 'A Very Polite and Considerate Revolution: The Scottish Women's Hospitals and the Russian Revolution, 1916–17', *Revolutionary Russia* 21, no. 2 (2008): 135–51.

10 Manuscript diary of L. C. Pocock, 25 May 1916 (also labelled 7 Jun. 1916), Documents. 3648, L. C. Pocock Papers, IWM.

11 Pares, *My Russian Memoirs*, 482.

12 Untitled note, written by Lady Muriel Paget, Box 14, LRA/MS 1405.

13 Minutes of committee meeting of Women and Children of Russian Relief Fund, 29 Jan. 1920, Box 14, LRA/MS 1405.

14 The model of Russian Orientalism was to become a central trope against which the 'Bolshevik Revolution of modernity' revolted: see Michael David-Fox, *Showcasing the Great Experiment: Cultural Diplomacy and Western Visitors to the Soviet Union, 1921–41* (New York: Oxford University Press, 2012), 9. Muriel Paget's evolving critique of the Orientalist view emerges in a series of letters she wrote to her husband in 1936 from a Ramakrishna Mission retreat near the River Ganges, in

which she denigrated the bourgeois materialist mode embodied by 'Western' bureaucrats and businessmen and valued instead a heightened 'spirit of the west' in conversation with the spirituality of the Ramakrishna monks: see Muriel Paget to (Richard) Artie Paget, 10–14 Feb. 1936, Correspondence Box H, LRA/MS 1405.

15 Untitled note, written by Lady Muriel Paget, Box 14, LRA/MS 1405.

16 Bernard Pares, *Russia and Reform* (London: Archibald Constable & Co. Ltd., 1907), ch. xiv.

17 Blunt, *Lady Muriel*, 59.

18 Pares, *My Russian Memoirs*, 398–9.

19 *The British Journal of Nursing*, 2 Oct. 1915, 276. For similar idealizations of the 'gift relationship' during the Second World War see Claire Knight, 'Mrs. Churchill Goes to Russia: The Wartime Gift Exchange Between Britain and the Soviet Union', in *A People Passing Rude*, ed. Anthony Cross, 253–68.

20 Rappaport, *Caught in the Revolution*, 212–13.

21 Bernard Pares to Muriel Paget, 24 Feb. 1931, Correspondence Box S, LRA/MS 1405.

22 Bernard Pares, 'Lady Muriel Paget', *The Slavonic and East European Review* 17, no. 49 (1938): 219.

23 On civil servants' and technocrats' repurposing of the model of philanthropic cultural patronage in the interwar period see Scott Anthony, *Public Relations and the Making of Modern Britain: Stephen Tallents and the Birth of a Progressive Media Profession* (Manchester: Manchester University Press, 2012).

24 'To Be Famous Figures: Picture Ball People and Paintings', *The Illustrated London News*, 29 Nov. 1913, 892; 'The Living-picture Ball', *The Manchester Guardian*, 3 Dec. 1913, 8. See also Lisa Tickner, 'The Popular Culture of *Kermesse*: Lewis, Painting and Performance, 1912–13', *Modernism/Modernity* 4, no. 2 (1997): 67–120.

25 Christopher Nevnison to Wyndham Lewis, quoted in Paul O'Keefe, *Some Sort of Genius: A Life of Wyndham Lewis* (Berkeley, CA: Counterpoint, 2015), 140. On the fashion for pre-war avant-garde art see Stella Tillyard, *The Impact of Modernism, 1900–1920: Early Modernism and the Arts and Crafts Movement in Edwardian England* (New York: Routledge, 1988).

26 Michael T. Saler, *The Avant-garde in Interwar England: Medieval Modernism and the London Underground* (New York: Oxford University Press, 1999), vii.

27 *Blast*, No. 1, June 20, 1914 ('Review of the Great English Vortex'), 26; 37. The Salvation Army was amongst the many things the Vorticist manifesto 'Bless[ed]' (rather than 'Blast[ed]'), 28.

28 Anthony Cross, 'Exhibiting Russia: The Two London Russian Exhibitions of 1917 and 1935', *Slavonica* 16, no. 1 (2010): 35.

29 'Preliminary Notice, Russian Exhibition: Descriptive of the Industries, Art, Literature and Customs of Russia', LBY EX. 231, IWM; *The British Journal of Nursing*, 5 May 1917, 306.

30 Richard Marks, 'Russian Icons through British Eyes, c. 1830–1930', in *A People Passing Rude*, ed. Anthony Cross, 80.

31 Rosa Newmarch, *The Russian Arts* (London: H. Jenkins, 1916), 285, quoted in Anthony Cross, 'By Way of Introduction: British Perception, Reception and Recognition of Russian Culture', in *A People Passing Rude*, ed. Anthony Cross, 31.

32 'Preliminary Notice, Russian Exhibition'; *Russian Exhibition Descriptive of the Industries, Art, Literature, and Customs of Russia* (London: Grafton Galleries, 1917), 7–8.

33 Pares, *My Russian Memoirs*, 256–7.

34 *Russian Exhibition Descriptive.*

35 Cross, 'Exhibiting Russia', 35.

36 *Russian Exhibition Descriptive*, 7; 77; 123.

37 'Child Welfare in Russia', *The Manchester Guardian*, 8 Jul. 1927, 14. See also USSR Society of Cultural Relations with Foreign Countries to Muriel Paget, 3 June 1926, Box 14, LRA/MS 1405.

38 Marks, 'Russian Icons', 69–88.

39 Muriel Paget to (Richard) Artie Paget, 29 May 1916, Correspondence Box F, LRA/MS 1405. The scene was documented in a postcard produced for the Anglo-Russian Hospital Fund series that was sold at the 1917 exhibition at the Grafton gallery: *Russian Exhibition Descriptive*, 14.

40 Lantern slide of an unnamed Russian Orthodox church, Box 5, LRA/MS 1405.

41 '"Star" Man's Diary', *The Star*, 6 Feb. 1931, 7. Evidence of Muriel Paget's developing collection of icons was recorded in an article for the SCF's journal in 1921 which noted that she was given an icon in late 1920/early 1921 during her visit to Dvinsk, Latvia: 'News from Stricken Lands', *The Record of the Save the Children Fund*, 15 Jan. 1921, 72.

42 Marks, 'Russian Icons', 70.

43 Pope-Hennessy, *Closed City*, 45. On the repatriation of British nationals from Russia in the early 1920s see M. V. Glenny, 'The Anglo-Soviet Trade Agreement, March 1921', *Journal of Contemporary History* 5, no. 2 (1970): 63–82.

44 Rappaport, *Caught in the Revolution*, 325.

45 Muriel Paget, 'Some Pictures of Soviet Russia II: Life in Moscow', *The Daily Telegraph*, 2 Feb. 1927, 9 and 'V: Hospitals and Clinics', *The Daily Telegraph*, 5 Feb. 1927, 7.

46 Robert Hodgson to Lady Muriel Paget, 10 May 1927, Box 26, LRA/MS 1405. Hodgson congratulated Paget on the success of her appeal for the BSRRA, which raised nearly £2,000.

47 'The Letters of Eve', *The Tatler*, 26 Aug. 1931, 344.

48 On women's negotiation and eventual formal inclusion in 1946 within the British diplomatic establishment, see Helen McCarthy, *Women of the World: The Rise of the Female Diplomat* (London: Bloomsbury, 2014).

49 Julian and Margaret Bullard eds., *Inside Stalin's Russia: the Diaries of Reader Bullard, 1930–34* (Charlbury: Day Books, 2000), 221–2. See also 'Echoes of the Town by Mr. Gossip', *Daily Sketch*, 10 Oct. 1936, 13. The BSRRA distributed the pensions that British companies continued to pay former employees.

50 Atticus, 'Men, Women, and Memories', *The Sunday Times*, 14 Feb. 1937, 15.

51 In 1930 the Soviet Government offered to assign twenty-five acres of land in Pushkin to the BSRRA and the British civic engineer Patrick Abercrombie drew up plans for the construction of a hostel, but these were rejected: L. E. Mather to USSR Government Representatives regarding 'Home for British Subjects in USSR', 17 Nov. 1930, Box 26, LRA/MS 1405.

52 Shelia Fitzpatrick, *Everyday Stalinism: Ordinary Life in Extraordinary Times: Soviet Russia in the 1930s* (Oxford: Oxford University Press, 1999), 47.

53 'Home for Needy Britons in Russia: Woman Who Works for their Comfort in a Forest Glade', *Daily Sketch*, 12 Oct. 1936, 12; 'Stranded Britons in Soviet Russia: Somerset's Lady Bountiful to Her Own People', *Evening World/Evening Times* (Bristol), 6 Jul. 1933, 13.

54 Pope-Hennessy, *Closed City*, 42. On the late-nineteenth-century discourse of hospitality as mandating an 'ongoing openness to the other' see Rachel Hollander, *Narrative Hospitality in Late Victorian Fiction: Novel Ethics* (New York: Routledge, 2012), 6.

55 Bennett, *Ilberts in India*, 33; 36; 38.

56 Bennett, *Ilberts in India*, 40.

57 Bennett, *Ilberts in India*, 104.

58 Lettice Fisher, 'Indian Memories', *The Cornhill Magazine* 154 (Sept. 1936), 346.

59 Bennett, *Ilberts in India*, 86.

60 Bennett, *Ilberts in India*, 193.

61 H. A. L. Fisher, *Autobiography*, vi-vii.

62 Fisher, *Autobiography*, 146.

63 Fisher, *Autobiography*, 150.

64 Lettice Fisher, *A Brief Survey of the British Empire* (London: Oxford University Press, 1932), 42; 110–11.

65 Lettice Fisher, *An Introductory History of England and Europe from the Earliest Times to the Present* (London: Victor Gollancz, 1935), 358.

66 Fisher, *Introductory History of England and Europe*, 723.

67 Fisher, *Citizen*, 254.

68 Lettice Fisher, *Life and Work in England: A Sketch of Our Social and Economic History* (London: Edward Arnold & Co., 1934).

69 T. W. Riker, 'Reviewed Work: *A History of Europe* by H. A. L. Fisher', *The Journal of Modern History* 9, no. 1 (1937), 64. The review described H. A. L. Fisher's three-volume history as aimed at the scholar and '[t]he well-read adult who

possesses an easy chair and taste for history . . . afforded the opportunity of passing – say – three delightful evenings'.

70 Berg, *Woman in History*, 11.

71 Berg, *Woman in History*, 244.

72 Mark Hewitson and Matthew D'Auria eds., *Europe in Crisis: Intellectuals and the European Idea, 1917–1957* (New York: Berghahn Books, 2012).

73 Stuart Woolf, 'Europe and its Historians', *Contemporary European History* 12, no. 3 (2003): 325.

74 Richard Overy, *The Morbid Age: Britain Between the Wars* (London: Allen Lane, 2009), 3–4.

75 H. A. L. Fisher, *A History of Europe* (London: Longman, 1935) 1:vi.

76 Hewitson and D'Auria eds., *Europe in Crisis*, 2.

77 Esme Wingfield-Stratford, *The Foundations of British Patriotism* (London: G. Routledge and Sons, 1939).

78 Fisher, *Introductory History of England and Europe*, 813.

79 Hardy ed., *Isaiah Berlin: Letters*, 265.

80 Graham Wallas, 'Introduction', in Élie Halévy, *A History of the English People in 1815* (London: T. Fisher Unwin, 1924-1934), trans. by E. I. Watkin and D. A. Barker, vi.

81 Fisher, *Introductory History of England and Europe*, 261.

82 Élie Halévy to Lettice Fisher, 26 Jul. 1934, MS Fisher 70, fol. 7, Papers of H. A. L. Fisher, BL.

83 See 114–16. See also John Stevenson, 'The Countryside, Planning and Civil Society in Britain, 1926–1947', in *Civil Society in British History: Ideas, Identities, Institutions*, ed. José Harris (Oxford: Oxford University Press, 2003), 191–212.

84 Untitled manuscript outlining aims of the Legal Subcommittee of the NCUMC, 5OPF/2/12/b, NCUMC Papers, TWL.

85 Secretary's Quarterly Report, 14 Nov. 1919, 5OPF/01/4/1, NCUMC Papers, TWL.

86 Frau Adele Schreiber, 'Status of the Illegitimate Child in Germany', *Maternity and Child Welfare: A Monthly Journal for Workers Among Mothers and Children* VII, no. 1 (Jan. 1923): 8–9. Schreiber's discussion of legislative reform was part of a wider strand of international sex reform campaigning which advocated that a healthy and moral populace would not be attained through the imposition of criminal law, and that the proper approach, for example, to abortion, would be to stop up the illegal sources by securing the welfare of all children. On the German context see Edward Ross Dickinson, *Sex, Freedom, and Power in Imperial Germany, 1880–1914* (Cambridge: Cambridge University Press, 2014), 291.

87 Mrs Edwin Gray, 'Illegitimacy in Norway: The Castberg Laws', *Maternity and Child Welfare: A Monthly Journal for Workers Among Mothers and Children* VII, no. 4 (Apr. 1923): 115–17.

88 Gray, 'Illegitimacy in Norway', 116. On her trip to Norway in 1920 Mrs Edwin Gray found that the law was circumvented in practice as a certain number of 'educated', expectant unmarried mothers went to Denmark or Sweden prior to giving birth 'in order to escape this law'.

89 Miss Musson to Miss Charlesworth (Intelligence Division of Ministry of Health), 4 Feb. 1924, 5OPF/9/1/2, NCUMC Papers, TWL. On Swedish child welfare policy in the period see Allan C. Carlson, *The Swedish Experiment in Family Politics: The Myrdals and the Interwar Population Crisis* (New Brunswick, NJ: Transaction Publications, 1990).

90 Adele Schreiber was a founding member of the Berlin Federal Maternity Board (established in 1908) and the German Society for Parental and Child Rights (1910), and in the 1920s she worked at a German hostel for mothers under the auspices of the Red Cross: see Ann Taylor Allen, 'Mothers of the New Generation: Adele Schreiber, Helene Stöcker, and the Evolution of a German Idea of Motherhood, 1900–1914', *Signs* 10, no. 3 (1985): 418–38. Mrs Edwin Gray had been an English Poor Law Guardian from the late 1890s to 1910s and was influential in the development of voluntary maternity services in York in the Edwardian period, before going on to sit on national committees for maternity hospitals and health and housing associations.

91 Mrs Edwin Gray, *Women's Work and Wages* (York: Coultas and Volans, 1908); *Women on Juries* (London: National Council of Women of Great Britain and Ireland, 1923); Adele Schreiber, *Mutterschaft: ein Sammelwerk für die Probleme des Wiebes als Mutter* (Muchen: A. Langen, 1912). On the centrality of female dignity to conceptions of European citizenship see Daniele Bussy Genevois [translated by Arthur Goldhammer], 'The Women of Spain from the Republic to Franco', in *A History of Women in the West*, Vol. 5: *Toward a Cultural Identity in the Twentieth Century*, eds. Georges Duby and Michelle Perrot (Cambridge, MA: Harvard University Press, 1994), 177–93.

92 Matt Houlbrook and Sarah Newman have identified this intersection as being critical also for the interpretation of the interwar press: Matt Houlbrook and Sarah Newman, 'Introduction: Special Issue: The Press and Popular Culture in Interwar Europe', *Journalism Studies* 14, no. 5 (2013): 642.

93 Gray, 'Illegitimacy in Norway', 117; Minutes of Meeting of the Legal Subcommittee of the NCUMC, 17 Dec. 1919, 5OPF/02/12, NCUMC Papers, TWL.

94 Minutes of meeting at Carnegie House, 15 Jul. 1936, 5OPF/01/4, NCUMC Papers, TWL.

95 Minutes of meeting of the Legal Subcommittee 19 Nov. 1918, 5OPF/02/12, NCUMC Papers, TWL. For example, Mr Hope felt strongly the limitations of making any observations on the proposals of the Reichstag Committee in view of the fact that 'the difficulties which they were designed to meet were so wholly different from those in England'.

96 Gray 'Illegitimacy in Norway', 117.

97 E. W. Bradford, 'World-Faring', *Our Own Gazette*, May 1935, 72.

98 'Why Not a Film Show?', *Blue Triangle Gazette*, Oct. 1935, 156.

99 Scott Anthony, 'The GPO Film Unit and "Britishness" in the 1930s', in *The Projection of Britain: A History of the GPO Film Unit*, eds. Scott Anthony and James Mansell (London: BFI, 2011), 14. Anthony has argued that these film showings sought to imbue in audiences a form of 'Britishness' that was active, engaged and participatory; I am arguing for the *relational* construction of national and cross-cultural identity.

100 See 103.

101 *A Study of the World's Young Women's Christian Association*, 11.

102 *Our Eighty Years*, 10 (see Introduction, note 67).

103 Bradford, 'World-Faring', 72 (see above, note 97).

104 D. E. C., 'Portuguese Girls', *Our Own Gazette*, Apr. 1926, 9.

105 Emily Kinnaird, 'What Of Portugal?', *Our Own Gazette*, Nov. 1923, 6. Kinnaird remembered subsequently that she had 'taught' the Portuguese campers to sit on the ground and drink tea at five o'clock and to have an open-air Bible Circle: see her *Reminiscences*, 152.

106 Kinnaird, 'What Of Portugal?', 5; 7.

107 *YWCA Bulletin* 3, no. 10 (1923): 4.

108 Trotter, *Literature in the First Media Age*, 225–6.

109 Kinnaird, *Reminiscences*, 122–5.

110 Elizabeth Wilson, *The Story of Fifty Years of the Young Women's Christian Association of India, Burma and Ceylon* (Calcutta: YMCA Association Press, 1925); 9–27.

111 Kinnaird, *Reminiscences*, 125; 130–2. See also Padmini Sengupta, *A Hundred Years of Service: Centenary Volume of the Y.W.C.A. of Calcutta, 1878–1978* (Calcutta: Bibhash Gupta (on behalf of Y.W.C.A. of Calcutta), 1987), 5.

112 Kinnaird, *My Adopted Country*, 35.

113 On journeys in interwar travel writing see Trotter, *Literature in the First Media Age*, 225–8.

114 Emily Kinnaird, 'News from Overseas: A Week's Travel in India', *Our Own Gazette*, Jan. 1922, 12. Kinnaird's reflection on the 'pretty Parsi girls' can also be read as a striking example of what Indira Ghose theorizes as the surveilling, as well as admiring, 'female gaze' of the western woman traveller upon the female subject of colonial India: Ghose, *Women Travellers in Colonial India*, 9.

115 Kinnaird, 'News from Overseas: A Week's Travel in India'.

116 Trotter, *Literature in the First Media Age*, 27–8.

117 Trotter, *Literature in the First Media Age*, 218–19.

118 Kinnaird, 'What Of Portugal?', 5.

119 Emily Kinnaird, 'Ceylon', *Blue Triangle Gazette*, Jan. 1929, 5.

120 Kinnaird, 'Ceylon', 5.

121 Jon Hoare, '"Go The Way the Material Calls You": Basil Wright and *The Song of Ceylon*', in *The Projection of Britain*, eds. Anthony and Mansell, 239. Hoare points out that the film in fact obscured the multiculturalism of the island's population.

122 Emily Kinnaird, 'South India. Week of World Fellowship. A Letter from Miss Emily Kinnaird', *Blue Triangle Gazette*, Feb. 1929, 8–9; and 'Ceylon', *Blue Triangle Gazette*, Jan. 1929, 6.

123 Kinnaird argued such an approach was still 'controversial' in the mid-1920s: Kinnaird, *Reminiscences*, 68.

124 Emily Kinnaird, 'South India. Week of World Fellowship', 8.

125 Cuttings book of Emily Kinnaird's visit to South Africa, 1908; Note about the 'Pan Anglican Thank-Offering Fund' (Transvaal Branch), 3 Mar. 1908, MSS 243/12/8, YWCA Records, MRC.

126 Nancy Marie Robertson, *Christian Sisterhood, Race Relations, and the YWCA, 1906–46* (Urbana: University of Illinois Press, 2007).

127 Kinnaird, *My Adopted Country*, 82.

128 Kinnaird, *Reminiscences*, 173.

129 Kinnaird, *Reminiscences*, 173.

130 Picton-Turbervill, *Life is Good*, 80.

131 Kinnaird, *Reminiscences*, 174.

132 A notice to *Our Own Gazette* readers at the end of the article covering Kinnaird's 1921–2 tour to India exhorted: '[i]f you are not an Overseas friend, then will you not become one by sending your name to Miss M. Lyne, the Secretariat, who will enroll you? Thus you will take your share in helping the girls of the East to find out from British girls some of the Christian possessions which Western girls enjoy': Emily Kinnaird, 'News from Overseas: A Week's Travel in India', *Our Own Gazette*, Jan. 1922, 13.

133 Emily Kinnaird, 'In India with Medical Missionaries', *The Girl's Own Paper*, 25 Jul. 1891, 686–7.

134 Kinnaird, *Reminiscences*, 125.

135 Kinnaird, *My Adopted Country*, 35.

136 'A Letter from India from Miss Kinnaird', *Blue Triangle Gazette*, Feb. 1930, 10–11. The article was illustrated with a photograph of a group of Indian girls country dancing at a YWCA summer school in Ootacamund.

137 Kinnaird, *Reminiscences*, 172–3.

138 Kinnaird, *My Adopted Country*, 83.

139 Kinnaird, *Reminiscences*, 176.

140 Kinnaird, *My Adopted Country*, 119.

141 On the progressive, anti-war narrative of the interwar period see Overy, *Morbid Age*, 240.

142 Kinnaird, *Reminiscences*, 177.

143 Helen Tracey to Muriel Paget, n. d. but approximately 8 Jul. 1920, SCF/A412/EJ214, Jebb Papers, CRL.

144 Fisher, *Life and Work in England*, 84. See also Fisher, *Getting and Spending*, 24–5 and Fisher, 'The Liberal Party's Woman Power', 20 (see Introduction, note 32).

145 Coombes, *Reinventing Africa*.

146 Peter Mandler, *Return From the Natives: How Margaret Mead Won the Second World War and Lost the Cold War* (New Haven, CT: Yale University Press, 2013). Mandler argues that these inter-cultural visions got caught up in the mire of the Cold War world.

5 Communication

1 'Evangeline Booth Returns For Rest: "Pillbox" on British Liner and a Passenger', *The New York Times*, 6 Dec. 1939, 7.

2 It is possible that Evangeline Booth was referring here to the attacks made by the third patrol of the German submarine *U-48* in late Nov/Dec. 1939.

3 Evangeline Booth to Mr and Mrs Frank O. Salisbury, 20 Dec. 1939, MS 100, vol. xviii, fol. 13, Frank O. Salisbury Papers, Heinz Archive and Library, National Portrait Gallery, London.

4 Evangeline Booth to Mr and Mrs Frank O. Salisbury, 20 Dec. 1939, MS 100.

5 Manuscript of Evangeline Booth's contribution to 'Famous Women', included with letter from Evangeline Booth to WCKY radio station, 15 Oct. 1942, Speeches I, 311/8, Booth Papers, SAA.

6 Charles L. Ponce de Leon, *Self-exposure: Human-interest Journalism and the Emergence of Celebrity in America, 1890–1940* (Chapel Hill: University of North Carolina Press, 2002), 5.

7 Evangeline Booth's activity, and the politics surrounding her position, were wired particularly frequently in these years between the London and the New York press, see e.g. 'General Booth Guest of Royalty', *The New York Times*, 23 June 1938, 23; 'Poll in Salvation Army: Majority Reported for Extension of General Booth's Tenure', *The New York Times*, 17 Aug. 1938, 8; 'General Booth To Stay: Retirement From the Salvation Army Delayed for Ten Months', *The New York Times*, 24 Aug. 1938, 2.

8 Trotter, *Literature in the First Media Age*, 2.

9 Trotter, *Literature in the First Media Age*, 8.

10 Trotter, *Literature in the First Media Age*, 28–9.

11 Prochaska, *The Voluntary Impulse*, 13.

12 Michael T. Saler, "'Clap If You Believe in Sherlock Holmes": Mass Culture and the Re-enchantment of Modernity, c. 1890–1940', *The Historical Journal* 46, no. 3 (2003): 599–622.

13 Fisher, *Twenty-one Years*, 3–5.

14 Fisher, *Twenty-one Years*, 5.

15 On 'opinion formers' as public intellectuals see Stefan Collini, *Absent Minds: Intellectuals in Britain* (Oxford: Oxford University Press, 2006), 26; 32.

16 Fisher, *Twenty-one Years*, 6.

17 Thane and Evans, *Sinners? Scroungers? Saints?*, 16–17; Keating, *Child for Keeps*, 6–7.

18 NCUMC Pamphlet, 'A Few points of the Law of England and Wales relating to Unmarried Mothers and Illegitimate Children', 3rd edn, 1927, 7, ACC/2201/B1/1/15, London Metropolitan Archives. Out-relief could be provided to unmarried mothers under the provision of Article XII of the Relief Regulation Order, 1911, but was at the discretion of Poor Law Guardians.

19 On mid-nineteenth-century discussions of baby-farming see Lionel Rose, *Massacre of the Innocents: Infanticide in Britain 1800–1939* (London: Routledge & Kegan Paul, 1986), 41–5.

20 'Provision For Unmarried Mothers and their Children': Policy adopted by a Conference held at Mansion House, London, 14 Feb. 1918 (see ch. 2, note 94); Thane and Evans, *Sinners? Scroungers? Saints?*, 14–16.

21 Laura E. Nym Mayhall, *The Militant Suffrage Movement: Citizenship and Resistance in Britain, 1860–1930* (Oxford: Oxford University Press, 2003), 15. Mayhall has argued that these methods, in continuum with direct action, characterized the militant politics of the suffrage movement.

22 Eve Colpus, '*Unmarried*: Unmarried Motherhood in Post-First World War British Film', in *Moral Panics, Social Fears, and the Media: Historical Perspectives*, eds. Siân Nicholas and Tom O'Malley (London: Routledge, 2013), 130–1.

23 Fisher, *Twenty-one Years*, 15.

24 Lettice Fisher, 'Unmarried Mothers', *The Times*, 24 Oct. 1922, 8.

25 Meetings of the Press and Publications Committee, 27 May 1918 and June 1918, 5OPF/2/18/A, NCUMC Papers, TWL.

26 Fisher, *Twenty-one Years*, 6.

27 'The Unmarried Mother', *The Times*, 29 Jan. 1919, 5.

28 Henry Russell Wakefield, *The Ethics of Birth Control. Statement by the Bishop of Birmingham* (Leicester: C. Killick Millard, 1919).

29 Eve Colpus, '*The Week's Good Cause*: Mass Culture and Cultures of Philanthropy at the Inter-war BBC', *Twentieth Century British History* 22, no. 3 (2011): 313.

30 Colpus, '*The Week's Good Cause*': 313.

31 See 115–18.

32 Susan Smulyan, *Selling Radio: The Commercialization of American Broadcasting, 1920–1934* (Washington: Smithsonian Institution Press, 1994), ch. 3.

33 On the British interpretation of the 'microphone personality' see 'All About the Week's Good Cause', *The Radio Times*, 4 Jan. 1935, 6.

34 Appeals Results: 1932, 1935, 1936, 1937, 1938, RS/282/2, BBC Written Archives Centre (hereafter cited as WAC).

35 On the early BBC's ambition for a nationwide reach see the first issue of *The Radio Times*, 9 Nov. 1923, 1.

36 The Legitimacy Act (1926) ruled that a child could be legitimated by the subsequent marriage of its parents in cases where neither parent had been married to someone else at the time of the child's birth: Thane and Evans, *Sinners? Scroungers? Saints?*, 50.

37 Manuscripts of Broadcast NCUMC appeals: Lettice Fisher, 'The Unwanted Child', 1925, 5OPF/2/2/7/1, NCUMC Papers, TWL.

38 David Trotter discusses this trend with relation to Graham Greene's writings in the 1930s, see *Literature in the First Media Age*, 28.

39 Fisher, 'The Unwanted Child', 1925.

40 Rose, *Massacre of the Innocents*, 186.

41 Colpus, *Unmarried*, 129–46.

42 Colpus, 'The Week's Good Cause', 321–2. On 'human-interest' stories in interwar British journalism see LeMahieu, *Culture for Democracy*, 17–55.

43 For discussion of the 'middle-class' world-view of domestic economy and savings see McKibbin, 'Social Class and Social Observation', 175–99. On the centrality of the conceit of respectability to debates about adoption in this period see Keating, *A Child for Keeps*, 15.

44 Colpus, 'The Week's Good Cause', 317.

45 'Advisory Committees: Appeals Advisory Committee Reports, File 1, 1928–1930': 'Appeals Advisory Committee, 29 October 1929, Secretary's Report, March to October', R6/1/1, WAC. For an extended commentary on the early ambitions for the interconnectedness of broadcasting see John Reith, *Broadcast Over Britain* (London: Hodder and Stoughton, 1924).

46 Winifred Holtby, 'Who'd Be a Baby?', *The Radio Times*, 27 Feb. 1931, 479.

47 Elspeth H. Brown, *The Corporate Eye: Photography and the Rationalization of American Commercial Culture, 1884–1929* (Baltimore: John Hopkins University Press, 2005), 167. See also Don Slater, *Consumer Culture and Modernity* (Cambridge, UK: Polity Press, 1997), 54–9.

48 Manuscripts of Broadcast NCUMC appeals: Neville Chamberlain, 4 May 1930, 5OPF/2/2/7/1, NCUMC, TWL. Chamberlain had also been an important ally of the NCUMC in Parliament, notably guiding the Bastardy Bill of 1920 through the House of Commons as a Private Members' Bill: see Thane, 'Voluntary Action in the "Welfare State"', 136.

49 'Index Books of Organisations: 'N-Q': 'National Council for the Unmarried Mother and her Child', R7/308/5, WAC.

50 By this time, Lettice Fisher's husband, H. A. L. Fisher was a member of the board of BBC Governors.

51 Script of BBC appeal on behalf of the NCUMC, delivered by Cyril Maude, 5OPF/2/2/7/1, NCUMC Papers, TWL.

52 'Index Books of Organisations: 'N-Q': NCUMC (see above, note 49).

53 Philip M. Taylor, *British Propaganda in the Twentieth Century: Selling Democracy* (Edinburgh: Edinburgh University Press, 1999), 2–3.

54 For a useful summary of this context see Mariel Grant, *Propaganda and the Role of the State in Inter-war Britain* (Oxford: Clarendon Press, 1994), ch. 2.

55 Anthony, *Public Relations*, 1.

56 Grant, *Propaganda and the Role of the State*, ch. 2; Taylor, *British Propaganda*, chs. 4–6; Temple Willcox, 'Projection or Publicity? Rival Concepts in the Pre-war Planning of the British Ministry of Information', *Journal of Contemporary History* 18, no. 1 (1983): 97–116.

57 See for example, Sarah Ellen Graham, *Culture and Propaganda: The Progressive Origins of American Public Diplomacy, 1936–1953* (Farnham: Ashgate, 2015).

58 Philip M. Taylor, *The Projection of Britain: British Overseas Publicity and Propaganda 1919–1939* (Cambridge: Cambridge University Press, 1981). Taylor notes that the culture was taken up reluctantly by government ministers in the late 1930s: 291–2.

59 Braithwaite, *The Voluntary Citizen*, 40.

60 Ray Strachey, 'Jebb, Eglantyne (1876–1928)', *Dictionary of National Biography, 1922–1930*, ed. J. R. H. Weaver (London: Oxford University Press, 1937), 451.

61 Strachey, 'Jebb, Eglantyne', 451.

62 Strachey, 'Jebb, Eglantyne', 451.

63 Emily Baughan, '"Every Citizen of Empire Implored to Save the Children!" Empire, Internationalism and the Save the Children Fund in Inter-war Britain', *Historical Research* 86, no. 231 (2013): 116–37.

64 Strachey, 'Jebb, Eglantyne', 452.

65 See 41.

66 Katherine Storr, *Excluded From the Record: Women, Refugees and Relief 1914–1929* (Oxford: Peter Lang, 2010), 237.

67 Buxton and Fuller, *White Flame*, 15.

68 Muriel Paget, Manuscript speech, 'Lecture to the Imperial Defence College, 1929', Box 38, LRA/MS 1405. Paget's schema read: 'First stage of Revolution October 1917 – Communist party overthrew Kerensky regime – to March 1921, Kronstadt rising [War Communism] ... Second phase of Revolution [New Economic Policy] which lasted until end of 1926/early 1927 – state enlarged powers ... We are now witnessing the third phase ... the inevitable struggle between Communist party and Peasantry'. The overall progression from war communism to the New Economic

Policy (NEP) and the 'great break' of Stalinist industrialization is now accepted, although some of Paget's dates would need amendment to fit this model (notably collectivization, which dates from 1931-2, the first Five Year Plan from 1928, and the war between Bolshevik leaders and the peasantry, which was actually a much wider social conflict), see e.g. Robert Service, *A History of Modern Russia: from Nicholas II to Putin* (London: Penguin, 2003), chs. 8-9.

69 Muriel Paget, 'Lecture to the Imperial Defence College, 1929'.

70 The context I am tracing here complements Madeleine Herren's interest in examining, through women's presence in the League of Nations after 1919, women's access to academic discussions within the new field of international relations: Madeleine Herren, 'Gender and International Relations Through the Lens of the League of Nations (1919-1945)', *Women, Diplomacy and International Politics Since 1500*, eds. Glenda Sluga and Carolyn James (London: Routledge, 2016), 182-201.

71 'Distressed British Subjects in Russia: Lady Muriel Paget's Record, October to December 1932', Box 29, LRA/MS 1405.

72 Muriel Paget, 'Personal Relations with the Soviet Government': Address given to the Institute of International Affairs, 13 Nov. 1930, Box 28, LRA/MS 1405. On Chatham House as a forum for multiple voices in the making of foreign policy, see Inderjeet Parmar, 'Anglo-American Elites in the Interwar Years: Idealism and Power in the Intellectual Roots of Chatham House and the Council On Foreign Relations', *International Relations* 16, no. 1 (2002): 53-75. See also Keith Neilson, *Britain, Soviet Russia and the Collapse of the Versailles Order, 1919-1939* (Cambridge: Cambridge University Press, 2006), 17.

73 Paget, 'Personal Relations with the Soviet Government'.

74 Blunt, *Lady Muriel*, 213.

75 Blunt, *Lady Muriel*, 257.

76 As Constance Braithwaite noted: *The Voluntary Citizen*, 43-9.

77 See 133-8.

78 Blunt, *Lady Muriel*, 233-4. The tour had been scheduled for late 1926 but was postponed due to Paget's ill health.

79 Paul Kennaday to Lady Muriel Paget, 10 Jan. 1927, Box 34, LRA/MS 1405. Some business leaders, social workers and journalists presented more diverse political and cultural pictures of Russia in this period, see e.g. Oswald Garrison Villard, 'Russia From a Car Window: V. The Soviets and the Human Being', *Nation*, 4 Dec. 1929, 654-7, quoted in Peter G. Filene ed., *American Views of Soviet Russia* (Homewood, ILL: Dorsey Press, 1968), 63-71.

80 Muriel Paget, Manuscript of Speech for the American Women's Club, 17 Dec. 1930, Box 38, LRA/MS 1405. Founded in 1899 as the Society of American Women, the American Women's Club of London provided social, cultural, educational and philanthropic activities for expatriated American women living in London.

81 William B. Feakins, *Feakins' Attractions* (New York: William B. Feakins, Inc., Lecture and Concert Management, 1929).

82 'Fall Bulletin (1925–6) of William M. Feakins Inc', Box 34, LRA/MS 1405.

83 Saler, 'Clap If You Believe in Sherlock Holmes': 6–7. Matt Houlbrook has described the genre as blending the 'everyday' and the 'fictional': '"A Pin to See the Peepshow": Culture, Fiction and Selfhood in Edith Thompson's Letters, 1921–22', *Past and Present* 207, no. 1 (2010): 241.

84 Light, *Forever England*, 158–66. Lea Jacobs has argued for a distinct American 'anti-sentiment' taste parameter that grew up during the 1920s, see *The Decline of Sentiment: American Film in the 1920s* (Berkeley: University of California Press, 2008).

85 William Feakins' offices to Lady Muriel Paget, 15 Oct. 1926, Box 34, LRA/MS 1405.

86 Blunt, *Lady Muriel*, 238.

87 'A Wrong Impression', *New York Herald Tribune*, 27 Mar. 1927, 8.

88 Mrs Franklin Roosevelt to William Feakins, 5 Jan. 1927, Box 34, LRA/MS 1405.

89 William Feakins' Publicity Pamphlet of Paget's American Tour, Jan. 1927, Box 34, LRA/MS 1405.

90 Muriel Paget extended the fundraising goals for the BSRRA and in 1930 launched an appeal to raise £5,000: see Muriel Paget, 'British Subjects in Russia', *The Times*, 29 Dec. 1930, 6.

91 Muriel Paget, 'Some Pictures of Soviet Russia: I After the Revolution', *The Daily Telegraph*, 1 Feb. 1927, 11–12.

92 Muriel Paget, 'Some Pictures of Soviet Russia: III: The Wild Children', *The Daily Telegraph*, 3 Feb. 1927, 9.

93 Shelia Fitzpatrick, *The Cultural Front: Power and Culture in Revolutionary Russia* (Ithaca, NY: Cornell University Press, 1992), 84. See also Alan M. Ball, *And Now My Soul is Hardened: Abandoned Children in Soviet Russia, 1918–1930* (Berkeley: University of California Press, 1994), 76–78.

94 Muriel Paget, 'The Wild Children', 9.

95 LeMahieu, *Culture for Democracy*, 17–55; Ponce de Leon, *Self-exposure*, 30–40; ch. 2; Adrian Bingham, *Gender, Modernity and the Popular Press* (Oxford: Clarendon Press, 2004); *Family Newspapers? Sex, Private Life and the British Popular Press, 1918–1978* (Oxford: Oxford University Press, 2009).

96 Founded in 1924, the organization the Societies for Cultural Relations was recognized as the British counterpart of VOKS.

97 'Child Welfare in Russia: "Matching-Up" a Pimple', *The Manchester Guardian*, 8 Jul. 1927, 14.

98 Shani D'Cruze has argued that human-interest journalism was a means by which 'readers were invited into a participatory relationship with the newspaper': 'Intimacy, Professionalism and Domestic Homicide in Interwar Britain: The Case of Buck Ruxton', *Women's History Review* 16, no. 5 (2007): 715.

99 Ponce de Leon, *Self-exposure*, ch. 2.

100 Linda Williams, *Playing the Race Card: Melodramas of Black and White from Uncle Tom's Cabin to O. J. Simpson* (Princeton: Princeton University Press, 2001), 29. See also Christine Gledhill, ed., *Home is Where the Heart Is: Studies in Melodrama and the Woman's Film* (London: British Film Institute, 1987).

101 Booth, *Will You Help?*

102 Booth, *Will You Help?*

103 See e.g. Seth Koven's discussion of Dr Barnardo's fundraising campaigns in the 1870s: *Slumming*, 112–24.

104 Deborah Cohen, *Household Gods: The British and Their Possessions* (New Haven, CT: Yale University Press, 2006),13.

105 Paula Bartley, *Emmeline Pankhurst* (London: Routledge, 2002), 112; Jill Rappoport, *Giving Women: Alliance and Exchange in Victorian Culture* (New York: Oxford University Press, 2012), 162.

106 Basil Nicholson, 'Salvation in a Poke Bonnet', *Daily Mirror*, 25 Feb. 1935, 10.

107 *Daily Mirror*, 25 Feb. 1935, 10.

108 *Daily Mirror*, 25 Feb. 1935, 10.

109 Walker, *Pulling the Devil's Kingdom Down*, 196.

110 Eve Colpus, 'Preaching Religion, Family and Memory in Nineteenth-Century England', *Gender & History* 22, no. 1 (2010): 42–3.

111 Dorothy Walworth, 'General of the Army: Evangeline Booth', *Reader's Digest*, Aug. 1947, 36, quoted in Diane Winston, 'All the World's a Stage: The Performed Religion of the Salvation Army, 1880–1920', in Stewart M. Hoover and Lynn Schofield Clark, eds., *Practicing Religion in the Age of the Media: Explorations in Media, Religion, and Culture* (New York: Columbia University Press, 2002), 122.

112 Winston, *Red Hot and Righteous*, 146; 'Evangeline Booth Pleads in Tatters', *The New York Times*, 7 May 1924, 21.

113 Winston, *Red Hot and Righteous*, 146.

114 On the constructed drama of the charitable encounter, see especially, Peel, *Miss Cutler*.

115 'The One Source', quoted in John D. Waldon, ed., *The World for God: Writings and Speeches of Evangeline Cory Booth* (New York: The Salvation Army, USA Eastern Territory, 1992), 2:189.

116 Muriel Harris, *Pulpits and Preachers* (London: Methuen & Co., 1935), 130–1.

117 Hannen Swaffer, 'Last of the Booths', *John Bull*, 15 July 1939, 15.

118 'Foreign News: World's Greatest Romance', *Time*, 16 Nov. 1936, 11. The magazine informed readers that Booth rehearsed this talk in late 1936 for an audience in Britain that included Mrs Wallace Simpson.

119 'Faith and Philanthropy', *The Church Times*, 14 Dec. 1934, 668.

120 Swaffer, 'Last of the Booths', 15.

121 Swaffer, 'Last of the Booths', 15.

122 Walker, *Pulling the Devil's Kingdom Down*, 175–6.

123 See e.g. S. P. B. Mais, 'Wanted! Work – Not Charity' (see ch. 1, note 37).

124 Booth, *Will You Help?*

125 'General Evangeline Booth: Women of 68 Chief of Salvation Army', *Daily Mirror*, 4 Sept. 1934, 1.

126 For discussion of the symbolism of Salvation Army women wearing hats see Rappoport, *Giving Women*, 111. For the description of the 'grey-headed leaders of the Army' see *Daily Mirror*, 4 Sept. 1934, 1.

127 Lynda Nauright, 'Politics and Power: A New Look at Florence Nightingale', *Nursing Forum* 21, no. 1 (1984): 6.

128 'General Booth's World's Tour', *The Manchester Guardian*, 7 Nov. 1936, 19.

129 Wilson, *The General*, 71; 73.

130 Booth, *Woman*, 21.

131 The consumer market for make-up was greatly stimulated in the interwar period by women's cinema-going, see Ina Zweiniger-Bargielowska, *Managing the Body: Beauty, Health, and Fitness in Britain, 1880–1939* (Oxford: Oxford University Press, 2010), 239.

132 On the American film industry's exploitation of the ambiguity of the 'Sallie's' attractiveness see Winston, *Red Hot and Righteous*, 195–7.

133 On the extension of middle-class women's public agency through shopping see Erika Diane Rappaport, *Shopping for Pleasure: Women in the Making of London's West End* (Princeton, NJ: Princeton University Press, 2000).

134 The term 'connective sociability' is David Trotter's: *Literature in the First Media Age*, 55.

135 The loudspeaker was referred to as an 'amplifier', see e.g. 'The Journal of the Motorcade', *The War Cry* (UK), 18 Jul. 1936, 5.

Conclusion

1   Stephen Pimpare, 'Toward a New Welfare History', *Journal of Policy History* 19, no. 2 (2007): 234–52.

2   Peel, *Miss Cutler*, 280.

3   Bernhard Rieger, *Technology and the Culture of Modernity in Britain and Germany, 1890–1945* (Cambridge: Cambridge University Press, 2005), 2.

4   Fisher, *Introductory History of England and Europe*, 813.

5   'Pioneers and "Skin-colour"', *Blue Triangle Gazette*, Oct. 1936, 164.

6   J. H. Oldham, *Christianity and the Race Problem* 2nd edn. (London: Student Christian Movement, 1924); Cox, 'From the Empire of Christ to the Third World', 99.

7 Fisher, *Life and Work in England*, 10.

8 For an exception that has stressed continuity of practice in elite women's philanthropic practice see Hinton, *Women and Social Leadership*.

9 Matthew Hilton and James McKay eds., *The Ages of Voluntarism: How We Got to the Big Society* (Oxford: Oxford University Press, 2011); McCarthy and Thane, 'The Politics of Association in Industrial Society'; Pat Thane, 'The Ben Pimlott Memorial Lecture 2011: The "Big Society" and the "Big State": Creative Tension or Crowding Out?', *Twentieth Century British History* 23, no. 1 (2012), 408–29.

10 William Beveridge and A. F. Wells eds., *The Evidence for Voluntary Action: Being Memoranda by Organisations and Individuals and Other Material Relevant to Voluntary Action* (London: George Allen and Unwin, 1949), 322.

11 Pamela Glenconner, 'Invalid Meals for London', *The Times*, 28 Mar. 1960, 11.

12 For a fictional critique see Ellen Wilkinson, *Clash* (1929; repr., London: Virago, 1989).

13 In the context of social work, Peel argues there were not rapid or comprehensive changes across time, but rather 'shades and shifts': *Miss Cutler*, 278–9.

14 'Work of Salvation Army: General Booth honoured', *The Times*, 22 Feb. 1939, 19.

15 Muriel Paget to Reverend F. Komlosy, 16 Mar. 1920, Box 12, LRA/MS 1405.

16 See 121–3.

17 'Lady Muriel Paget: An Appreciation', *The Times*, 22 June 1938, 18.

18 Florence Nightingale's reputation had been complicated, not least, following the publication of Lytton Strachey's biography, *Eminent Victorians* (1918; repr., Oxford: Oxford University Press, 2003).

19 See 98.

20 Alison Light has read this concern as taking shape in middle-class women's lives in the interwar period around a realignment of the public and private behaviours, values and norms of the pre-war years that was expressed through a new language of reticence: Light, *Forever England*; 12; 59; 108.

21 'Hold the Light Steady' (1918), MSS 243/14/22/6, YWCA Records, MRC.

22 Lewis, *Women and Social Action in Victorian and Edwardian England*; Bush, *Edwardian Ladies and Imperial Power*.

23 A discussion that took place at '30 Years of ChildLine: A Witness Seminar', held at the BT Tower, London, 1 June 2016, organized by Eve Colpus and Jenny Crane. See Valerie Howarth and Anne Houston, in '30 Years of ChildLine (1986–2016)', transcript held at the Modern Records Centre, University of Warwick, Coventry, 32–3.

Bibliography

Primary sources

Manuscript collections

'A Few points of the Law of England and Wales relating to Unmarried Mothers and Illegitimate Children', NCUMC Pamphlet, 3rd edn, 1927 [ACC/2201/B1/1/15]. London Metropolitan Archives, London.

BBC *Week's Good Cause*, Records. Appeals Advisory Committee Reports [R6/1/1], Appeals Results [RS/282/2] and Index Books of Organisations [Charity Appeals] N–Q [R7/308/5]. BBC Written Archives Centre, Caversham, Reading.

Booth, Evangeline, Papers. The Salvation Army National Archives and Research Center, Alexandria, Virginia.

Booth, Evangeline to Frank O. Salisbury, Letter. Frank O. Salisbury Papers. Heinz Archive, National Portrait Gallery, London.

Fisher H. A. L., Additional Papers [MSS Eng. d.3779–80]. Bodleian Libraries, University of Oxford, Oxford.

Fisher, H. A. L., Papers [MSS Fisher]. Bodleian Libraries, University of Oxford, Oxford.

Fisher, Lettice to Frances Stevenson, Letter. Frances Stevenson Papers [FCG2]. National Library of Wales, Aberystwyth.

Ilbert Family Papers, Photographs and Press Cuttings. Private collection, Sophie Ilbert Decaudaveine (and the late Robert Ilbert).

Jebb, Eglantyne, Papers [SCF/A409/EJ]. Save the Children Fund Papers. Cadbury Research Library: Special Collections, University of Birmingham, Birmingham.

Kinnaird, Emily to Olga Nethersole, 20 June 1918, Letter. Papers of the People's League of Health [PLH/1]. London School of Economics Library, London.

'London School of Economics and Political Science, Papers 1898–99: Arrangements for the Session 1898–99', LSE/Unregistered/27/2/1A (Year Books 1895–1903). London School of Economics Library, London.

National Council for the Unmarried Mother and her Child, Papers [5OPF]. London School of Economics Library, The Women's Library Collection, London.

Oral Evidence on the Suffrage and Suffragette Movements, the Brian Harrison Interviews [8SUF]. London School of Economics Library, The Women's Library Collection, London.

Paget, Lady Muriel, Papers [LRA/MS 1405]. Leeds Russian Archive, Special Collections, Leeds University Library, Leeds.

Pocock, G. M. and L. C. Pocock, Papers [Documents.3648]. Imperial War Museum, London.

'The Bastardy Bill, 1920', Special Collections Pamphlets [346.017 BAS]. London School of Economics Library, The Women's Library Collection, London.

Young Women's Christian Association, Records [MSS 243]. The Modern Records Centre, University of Warwick, Coventry.

Printed primary sources

A. J. R., ed. *The Suffrage Annual and Women's Who's Who*. London: Stanley, Paul and Co., 1913.

Attlee, C. R. *The Social Worker*. London: G. Bell, 1920.

Baldwin, Stanley. *Our Inheritance: Speeches and Addresses*. London: Hodder and Stoughton Ltd., 1928.

Barnett, Canon and Mrs S. A. *Practicable Socialism*. New ser. London: Longmans, Green and Co., 1915.

Begbie, Harold. 'Booth, William (1829–1912)'. In *Dictionary of National Biography, 1912-1921*, edited by H. W. C. Davis and J. R. H. Weaver, 50–2. London: Oxford University Press.

Bell, Anne Olivier ed. *The Diary of Virginia Woolf*, Vol. 4. London: The Hogarth Press, 1982.

Bennett, Mary. *The Ilberts in India, 1882-1886: An Imperial Miniature*. London: BACSA, 1995.

Bennett, Mary. *An Autobiography*. Privately published, 1997.

Berry, Paul and Alan Bishop eds. *Testament of a Generation: The Journalism of Vera Brittain and Winifred Holtby*. London: Virago, 1985.

Beveridge, William and A. F. Wells eds. *The Evidence for Voluntary Action: Being Memoranda by Organisations and Individuals and Other Material Relevant to Voluntary Action*. London: George Allen and Unwin, 1949.

Booth, Catherine. *Papers on Practical Religion*. London, 1879.

Booth, Catherine. *Papers on Aggressive Christianity*. London, 1880.

Booth, Evangeline. 'Around the World with the Salvation Army', *National Geographic Magazine* 37, no. 4 (1920): 347–68.

Booth, Evangeline. *Toward a Better World*. London: Salvationist Publishing and Supplies, 1929.

Booth, Evangeline. *Woman*. New York: Fleming H. Revell Company, 1930. Reprint, London: Salvationist Publishing and Supplies, 1936.

Booth, Evangeline. *Love is All*. London: Marshall, Morgan and Scott, 1935.

Booth, Evangeline. *This Brotherhood of Nations*. St. Albans: The Campfield Press, 1937.

Booth, Evangeline. *Will You Help? . . . A Call from Evangeline Booth*. London: Salvation Army, 1937.

Booth, Evangeline and Grace Livingston Hill. *The War Romance of the Salvation Army*. Philadelphia: J. B. Lippincott Co., 1919.

Booth, William. *In Darkest England and the Way Out*. London, 1890.

Bosanquet, Helen. *Rich and Poor*. London, 1898.

Bourdillon, A. F. C. ed. *Voluntary Social Services: Their Place in the Modern State*. London: Methuen & Co., 1945.

Braithwaite, Constance. *The Voluntary Citizen: An Enquiry into the Place of Philanthropy in the Community*. London: Methuen & Co., 1938.

Brittain, Vera. *Women's Work in Modern England*. London: Douglas, 1928.

Brittain, Vera and Geoffrey Handley-Taylor eds. *Selected Letters of Winifred Holtby and Vera Brittain, 1920–1935*. London: A. Brown, 1960.

Burdett-Coutts, Angela. *Woman's Mission: A Series of Congress Papers on the Philanthropic Work of Women*. London, 1893.

Burt, Cyril. *The Yong Delinquent*. New York: D. Appleton and Co., 1925.

Butler, C. V. *Social Conditions in Oxford*. London: Sidgwick & Jackson, 1912.

Butler, C. V. 'Review: *Getting and Spending: An Introduction to Economics*, by Lettice Fisher'. *The Economic Journal* 32, no. 127 (1922): 393–4.

Buxton, Dorothy and Edward Fuller. *The White Flame: The Story of the Save the Children Fund*. London: Longmans, Green & Co. Ltd., 1931.

Carnegie, Dale. *Five Minute Biographies*. Surrey: The World's Work, 1946.

C.O.P.E.C. Commission Report, *The Social Function of the Church*. London: C.O.P.E.C. Continuation Committee, 1924.

Cullis, W. C. 'Scharlieb, Dame Mary Ann Dacomb (1845–1930)'. In *Dictionary of National Biography, 1922–1930*, edited by J. R. H. Weaver, 749–51. Oxford: Oxford University Press, 1937.

Deneke, Helena. *Grace Hadow*. London: Oxford University Press, 1946.

Feakins, William B. *Feakins' Attractions*. New York: William B. Feakins, Inc., Lecture and Concert Management, 1929.

Fisher, H. A. L. *A History of Europe*, 3 vols. London: Longman, 1935.

Fisher, H. A. L. *An Unfinished Biography*. London: Oxford University Press, 1940.

Fisher, Lettice. 'Labourers' Dwellings'. *The Economic Journal* 9, no. 36 (1899): 605–11.

Fisher, Lettice. 'Review of C. J. Stewart, "The Housing Question in London"'. *The Economic Journal* 11, no. 41 (1901): 56–8.

Fisher, Lettice. 'Local Authorities and the Housing Problem in 1901'. *The Economic Journal* 12, no. 46 (1902): 263–71.

Fisher, Lettice. 'The Town Housing Problem'. *The Economic Journal* 15, no. 57 (1905): 23–36.

Fisher, Lettice. 'The Unmarried Mother'. Issued by The Six Point Group (Women's Printing Society, Brick Street, Piccadilly, n.d.). Reprinted from *Time and Tide*, 21 January 1921.

Fisher, Lettice. *Getting and Spending: An Introduction to Economics*. London: Collins Clear-Type Press, 1922.

Fisher, Lettice. 'The Economic Position of the Married Woman'. The Stansfield Trust Lecture, University of London, 1924. London: Oxford University Press, 1924.

Fisher, Lettice. *Then and Now: Economic Problems After the War a Hundred Years Ago*. London: Oxford University Press, 1925.

Fisher, Lettice. *The Citizen: A Simple Account of How We Manage our National and Local Affairs.* London: W. and R. Chambers, 1927.

Fisher, Lettice. *The Facts Behind the Crisis.* London: Oxford University Press, 1931.

Fisher, Lettice. *A Brief Survey of the British Empire.* London: Oxford University Press, 1932.

Fisher, Lettice. *Mothers and Families.* London: Ernest Benn Ltd., 1932.

Fisher, Lettice. *The Housewife and the Town Hall.* London: Ivor Nicholson and Watson Ltd., 1934.

Fisher, Lettice. *Life and Work in England: A Sketch of Our Social and Economic History.* London: Edward Arnold & Co., 1934.

Fisher, Lettice. *An Introductory History of England and Europe: From The Earliest Times to the Present Day.* London: Victor Gollancz, 1935.

Fisher, Lettice. 'Indian Memories'. *The Cornhill Magazine* 154 (Sept. 1936): 344–6.

Fisher, Lettice. *Earning and Spending: An Introduction to Economics.* London: Collins Clear-Type Press, 1938.

Fisher, Lettice. *Twenty-one Years 1918–1939* [A history of the National Council for the Unmarried Mother and her Child]. London: National Council for the Unmarried Mother and her Child, 1939.

Gates, Evelyn G. ed. *The Woman's Year Book 1923–1924.* London: Women Publishers Ltd., 1924.

Gesell, Arnold. 'Scientific Approaches to the Study of the Human Mind'. *Science* 88, no. 2280 (1938): 225–30.

Gray, Mrs Edwin. *Women's Work and Wages.* York: Coultas and Volans, 1908.

Gray, Mrs Edwin. 'Illegitimacy in Norway: The Castberg Laws'. *Maternity and Child Welfare: A Monthly Journal for Workers Among Mothers and Children* VII, no. 4 (Apr. 1923): 115–17.

Gray, Mrs Edwin. *Women on Juries.* London: National Council of Women of Great Britain and Ireland, 1923.

Hadow, William Henry. *Citizenship.* Oxford: Clarendon Press, 1923.

Haldane, Charlotte. *Motherhood and its Enemies.* London: Chatto & Windus, 1927.

Hardy, Henry ed. *Isaiah Berlin: Letters 1928–1946.* Cambridge: Cambridge University Press, 2004.

Harris, Muriel. *Pulpits and Preachers.* London: Methuen & Co., 1935.

Heseltine, Olive. *Conversation.* London: Methuen, 1927.

Heseltine, Olive. *Lost Content.* London: Spottiswoode, Ballantyne and Co., 1953.

Hill, L. 'Advertising Local Government in England'. *Public Opinion Quarterly* 1, no. 2 (1937): 62–72.

Hutton, Isabel Emslie. *With a Woman's Unit in Serbia, Salonika and Sebastopol.* London: Williams and Norgate, 1928.

Hutton, Isabel Emslie. *Memories of a Doctor in War and Peace.* London: Heinemann, 1960.

Ilbert, Mrs Courtenay. *Six Lectures on Practical Nursing.* Calcutta: Superintendent of Government Printing India, 1885.

Ilbert, Lettice. 'Pioneers in Housing'. *Economic Review* 9 (1899): 450–62.

James, Henry. *The Princess Casamassima.* London: Macmillan, 1886. Reprint, Harmondsworth: Penguin, 1987.

Kenealy, Arabella. *Feminism and Sex-Extinction.* London: T. Fisher Unwin Ltd., 1920.

Kinnaird, Emily. *Reminiscences.* London: Murray, 1925.

Kinnaird, Emily. *My Adopted Country 1889–1944.* Lucknow: E. Kinnaird, 1944.

LeBon, Gustav. *The Crowd: A Study of the Popular Mind.* London, 1896.

Macadam, Elizabeth. 'The Universities and the Training of the Social Worker'. *Hibbert Journal: A Quarterly Review of Religion, Theology, and Philosophy* 12, no. 2 (1914): 283–94.

Macadam, Elizabeth. *The Equipment of the Social Worker.* London: G. Allen and Unwin Ltd., 1925.

Macadam, Elizabeth. *The New Philanthropy: A Study of the Relations Between the Statutory and Voluntary Social Services.* London: G. Allen and Unwin Ltd., 1934.

Macadam, Elizabeth. *The Social Servant in the Making: A Review of the Provision of Training for the Social Services.* London: G. Allen and Unwin Ltd., 1945.

Oldham, J. H. *Christianity and the Race Problem.* 2nd edn., London: Student Christian Movement, 1924.

Paget, Louise Margaret Leila Wemyss. *With Our Serbian Allies.* London: Serbian Relief Fund, 1915.

Palmer, Agnes Lizzie Page. *1904–1926. The Time Between: Reviewing the Progress of the Salvation Army in the United States Under the Leadership of Commander Evangeline Booth.* New York: Salvation Army Printers, 1926.

Parcq, Herbert du. *Life of Lloyd George,* Vol. 4. London: Caxton Publishing Company, 1912–13.

Pares, Bernard. *Russia and Reform.* London: Archibald Constable & Co. Ltd., 1907.

Pares, Bernard. *My Russian Memoirs.* London: Jonathan Cape, 1931.

Pares, Bernard. 'Lady Muriel Paget'. *The Slavonic and East European Review* 17, no. 49 (1938): 218–9.

Picton-Turbervill, Edith. *Life is Good: An Autobiography.* London: Frederick Muller, 1939.

Pope-Hennessy, Una. *The Closed City: Impressions of a Visit to Leningrad.* London: Hutchinson and Co., 1938.

Pringle, John Christian, *The Nation's Appeal to the Housewife and Her Response.* London: Longmans, Green & Co. and [London] Charity Organization Society, 1933.

Reeves, Mrs M. S. Pember. *Round About a Pound a Week.* London: G. Bell and Sons Ltd., 1913.

Reith, John. *Broadcast Over Britain.* London: Hodder and Stoughton, 1924.

Riker, T. W. 'Reviewed Work: *A History of Europe* by H. A. L. Fisher'. *The Journal of Modern History* 9, no. 1 (1937): 64–66.

Russian Exhibition Descriptive of the Industries, Art, Literature, and Customs of Russia. London: Grafton Galleries, 1917.

Schreiber, Adele *Mutterschaft: ein Sammelwerk für die Probleme des Wiebes als Mutter.* Muchen: A. Langen 1912.

Schreiber, Frau Adele. 'Status of the Illegitimate Child in Germany'. *Maternity and Child Welfare: A Monthly Journal for Workers Among Mothers and Children* VII, no. 1 (Jan. 1923): 8–9.

Strachey, Lytton. *Eminent Victorians.* Oxford: Oxford University Press, 2003. First Published, London: Chattus & Windus, 1918.

Strachey, Ray. 'Jebb, Eglantyne (1876–1928)'. In *Dictionary of National Biography, 1922–1930,* edited by J. R. H. Weaver, 451–2. London: Oxford University Press, 1937.

Wakefield, Henry Russell. *The Ethics of Birth Control. Statement by the Bishop of Birmingham.* Leicester: C. Killick Millard, 1919.

Wallas, Graham. 'Introduction'. In Élie Halvéy, *A History of the English People in 1815,* translated by E. I. Watkin and D. A. Barker, v–viii. London: T. Fisher Unwin, 1924–1934.

Ward, Charlotte. *Lending a Hand, or Help for the Working Classes.* London, 1866.

Webb, Beatrice. *My Apprenticeship.* London: Longmans, Green & Co., 1926. Reprint, Cambridge: Cambridge University Press, 1979.

Webb, Ewing T. and John B. Morgan. *Strategy in Handling People.* New York: Garden City Publishing Co., 1930.

Wilkinson, Ellen. *Clash.* London: Harrap, 1929. Reprint, London: Virago, 1989.

Wilson, Elizabeth. *The Story of Fifty Years of the Young Women's Christian Association of India, Burma and Ceylon.* Calcutta: YMCA Association Press, 1925.

Wilson, P. W. *The General: The Story of Evangeline Booth.* London: Hodder and Stoughton Ltd., 1935.

Wingfield-Stratford, Esme. *The Foundations of British Patriotism.* London: G. Routledge and Sons, 1939.

Woolf, Virginia. *Carlyle's House and Other Sketches,* edited by David Bradshaw. London: Hesperus, 2003.

World's Young Women's Christian Association. *A Study of the World's Young Women's Christian Association.* London: World's Young Women's Christian Association, 1924.

Newspapers and journals

Aeroplane (1933)

Birmingham Mail (1911)

Blast (1914)

The British Journal of Nursing (1915–1916; 1920)

British Medical Journal (1916)

Christian World (1919)

The Church Times (1934)

Daily Mail (1918–39)

Daily Mirror (1918–39)

Daily Sketch (1936)

The Daily Telegraph (1927)

Evening World / Evening Times (Bristol, 1933)

The Field Officer (1906)

Flight: The Aircraft Engineer (1919)

The Gentlewoman (1901–26)

The Girl's Own Paper (1891)

The Illustrated London News (1913)

John Bull (1939)

Journal of Public Health (1931)

The Listener (1929–38)

The Manchester Guardian (1913; 1918–39)

Mothers' Union Journal (1932)

New York Herald Tribune (1927)

The New York Times (1918–39)

The North American Review (1921)

Our Own Gazette [becoming *The Blue Triangle Gazette* in 1928] (1884; 1918–36)

Pall Mall Gazette (1885)

The Queen, the Lady's Newspaper and Court Chronicle (1895; 1901; 1921)

The Quiver (1916)

The Radio Times (1923–39)

The Record of the Save the Children Fund (1920–22)

Red Cross World (1920)

The Rotarian (1931)

The Star (1931)

The Sunday Times (1931; 1937)

Tatler (1931; 1935)

Time (1936)

The Times (1903; 1911; 1918–39)

Times Literary Supplement (1919; 1922; 1934)

Toronto Star (1913)

The War Cry, UK (1934–9)

The War Cry, US (1919)

The Woman's Leader (1920–4)

Woman's Own (1933)

YWCA Bulletin (1923)

Audio-visual sources

'"100 Voices": History of the BBC', Interview with John Snagge, Part 1, http://www.bbc.co.uk/historyofthebbc/bbc-memories/john-snagge [accessed 28 Mar. 2017].

'Salvation Army General-Elect', Video newsreel film, 5 September 1934, http://www. britishpathe.com/record.php?id=5051 [accessed 2 Mar. 2017].

Secondary sources

Agathocleous, Tanya. *Urban Realism and the Cosmopolitan Imagination in the Nineteenth Century: Visible City, Invisible World*. Cambridge: Cambridge University Press, 2011.

Akiyama, Yuriko. *Feeding the Nation: Nutrition and Health in Britain Before World War One*. London: Tauris Academic Studies, 2008.

Allen, Ann Taylor. 'Mothers of the New Generation: Adele Schreiber, Helene Stöcker, and the Evolution of a German Idea of Motherhood, 1900–1914'. *Signs* 10, no. 3 (1985): 418–38.

Andrews, Maggie. *The Acceptable Face of Feminism: The Women's Institute as a Social Movement*. London: Lawrence and Wishart, 1997.

Andrews, Maggie. *Domesticating the Airwaves: Broadcasting, Domesticity and Femininity*. London: Continuum, 2012.

Anthony, Scott. 'The GPO Film Unit and "Britishness" in the 1930s'. In *The Projection of Britain: A History of the GPO Film Unit*, edited by Scott Anthony and James Mansell, 10–17. London: BFI, 2011.

Anthony, Scott. *Public Relations and the Making of Modern Britain: Stephen Tallents and the Birth of a Progressive Media Profession*. Manchester: Manchester University Press, 2012.

Ball, Alan M. *And Now My Soul is Hardened: Abandoned Children in Soviet Russia, 1918–1930*. Berkeley: University of California Press, 1994.

Bartley, Paula. *Prostitution: Prevention and Reform in England, 1860–1914*. London: Routledge, 2000.

Bartley, Paula. *Emmeline Pankhurst*. London: Routledge, 2002.

Baughan, Emily. '"Every Citizen Of Empire Implored to Save the Children!" Empire, Internationalism and the Save the Children Fund in Inter-war Britain'. *Historical Research* 86, no. 231 (2013): 116–37.

Beaumont, Caitríona. 'Citizens Not Feminists: The Boundary Negotiated Between Citizenship and Feminism by Mainstream Women's Organisations in England, 1928–39'. *Women's History Review* 9, no. 2 (2000): 411–29.

Beaumont, Caitríona. *Housewives and Citizens: Domesticity and the Women's Movement in England, 1928–64*. Manchester: Manchester University Press, 2013.

Beaumont, Caitríona. 'Fighting for the "Privileges of Citizenship": The Young Women's Christian Association (YWCA), Feminism and the Women's Movement, 1928–1945', *Women's History Review*, 23, 3 (2014): 463–79.

Bebbington, David W. *Evangelicalism in Modern Britain: A History from the 1730s to the 1980s*. London: Unwin Hyman, 1989.

Behdad, Ali. *Belated Travelers. Orientalism in the Age of Colonial Dissolution.* Durham, NC: Duke University Press, 1994.

Berg, Maxine. 'The First Women Economic Historians'. *The Economic History Review* 45, no. 2 (1992): 308–29.

Berg, Maxine. *A Woman in History: Eileen Power, 1889–1940.* Cambridge: Cambridge University Press, 1996.

Bingham, Adrian. *Gender, Modernity and the Popular Press in Inter-war Britain.* Oxford: Clarendon Press, 2004.

Bingham, Adrian. *Family Newspapers? Sex, Private Life and the British Popular Press, 1918–1978.* Oxford: Oxford University Press, 2009.

Blunt, Alison. *Travel, Gender, and Imperialism: Mary Kingsley and West Africa.* New York: Guilford Press, 1994.

Blunt, Wilfrid. *Lady Muriel: Lady Muriel Paget, Her Husband, and Her Philanthropic Work in Central and Eastern Europe.* London: Methuen, 1962.

Bock, Gisela and Pat Thane eds. *Maternity and Gender Policies: Women and the Rise of the European Welfare States 1880s–1950s.* London: Routledge, 1991.

Booth, Alan. 'Corporatism, Capitalism and Depression in Interwar Britain'. *The British Journal of Sociology* 33, no. 2 (1982): 200–23.

Booth, Alison. *How to Make It As A Woman: Collective Biographical History from Victoria to the Present.* Chicago: University of Chicago Press, 2004.

Borkman, Thomasina. 'Experiential Knowledge: A New Concept for the Analysis of Self-Help Groups'. *Social Service Review* 50, no. 3 (1976): 445–56.

Bourke, Joanna. *Dismembering the Male: Men's Bodies, Britain and the Great War.* London: Reaktion, 1996.

Bowler, Peter J. *Reconciling Science and Religion: The Debate in Early-Twentieth Century Britain.* Chicago: Chicago University Press, 2001.

Brassley, Paul, Jeremy Burchardt and Lynne Thompson, eds. *The English Countryside Between the Wars: Regeneration or Decline?* Woodbridge: Boydell, 2006.

Braude, Ann. 'Women's History *Is* American Religious History'. In *Retelling U.S. Religious History,* edited by Thomas A. Tweed, 87–107. Berkeley: University of California Press, 1997.

Brooker, Peter. 'Afterword: "Newness" in Modernisms, Early and Late'. In *The Oxford Handbook of Modernisms,* edited by Peter Brooker, Andrzej Gasiorek, Deborah Longworth and Andrew Thacker, 1012–1036. Oxford: Oxford University Press, 2010.

Brouwer, Ruth Compton. *Modern Women Modernizing Men: The Changing Missions of Three Professional Women in Asia and Africa.* Vancouver: UBC Press, 2002.

Brown, Elspeth H. *The Corporate Eye: Photography and the Rationalization of American Commercial Culture, 1884–1929.* Baltimore: John Hopkins University Press, 2005.

Bullard, Julian and Margaret Bullard eds. *Inside Stalin's Russia: The Diaries of Reader Bullard, 1930–34.* Charlbury: Day Books, 2000.

Burchardt, Jeremy. *Paradise Lost: Rural Idyll and Social Change in England Since 1800.* London: Tauris, 2002.

Bush, Julia. *Edwardian Ladies and Imperial Power*. London: Leicester University Press, 2000.

Cabanes, Bruno. *The Great War and the Origins of Humanitarianism, 1918–1924*. New York: Cambridge University Press, 2014.

Callan, Hilary and Shirley Ardener, eds. *The Incorporated Wife*. London: Croom Helm, 1984.

Capet, Antoine. 'Photographs of the British Unemployed in the Inter-war Years: Representation or Manipulation?' In *The Representation of the Working People in Britain and France: New Perspectives*, edited by Antoine Capet, 93–105. Newcastle-upon-Tyne: Cambridge Scholars Publishing, 2009.

Carlson, Allan C. *The Swedish Experiment in Family Politics: The Myrdals and the Interwar Population Crisis*. New Brunswick, NJ: Transaction Publications, 1990.

Cheffins, B. R. *Corporate Ownership and Control: British Business Transformed*. Oxford: Oxford University Press, 2008.

Clavin, Patricia. 'Defining Transnationalism'. *Contemporary European History, special issue on 'Transnational Communities in European History, 1920–1970'* 14, no. 4 (2005): 421–39.

Clements, S. 'Feminism, Citizenship and Social Activity: The Role and Importance of Local Women's Organisations, Nottingham, 1918–1969'. PhD diss., University of Nottingham, 2008.

Cocks, R. C. J. 'Ilbert, Sir Courtenay Peregrine (1841–1924)'. In *Oxford Dictionary of National Biography*, Oxford University Press, 2004; online edn, Jan 2008, http://ezproxy.ouls.ox.ac.uk:2117/view/article/34090 [accessed 2 Mar. 2017].

Cohen, Deborah. *Household Gods: The British and Their Possessions*. New Haven, CT: Yale University Press, 2006.

Cohen, Stanley. *States of Denial: Knowing About Atrocities and Suffering*. Cambridge, UK: Polity, 2001.

Collini, Stefan. *Absent Minds: Intellectuals in Britain*. Oxford: Oxford University Press, 2006.

Colpus, Eve. 'Preaching Religion, Family and Memory in Nineteenth-Century England'. *Gender & History* 22, no. 1 (2010): 38–54.

Colpus, Eve. 'Landscapes of Welfare: Concepts and Cultures of British Women's Philanthropy, 1918–1939'. DPhil thesis, University of Oxford, 2011.

Colpus, Eve. 'The Week's Good Cause: Mass Culture and Cultures of Philanthropy at the Inter-war BBC'. *Twentieth Century British History* 22, no. 3 (2011): 305–29.

Colpus, Eve. '*Unmarried*: Unmarried Motherhood in Post-First World War British Film'. In *Moral Panics, Social Fears, and the Media: Historical Perspectives*, edited by Siân Nicholas and Tom O'Malley, 129–46. London: Routledge, 2013.

Colpus, Eve. 'Women, Service and Self-actualization in Inter-war Britain'. *Past and Present* (forthcoming, 2018).

Coombes, Annie. *Reinventing Africa: Museums, Material Culture and Popular Imagination in Late Victorian and Edwardian England*. New Haven, CT: Yale University Press, 1994.

Cox, Jeffrey. 'From the Empire of Christ to the Third World: Religion and the Experience of Empire in the Twentieth Century'. In *Britain's Experience of Empire in the Twentieth Century*, edited by Andrew Thompson, 76–121. Oxford: Oxford University Press, 2012.

Cross, Anthony. 'Exhibiting Russia: The Two London Russian Exhibitions of 1917 and 1935'. *Slavonica* 16, no. 1 (2010): 29–39.

Cross, Anthony. 'By Way of Introduction: British Perception, Reception and Recognition of Russian Culture'. In *A People Passing Rude: British Responses to Russian Culture*, edited by Anthony Cross, 1–36. Cambridge, UK: Open Book Publishers, 2012.

Cross, Anthony, ed. *A People Passing Rude: British Responses to Russian Culture*. Cambridge, UK: Open Book Publishers, 2012.

Curthoys, M. C. and Janet Howarth. 'Origins and Destinations: The Social Mobility of Oxford Men and Women'. In *The History of the University of Oxford*. Vol. 7: *Nineteenth-Century Oxford Part 2*, edited by M. J. Brock and M. C. Curthoys, 571–95. Oxford: Clarendon Press, 2000.

Dahrendorf, Ralf. *LSE: A History of the London School of Economics and Political Science 1895–1995*. Oxford: Oxford University Press, 1995.

Darlington, Tim. 'Trustees, Committees and Boards'. In *Introduction to the Voluntary Sector*, edited by Rodney Hedley, Colin Rochester and Justin Davis-Smith, 211–26. London: Routledge, 1995.

David-Fox, Michael. *Showcasing the Great Experiment: Cultural Diplomacy and Western Visitors to the Soviet Union, 1921–41*. New York: Oxford University Press, 2012.

Davin, Anna. 'Imperialism and Motherhood'. *History Workshop Journal* 5, no. 1 (1978): 9–65.

Davis, Natalie Zemon. 'Conclusion'. In *Poverty and Charity in Middle Eastern Contexts*, edited by Michael Bonner, Mine Ener and Amy Singer, 315–24. Albany: State University of New York Press, 2003.

D'Cruze, Shani. 'Intimacy, Professionalism and Domestic Homicide in Interwar Britain: The Case of Buck Ruxton'. *Women's History Review* 16, no. 5 (2007): 701–22.

Delap, Lucy. *Knowing Their Place: Domestic Service in Twentieth-Century Britain*. Oxford: Oxford University Press, 2011.

Delap, Lucy. 'Conservative Values, Anglicans, and the Gender Order in Inter-war Britain'. In *Brave New World: Imperial and Democratic Nation-Building in Britain Between the Wars*, edited by Laura Beers and Geraint Thomas, 149–68. London: Institute of Historical Research, 2012.

Dickinson, Edward Ross. *Sex, Freedom, and Power in Imperial Germany, 1880–1914*. Cambridge: Cambridge University Press, 2014.

Doughan, David and Peter Gordon. *Women, Clubs and Associations in Britain*. Abingdon: Routledge, 2006.

Dyhouse, Carol. *No Distinction Of Sex? Women in British Universities, 1870–1939*. London: UCL Press, 1995.

Eason, Andrew Mark. *Women in God's Army: Gender and Equality in the Early Salvation Army*. Waterloo, Ont.: Wilfrid Laurier University Press, 2003.

Edgerton, David. *The Shock of the Old: Technology and Global History Since 1900.* London: Profile Books, 2006.

Edwards, Martin. *Control and the Therapeutic Trial: Rhetoric and Experimentation in Britain, 1918–1948.* Amsterdam: Editions Rodopi B.V., 2007.

Erdmann, Martin. *Building the Kingdom of God on Earth: The Churches' Contribution to Marshal Public Support for World Order and World Peace, 1919–1945.* Eugene, Or.: Wipf and Stock, 2005.

Fairbank, Jenty. *Booth's Boots: The Beginnings of Salvation Army Social Work.* London: International Headquarters of the Salvation Army, 1983.

Fehrenbach, Heide and Davide Rodogno, eds. *Humanitarian Photography: A History.* Cambridge: Cambridge University Press, 2015.

Ferrall, Charles and Dougal McNeill. *Writing the 1926 General Strike: Literature, Culture, Politics.* Cambridge: Cambridge University Press, 2015.

Filene, Peter G., ed. *American Views of Soviet Russia, 1917–1965.* Homewood, ILL: The Dorsey Press, 1968.

Finstuen, Andrew S. *Original Sin and Everyday Protestants: The Theology of Reinhold Niebuhr, Billy Graham, and Paul Tillich in an Age of Anxiety.* Chapel Hill: University of North Carolina Press, 2009.

Fitzpatrick, Sheila. *The Cultural Front: Power and Culture in Revolutionary Russia.* Ithaca, NY: Cornell University Press, 1992.

Fitzpatrick, Sheila. *Everyday Stalinism: Ordinary Life in Extraordinary Times: Soviet Russia in the 1930s.* Oxford: Oxford University Press, 1999.

Gandhi, Leela. *Affective Communities: Anticolonial Thought, Fin-de-Siècle Radicalism, and the Politics of Friendship.* Durham, NC: Duke University Press, 2006.

Garnett, Jane. 'Political and Domestic Economy in Victorian Social Thought: Ruskin and Xenophon'. In *Economy, Polity and Society: British Intellectual History 1750–1950,* edited by Stefan Collini, Richard Whatmore and Brian Young, 205–223. Cambridge: Cambridge University Press, 2000.

Garnett, Jane. 'Kinnaird, Mary Jane, Lady Kinnaird (1816–1888)'. In *Oxford Dictionary of National Biography,* Oxford University Press, 2004; online edn, May 2006, http://ezproxy.ouls.ox.ac.uk:2117/view/article/15636 [accessed 22 Apr. 2017].

Garnett, Jane. 'At Home in the Metropolis: Gender and Ideals of Social Service'. In *'Nobler Imaginings and Mightier Struggles': Octavia Hill, Social Activism and the Remaking of British Society,* edited by Elizabeth Baigent and Ben Cowell, 243–54. London: Institute of Historical Research, 2016.

Genevois, Daniele Bussy [translated by Arthur Goldhammer]. 'The Women of Spain from the Republic to Franco'. In *A History of Women in the West.* Vol. 5, *Toward a Cultural Identity in the Twentieth Century,* edited by Georges Duby and Michelle Perrot, 177–93. Cambridge, MA: Harvard University Press, 1994.

Geniesse, Jane Fletcher. *Passionate Nomad: The Life of Freya Stark.* New York: Modern Library, 2001.

Gerard, Jessica. '"Lady Bountiful": Women of the Landed Classes and Rural Philanthropy'. *Victorian Studies* 30, no. 2 (1987): 183–210.

Gibson, Lorna. *Beyond Jerusalem: Music in the Women's Institute, 1919–1969*. Aldershot: Ashgate, 2008.

Gilbert, Bentley B. *The Evolution of National Insurance in Great Britain: The Origins of the Welfare State*. London: Michael Joseph, 1966.

Glasman, Maurice. 'Politics, Employment Policies and the Young Generation'. *Economia Politica* / a. xxx, n. 2 August 2013.

Gleadle, Kathryn. *Borderline Citizens: Women, Gender and Political Culture in Britain, 1815–1867*. Oxford: Oxford University Press for the British Academy, 2009.

Gledhill, Christine, ed. *Home Is Where the Heart Is: Studies in Melodrama and the Woman's Film*. London: British Film Institute, 1987.

Glenny, M. V. 'The Anglo-Soviet Trade Agreement, March 1921'. *Journal of Contemporary History* 5, no. 2 (1970): 63–82.

Glew, Helen. *Gender, Rhetoric and Regulation: Women's Work in the Civil Service and the London County Council, 1900–55*. Manchester: Manchester University Press, 2016.

Goldman, Lawrence. 'Victorian Social Science: From Singular to Plural'. In *The Organization of Knowledge in Victorian Britain*, edited by Martin Daunton, 87–114. Oxford: Published for the British Academy by Oxford University Press, 2005.

Gottlieb, Julie V. and Richard Toye. 'Introduction'. In *The Aftermath of Suffrage: Women, Gender and Politics in Britain, 1918–1945*, edited by Julie V. Gottlieb and Richard Toye, 1–18. Basingstoke: Palgrave Macmillan, 2013.

Graham, Sarah Ellen. *Culture and Propaganda: The Progressive Origins of American Public Diplomacy, 1936–1953*. Farnham, Surrey: Ashgate, 2015.

Grant, Mariel. *Propaganda and the Role of the State in Inter-War Britain*. Oxford: Clarendon Press, 1994.

Grant, Peter. *Philanthropy and Voluntary Action in the First World War: Mobilizing Charity*. London: Routledge, 2014.

Hagedorn, Nancy L. '"A Friend to Go Between Them": The Interpreter as Cultural Broker During Anglo-Iroquois Councils, 1740–70'. *Ethnohistory* 35, no. 1 (1988): 60–80.

Hannah, Leslie. *The Rise of the Corporate Economy*. London, Methuen, 1979.

Harmer, Michael H. *The Forgotten Hospital: An Essay*. Chichester, Springwood Books, 1982.

Harris, Bernard. 'Health by Association'. *International Journal of Epidemiology* 34, no. 2 (2005): 488–90.

Harris, José. 'Political Thought and the State'. In *Boundaries of the State in Modern Britain*, edited by S. J. D. Green and R. J. Whiting, 15–28. Cambridge: Cambridge University Press, 1996.

Harris, José. 'Political Thought and the Welfare State 1870–1940: An Intellectual Framework for British Social Policy'. In *Before Beveridge: Welfare Before the Welfare State*, edited by David Gladstone, 43–63. London: Institute of Economic Affairs, 1999.

Hayward, Rhodri. 'Desperate Housewives and Model Amoebae: The Invention Of Suburban Neurosis in Inter-war Britain'. In *Health and the Modern Home*, edited by Mark Jackson, 42–62. New York: Routledge, 2007.

Herren, Madeleine. 'Gender and International Relations Through the Lens of the League of Nations (1919–1945)'. In *Women, Diplomacy and International Politics Since 1500*, edited by Glenda Sluga and Carolyn James, 182–201. London: Routledge, 2016.

Hewitson, Mark and Matthew D'Auria eds. *Europe in Crisis: Intellectuals and the European Idea, 1917–1957*. New York: Berghahn Books, 2012.

Higginbotham, Ann R. 'Respectable Sinners: Salvation Army Rescue Work With Unmarried Mothers, 1884–1914'. In *Religion in the Lives of English Women, 1760–1930*, edited by Gail Malmgreen, 216–33. Bloomington: Indiana Press, 1986.

Hilton, Matthew and James McKay eds. *The Ages of Voluntarism: How We Got to the Big Society*. Oxford: Oxford University Press, 2011.

Hindmarsh, D. Bruce. *The Evangelical Conversion Narrative: Spiritual Autobiography in Early Modern England*. Oxford: Oxford University Press, 2005.

Hinton, James. 'Voluntarism and the Welfare/Warfare State: Women's Voluntary Services in the 1940s'. *Twentieth Century British History* 9, no. 2 (1998): 274–305.

Hinton, James. *Women, Social Leadership and the Second World War: Continuities of Class*. Oxford: Oxford University Press, 2002.

Hoare, Jon. '"Go The Way The Material Calls You": Basil Wright and *The Song of Ceylon*'. In *The Projection of Britain: A History of the GPO Film Unit*, edited by Scott Anthony and James Mansell, 233–43. London: BFI, 2011.

Hogg, William Richey. *Ecumenical Foundations: A History of the International Missionary Council and its Nineteenth Century Background*. New York: Harper and Brothers, 1952.

Hollander, Rachel. *Narrative Hospitality in Late Victorian Fiction: Novel Ethics*. New York: Routledge, 2012.

Hollis, Patricia. *Ladies Elect: Women in English Local Government 1865–1914*. Oxford: Clarendon Press, 1987.

Holmes, Vicky. 'Finding a Bed: The Experiences of Unmarried Mothers in Working-Class Victorian Society'. Paper presented at the Women's History Network Conference, Leeds Trinity, September 2016.

Houlbrook, Matt. '"A Pin to See the Peepshow": Culture, Fiction and Selfhood in Edith Thompson's Letters, 1921–22'. *Past and Present* 207, no. 1 (2010): 215–49.

Houlbrook, Matt and Sarah Newman. 'Introduction: Special Issue: The Press and Popular Culture in Interwar Europe'. *Journalism Studies* 14, no. 5 (2013): 640–50.

Howse, Carrie. 'From Lady Bountiful to Lady Administrator: Women and the Administration of Rural District Nursing in England, 1880–1925'. *Women's History Review* 15, no. 3 (2006): 423–41.

Humble, Nicola. *The Feminine Middlebrow Novel, 1920s to 1950s: Class, Domesticity and Bohemianism*. Oxford: Oxford University Press, 2001.

Hunt, Karen and June Hannam. 'Towards an Archaeology of Interwar Women's Politics: The Local and the Everyday'. In *The Aftermath of Suffrage: Women, Gender, and*

Politics in Britain, 1918–1945, edited by Julie V. Gottlieb and Richard Toye, 124–41. Basingstoke: Palgrave Macmillan, 2013.

Hutchinson, John F. '"Custodians of the Sacred Fire": The ICRC and the Postwar Reorganisation of the International Red Cross'. In *International Health Organisations and Movements 1918–1939*, edited by Paul Weindling, 17–35. Cambridge: Cambridge University Press, 1995.

Huyssen, Andreas. *After the Great Divide: Modernism, Mass Culture, Postmodernism.* Bloomington: Indiana University Press, 1986.

Jacobs, Lea. *The Decline of Sentiment: American Film in the 1920s.* Berkeley: University of California Press, 2008.

Jones, Kathleen W. *Taming the Troublesome Child: American Families, Child Guidance, and the Limits of Psychiatric Authority.* Cambridge, MA: Harvard University Press, 1999.

Keating, Jenny. *A Child for Keeps: The History of Adoption in England, 1918–45.* Basingstoke: Palgrave Macmillan, 2009.

Kent, Susan Kingsley. *Aftershocks: Politics and Trauma in Britain, 1918–1931.* Basingstoke: Palgrave Macmillan, 2009.

Kiernan, Kathleen, Hilary Land and Jane Lewis. *Lone Motherhood in Twentieth-Century Britain: From Footnote to Front Page.* Oxford: Clarendon Press, 1998.

King, Laura. 'Future Citizens: Cultural and Political Conceptions of Children in Britain, 1930s–1950s'. *Twentieth Century British History* 27, no. 3 (2016): 389–411.

Knight, Claire. 'Mrs. Churchill Goes to Russia: The Wartime Gift Exchange Between Britain and the Soviet Union'. In *A People Passing Rude: British Responses to Russian Culture,* edited by Anthony Cross, 253–68. Cambridge, UK: Open Book Publishers, 2012.

Koven, Seth. *Slumming: Sexual and Social Politics in Victorian Britain.* Princeton: Princeton University Press, 2004.

Koven, Seth. *The Match Girl and the Heiress.* Princeton: Princeton University Press, 2015.

Koven, Seth and Sonya Michel eds. *Mothers of a New World: Maternalist Politics and the Origins of Welfare States.* New York: Routledge, 1990.

Kymlicka, Will and Wayne Norman. 'Return of the Citizen: A Survey of Recent Work On Citizenship Theory'. *Ethics* 104, no. 2 (1994): 352–81.

Larsson, John. *1929: A Crisis that Shaped the Salvation Army's Future.* London: Salvation Army, 2009.

Lavine, Sigmund A. *Evangeline Booth: Daughter of Salvation.* New York: Dodd, Mead and Co., 1970.

Lawrence, Christopher. *Rockefeller Money, the Laboratory, and Medicine in Edinburgh 1919–1930: New Science in an Old Country.* Rochester, NY: University of Rochester Press, 2005.

Laybourn, Keith. 'The Guild of Help and the Changing Face of Edwardian Philanthropy'. *Urban History* 20, no. 1 (1993): 43–60.

Lears, T. J. Jackson. 'From Salvation To Self-Realization: Advertising and the Therapeutic Roots of the Consumer Culture, 1880–1930'. In *The Culture of Consumption: Critical*

Essays in American History, 1880–1980, edited by Richard Wightman Fox and T. J. Jackson Lears, 1–38. New York: Pantheon Books, 1983.

Lears, T. J. Jackson. *No Place of Grace: Antimodernism and the Transformation of American Culture 1880–1920*. Chicago: University of Chicago Press, 1994.

LeMahieu, Dan. *A Culture for Democracy: Mass Communication and the Cultivated Mind in Britain Between the Wars*. Oxford: Clarendon Press, 1988.

Lewis, Jane. *Women and Social Action in Victorian and Edwardian England*. Aldershot: Elgar, 1991.

Lewis, Jane. *The Voluntary Sector, the State and Social Work in Britain: The Charity Organisation Society/Family Welfare Association since 1869*. Aldershot: Elgar, 1995.

Lewis, Jane. 'Women, Social Work and Social Welfare in Twentieth-century Britain: From (Unpaid) Influence to (Paid) Oblivion'. In *Charity, Self-Interest and Welfare in the English Past*, edited by Martin Daunton, 203–24. London: UCL Press, 1996.

Lewis, Jane. 'Reviewing the Relationship Between the Voluntary Sector and the State in Britain in the 1990s'. *Voluntas: International Journal of Voluntary and Nonprofit Organizations* 10, no. 3 (1999): 255–70.

Light, Alison. *Forever England: Femininity, Literature and Conservatism Between the Wars*. London: Routledge, 1995.

Light, Alison. *Mrs Woolf and the Servants: The Hidden Heart of Domestic Service*. London, Fig Tree, 2007.

Lister, Ruth. *Citizenship: Feminist Perspectives*. Basingstoke: Macmillan, 1997.

Lloyd, Genevieve. *The Man of Reason: 'Male' and 'Female' in Western Philosophy*. London: Methuen, 1984.

Lorcin, Patricia M. E. *Historicizing Colonial Nostalgia: European Women's Narratives of Algeria and Kenya 1900–Present*. New York: Palgrave Macmillan, 2012.

Lowe, Rodney. 'Welfare's Moving Frontier'. *Twentieth Century British History* 6, no. 3 (1995): 369–76.

McCarthy, Helen. 'Service Clubs, Citizenship and Equality: Gender Relations and Middle-class Associations in Britain Between the Wars'. *Historical Research* 81, no. 213 (2008): 531–52.

McCarthy, Helen. 'The Lifeblood of the League? Voluntary Associations and League of Nations Activism in Britain'. In *Internationalism Reconfigured: Transnational Ideas and Movements Between the Wars*, edited by Daniel Laqua, 187–208. London: I.B. Tauris, 2011.

McCarthy, Helen. *Women of the World: The Rise of the Female Diplomat*. London: Bloomsbury, 2014.

McCarthy, Helen and Pat Thane. 'The Politics of Association in Industrial Society'. *Twentieth Century British History* 22, no. 2 (2011): 217–29.

McCarthy, Kathleen D., ed. *Lady Bountiful Revisited: Women, Philanthropy and Power*. New Brunswick, NJ: Rutgers University Press, 1990.

McDermid, Jane. 'A Very Polite and Considerate Revolution: The Scottish Women's Hospitals and the Russian Revolution, 1916–17'. *Revolutionary Russia* 21, no. 2 (2008): 135–51.

McEwan, Cheryl. *Gender, Geography and Empire: Victorian Women Travellers in West Africa*. Aldershot: Ashgate, 2000.

McKibbin, Ross. 'Social Class and Social Observation in Edwardian England'. *Transactions of the Royal Historical Society* 5th series, no. 28 (1978): 175–99.

McKibbin, Ross. *Classes and Cultures: England 1918–1951*. Oxford: Oxford University Press, 2000.

Macalister-Smith, Peter. *International Humanitarian Assistance: Disaster Relief Actions in International Law and Organization*. Dordrecht: Martinus Nijhoff Publishers, 1985.

Maiden, John. 'Evangelical and Anglo-Catholic Relations, 1928–1983'. In *Evangelicalism and the Church of England in the Twentieth Century: Reform, Resistance and Renewal*, edited by Andrew Atherstone and John Maiden, 136–61. London: The Boydell Press, 2014.

Mandler, Peter. *Return From the Natives: How Margaret Mead Won the Second World War and Lost the Cold War*. New Haven, CT: Yale University Press, 2013.

Marks, Richard. 'Russian Icons through British Eyes, c. 1830–1930'. In *A People Passing Rude: British Responses to Russian Culture*, edited by Anthony Cross, 69–88. Cambridge, UK: Open Book Publishers, 2012.

Marland, Hilary. *Health and Girlhood in Britain, 1874–1920*. Basingstoke: Palgrave Macmillan, 2013.

Marsh, Sabine Noelle. 'Religious Women in Modern American Social Reform: Evangeline Booth, Aimee Semple McPherson, Dorothy Day, and the Rhetorical Invention of Humanitarian Authority'. PhD diss., Graduate College of the University of Illinois at Urbana-Champaign, 2012.

Mathias, Jörg. 'Unity in Christ or Pan-Europeanism? Nathan Söderblom and the Ecumenical Peace Movement in the Interwar Period'. *Religion, State and Society* 42, no. 1 (2014): 5–22.

Mauss, Marcel. *The Gift: The Form and Reason for Exchange in Archaic Societies*, translated by W. D. Halls. London: Routledge, 1990. First published, Presses Universitaires de France, 1950.

Mawson, Andrew. *The Social Entrepreneur: Making Communities Work*. London: Atlantic Books, 2008.

Mayhall, Laura E. Nym. *The Militant Suffrage Movement: Citizenship and Resistance in Britain, 1860–1930*. Oxford: Oxford University Press, 2003.

Melnyk, Julie. 'Women, Writing and the Creation of Theological Cultures'. In *Women, Gender and Religious Cultures in Britain, 1800–1940*, edited by Sue Morgan and Jacqueline de Vries, 32–53. Abingdon: Routledge, 2010.

Metzger, Barbara. 'Towards an International Human Rights Regime during the Interwar Years: The League of Nations' Combat of Traffic in Women and Children'. In *Beyond Sovereignty: Britain, Empire and Transnationalism, c.1880–1950*, edited by Kevin Grant, Philippa Levine and Frank Trentmann, 54–79. Basingstoke: Palgrave Macmillan, 2007.

Michail, Eugene. *The British and the Balkans: Forming Images of Foreign Lands, 1900–1950*. London: Continuum, 2011.

Middlemas, Keith. *Politics in Industrial Society: The Experience of the British System Since 1911*. London: A. Deutsch, 1979.

Miller, Carol. 'Women in International Relations? The Debate in Inter-war Britain'. In *Gender and International Relations*, edited by Rebecca Grant and Kathleen Newland, 64–82. Milton Keynes: Open University, 1991.

Miller, Carol. 'Lobbying the League: Women's International Organisations and the League of Nations'. DPhil thesis, University of Oxford, 1992.

Miller, Carol. "Geneva – the Key to Equality": Inter-war Feminists and the League of Nations', *Women's History Review* 3, no. 2 (1994): 219–45.

Mills, Sara. *Discourses of Difference: An Analysis of Women's Travel Writing and Colonialism*. London: Routledge, 1991.

Mitchell, David. *Women on the Warpath: The Story of the Women of the First World War*. London: Cape, 1966.

Moeller, Susan D. *Compassion Fatigue: How the Media Sell Disease, Famine, War and Death*. New York: Routledge, 1999.

Moore, Henrietta L. *Still Life: Hopes, Desires and Satisfactions*. Cambridge, UK: Polity Press, 2011.

Moorehead, Caroline. *Dunant's Dream: War, Switzerland and the History of the Red Cross*. London: HarperCollins, 1998.

Mort, Frank. *Dangerous Sexualities: Medico-Moral Politics in England Since 1830*. London: Routledge & Kegan Paul, 1987.

Mouffe, Chantal. 'Democratic Citizenship and Political Community'. In *Dimensions of Radical Democracy: Pluralism, Citizenship, Community*, edited by Chantal Mouffe, 225–239. London: Verso, 1992.

Moyse, Cordelia. *A History of the Mothers' Union: Women, Anglicanism and Globalization*. London: The Boydell Press, 2009.

Muckle, James. 'Saving the Russian Children: Materials in the Archive of the Save the Children Fund Relating to Eastern Europe in 1920–23'. *The Slavonic and East European Review* 68, no. 3 (1990): 507–11.

Mumm, Susan. 'Women and Philanthropic Cultures'. In *Women, Gender and Religious Cultures in Britain, 1800–1940*, edited by Sue Morgan and Jacqueline de Vries, 54–71. London: Routledge, 2010.

Nauright, Lynda. 'Politics and Power: A New Look at Florence Nightingale'. *Nursing Forum* 21, no. 1 (1984): 5–8.

Neilson, Keith. *Britain, Soviet Russia and the Collapse of the Versailles Order, 1919–1939*. Cambridge: Cambridge University Press, 2006.

Nussbaum, Martha C. *Political Emotions: Why Love Matters for Justice*. Cambridge, MA: The Belknap Press of Harvard University, 2013.

O'Keefe, Paul. *Some Sort of Genius: A Life of Wyndham Lewis*. Berkeley, CA.: Counterpoint, 2015.

Oldfield, Adrian. *Citizenship and Community: Civic Republicanism and the Modern World*. London: Routledge, 1990.

Oldfield, Sybil. *Women Humanitarians: A Biographical Dictionary of British Women Active Between 1900 and 1950*. London: Continuum, 2001.

Oppenheimer, Melanie. "'We All Did Voluntary Work of Some Kind": Voluntary Work and Labour History'. *Labour History* 81 (2001): 1–11.

Overy, Richard. *The Morbid Age: Britain Between the Wars*. London: Allen Lane, 2009.

Parmar, Inderjeet. 'Anglo-American Elites in the Interwar Years: Idealism and Power in the Intellectual Roots of Chatham House and the Council on Foreign Relations'. *International Relations* 16, no. 1 (2002): 53–75.

Parratt, Catriona M. 'Making Leisure Work: Women's Rational Recreation in Late Victorian and Edwardian England'. *Journal of Sport History* 26, no. 3 (1999): 471–88.

Pedersen, Susan. *Eleanor Rathbone and the Politics of Conscience*. New Haven, CT: Yale University Press, 2004.

Pedersen, Susan. 'Macadam, Elizabeth (1871–1948)'. In *Oxford Dictionary of National Biography*. Oxford: Oxford University Press, 2004, http://www.oxforddnb.com/view/article/53582 [accessed 22 Apr. 2017].

Pedersen, Susan. 'Metaphors of the Schoolroom: Women Working the Mandates System of the League of Nations'. *History Workshop Journal* 66, no. 1 (2008): 188–207.

Peel, Mark. *Miss Cutler and the Case of the Resurrected Horse: Social Work and the Story of Poverty in America, Australia, and Britain*. Chicago: University of Chicago Press, 2012.

Peretz, Elizabeth. 'Infant Welfare Between the Wars'. In *Oxford: Studies in the History of a University Town Since 1800*, edited by R. C. Whiting, 131–45. Manchester: Manchester University Press, 1993.

Perriton, Linda. 'The Education of Women for Citizenship: The National Federation of Women's Institutes and the British Federation of Business and Professional Women 1930–1959'. *Gender and Education* 21, no. 1 (2009): 81–95.

Perrone, Fernanda. 'Women Academics in England, 1870–1930'. *History of Universities* XII (1993): 339–67.

Pimpare, Stephen. 'Toward a New Welfare History'. *Journal of Policy History* 19, no. 2 (2007): 234–52.

Ponce de Leon, Charles L. *Self-exposure: Human-interest Journalism and the Emergence of Celebrity in America, 1890–1940*. Chapel Hill: University of North Carolina Press, 2002.

Preston, Margaret H. *Charitable Words: Women, Philanthropy and the Language of Charity in Nineteenth-century Dublin*. Westport, CT: Praeger, 2004.

Prochaska, Frank. *Women and Philanthropy in Nineteenth-century England*. Oxford: Clarendon Press, 1980.

Prochaska, Frank. *The Voluntary Impulse in Modern Britain*. London: Faber & Faber, 1988.

Prochaska, Frank. *Christianity and Social Service in Modern Britain: The Disinherited Spirit*. Oxford: Oxford University Press, 2006.

Rappaport, Erika Diane. *Shopping for Pleasure: Women in the Making of London's West End*. Princeton, NJ: Princeton University Press, 2000.

Rappaport, Helen. *Caught in the Revolution: Petrograd 1917.* London: Hutchinson, 2016.

Rappoport, Jill. *Giving Women: Alliance and Exchange in Victorian Culture.* New York: Oxford University Press, 2012.

Read, John. *Catherine Booth: Laying the Theological Foundations of a Radical Movement.* Cambridge: The Lutterworth Press, 2013.

Reynolds, K. D. *Aristocratic Women and Political Society in Victorian Britain.* Oxford: Clarendon Press, 1998.

Rieger, Bernhard. *Technology and the Culture of Modernity in Britain and Germany, 1890–1945.* Cambridge: Cambridge University Press, 2005.

Roberts, Elizabeth. *A Woman's Place: An Oral History of Working-Class Women 1890–1940.* Oxford: Basil Blackwell, 1984.

Robertson, Nancy Marie. *Christian Sisterhood, Race Relations, and the YWCA, 1906–46.* Urbana: University of Illinois Press, 2007.

Rose, Lionel. *Massacre of the Innocents: Infanticide in Britain 1800–1939.* London: Routledge & Kegan Paul, 1986.

Ross, Ellen, ed. *Slum Travelers: Ladies and London Poverty, 1860–1920.* Berkeley: University of California Press, 2007.

Rosser, Gervase. *The Art of Solidarity in the Middle Ages: Guilds in England, 1250–1550.* Oxford: Oxford University Press, 2015.

Rouse, Ruth and Stephen Charles Neill, eds. *A History of the Ecumenical Movement 1517–1948.* 2nd edn, London: SPCK, 1967. First published 1954 by SPCK.

Sacks, Jonathan. *The Dignity of Difference: How to Avoid the Clash of Civilizations.* London: Bloomsbury, 2002.

Saler, Michael T. *The Avant-garde in Interwar England: Medieval Modernism and the London Underground.* New York: Oxford University Press, 1999.

Saler, Michael T. '"Clap If You Believe in Sherlock Holmes": Mass Culture and the Re-enchantment of Modernity, c.1890–c.1940'. *The Historical Journal* 46, no. 3 (2003): 599–622.

Sasson, Tehila. 'From Empire to Humanity: The Russian Famine and the Imperial Origins of International Humanitarianism'. *Journal of British Studies* 55, no. 3 (2016): 519–37.

Satter, Beryl. *Each Mind a Kingdom: American Women, Sexual Purity, and the New Thought Movement, 1875–1920.* Berkeley: University of California Press, 1999.

Searle, G. R. *The Quest for National Efficiency: A Study in Politics and Political Thought, 1889–1914.* Oxford: Basil Blackwell, 1971.

Sen, Amartya. *Development As Freedom.* Oxford: Oxford University Press, 1999.

Sengupta, Padmini. *A Hundred Years of Service: Centenary Volume of the Y.W.C.A. of Calcutta, 1878–1978.* Calcutta: Bibhash Gupta (on behalf of Y.W.C.A. of Calcutta), 1987.

Service, Robert. *A History of Modern Russia: from Nicholas II to Putin.* London: Penguin, 2003.

Shapiro, Laura. *Perfection Salad: Women and Cooking at the Turn of the Century.* 2nd edn, Berkeley: University of California Press, 2009.

Sheard, Jos. 'From Lady Bountiful to Active Citizen: Volunteering and the Voluntary Sector'. In *An introduction to the Voluntary Sector*, edited by Justin Davis Smith, Colin Rochester and Rodney Hedley, 114–27. London: Routledge, 1995.

Simonton, Deborah. *Women in European Culture and Society: Gender, Skill and Identity from 1700*. London: Routledge, 2011.

Slater, Don. *Consumer Culture and Modernity*. Cambridge, UK: Polity Press, 1997.

Sluga, Glenda. *The Nation, Psychology, and International Politics, 1870–1919*. Basingstoke: Palgrave Macmillan, 2006.

Smart, Judith. 'Modernity and Mother-heartedness: Spirituality and Religious Meaning in Australian Women's Suffrage and Citizenship Movements, 1890s–1920s'. In *Women's Suffrage in the British Empire: Citizenship, Nation and Race*, edited by Ian Christopher Fletcher, Philippa Levine, Laura E. Nym Mayhall, 51–67. London: Routledge, 2000.

Smith, George, Elizabeth Peretz, Teresa Smith. *Social Enquiry, Social Reform and Social Action: One Hundred Years of Barnett House*. Oxford: University of Oxford Department of Social Policy and Intervention, 2014.

Smulyan, Susan. *Selling Radio: The Commercialization of American Broadcasting, 1920–1934*. Washington: Smithsonian Institution Press, 1994.

Smuts, Alice Boardman. *Science in the Service of Children, 1893–1935*. New Haven, CT: Yale University Press, 2006.

Staeheli, Lynn. 'Political Geography: Where's Citizenship?'. *Progress in Human Geography* 35, no. 3 (2010): 393–400.

Stanley, Brian. *The World Missionary Conference, Edinburgh 1910*. Grand Rapids, MI: William B. Eerdmans Pub. Co., 2009.

Stevenson, John. 'The Countryside, Planning and Civil Society in Britain, 1926–1947'. In *Civil Society in British History: Ideas, Identities, Institutions*, edited by José Harris, 191–212. Oxford: Oxford University Press, 2003.

Stewart, John. 'The Mixed Economy of Welfare in Historical Perspective'. In *Understanding the Mixed Economy of Welfare*, edited by Martin Powell, 23–40. Bristol: The Policy Press, 2007.

Stewart, John. *Child Guidance in Britain, 1918–55: The Dangerous Age of Childhood*. London: Pickering & Chatto, 2013.

Storr, Katherine. *Excluded From the Record: Women, Refugees and Relief 1914–1929*. Oxford: Peter Lang, 2010.

Sturdy, Steve and Roger Cooter. 'Science, Scientific Management, and the Transformation of Medicine in Britain c. 1870–1950', *History of Science* 36, no. 4 (1998): 421–66.

Summers, Anne. 'A Home from Home – Women's Philanthropic Work in the Nineteenth Century'. In *Fit Work for Women*, edited by Sandra Burman, 33–63. London: Croom Helm, 1979.

Sutherland, Gillian. *In Search of the New Woman: Middle-Class Women and Work in Britain 1870–1914*. Cambridge: Cambridge University Press, 2015.

Sweet, Helen and Sue Hawkins. 'Introduction: Contextualising Colonial and Post-colonial Nursing'. In *Colonial Caring: A History of Colonial and Post-colonial Nursing*, edited by Helen Sweet and Sue Hawkins, 1–17. Manchester: Manchester University Press, 2015.

Szreter, Simon. *Fertility, Class and Gender in Britain, 1860–1940*. Cambridge: Cambridge University Press, 1996.

Taiz, Lillian. *Hallelujah Lads and Lasses: Remaking the Salvation Army in America, 1880–1930*. Chapel Hill: University of North Carolina Press, 2001.

Tate, Cassandra. *Cigarette Wars: The Triumph of the Little White Slaver*. New York: Oxford University Press, 1999.

Taylor, Philip M. *The Projection of Britain: British Overseas Publicity and Propaganda 1919–1939*. Cambridge: Cambridge University Press, 1981.

Taylor, Philip M. *British Propaganda in the Twentieth Century: Selling Democracy*. Edinburgh: Edinburgh University Press, 1999.

Thackeray, David. 'From Prudent Housewife to Empire Shopper: Party Appeals to the Female Voter, 1918–1928'. In *The Aftermath of Suffrage: Women, Gender, and Politics in Britain, 1918–1945*, edited by Julie V. Gottlieb and Richard Toye, 37–53. Basingstoke: Palgrave Macmillan, 2013.

Thane, Pat. 'Women of the British Labour Party and Feminism, 1906–45'. In *British Feminism in the Twentieth Century*, edited by Harold Smith, 124–143. Aldershot: Elgar, 1990.

Thane, Pat. 'The Ben Pimlott Memorial Lecture 2011: The "Big Society" and the "Big State": Creative Tension or Crowding Out?', *Twentieth Century British History* 23, no. 1 (2012), 408–29.

Thane, Pat. 'Voluntary Action in the "Welfare State": The National Council for the Unmarried Mother and her Child'. In *People, Places and Identities: Themes in British Social and Cultural History 1700s–1980s*, edited by Alan Kidd and Melanie Tebbutt, 132–51. Manchester: Manchester University Press, 2017.

Thane, Pat and Tanya Evans. *Sinners? Scroungers? Saints? Unmarried Motherhood in Twentieth-Century England*. Oxford: Oxford University Press, 2012.

Thompson, Lynne. 'Agricultural Education in the Interwar Years'. In *The English Countryside Between the Wars: Regeneration or Decline?*, edited by Paul Brassley, Jeremy Burchardt and Lynne Thompson, 53–72. Woodbridge: Boydell, 2006.

Thomson, Mathew. *Psychological Subjects: Identity, Culture, and Health in Twentieth-Century Britain*. Oxford: Oxford University Press, 2006.

Tice, Karen. *Tales of Wayward Girls and Immoral Women: Case Records and the Professionalization of Social Work*. Urbana: University of Illinois Press, 1998.

Tickner, Lisa. *The Spectacle of Women: Imagery of the Suffrage Campaign, 1907–1914*. Chicago: University of Chicago Press, 1988.

Tillyard, Stella. *The Impact of Modernism, 1900–1920: Early Modernism and the Arts and Crafts Movement in Edwardian England*. New York: Routledge, 1988.

Todd, Selina. *Young Women, Work, and Family in England 1918–1950*. Oxford: Oxford University Press, 2005.

Todd, Selina. 'Domestic Service and Class Relations in Britain, c. 1900–1950'. *Past and Present* 203, no. 1 (2009): 181–204.

Tolley, Christopher. *Domestic Biography: The Legacy of Evangelicalism in Four Nineteenth-Century Families.* Oxford: Clarendon Press, 1997.

Towers, Bridget. 'Red Cross Organisational Politics, 1918–1922: Relations of Dominance and the Influence of the United States'. In *International Health Organisations and Movements, 1918–1939*, edited by Paul Weindling, 36–55. Cambridge: Cambridge University Press, 1995.

Trotter, David. *Literature in the First Media Age: Britain Between the Wars.* Cambridge, MA: Harvard University Press, 2013.

Troutt, Margaret. *The General Was a Lady: The Story of Evangeline Booth.* Nashville: A. J. Holman, 1980.

Tusan, Michelle. 'Crimes Against Humanity: Human Rights, the British Empire, and the Origins of the Response to the Armenian Genocide'. *American Historical Review* 119, no. 1 (2014): 47–77.

Twells, Alison. 'Missionary Domesticity, Global Reform and "Woman's Sphere" in Early Nineteenth-Century England'. *Gender & History* 18, no. 2 (2006): 266–84.

Valenze, Deborah M. *Prophetic Sons and Daughters: Female Preaching and Popular Religion in Industrial England.* Princeton, NJ: Princeton University Press, 1985.

Vernon, James. *Hunger: A Modern History.* Cambridge, MA: The Belknap Press of Harvard University Press, 2007.

Vicinus, Martha. *Independent Women: Work and Community for Single Women, 1850–1920.* Chicago: Chicago University Press, 1985.

Walby, Sylvia. 'Is Citizenship Gendered?'. *Sociology* 28, no. 2 (1994): 379–95.

Waldon, John D. ed. *The World for God: Writings and Speeches of Evangeline Cory Booth*, Vol. 2. New York: The Salvation Army, USA Eastern Territory, 1992.

Walker, Pamela J. *Pulling the Devil's Kingdom Down: The Salvation Army in Victorian Britain.* Berkeley: University of California Press, 2001.

Walkowitz, Daniel. *Working With Class: Social Workers and the Politics of Middle-Class Identity.* Chapel Hill: University of North Carolina Press, 1999.

Walkowitz, Judith R. *City of Dreadful Delight: Narratives of Sexual Danger in Late-Victorian London.* London: Virago, 1992.

Walton, Ronald G. *Women in Social Work.* London: Routledge & Kegan Paul, 1975.

Weindling, Paul. *Epidemics and Genocide in Eastern Europe, 1890–1945.* Oxford: Oxford University Press, 2000.

Westwood, Louise. 'Explorations of Scottish, German and American Psychiatry: The Work of Helen Boyle and Isabel Hutton in the Treatment of Noncertifiable Mental Disorders in England, 1899–1939'. In *International Relations in Psychiatry: Britain, Germany, and the United States to World War II*, edited by Volker Rolecke, Paul J. Weindling and Louise Westwood, 179–96. Rochester, NY: University of Rochester Press, 2010.

Wightman, Clare. *More than Munitions: Women, Work and the Engineering Industries. 1900–1950.* London: Longman, 1999.

Willcox, Temple. 'Projection or Publicity? Rival Concepts in the Pre-war Planning of the British Ministry of Information'. *Journal of Contemporary History* 18, no. 1 (1983): 97–116.

Williams, Linda. *Playing the Race Card: Melodramas of Black and White from Uncle Tom's Cabin to O. J. Simpson.* Princeton, NJ: Princeton University Press, 2001.

Winston, Diane. *Red Hot and Righteous: The Urban Religion of the Salvation Army,* Cambridge, MA: Harvard University Press, 1999.

Winston, Diane. 'All the World's a Stage: The Performed Religion of the Salvation Army, 1880–1920'. In *Practicing Religion in the Age of the Media: Explorations in Media, Religion, and Culture*, edited by Stewart M. Hoover and Lynn Schofield Clark, 113–137. New York: Columbia University Press, 2002.

Woolf, Stuart. 'Europe and its Historians'. *Contemporary European History* 12, no. 3 (2003): 323–37.

Woollacott, Angela. 'From Moral to Professional Authority: Secularism, Social Work, and Middle-Class Women's Self-Construction in World War I Britain'. *Journal of Women's History* 10, no. 2 (1998): 85–111.

Yeo, Eileen Janes. *The Contest for Social Science: Relations and Representations of Gender and Class.* London: Rivers Oram, 1996.

Zahra, Tara. *The Lost Children: Reconstructing Europe's Families After World War II.* Cambridge, MA: Harvard University Press, 2011.

Zweiniger-Bargielowska, Ina. *Managing the Body: Beauty, Health, and Fitness in Britain, 1880–1939.* Oxford: Oxford University Press, 2010.

Index

Page numbers in italics denote an image.

academia. *See also* Fisher, Lettice
    critique of academic methods 8, 66,
        68–9
    entertaining in 83–6
    gendered models of 66–7, 77–8, 83, 95,
        218 n.68
    inequalities for women 78
adult education 76, 116. *See also* Home
        University Library; Workers'
        Educational Association
aeroplane (mode of connective
        technology) 154, 160
Affiliation Orders Act, 1918 80, 109, 148,
        167. *See also* National
        Council for the Unmarried
        Mother and her Child
Aitken, William Hay 55, 57
All-Union Society for Cultural Relations
        with Foreign Cultures
        (VOKS) 27, 129. *See also*
        Paget, (Lady) Muriel
alms-giving (critique of) 32–3, 36, 39–40.
        See also Children's Order of
        Chivalry, The; Guild of Help
Anglo-Russian Hospital 26–7, 86, 132, 134,
        136, 182. *See also* Paget,
        (Lady) Muriel; Pares, (Sir)
        Bernard; Pocock, Lyndall
    established in Grand Duke Dmitri
        Pavlovich's palace 134
    exhibition at Grafton Galleries 136–7
    field hospitals blessed 138, 235 n.39
    form of gift exchange 134
    fundraising 86
    Paget gives talks in America on 182
    publicity uses clinical medical language
        86
Anglo-Russian relations 132–41, 178–9.
        See also cultural diplomacy;
        Paget, (Lady) Muriel

anthropology
    cultural relativism 160
    imperialist notions of thought 6
art 132–8. *See also* avant-gardism;
        Paget, (Lady) Muriel;
        Vorticism
    cross-cultural medium 135–8
    internationalism of 151
    Russian artists 132
Astor, (Lady) Nancy 112
Attlee, Clement 12, 96
avant-gardism. *See also* Lewis, Percy
        Wyndham; Modernism;
        Nevinson, Christopher;
        Vorticism
    artistic method 136
    culture of modernity 8

baby-farming 168
Baird, Dorothea. *See* Irving, Mrs H. B.
Baldwin, Stanley (first Earl Baldwin of
        Bewdley) 12
Ballets Russes 132
Baltic States 1, 27, 41, 43–5, 90–1, 138,
        178–9
    governments of 44
Barnardo, Thomas 54, 185
Barnett, Henrietta. *See also* Toynbee Hall
    advocates education of care-giving 66
    (and Canon Barnett) principles of
        service 32–3
Bastardy Act, 1923 80, 148, 167. *See also*
        National Council for the
        Unmarried Mother and her
        Child
Bastardy Bill, 1920 81, 110, 243 n.48
Bennett, Mary 109, 115
    looks like mother 8
Berlin, Isaiah 85
    book on Karl Marx 146

critiques Fishers' dinner parties 85,
         220 n.104
Beveridge, William 85
    *Report on Voluntary Action as a Means
         of Social Advance* 196
Bible study. *See* Young Women's Christian
         Association: UK
book-learning. *See* libraries
Booth, Catherine 4, 20, 72–5
    argues for women's capacities as
         preachers 73
    better educated than her husband 72
    blue-stocking 73
    theology of salvation 73–5
Booth, Evangeline 1–2, 4–10, 14–15, 17,
         19–21, *21*, 29, 31, 33, 45–54,
         67–76, 95, 100, 118–27,
         163–7, *164*, 183–92, 195–6,
         198–9
    adopts four children 21
    ageing 189–90
    body
         contrast with male Salvation Army
              leaders 189
         hands 52
         like a soldier's 189–90
    books she owned 69, 216 n. 24
    celebrity status 20–1, 163–5, 186–7
         public image 163–4, 192
    on Christian housekeeping 118–19
    cites parable of the Good Samaritan
         51
    'Commander in Rags' 186–7
    denies the social can be separated from
         the spiritual 46
    evangelism, defines 124–5
    on female beauty 190–1
    imagines God's artists 70
    international news of 165, 241 n.7
    methods appropriated by business
         psychologists 52–4
    mother, a model for inspiration 73
    non-academic credentials 68–9
    personality 186–7
    portrait by Frank O. Salisbury 163–5, *164*
    preaching style critiqued 186–8
    quotes Thomas Carlyle, Shakespeare,
         Abraham Lincoln 69–70
    religious selfhood 163–5, 190

Salvation Army
    addresses Home League 72, 74
    describes as non-political 124, 198
    describes Salvation Army as
         cosmopolitan 123–4
    manages International Training
         Centre, London 69
    National Commander in America
         20
         expansion of role 46–7
         launched fundraising drives 47
         William Booth advises on the
              work 45–6
    National Commander in Canada 20
         with Soapy Smith 52
    World General 20, 187, 190
         accession 189
         retirement 72, 163, 165, 187
    works for in London as girl 20
on social motherhood 71
social science methods 70–1
St Paul, teachings 51, 75
urban crowd, the 51–2
uses imperialist language 120
women's social work 73–6, 118–19
women's suffrage
    defines the 'woman's movement' 119
    Woman 69–71, 73, 118–19, 190
Booth, William 20
    anxieties about social work 45–6
    In Darkest England (1890) 123
Booth, William Bramwell 47, 187
Bosanquet, Bernard 11
Bosanquet, Helen 11, 38
Bourdillon, Anne 114
brain, science of. *See under* psychology
Braithwaite, Constance 11, 33, 62, 99, 176,
         245 n.76
British Broadcasting Corporation (BBC).
         See also Fisher, Lettice;
         Week's Good Cause
charity appeals 38, 111, 170–5
cultural elites 38
cultural uplift 117
early history 201 n.2
family audience 117
and General Strike (1926) 3
Listener, The (magazine) 39
national culture 45, 243 n.35

Radio Times, The (magazine) 166
British Subjects in Russia Relief
    Association (BSRRA) 26,
    129, 138–41. *See also*
    Hodgson, (Sir) Robert; Paget,
    (Lady) Muriel
    cultural-political project 139–41, 178
    dacha (Sosnovka) 139–41, *140*, 179,
        236 n.51
    fundraising 138, 182, 235 n.46,
        246 n.90
    Relief Centre (Krasnaia Ulitsa) 129,
        139
Brittain, Vera 31–3, 62, 209 n.27
Brotherhood of Nations, This (Salvation
    Army international appeal,
    1937) 121–2, *122*, 198. *See*
    also universalism
Buddhism (in Ceylon) 155. *See also*
    Kinnaird, (Hon.) Emily
Butler, (Christina) Violet (C. V.) 67, 79, 116
Butler, Josephine 73–5, 189
Buxton, Dorothy 43, 177

Carnegie, Dale 52–3
celebrity. *See also* Booth, Evangeline; Paget,
    (Lady) Muriel; *Week's Good*
    Cause
    celebrity endorsement of charities 171
    celebrity persona 165, 180–1
    female philanthropist as 165, 167,
        191–2
    human-interest journalism 182–3
    literary celebrity 179–82
Chamberlain, (Arthur) Neville 175,
    243 n.48
charity. *See also* alms-giving
    Christian concept 46
    critique of chauvinism of 197
    definitions of 11–12, 32, 36, 39
    friendliness as alternative to 39–40
    the 'look' of 19
    personal service distinguished from
        32
    recipients of 15–16
    relationship between 'giver' and
        'receiver' 38
Chatham House 178–9, 245 n.72. *See also*
    Paget, (Lady) Muriel

child welfare work. *See also* National
    Council for the Unmarried
    Mother and her Child; Paget,
    (Lady) Muriel
    methods of 44
    public policy 80–1, 147–9, 167–8
    in Russia 179
    social sciences 89–92
    therapeutic practice 92–3
    women's medical expertise in 87–90
Children's Order of Chivalry, The 39–40
Christianity. *See also* evangelicalism;
    Salvation Army;
    universalism
    Christian conscience 67, 74–5
    Christianisation 120, 151
    ecumenical movement 61–2, 104, 124
    examples of womanhood 54–6, 71–6,
        118–19
    Gospels, the 102, 124–5
    missionary work 120–6, 131, 150–9
    purposeful life, models of 3
    self-sacrifice, ideal 185–6
Church Missionary Society (CMS) 155.
    See also Gollock, Minna
citizenship. *See also* cosmopolitanism;
    democracy; Fisher, Lettice;
    social contract
    children's 110–11
    discourse of 'futurity' 12, 111
    ethics of social connection, central to
        11
    global citizenship 118–26
    history writing 143–7
    mass democracy 12, 100, 108, 111–13,
        146
    pastoral traditions 115–16, 141, 146–7
    women's 12, 32, 98–100, 108–9, 114,
        126–7, 148
        housewife, the 113–18
        role of religion 57–62, 118–20, 199
        voluntary women's organizations
        100, 107–8
Civil Service
    forum for public relations 176
    opens up to women 96
    social engagement 96
Cole, George Douglas Howard (G. D. H.)
    80, 117

committee work. *See also* Kinnaird, (Hon.)
　　　　Emily
　　Christianity and 101–3
　　committee women (critique of) 101
　　gendered approaches 101
　　part of voluntary motive 101–3
communication. *See also* Booth,
　　　　Evangeline; celebrity;
　　　　expertise; National Council
　　　　for the Unmarried Mother
　　　　and her Child; opinion-
　　　　forming; propaganda; radio
　　connective communication 166
　　infrastructure 144
　　modernizing force 116
　　philanthropy, project of 191–2
　　practices 164–7
　　technologies 165–6, 195–6
　　visceral modes of 185–6
communism 176
　　judgement on history 125
community. *See also* citizenship;
　　　　committee work;
　　　　democracy
　　Christian concept 58–60, 99–108,
　　　　106–7, 118, 121–4, 151, 199
　　community centres 11
　　community development 32, 59–62,
　　　　99–102, 110, 115, 118–19
　　integrates detached social units
　　　　110–11, 172
　　inter-class relations 196
　　and new media 166
　　racial and ethnic divisions 157–8
　　relationship to individual 111–13
　　relationship to mass democracy 112
　　rural setting 114, 116
Conference on Christian Politics,
　　　　Economics and Citizenship
　　　　(COPEC) 59, 104
conferences
　　child welfare 17
　　Christian method 22, 103–4. *See also*
　　　　COPEC; World Missionary
　　　　Conference; World's YWCA;
　　　　YWCA
Cooper, Anthony Ashley (seventh earl of
　　　　Shaftesbury) 22
Cooper, (Sir) Edward 170

cooperation
　　cross-sector 80
　　principle of voluntary engagement
　　　　104–7, 127
corporatism 3, 105
cosmopolitanism 123–4. *See also*
　　　　citizenship
crowd (theories of) 51–2, 60. *See also*
　　　　Booth, Evangeline; mass
cultural diplomacy 130, 175–81. *See also*
　　　　Paget, (Lady) Muriel;
　　　　All-Union Society for
　　　　Cultural Relations with
　　　　Foreign Cultures
　　vernacular emphases 181
cultural patronage 135–8, 234 n.23. *See
　　　　also* Paget, (Lady) Muriel
Czechoslovakia 1, 4, 27, 40–2, 44, 86–7,
　　　　90–2, 177, 222 n.138. *See also*
　　　　Masaryk Alice; Masaryk,
　　　　Thomas; Paget, (Lady)
　　　　Muriel

democracy. *See also* citizenship;
　　　　Representation of the People
　　　　Act 1918; Representation of
　　　　the People (Equal Franchise)
　　　　Act 1928
　　active citizenship 111–13
　　democratic subjectivity 97–108,
　　　　113–18
　　mass democracy (interwar) 12, 97,
　　　　99–100, 108–9, 111–13, 146
　　women and 97–120
diary-keeping (evangelical practice) 102–3
documentary films 151, 155, 239 n.99. *See
　　　　also Song of Ceylon, The*
domestic economy
　　feminist issue 108–9
　　middle-class ideal 243 n.43
　　women's expertise in 116–19, 173, 180
domestic science 74, 94
domestic service. *See also* Fisher, Lettice
　　economy of 109
　　family servants 6, 109
　　YWCA campaigns 104
donor, category of 11, 121, 172–5, 185–6.
　　　　See also identification
Dostoevsky, Fyodor 132

dress
  charitable subjects 155
  women's styles of 3, 98–9
Dykes, Oswald 54

East London. *See also* Booth, Evangeline
  IKL targets poverty in 34–5
  slums 186
  trades unions' campaigns for workers'
    wages 188
economics 76–80. *See also* Fisher, Lettice
  gendered approaches 80
  study of as training in citizenship
    78
  theories of 79–80
education. *See also* adult education
  gendered models 75–6
  illiteracy 75–6
  theories of 65–9, 77–80
Emslie, Isabel. *See* Hutton, Isabel Emslie
European
  idea, crisis of 145–6
  imagination 141–9
evangelicalism. *See also* Booth, Evangeline;
    Kinnaird, (Hon.) Emily
  ambitions in early-twentieth century
    57–9
  interdenominational enthusiasm
    61–2
  nineteenth-century evangelical fervour
    21–2, 54–6
  split between conservative and liberal
    wings post-1918 54, 104
  transatlantic networks 54
experiential authority 68, 74, 182
expertise 166–7, 191–2. *See also* celebrity;
    experiential authority;
    knowledge; social science
  in foreign policy 177–9
  in humanitarian projects 17, 44, 130
  women's 62, 68, 71–2, 87–9, 116–18

factory work
  social work during the First World War
    9–10
  women's 57, 213 n.112
family servants. *See under* domestic
    service
female gaze 239 n.114

female philanthropy. *See also*
    philanthropy
  Christian commitment 14, 16, 31, 56,
    58, 198
  class identity 15
  communication practices 9, 164–5,
    166–7, 191–2
  comparative thinking 131–2
  conceptual elasticity of 65
  creative force 6
  and cultural narratives 12–13, 130–1,
    159–61
  definitions 1–2
  Edwardian models of 11
  epistemologies of 65–8, 74, 94–6
  female solidarity 3–4
  gendered category of analysis
    27–8
  and growth of welfare state 196
  historiography of 13–16
  intellectual project 7, 14, 27–8, 91
  interleaved with professionalization
    197–8
  and interpersonal relationships 33–4,
    63, 194
  language of tact 93
  linked to emotions 12–13, 167,
    181
  marshals psychological insights 33
  metaphors of inter-class subjectivity
    97–9, *98*, 100
  movement between theoretical and
    practical 67
  not one model of 19–20
  parish visiting, model 41
  personal methods of 34–5
  politics 15–16, 106, 114, 177, 191, 198,
    204 n.51
    of community development 100
    feminism 100
  relationship to modernity 1, 4, 7–9,
    194–6
  seen as extension of running a home
    34
  selfhood 6, 28, 62, 126–7, 199
  social connectedness 3–6, 16, 19
  structural inequalities 6
  'unnatural' 13
  Victorian exemplars 73–5, 189, 199

feminism 12, 31–2, 100, 148. *See also*
   Fisher, Lettice; National
   Union of Societies for
   Equal Citizenship; Six
   Point Group
 Christian feminism 72–3
 and economic history 76
 feminist literature 109
Fight the Famine Council. *See* Save the
   Children Fund
Finch-Hatton, Murray Edward Gordon
   (twelfth earl of Winchilsea
   and seventh earl of
   Nottingham) 25, 39,
   207 n.78
First World War. *See also*
   humanitarianism; Ministry
   of Munitions; Salvation
   Army; Young Women's
   Christian Association
 and citizenship 97
 distortions of publicity during 176
 growth of domestic charities 10–11
 and history writing 145
 humanitarian relief work 27, 87
 social work 9–10
 thrift meetings 118
 trauma 107
 trench warfare as a site for social work
  49
 women's war work 23, 181–2
Fisher, Herbert Albert Laurens (H. A. L.)
 defines purpose of scholarship 77–8
 depiction of Canada 143
 foreign travel 142–3
 History of Europe, 145, 236 n.69
 history tutor 25
 Lloyd George Liberal 25, 83
 marriage 25
 member of board of BBC Governors
  244 n.50
 Warden, New College, Oxford 82–6
Fisher, Lettice 1–2, 4–10, 12–13, 15, 17, 19,
  23–5, *24,* 29, 67, 76–86, 95,
  100, 108–18, 126–7, 131,
  141–9, 160, 166–75, 191–2,
  194–6, 199. *See also* National
  Council for the Unmarried
  Mother and her Child

Armstrong, Edward, supports 83
Brief Survey of the British Empire, A
  143
childhood memories of India 141–2
on citizenship 12, 78, 108–18, 143–4,
  146–7, 172
 Citizen, The 112–13, 127, 144
'Commonwealth of nations', the 144
community, defines 113
daughter, Mary (b. 1913) 78
'democratic woman' 25
on domestic economy 108–9
economic history 76–80
essentializes Canadian identity 143
friendship with Frances Stevenson 85
Getting and Spending 78–80, 109, 111
hospitality
 Salon culture 83
 unorthodox 23
 as Warden's wife 82–6
indifferent to fine arts 25
international travel 141–3
Introductory History of England and
  Europe, An 144–6
mutual interests with husband 25
NCUMC
 defends unmarried mothers 169
 first BBC radio charity appeal 111,
  170–5
 press work 110–11, 166–9
NCW, member of 17
NFWI 25, 100
 BBC broadcasts 115–18
 Facts Behind the Crisis, The
  118
 Housewife and the Townhall, The
  116–18
 speaks about laws against
  pollution 116
NUSEC, works with 100
NUWSS, stands for leadership 12
pastoral living 115–16
pet goat
 and economics 79
 keeps at the family home 115
postgraduate study at LSE 76–7
relationship with domestic servant,
  Kate Smith 109, 115
reviews Halévy's work 146–7

Six Point Group, works with 100
social work in Oxford 25, 77
teetotalism 25
tutor at St. Hugh's, Oxford 23
undergraduate at Oxford 23
uses the term 'elasticity' 194
on women's employment opportunities
 108–9
Woolf, Virginia (critical of the
 Fishers) 7–8
flame (metaphor) 97–9, 198–9
food aid. *See* Paget, (Lady) Muriel:
 'humanitarianism'
friendship
 Christian ideal 31, 56, 58
 community work as 40
 cross-cultural 27, 136
 international diplomacy 1, 6, 19, 136
Fry, Elizabeth 73–5

Galsworthy, John 136
Gandhi, Mahatma 23, 158–9
Garnett, Elizabeth 55–6
General Strike (1926) 2–3, 201 n.1–2
George, David Lloyd. *See also* Fisher,
 Herbert Albert Laurens
 language of New Liberalism 111
 wartime coalition cabinet 83
Gollock, Minna 60–1
Graffa, Margaret 75–6
Gray, Mrs Edwin 147–9, 238 n.90
Great War. *See* First World War
Guild of Help 35–6, 39–40. *See also* Paget,
 (Lady) Muriel
guilds 36, 113

Hadow, Grace 116, 228 n.80
Hadow, William Henry 112, 228 n.80
Halvéy, Élie 84–5, *84*, 146–7
Hammond, Barbara 85
Hammond, Lawrence 85
hands. *See also* Booth, Evangeline
 metaphor of women's social action 68
Hill, Octavia 11, 77
history (discipline). *See also* Fisher,
 Herbert Albert Laurens;
 Fisher, Lettice; Halévy, Élie;
 Wingfield-Stratford, Esme
 economic history 76–7, 79–80

and histories of Europe 145–6
 in interwar period 144–7
Hodgson, (Sir) Robert 138, 235 n.46
Hogg, Quintin 101
Holland, George 54
Holtby, Winifred 32
home. *See also* domestic science; domestic
 service; hospitality;
 housekeeping; housewife
 institutional homes
 BSRRA home 139–41
 NCUMC 168
 North London Home for young
 women 54, 58
 Salvation Army 49–50, 120–1,
 184–5, 188
 managing akin to running
 philanthropic enterprise 34
 women
 and arts of homelife 74
 'heroines of home' 119
 'homely countenance' 71
 home-makers 57, 116, 121
 working in 109, 116
Home University Library 83, 112, 146. *See
 also* Berlin, Isaiah; Fisher,
 Lettice
hospitality. *See also* Fisher, Lettice;
 Kinnaird, (Hon.) Emily;
 Paget, (Lady) Muriel
 diplomatic practice 140–1, 236 n.54
 evangelicalism and 61
 political 83
 and psychology 83–4
 reciprocal exchange 157
housekeeping
 Christian concept 118–19
 for prevention of poverty 114
housewife 113–18. *See also* citizenship;
 Fisher, Lettice
 category of interwar democracy
 114–15
 cross-class identity 115–18
 economic and political agency of
 117–18
 in Edwardian tariff reform campaigns
 114
 in middlebrow and popular culture
 115

humanitarianism 40-5. *See also* Booth,
        Evangeline; Paget, (Lady)
        Muriel
    data collection 89-92
    differences between American and
        British/European agencies
        44-5
    humanitarian governance 44-5,
        89-92
    'mixed economy' of 44, 95, 179
    political project 198
    transnationalization of 40, 45,
        209 n.40
    women's medical expertise 87-9
Hutton, Isabel Emslie 87-90

identification
    between donors and charitable subject
        170-5, 185-6
    cross-class 115-18
    kinship 121-3
identity 14, 18-19, 192, 197. *See also*
        democracy; housewife;
        selfhood
    civic 117
    class 15, 115
    collective 100, 124, 126-7, 166
    models of 99
    national 17, 132-3, 135, 137, 146, 155
Ilbert, (Sir) Courtenay Peregrine 23, 76,
        141
Ilbert, Jessie 23, 77, 141
illegitimacy. *See also* National Council for
        the Unmarried Mother and
        her Child
    Christian perspectives 169-70
    deaths of illegitimate infants 172
    economic issue 81
    increase in rates during wartime 167
    moral issue 169
    research on illegitimacy policy 147-9
    and social science 82
Imperial Defence College (IDC) 178
imperialism. *See also* Booth, Evangeline;
        Fisher, Lettice; Kinnaird,
        (Hon.) Emily; Paget, (Lady)
        Muriel
    anthropological thought 6
    British imperial history 143-4, 157

humanitarianism and
    imperial anxieties 44
    imperial social knowledge 92
Imperial India 141-2
international relief work 19
language of Christian mission 120, 123
individualism 3, 14, 101, 192
    liberal democracy, a form of 146
Infant Life Protection Act, 1905 173
infant mortality. *See also* baby-farming;
        illegitimacy; Infant Life
        Protection Act, 1905
    rates 81, 169
inhabitant, identity of 131, 142-3, 157
inspection, logic of 89-92
inter-cultural exchange 130-2, 139-41,
        144, 151-61
    and historicization 132
international exchange. *See* inter-cultural
        exchange
International Missionary Council (IMC)
        124-5
interwar years. *See also* modernity; social
        connectedness
    principle of social connection 11, 193
    transformative change 1
Invalid Kitchens of London (IKL) 34-40,
        93-4, 135, 196. *See also* Paget,
        (Lady) Muriel
    charity balls 135
    establishment of 34
    expansion during First World War 36
    gave evidence to Beveridge's enquiry
        into voluntary action 196
    language of psychological development
        36-8
    London County Council administers 196
    medical research 93-4
    portrait of secretary at an IKL branch 37
    source of data on London poor 35
    welfare work 36-7
Irving, Mrs H. B. 169-70

Jebb, Eglantyne 43, 88, 177. *See also* Paget,
        (Lady) Muriel; Save the
        Children Fund
Joint University Council for Social Studies
        (JUC) 10, 32. *See also*
        Macadam, Elizabeth

Kelly, Eleanor T. 36–7
Kinnaird, Arthur Fitzgerald (tenth Lord
    Kinnaird of Inchture and
    second Baron Kinnaird of
    Rossie) 21
Kinnaird, Arthur Fitzgerald (eleventh
    Lord Kinnaird of Inchture
    and third Baron Kinnaird of
    Rossie) 17, 22, 101
Kinnaird, (Hon.) Emily 1–2, 4–10, 14–15,
    17, 19, 21–3, *22*, 29–31, 33,
    54–63, 97, 100, 101–8, 126–7,
    149–59, 195–6, 199. *See also*
    World's Young Women's
    Christian Association; Young
    Women's Christian
    Association
  ambitions for pan-Christian
    engagement 156, 158–9
  on committee work 101–3
  criticizes voluntary women's
    organizations 106
  defends principle of conferences 103–4
  defines Christian friendship 56
  describes herself as a beggar 5
  educated at home 22
  family home (2 Pall Mall Street East,
    London) 21, 61, 157
  friendship with Gandhi 23, 158–9
  Labour Party, member of 106
  laments fear of 'danger of emotion' 55
  My Adopted Country 156, 158
  'navvies' (her first love) 63
  NCW, member of 17
  personal work, defines 63
  Presbyterian background 21
  Reminiscences 54–6, 61, 63, 97, 101–7,
    153, 155, 157, 159
  on teachings of karma 61
  UK YWCA
    concern about ageing membership
      105, 107
    critiques use of outdated
      evangelical books 55
    finance secretary 23
    leads new Religious Activities
      Department after 1913 58
    rallies support for eightieth
      anniversary 97
  taught at training centre for student
    secretaries 102
  uses metaphor of torchbearers 98
  works with WAAC 23
  Vice-President of Scottish Zenana
    Bible and Medical Mission
    23
  Vice-President of World's YWCA 23
  visits Portugal 152
  works fourteen-hour day 23
  YWCA mission in India and South
    East Asia 153–9
    fears revivalism of Buddhism in
      Ceylon 155
    founded the Madras YWCA (1900)
      153
    on tea industry (Ceylon) 154–5
    travels in India 153–8
Kinnaird, (Hon.) Gertrude 4, 17, 23, 153,
    156–8
Kinnaird, (Lady) Mary Jane 3, 21, 54, 106
Kipling, Rudyard 141
knowledge. *See also* education; expertise;
    inter-cultural exchange;
    libraries; philanthropy, social
    science
  experiential 65–6, 68, 71–2, 74–6,
    88–9
  inter-class relations 185–6
  scientific 86, 93–4

Labour Party. *See also* Kinnaird, (Hon.)
    Emily; Picton-Turbervill,
    Edith
  clubs 158
  route for social work 32
  slum clearance policy 188
Lady Bountiful 15. *See also* Paget, (Lady)
    Muriel
League of Nations 76, 131
League of Red Cross Societies (LORCS)
  NCUMC in discussion with 147
  Paget works with 40, 91, 222 n.138
Leningrad 129, 138–41, 178, 181–2. *See
    also* Paget, (Lady) Muriel;
    Soviet policy
Lewis, Percy Wyndham 135–6. *See also*
    avant-gardism; Nevinson,
    Christopher; Vorticism

libraries
    critique of learning in 65–8, 78–9
    travelling libraries 117
local government
    critique of women's minority position
        in 117, 230 n.117
    housewives' contribution to 115–16
    policies in relation to charities' 77
Loch, Charles 11
London County Council (LCC) 77, 196
London School of Economics (LSE) 76–7.
        See also Fisher, Lettice
love
    Christian concept of service 39, 46, 48,
        75, 121
    working through women 71, 75–6, 97, 190

Macadam, Elizabeth
    defines charity and philanthropy 11, 32
    member of NUSEC 32
    New Philanthropy, The 65–6, 95
    secretary of JUC 10
    social servant, concept of 95–6
    on the traits of a social worker 66
    university social work training 10,
        67–8, 202 n.21
    on voluntary engagement and the state
        99
    works for Ministry of Munitions 9–10
    works in women's settlements 10
Macpherson, Annie 54
Mais, Stuart Petre 39–40
Marsh, Catherine 55–6
Masaryk, Alice 4, 41
Masaryk, Thomas 27
mass (theory of) 60–1. *See also* crowd
Maude, Cyril 175
Mauss, Marcel 28
media
    connective media 166
    interwar age of 9, 165–7, 191–2
melodrama 173, 184
Meyendorff, Olga 152. *See also* World's
        Young Women's Christian
        Association
Ministry of Munitions 9–10
missionary work. *See* Christianity
mixed economy
    of humanitarianism 44, 95, 133–4, 179

of welfare 65, 95
Modernism. *See also* avant-gardism;
        Woolf, Virginia
    autonomy of self 3
    Bloomsbury 7–8
    critique of historical modernity 7–8
    and female philanthropists 8–9
modernity
    information age 9, 167
    interwar, models of 3, 194–5, 203 n.35
    mass transport technologies 7, 9, 12
    philanthropists as critics of 1, 2, 5, 7–9,
        193–5, 199
    varied responses to 7–9
    vocational 'resistance' to 29
Moody, Dwight 54
Mother of Israel 71
motherhood. *See also* unmarried mother
    Christian model 71, 74
    complements women's
        professionalization 88
    cross-class identity 115

National Council of Social Service
        (NCSS) 80, 111
National Council of Women (NCW) 17,
        101
National Council for the Unmarried
        Mother and her Child
        (NCUMC) 25, 80–2, 85–6,
        100, 109–11, 147–9, 167–75,
        180. *See also* Fisher, Lettice;
        Gray, Mrs Edwin; infant
        mortality; Schreiber, Adele;
        unmarried mother
    Affiliation Orders Act, 1918 80, 109,
        148, 167
    Bastardy Act, 1923 80, 148, 167
    Bastardy Bill, 1920 81, 110, 243 n.48
    Castberg Laws, The (Norway) 148–9
    comparative research 147–9
    'correlating and connecting agency' 111
    defines unmarried mothers 82
    infant life preservation 173
    and language of New Liberalism 111
    lobbying work 80–1, 148, 168
    press policy 169–70
    seeks attitudinal change 168–75
    and social science 81–2

national efficiency 35–6
National Federation of Women's Institutes
(NFWI) 4, 12, 25, 106,
115–18, 171, 174. *See also*
Fisher, Lettice; Hadow, Grace
National Insurance Act, 1911 111
National Union of Societies for Equal
Citizenship (NUSEC). *See
also* Fisher, Lettice;
Macadam, Elizabeth
Woman's Leader, The (magazine) 32,
101
Woman's Year Book 1923–1924 36–7
National Union of Women's Suffrage
Societies (NUWSS) 12
nationalism
ideology 121, 124–5, 131
Indian movement 158–9
'nascent nationalism' 178
neighbourhood
neighbourliness as Christian principle
50–1
social unit 106–7
women's influence within 107, 113
Nevinson, Christopher 135–6
New College, Oxford 83–6. *See also* Fisher,
Herbert Albert Laurens;
Fisher, Lettice
Newmarch, Rosa 136
Nightingale, Florence 73–5, 95, 189, 199,
249 n.18

opinion-forming 167, 171, 242 n.15
Orientalism 133, 233 n.14
original sin 55
Orthodox, Russian (church) 132, 137–8

Paget, (Lady) Muriel 1–2, 4–10, 14–15, 17,
19, 25–7, *26*, 29–31, 33–45,
67, 86–95, 129–41, 160,
166–7, 175–83, 191–2, 194–9.
See also Anglo-Russian
Hospital; British Subjects in
Russia Relief Association;
Invalid Kitchens of London;
Orthodox, Russian; Russian,
the
addresses Dudley Guild of Help 35–6
aeroplane travel 7, 207 n.77

Anglo-Russian Hospital 26, 86, 134,
136–8, 182
and British Intelligence Service 27
BSRRA 26, 129, 138–41, 178–9, 181–2
accused of Lady Bountiful 139
hospitality, models of 139–40
celebrity
American lecture tour 179–82
human-interest journalism 182–3
Society celebrity 25, 35
women's war work 181–2
collects modern art 135–6
education 25
foreign policy expertise 177–9
friendship with Masaryk family 4, 27,
41, 90, 177
friendship with Pares 86, 134–5
fundraises for Zenana Bible and
Medical Mission 17
humanitarianism 1, 17, 27, 40–5, 86–93,
139, 177, 182–3, 194, 198
in association with SCF 27, 40–4, *43*
in Baltic States 1, 41, 90–2
in Czechoslovakia 1, 27, 40–2, 44,
86–7, 90–2, 177, 210 n.47,
222 n.138
data collection 89–92
endorses women's medical expertise
87–9
joins British Red Cross 26
relief programmes distinguished
from American ones 44
in Romania 27, 40, 91–2, 222 n.138
works with LORCS, 40, 91,
222 n.138
IKL
appointed Honorary Secretary 34
broadcast radio charity appeal 38
charity ball at the Albert Hall,
London 135
juvenile policy, interest in 92–3
marriage 25
Mission for Children in the Crimea
87–90
Mission to Eastern Europe 41–2, *42*,
44, 160
headquarters in Dvinsk 41
Roosevelt, Eleanor, a supporter of
181–2

Russia
    access to Soviet Russia, 139,
        223 n.142
    active in Society for Cultural
        Relations between the
        Peoples of the British
        Commonwealth and the
        Union of Socialist Soviet
        Republics 137
    on Anglo-Soviet Trade Agreements
        178
    associates with Prince Yusupov 135
    collection of Russian icons 138,
        235 n.41
    constructs Russophile narratives
        135
    historical narratives of 133–4, 178,
        244 n.68
    meets with Soviet Ministers 139, 179
    Russian Revolution 135, 182
    supporter of VOKS 27
    tracked by Soviet intelligence
        service 179
    writes about homeless children in
        92–3, 182–3
Paget, (Sir) Richard Arthur Surtees 25,
        34–5, 222 n.134
Pares, (Sir) Bernard
    Anglo-Russian committee (secretary)
        134, 136
    describes Paget's 'likeness' for a
        'Russian' 135
    Director of the School of Slavonic and
        East European Studies 135
    observer of Russian army on eastern
        front 86, 134
    Russia and Reform (1907) 134
Paul, St (teachings of) 51, 74–5. *See also*
        Salvation Army
personality. *See also* radio
    Christian concept 60
    combined with ethics of service 60–1,
        104
    development of women's 32, 58–9, 104
    part of public performance 186–8
philanthropic relationship
    and class 15
    concept rooted in institutions 46
    giver and receiver in 40, 44, 63, 193

model of
    interpersonal 38
    and nineteenth-century traditions
        of women's service 36–7
    registers of 34
philanthropy. *See also* philanthropic
        relationship
    and associational culture 137
    centrality of relationships to 27, 29
    Christian philanthropy 198
    and class 15
    commodification of 183
    conceptual history of 14, 28
    and First World War 10–11
    fundraising 36, 38, 85–6, 134, 138, 166,
        177, 182, 185–6, 246 n.90
    and celebrity endorsement 171
    cultural 135–7
    donors' experiences of giving 185
    as participation 98
    projects medical knowledge 93–4
    relation to practical social work
        47–8
    'international philanthropy' 176, 179
    interwar civic landscape 5, 95
    interwar taxonomies of 11–12
    and language 4–5
    and melodrama 173, 184
    methods 32, 36
    and power relationships 53–4, 63, 197
    project of communication 191
    relationship to culture 130–2, 159–60
    response to modernity 4, 194–5
    revelatory practice 28, 197, 199
    and socially-constructed selfhood 6
    tool for negotiating social and cultural
        change 14, 28–9, 193, 198
    transnational 6, 19
Picton-Turbervill, Edith 4, 106, 157
Pocock, Lyndall 86
    reads Stephen Graham 132
Poor Laws
    ineligibility for relief 35
    'outdoor relief' for unmarried mothers
        242 n.18
    principle of deterrent 168
    women on Poor Law Boards 114
Pope-Hennessy, Una 129
    on the concept of hospitality 139–40

poverty. *See also* Poor Laws
  in Baltic States 90
  charities gatekeeping definitions of 35
  child poverty 39
  'deserving' and 'undeserving' poor 40,
    174
  fear that poverty stifled independence
    42–3
  narratives of 15
  National Insurance Act, 1911 111
  romanticization of 76
  in South India 154
  urban poverty 35, 39
  visual representations 121
  working-class poverty 77, 114
Power, Eileen 145
professionalization
  social service 65
  social work 13, 35, 37
  voluntary commitment 31
  women's 28, 95–6, 197
    in medicine 87–9
propaganda
  associated with communism and
    fascism 176
  films 155, 174
  international social work as a route to
    91
  philanthropy as 11, 176–80
psychiatry 49, 82
psychology
  behavioural 34, 52–4
  brain, science of 75–6
  child 49, 92–3
  of hostess 83–5
  national 12, 107
  overcomes 'silences' in nature 95
  popular 33
  relational 62–3
public relations 175–6, 184. *See also*
    propaganda

race. *See also* national efficiency
  Christian groups challenge racism
    194–5
  Christian universalism transcends
    120–1, 123–5
  and instincts for independence 159
  racial divisions 143

radio (wireless). *See also* British
    Broadcasting Corporation;
    Stone, Christopher; *Week's*
    Good Cause
  charity appeals
    IKL 38
    NCUMC 111, 170–5
  cost of licenses 230 n.110
  cross-class identification 116–17
  listeners 38, 116–17, 165, 174–5
  microphone personality 171
  technology effects cultural change 160
Ramabai, Pandita 157
Ranyard, Ellen 54
Red Cross. *See* League of Red Cross
    Societies; *see under* Paget,
    (Lady) Muriel
refugees. *See also* Paget, (Lady) Muriel
  children 160
  Fund for Russian Refugees 136
relationships. *See also* citizenship;
    democracy; philanthropic
    relationship; philanthropy;
    social contract
  between women 3–4, 15, 49–50
  Christian models 39, 72
  family 53, 99
  and female philanthropy
    confronts everyday power
      relationships 62–3
    logic of combined with other
      modes of expertise 182–3
    public responsibility in harnessing
      163
    shapes imaginations of 6
  social relationships 3, 9, 95, 163, 172
    economy of 79–80, 196
    and media age 165–6
    modern forms 32
    theory of 28–9
rent collecting 77
Representation of the People Act, 1918 12,
    97, 108, 114
Representation of the People (Equal
    Franchise) Act, 1928 12, 99,
    112, 114
Rhondda, Viscountess (Margaret Haig
    Thomas) 109
Roosevelt, Eleanor 181–2

Russia. *See also* Russian Revolution; Soviet
        policy; Soviet state
    politics 133–4
Russian, the
    'English "Russian myth"' 132, 135,
        137, 141
    peasantry 86, 134, 137
    stereotype 129, 135
Russian Revolution (1917) 27, 133–5
    news reports of 182

Salisbury, Frank O. 163–5, *164*
Sallies. *See under* Salvation Army
Salon (women's influence in) 83
Salvation Army 2, 8–9, 20–1, 45–54, 67–76,
        95, 118–26, 163–5, 184–92,
        198
    in America
        First World War 20, 48–50
        social work projects 45–8
        Thirteen Million Dollar Campaign
            47
    'Blood-and-Fire' theology 46
    'close-touchness' of methods 50–1
    Commissioners' Conference (1939) 125
    conversion (religious)
        model of 52–3
        narratives 71
    electoral system for selecting World
        General 51
    Emergency Relief Unit 48
    in First World War 48–50, 190
    founded (1865) 20
    fundraising 47–8, 121, 184–7
        self-denying week 185
    Holiness theology 72
    Home League 74, 119, 121–2
    Homes 121, 184
    international expansion 120
        support from Emperor Taishō 120
    neighbourhood activism 50
    populism of 69, 73
    and 'practical Christianity' 68, 73
    regeneration, concept of 21, 46–8, 119,
        125
    response to natural disasters 48
    Sallies 49–50, 212 n.83
    and social sciences 70–1
    social service 46

        beginnings 46
        presentation of 70
        rescue work 46
        training of officers 45, 69
        War Cry, The (magazine) 45
        women preachers 186
        women wearing hats 189, 248 n.126
Sankey, Ira D. 54
Save the Children Fund (SCF) 27, 40–5,
        89–91, 176–7, *43*. *See also*
        Jebb, Eglantyne; Paget,
        (Lady) Muriel
Scharlieb, Mary 88
Schreiber, Adele 147–9; 237 n. 86, 238 n. 90
Scottish Women's Hospitals 88, 132
self-denial
    principle of charity fundraising 185–6
    and suffrage movement 185
self-development. *See under* selfhood
self-help
    assisted 38, 173, 194
    ethic of 38–40
    in humanitarian practice 41–3
selfhood. *See also* celebrity; democracy
    constructed within family
        relationships 53
    and democracy 12, 100, 173
    inter-class subjectivity 6, 115
    malleable construction 54
    philanthropic selfhood 5–6
    religious selfhood 55, 61, 190, 198
    self-development 3, 12, 15, 38
        Christian models 59, 104–8, 195,
            198
    and service 31–4, 125
    socially-constructed 6, 15, 63, 99, 199,
        232 n.154
    women's 3, 31, 63
        outward-facing model 126, 199,
            232 n.154
        political selfhood 100, 119
        religious models 5, 55, 61, 99
service. *See also* selfhood
    scholarship as 78
    self-sacrificial 20, 103
    service ethics
        Christian teaching of
            neighbourliness 51
        cosmopolitanism 119–20, 123

and humanitarian politics 44–5
and model of friendliness 40
personal service 36–7, 176
personal work 62–3
principle of community 112–13
Victorian ethos 14
women's service
    basis for psychological
        transformation 38
    critiqued 31–4
    everyday work of 74–6
    Lamp of 97–8, *98*
    linked to professional and extra-
        professional practice 36
    mutual service 56–9, 72, 102–3
    and relational psychology 47–50, 62
    and self-development 3
settlement movement 10, 32, 65, 66. *See
    also* Toynbee Hall
settlements. *See* settlement movement
Sex Discrimination Removal Act, 1919 12,
    108
shopping (forum for women's agency) 191
Six Point Group 32, 100, 109. *See also*
        Rhondda, Viscountess
        (Margaret Haig Thomas)
Time and Tide 31–2, 109
Slump (Great) 38–9, 175. *See also*
        unemployed
slums. *See also* Booth, Evangeline
    Guild of Help do social work in 36
    Salvation Army work in 20, 123, 184,
        186–8
social connectedness
    and class 186
    First World War 11
    inequalities remain 19
    interwar idea 6
        contested 197
        female philanthropists explore 16,
            163, 173, 183, 185
    stimulated by new technologies 9
social connectivity 9, 114
social contract 97, 99–100, 107–8, 126. *See
        also* democracy;
        Representation of the People
        Act, 1918; Representation of
        the People (Equal Franchise)
        Act, 1928

social motherhood 66, 71. *See also* Mother
    of Israel
social sciences
    method 70
    and motherhood 71, 91
    rationalism of 79
    specialist authority 66, 198
    women's relationship to 66–7, 71, 95
social services
    fear of state services usurping
        voluntary spirit 112–14
    motives for 62
    personal attitude towards clients is
        vital 33
    professionalization of 65
    voluntary social services post-1918 11,
        80, 112–14
social work
    casework 35
    First World War 9–10
    politics of social justice 12
    professionalization of sector 13, 16, 32,
        35–6, 93 198
    social worker 36, 65–6, 90, 115, 200
    theories of 65–6, 95–6
    training for
        compared to philanthropy 37,
            209 n.27
        university programmes 10, 65, 76
    welfare worker 10, 36–7, 167
    women and 34–5, 66–8, 71–2, 78, 114,
        189
        class problems 115
Song of Ceylon, The (1934) 155,
        240 n.121
Sorabji, Cornelia 157
Soviet policy
    children's institutions 133
    Five Year Plan 180
    housing 139–41
    intelligence 179
    international visitors 141, 223 n.142
Soviet state
    history of 178, 244 n.68
Stead, William Thomas (W. T.) 46
Stephens, Winifred 136
Stevenson, Frances 85
Stone, Christopher 171
Strachey, Ray 85, 176–7

Student Christian Movement 103
    publications of 55
suffrage movement 25, 148, 169
    after 1918 12, 112
    Christian suffragism 119
    imagery 17
    principle of self-denial 185
Swaffer, Hannen 187–8

Tagore, Rabindranath 23, 158
time-space compression 12, 203 n.35
Toynbee Hall 32
trades unions. *See also* Young Women's
            Christian Association
    community work 32
    critique cross-class methods 104
    methods compared to Salvation Army's
            188
transit
    mode of connectivity 154
    transit writing 154–5
travel
    missionary 23, 153–8
    thrill of journey 154
    tourism 129, 144, 153
    traveller (identity) 142–3, 156
    women's travel writings 130, 153–5

unemployed
    psychology of 40
    and Slump (Great) 38–40
    social work for 184
universalism. *See also Brotherhood of
            Nations, This*
    Christian concept 60–1, 119–23, 125–6,
            231 n.139
    cultural universalism 160
Unmarried (film) 173–4, *174*
unmarried mother. *See also* illegitimacy;
            motherhood; National
            Council for the Unmarried
            Mother and her Child
    active citizen 148, 169
    dignity of 81
    portrait of 172–3
    respectable 173
    social category 82
    social criticism of 168
    social unit, rhetorical construction 110
    support from family and kin 110

village
    unit of democracy 114, 116–17
voluntary citizen, concept of 11, 33, 99. *See
            also* Braithwaite, Constance
voluntary women's organizations 11, 100,
            106. *See also* National
            Federation of Women's
            Institutes; Young Women's
            Christian Association
Vorticism 135–6. *See also* art; avant-gardism;
            Lewis, Percy Wyndham; Paget,
            (Lady) Muriel
    manifesto (1914) 136, 234 n.27

Wakefield, Henry Russell (bishop of
            Birmingham) 170
Webb, Beatrice 16, 32–3
Week's Good Cause 38, 171, 175. *See also*
            British Broadcasting
            Corporation; radio
welfare state 13, 196, 200
welfare worker 10, 36–7
    child welfare worker
            NCUMC campaigns for support 167
            trained in psychotherapy 93
White Russian Army (Russia) 86, 88
White, W. W. 54
Wingfield-Stratford, Esme 145
women
    agency 14, 16
    civil rights 108–9
    portrayals of in interwar era 3
    self-development 3–4
    social activism 7, 27–8
    social duty 31
    spiritual strength 49, 71–2, 75–6
Women's Army Auxiliary Corps (WAAC)
            23, 105
Women's Institutes. *See* National
            Federation of Women's
            Institutes
Woolf, Virginia 7–8
Workers' Educational Association (WEA)
            25, 32
working class
    critique of philanthropy in working-
            class communities 197
    social work in working-class
            communities 50, 56, 77
    stereotype of masculine culture 38

World Fellowship Week (YWCA) 149–53,
    156, 194–5
  history of 151
  in 1935 150–1, *150*
World Missionary Conference 124
World's Young Women's Christian
    Association (World's
    YWCA). *See also* Kinnaird,
    (Hon.) Emily
  beginnings (1894) 22, 151
  Commission in Salzburg (1922) 107–8
  first Conference in London 103
  membership 22
  Meyendorff, Olga (Secretary) 152
  Stockholm Conference (1914) 3, 58, 102
  UK YWCA annual week of prayer as
    fundraiser 151

X-ray equipment. *See also* Pocock, Lyndall
  at Anglo-Russian field hospital 86, *87*,
    132

Young Men's Christian Association
    (YMCA)
  in America 47
  Indian National Council 158
young women. *See also* Young Women's
    Christian Association
  economic status 108
  using cosmetics 190
Young Women's Christian Association
    (YWCA) 2–5, 9, 17–18,
    21–3, 54–63, 97–108, 149–59,
    194–5, 199. *See also*
    Kinnaird, (Hon.) Emily;
    Kinnaird, (Hon.)Gertrude;
    Kinnaird, (Lady) Mary Jane;
    Picton-Turbervill, Edith;

World Fellowship Week;
    World's Young Women's
    Christian Association
  Ceylon 153–5
  India 153–4, 158
  Portugal 152–4
  South Africa 156
  UK
    addresses the mass and the
      individual 60–1
    Bible study 59, 153, 156
    Blue Triangle clubs 105
    Commission (1910–13) 57–8
    concern about 'worldy drift' 56
    conferences 59, 103–4, 106
    cooperation, an ideal 105–8
    development of women's
      personality 58–9, 195
    eightieth anniversary 59, 97–9, *98*,
      199
    fiftieth anniversary 56
    in First World War 23, 199
    'fourfold method' 56
    interdenominationalism 61–2
    internationalism 149–59
    membership 56
    motto 97, 103
    Our Own Gazette (magazine) 56,
      153–4
    publicity campaign (1923) 17–18,
      18
    service ethics 56–9, 61, 97, 101–5
    splits within the organization 54–6
    training centre for secretaries 102

Zenana Bible and Medical Mission 17, 23.
    See also Kinnaird, (Hon.)
    Emily; Paget, (Lady) Muriel